MW01713760

English in Middle and Secondary Classrooms: Creative and Critical Advice from Canada's Teacher Educators

Kedrick James
University of British Columbia

Teresa M. Dobson
University of British Columbia

Carl Leggo
University of British Columbia

PEARSON

Toronto

This book is dedicated to our former and future students.

Vice-President, Editorial Director: Gary Bennett
Editor-in-Chief: Michelle Sartor
Acquisitions Editor: Carolin Sweig
Marketing Manager: Loula March
Supervising Developmental Editor: Madhu Ranadive
Developmental Editor: Rachel Stuckey
Project Manager: Richard di Santo
Manufacturing Manager: Jane Schell
Production Editor: Rohini Deb, Cenveo Publisher Services
Copy Editor: Kelly Coleman
Proofreader: Kelli Howey
Compositor: Cenveo Publisher Services
Art Director: Julia Hall
Interior and Cover Designer: Anthony Leung
Cover Image: Farinaz Taghavi/PhotoDisc

Credits: Pages 19, 28, 44, 63, 82, 89, 105, 118, 126, 135, 146, 164, 179, 192, 204, 217, 232: Words copyright © 2012 Carl Leggo, images copyright © 2012 Donal O'Donoghue. All other credits and acknowledgments borrowed from other sources and reproduced, with permission, in this textbook appear on the appropriate page within the text.

Copyright © 2013 Pearson Canada Inc. All rights reserved. Manufactured in Canada. This publication is protected by copyright and permission should be obtained from the publisher prior to any prohibited reproduction, storage in a retrieval system, or transmission in any form or by any means, electronic, mechanical, photocopying, recording, or likewise. To obtain permission(s) to use material from this work, please submit a written request to Pearson Canada Inc., Permissions Department, 26 Prince Andrew Place, Don Mills, Ontario, M3C 2T8, or fax your request to 416-447-3126, or submit a request to Permissions Requests at **www.pearsoncanada.ca**.

10 9 8 7 6 5 4 3 2 1 WC

Library and Archives Canada Cataloguing in Publication

James, Kedrick,
English in middle and secondary classrooms : creative and critical advice from Canada's teacher educators / Kedrick James, Teresa M. Dobson, Carl Leggo.

Includes index.
ISBN 978-0-13-296347-3

1. Language arts (Middle school)—Canada. 2. Language arts (Secondary)—Canada. 3. Middle school education—Canada. 4. Education, Secondary—Canada. 5. Active learning—Canada. 6. Multicultural education—Canada. 7. Teaching—Canada. I. Dobson, Teresa Mary, 1967– II. Leggo, Carl, 1953– III. Title.

LB1631.J34 2012 428.0071'2 C2012-905745-2

PEARSON

ISBN 978-0-13-296347-3

Contents

Preface

This book presents a collective, scholarly envisioning of what we, as Canadians, ought to be integrating into English language arts curriculum—that is, what we should be doing in classrooms to facilitate learning and to help students navigate the new conditions of meaning making in the twenty-first century. Conceptualizing and collecting the contents of this publication involved two years of lively discussion, research, and reaching out to colleagues with the general query: *What are the most pressing issues that English teachers face today?* We asked them to begin their answer with a frequently asked question and to respond to it with their best advice. The response was immediately encouraging. Leading Canadian scholars and teacher educators joined our cause, specialists in English teaching methods, Language Arts curriculum, Canadian literature, and adolescents' multiple literacies in the context of language education. These contributors, who themselves help prepare middle and secondary school teacher candidates for their practicum and professional certification, have shared their wisdom in the present volume.

With such rapid change in technology, modalities, genres, literacies, and social and identity formations, it can be very difficult to gain a broad enough perspective on the Humanities to re-conceive language study, literacy practice, and the transmission of cultural knowledge and literary heritage. The questions and responses authored for this book highlight the many possibilities for enhancing creativity and critical engagement in classroom activities. They suggest the kinds of teaching strategies and resources needed to make English classes relevant and rewarding for students, and they give excellent advice on how to get the job of teaching language and literacy done—even when up against the odds of tight schedules, standardized testing, diverse student needs, and so on. Instead of solely providing answers, the authors offer pedagogical suggestions, theoretical frames, anecdotal experiences, and background resources to aid a teacher's self-directed inquiry, all the while pondering the immediate issues of planning and delivering English lessons. We invite the reader to see each of the questions posed as an entry point, a portal to further inquiry and classroom-based research.

English teachers fill an important role in society: they set free intrepid imagination and help students discover how to make good use of it; they are the midwives of vibrant cultural engagement by working to bring forth a commitment to conscientious and informed citizenship. With ardent determination we can meet the classroom challenges ahead, so long as we are forward-looking and willing to question our favoured assumptions. Take, for example, the typical categories used in ELA instructional textbooks. Modalities—listening, speaking, reading, writing, viewing, and representing—provide the basic structural principles of the discipline. Our confidence in this basic taxonomy has been profoundly and justifiably shaken in an age where wireless digital devices like "smart" phones can include all of those modes of communication in a single dialogical exchange. By contrast, the sections of this book reflect a renewed sense of priorities, areas of concern that require attention *now* in Canadian ELA education, namely: 1. Including Diverse Learners; 2. Engaging Diverse Knowledge Frameworks; 3. Inspiring

Imagination and Creativity; and 4. Exploring Processes and Products of Learning. These constitute, in our estimation, an emerging framework for the challenges facing English language arts educators today.

The educational perspectives offered in each section, as diverse as they are, outline a game plan for what should be studied (evolving ELA curriculum), how it can best be taught (evolving ELA methods), and why we need to make these changes (evolving ELA theory). In practical terms, these initiatives require more than the occasional experiment in curriculum design. They require continual effort and steadfast support, innovative leadership and a perpetual, lifelong love of learning. From our collective experience working with novice and veteran teachers in and out of school settings, we understand that teacher candidates need a resource that can help them breathe new life into their profession, expand curriculum, innovate with new methods, and do all this in the midst of a busy life and the many daily demands habitual to an English teacher's schedule.

Although this collection of pedagogical provocations is directed first and foremost to classroom teachers, in so far as it addresses curriculum development and teaching strategies, we anticipate that it will be useful across the diverse educational settings in which English teachers are employed. Many English teachers certified in Canada do not spend the majority of their time instructing in Canadian schools. Many travel and teach overseas; others find work as private tutors or work in community-based settings; still others might go on to work as professional or technical writers, or pursue further studies and enter adjunct professions like law, counseling, and so on. Others might abandon the career entirely; but few regret the opportunity to experience classrooms from the teacher's point of view. Engaging a group of adolescent minds through stellar works of literature, honing their understanding of how language works, and awakening imagination lets English teachers share in the intimate rewards of helping students reach personal and intellectual goals. This book is meant to inspire all English teachers to make the most of their pedagogical opportunities. As a result, the creative and critical advice we have prepared is Canadian in origin—in some ways also in mood and sentiment—but is certainly not limited to Canadian classroom teachers in terms of its applied value.

Thus, we present an overview of a subject area under continuous, momentous change. One message is clear. Teachers cannot sit back and remain reticent in the face of these critical and creative challenges. Such challenges include how to incorporate new ways of finding, making, and sharing meaning; how to engage with all kinds of texts and to read, listen, and view extensively; how to broaden cultural points of reference and reverse processes of marginalization; and how to adapt teaching methods and curriculum not only to give students the best possible preparation for their adult lives but also to make them conscious of how language constructs the way they see others and themselves. We hope that this book does just that, providing points of entry for teachers into a wide array of topics with sufficient resources to facilitate more in-depth inquiry, having at their disposal good advice that can save time, build confidence, and turn repetition and imitation into inspiration and innovation.

ACKNOWLEDGMENTS

We wish to thank all of our colleagues, with special thanks to Barrie Barrell, Joel Gladstone, Geoff Roeder, Geoff Williams, and the University of British Columbia.

SUPPLEMENTS

MyEducationLab

Discover where the classroom comes to life! From video clips of teachers and students interacting to sample lessons, portfolio templates, and standards integration, MyEducationLab gives students the tools they will need to succeed in the classroom—with content easily integrated into existing courses. MyEducationLab gives students powerful insights into how real classrooms work and also gives them a rich array of tools that will support them on their journey from their first class to their first classroom.

peerScholar

Firmly grounded in published research, peerScholar is a powerful online pedagogical tool that helps develop your students' critical and creative thinking skills. peerScholar facilitates this through the process of creation, evaluation and reflection. Working in stages, students begin by submitting a written assignment. peerScholar then circulates their work for others to review, a process that can be anonymous or not depending on your preference. Students receive peer feedback and evaluations immediately, reinforcing their learning and driving the development of higher-order thinking skills. Students can then re-submit revised work, again depending on your preference. Contact your Pearson representative to learn more about peerScholar and the research behind it.

CourseSmart for Instructors (ISBN 9780133088151)

CourseSmart goes beyond traditional expectations–providing instant, online access to the textbooks and course materials you need at a lower cost for students. And even as students save money, you can save time and hassle with a digital eTextbook that allows you to search for the most relevant content at the very moment you need it. Whether it's evaluating textbooks or creating lecture notes to help students with difficult concepts, CourseSmart can make life a little easier. See how when you visit www.coursesmart.com/instructors.

CourseSmart for Students (ISBN 9780133088151)

CourseSmart goes beyond traditional expectations–providing instant, online access to the textbooks and course materials you need at an average savings of 60%. With instant access from any computer and the ability to search your text, you'll find the content you need quickly, no matter where you are. And with online tools like highlighting and note-taking, you can save time and study efficiently. See all the benefits at www.coursesmart.com/students.

About the Editors

Kedrick James is a writer, teacher, and arts-based researcher specializing in secondary English curriculum and teacher education. Through his literary pursuits, which include collaborations with musicians, video artists, visual artists, poets and programmers, he is continually prodding the pedagogical possibilities of creative living, teaching, and research. His research interests focus on information environments, cultural recycling, language automation, and assessment of written English. He is an instructor at the University of British Columbia, Department of Language and Literacy Education.

Teresa M. Dobson is Associate Professor in the Department of Language and Literacy Education at the University of British Columbia. Her primary areas of research are literary education, digital literacy, and digital humanities. She is a member of several funded international teams conducting research in these areas, and has published widely in education and humanities journals. Prior to her work in higher education she was a teacher of English in middle and high schools.

Carl Leggo is a poet and Professor in the Department of Language and Literacy Education at the University of British Columbia. His books include: *Growing Up Perpendicular on the Side of a Hill*; *View from My Mother's House*; *Come-By-Chance*; *Teaching to Wonder: Responding to Poetry in the Secondary Classroom*; *Lifewriting as Literary Métissage and an Ethos for Our Times* (co-authored with Erika Hasebe-Ludt and Cynthia Chambers); *Being with A/r/tography* (co-edited with Stephanie Springgay, Rita L. Irwin, and Peter Gouzouasis); *Creative Expression, Creative Education* (co-edited with Robert Kelly); and *Poetic Inquiry: Vibrant Voices in the Social Sciences* (co-edited with Monica Prendergast and Pauline Sameshima).

About the Contributors

Allyson Eamer is Assistant Professor of English as a Second Language Education at the Faculty of Education, University of Ontario Institute of Technology. Her research interests are in the areas of language practice and identity negotiation, online language learning, narrative inquiry, and language shift and maintenance. She has written on identity and language in both elementary and secondary settings, and is currently researching online learning of First Nations' languages.

Anne Burke is Assistant Professor of Literacy Education and Early Childhood Learning at the Faculty of Education, Memorial University of Newfoundland. Her research focuses on digital reading practices, assessment of new literacies, multimodal artifact literacies, family literacy, and virtual play worlds for the young child. She recently published *Ready to Learn: Using Play to Build Literacy Skills* (2010), and has two earlier books in the area of pop culture for youth: *The Beat: Behind the Music* (2006) and *That's Entertainment* (2007). She also co-edited *Assessment of New Literacies: Perspectives from the Classroom* with Roberta Hammett. Anne has published in *English Journal, E-Learning, JAAL, Changing English, International Journal of Learning,* and has made several book-chapter contributions. She has researched and written widely in the area of multimodality, multiliteracies, and new literacies. Currently, she is researching adolescents' reading and authoring in digitals spaces (funded by SSHRC).

Barrie Barrell was born in London, England and educated in New York and Toronto. He teaches and researches in the area of secondary English education at Memorial University of Newfoundland. The author or co-author of five books on English education and technology, he is now focused on *ekphrasis* and the building of texts that juxtapose images, poetry, and prose. Informing his academic writing is twenty years of middle and secondary school teaching at public, private, and Catholic schools in the United States and Canada.

Bill Hay has been teaching courses in curriculum, instruction, language, and the humanities in the School of Education at the University of Northern British Columbia for the past six years. For a number of years before that, he taught high school English, journalism, and Canadian literature in New Brunswick. He has also completed projects in Canadian literature curriculum for the NB Department of Education, acted as an editor for the Canadian Council Teachers of English Language Arts, and as a head Canadian judge of literary magazines for the National Council of Teachers of English.

Bronwen Low is Associate Professor in the Faculty of Education, McGill University. In her research she explores the implications and challenges of popular youth culture, including hip-hop and spoken word, for curriculum theory, literacy studies, and pedagogy. Recent publications include *Slam School: Learning through Conflict in the Hip-Hop and Spoken Word Classroom* (Stanford, 2011) and *Reading Youth Writing* (Lang, 2008) with Michael Hoechsmann. Other research and teaching interests include informal, community video, and digital storytelling projects, and the educational possibilities of life stories of Montrealers displaced by human rights violations.

Danika Barker is a secondary school English teacher fascinated by the ways in which technology and literacy intersect. She maintains a professional blog at www.dbarker.edublogs.org and recently spoke at the TEDxOntarioEd Event about the ways she engages her students using new literacies practices.

Deborah Begoray is Professor of Language and Literacy in the Department of Curriculum and Instruction, Faculty of Education, University of Victoria. She does literacy teaching and research in a variety of contexts and with a wide range of learners including students and teachers in K–12 language arts and in adult literacy education (in health contexts specifically). Deborah also works in other school curricula (such as the teaching of reading in mathematics, history, and science). Her work on visual literacies includes media and arts applications. Deborah also writes extensively on literacy research in Aboriginal communities both rural and urban.

Dennis Sumara is Professor and Dean of Education at the University of Calgary, Canada. His areas of research include curriculum theory, teacher education, and literacy education, as oriented by conceptual interests in hermeneutic phenomenology, literary response theory, and complexity science. Specific topics of research include literary engagement and curriculum, problems and possibilities of learning and teaching, as well as normativity and counternormativity in teacher education. He is the author of many research papers and several books, including *Why Reading Literature in School Still Matters: Imagination, Interpretation, Insight* (2002, Erlbaum), recipient of the 2003 National Reading Conference's (USA) Ed Fry Book Award.

D.M.R. Bentley is a Distinguished University Professor and the Carl F. Klinck Professor in Canadian Literature at Western University. He has taught Canadian literature extensively at both the undergraduate and the graduate levels and has published widely in the field, as well as on nineteenth-century British literature and art. Among his publications on Canadian literature are *The Gay]Grey Moose: Essays on the Ecologies and Mythologies of Canadian Poetry, 1690–1990, Mimic Fires: Accounts of Early Long Poems on Canada, Mnemographia Canadensis: Essays on Memory, Community, and Environment in Canada, The Confederation Group of Canadian Poets, 1880–1897*, and *Canadian Architexts: Essays on Literature and Architecture in Canada, 1759–2006.*

Douglas Gosse is Associate Professor of Teaching and Learning Methods in the Schulich School of Education at Nipissing University, North Bay, Ontario. Dr. Gosse received the Nipissing University Research Achievement Award and has also been recognized for teaching excellence by the Governor-General of Canada. He is the author of *A Celtic Cross: A Vampire Journal* (1995), and *The Romeo & Juliet Murders* (1997). His educational novel on masculinities, power, and identity, *Jackytar* (2005), followed by *Breaking Silences & Exploring Masculinities: A Critical Supplement to the Novel Jackytar* (2008), are applicable to diverse high school and university courses.

Erika Hasebe-Ludt is Associate Professor in the Faculty of Education, the University of Lethbridge, Alberta. She researches and teaches in the areas of teacher education and curriculum studies in connection with language, literacy, and culture. Her current research focuses on rewriting literacy curricula in cosmopolitan Canadian schools, and on investigating languages and cultures in transnational contexts through interpretive inquiry and life writing. Her publications include the co-edited *Curriculum Intertext: Place/Language/Pedagogy* (2003; with Wanda Hurren) and co-authored *Life Writing and Literary Métissage as an Ethos for Our Times* (2009; with Cynthia Chambers and Carl Leggo).

George Belliveau is Associate Professor in the Faculty of Education at the University of British Columbia where he teaches undergraduate and graduate courses in Theatre/ Drama Education. His research interests include research-based theatre, ethnotheatre, drama and social justice (bullying), drama and L2 learning, drama across the curriculum, and Canadian theatre. His co-authored book with Lynn Fels, *Exploring Curriculum: Performative Inquiry, Role Drama and Learning* (2008), is published by Pacific Educational Press.

Ingrid Johnston is Professor of English Education and Curriculum Studies in the Department of Secondary Education at the University of Alberta, Edmonton. Her research and teaching interests focus on postcolonial theories and pedagogies, literature for children and adolescents, and questions of cultural difference and teacher education. Her book *Re-mapping Literary Worlds: Postcolonial Pedagogy in Practice* (Peter Lang, 2003) also appears in Chinese translation, and she has recently co-edited a book with James Nahachewsky entitled *Beyond 'Presentism': Re-imagining the Historical, Personal, and Social Spaces of Curriculum* (Sense Publishers, 2009). Her forthcoming book, co-authored with Jyoti Mangat, is entitled *Reading Practices, Postcolonial Literature, and Cultural Mediation in the Classroom* (Sense Publishers, 2011).

Jan Hare is an Anishinaabe scholar and educator from the M'Chigeeng First Nation. She is Associate Professor in the Department of Language and Literacy Education at the University of British Columbia. Her research interests include the social practices of literacy in Aboriginal families, schools, and communities. She has a particular interest in Aboriginal early learning and youth issues. She teaches courses related to Indigenous Education including Indigenous Storytelling in Education.

Janette Hughes is Assistant Professor of Language and Literacy Education at the Faculty of Education, University of Ontario Institute of Technology. Her research focuses on digital reading and writing practices, multimodal literacies, and digital transformations of literacy. Janette has researched and written widely in the areas of multimodality, multiliteracies, and new literacies. She has published articles in the journals *English in Education, E-Learning, Voices from the Middle, Children's Literature in Education, Language and Literacy,* and *English Teaching: Practice and Critique*. Currently, Janette is researching adolescents' authoring of digital texts, specifically digital poetry (a project funded by SSHRC).

Jean Baird has been an English professor, program director for an arts facility, managing editor for business publications, consultant for non-profit organizations, and creative director of Canada Book Week for the Writers' Trust of Canada. In 2007–2008 she worked on a BC-based project about the use of Canadian literature in secondary schools. She is the co-editor with George Bowering of an anthology on grief and mourning, *The Heart Does Break.* Her current research is an examination of prize and celebrity culture and its impact on the Canadian publishing industry. She is the founder of The Al Purdy A-frame Trust.

Jeff Park is an educator and writer, working in a number of genres including short fiction, poetry, and drama. He has published a book on writing theory and narrative entitled *Writing at the Edge* (Peter Lang, New York, 2005), and recently had three stories published by Oberon (2009) in *Coming Attractions 09.* His book of poetry *The Cellophane Sky: Jazz Poems* was published by Hagios Press in 2011. He is now in the process of finishing a collection of short stories, and two new poetry manuscripts. He is currently at the University of Saskatchewan, where he teaches courses in English language arts, writing, curriculum, and literacy.

Jill Kedersha McClay is Professor of Language and Literacy Education at the University of Alberta. Her research on writing theory and pedagogy is often classroom-based and focused on teachers' and students' literacy practices.

John J. Guiney Yallop is a parent, a partner, and a poet. He is also Assistant Professor in the School of Education at Acadia University where he teaches teachers about literacy and arts-based research, and where he writes poetry to come to a better understanding of how to be in the world.

John Willinsky is Khosla Family Professor of Education at Stanford University and Professor (Limited Term) of Publishing Studies at Simon Fraser University, where he directs the Public Knowledge Project. The project is dedicated to conducting research and developing software aimed at improving the public and scholarly quality of academic publishing. His books include the *Empire of Words: The Reign of the OED* (Princeton, 1994), *Learning to Divide the World: Education at Empire's End* (Minnesota, 1998), *Technologies of Knowing* (Beacon 2000), and *The Access Principle: The Case for Open Access to Research and Scholarship* (MIT Press, 2006).

Kathy Hibbert is Assistant Professor, Adolescent Literacy at the Faculty of Education, University of Western Ontario. As a classroom teacher for sixteen years working with students of all grades, abilities, and levels of motivation, she is keenly interested in what we, as teachers, can learn together with our students. She is currently President of the Language and Literacy Researchers of Canada, and author of *The Salty Chip: A Canadian Multiliteracies Collaborative* (www.saltychip.com). Her professional website is www.kathyhibbert.com.

Kathy Sanford is Associate Professor in the Faculty of Education at University of Victoria. Her literacy research and teaching interests include issues of gender, new literacies, and assessment. Current research projects involve videogame playing and creating, exploring the learning that happens as youth engage critically and creatively in virtual worlds. Additionally, she has been actively involved in issues related to teacher education programs, and her current writing and research involves school-based teacher education and professional electronic portfolios.

Kelly Young is Associate Professor at the School of Education and Professional Learning at Trent University, in Peterborough, Ontario, where she teaches courses in English Language Arts, Curriculum Methods, and Classroom Management. Her research areas include curriculum theorizing, language and literacy, arts-based inquiry, and leadership in environmental and eco-justice education. She has published articles in *Language and Literacy: A Canadian Educational E-Journal, The Journal of Curriculum Theorizing* (JCT), and the *Journal of the Canadian Association for Curriculum Studies* (JCACS).

Her most recent edited book is titled *Approaches to Educational Leadership and Practice* (Smale & Young, 2007).

Leah C. Fowler works with graduate students and with pre-service teachers in the Faculty of Education, University of Lethbridge, supervises students in teaching practica, and conducts research in Curriculum Studies, difficulty in teaching, and narrative inquiry. She has 30 years of teaching experience at the secondary and post-secondary levels. "As an old biologist," she writes, "I like to kayak and garden. Music, meditation, Tai Chi, art, literature and gentle, sentient people contribute to my best consciousness. The process of acquiring a Ph.D., M.Ed., B.Ed., B. Sc. were all remarkable adventures: I highly recommend lifelong learning."

Lee Gunderson is Professor and former Head of the Department of Language and Literacy Education at the University of British Columbia. He received the David Russell Award for Research, the Killam Teaching Prize, and the Kingston Prize for contributions to the National Reading Conference. He was awarded the British Columbia Deans of Education Media Contributor of the Year Award, the UBC President's Award for Education through the Media, the BC TEAL Lifetime Contributors Award, and an Honorary Life Membership in the Learning Disabilities Association of Vancouver. He has published articles, books, and commentaries, and in 2009 his research formed the basis for a documentary film called *Planet Vancouver*.

Linda Coles was born in Newfoundland and educated in St. John's. She teaches language arts curriculum and literacy courses in the Faculty of Education at Memorial University of Newfoundland. Her focus on visual literacy (early childhood to adult) has been influenced and informed by her teaching and research in the area of literacy at the post-secondary level; her work with literacy development at the provincial and national levels; and her ongoing focus, as a visual artist, on creating visual representations of the culture and way of life of the people of Newfoundland.

Linda MacKinley-Hay has been instructing courses in Canadian, First Nations, comparative, and British literature, literary theory, and expository writing at the University of Northern British Columbia for the past seven years. Prior to that, she received undergraduate degrees in Canadian literature at the University of New Brunswick, where she also completed her Doctorate and instructed courses in Canadian literature, short fiction, and composition. In addition, she was employed by the English Language Assessment Branch of the NB Department of Education as an exemplar and scorer for provincial examinations.

Liz Merkel is completing her master's degree at the University of Victoria and has been researching in the area of videogames for the past two years. She has taught extensively in international and rural settings, as well as in the teacher education program at University of Victoria. She has explored alternative research methodologies including autoethnography and metissage; research interests include teacher education, alternative modes of representation, and digital literacies.

Lorri Neilsen Glenn is an award-winning ethnographer, teacher, essayist, and poet whose publications include a memoir, *Threading Light: Explorations in Loss and Poetry* (Hagios Press, 2011), four poetry collections (including *Lost Gospels,* 2010, and *Combustion,* 2007, Brick Books), and three books on literacy research and education.

She has also edited an anthology about mothers and co-edited three collections of arts-informed inquiry. Neilsen Glenn was Halifax Poet Laureate for 2005–2009. She leads writing workshops in Canada and internationally, has taught in public schools, and currently is Professor of Literacy at Mount Saint Vincent University in Halifax.

Lynne Wiltse is Associate Professor in the Faculty of Education at the University of Alberta where she teaches courses in language and literacy and children's literature. Previously, Lynne taught in the School of Education at Thompson Rivers University in Kamloops, BC. Her areas of research expertise include minority language education, literacy pedagogy, multicultural children's literature, sociocultural theory, teacher education, and qualitative methodologies. Recent research projects range from a national study exploring pre-service teachers' perspectives on Canadian identity in multicultural children's literature to a school-university collaboration examining ways to merge out-of-school literacy resources with school literacy practices for Aboriginal youth.

Margaret Mackey is Professor in the School of Library and Information Studies at the University of Alberta. She teaches courses on theories and practices of reading, multimedia literacies, and young adult literature. She has published widely in all these areas, and her most recent book is *Mapping Recreational Literacies: Contemporary Adults at Play* (Peter Lang, 2007). For eleven years she served as North American editor *of Children's Literature in Education: An International Quarterly.*

Mary Clare Courtland is Professor in the Faculty of Education, Lakehead University, where she teaches preservice courses in media, multiliteracies, and literacy as well as graduate courses in curriculum, literacy, and qualitative research. She supervises master's and doctoral researchers. She is currently involved in a national research study on how collaborative inquiry groups of practising literacy teachers can support teachers' use of Canadian literature to promote social justice. She and a colleague are also conducting a longitudinal case study that describes one young teacher candidate's journey into teaching and the influences on her understanding of literacy teaching, learning, and diversity.

Meredith Rogers Cherland, formerly an elementary and secondary English teacher in the United States and Canada, has been Professor of Literacy Education at the University of Regina for more than thirty years. Grounded in the assumption that literacy is a social practice, her scholarship investigates the ways in which cultural beliefs are enacted in daily reading practices, and how learning to critique popular fiction can help teens understand the roots of social injustice. Cherland is the author of *Private Practices: Girls Reading Fiction and Constructing Identity* and (with Helen Harper) *Advocacy Research in Literacy Education: Seeking Higher Ground.*

Rebecca Luce-Kapler is Associate Dean of Graduate Studies and Research and an instructor for secondary English curriculum in the Faculty of Education, Queen's University. Her research interests focus on the integral role of literary practices, particularly writing, in the development of human consciousness and identity. Her book, *Writing With, Through, and Beyond the Text: An Ecology of Writing,* details the writing practices she uses in research and teaching. Rebecca is also a poet with a published collection of poetry, *The Gardens Where She Dreams.*

Roberta F. Hammett is Professor, Faculty of Education, Memorial University. Her research interests include new literacies, the literacy implications and applications of digital and Web 2.0 technologies, teacher education, and critical media literacy. She teaches courses in intermediate and secondary English education, technology integration, media literacy, and feminist epistemology and research methodologies. Her recent publications include five co-edited texts: *Assessment and New Literacies: Perspectives from the Classroom* (Peter Lang, 2009), *Boys, Girls, and the Myths of Literacies and Learning* (Canadian Scholars Press Inc., 2008), *Teaching English Today: Advocating for Change in the Secondary Curriculum* (Teachers College Press, 2004), *Digital Expressions: Media Literacy and English Language Arts* (Detselig, 2002) and *Advocating Change: Contemporary Issues in Subject English* (Irwin, 2000).

Robin M. Bright is Professor in the University of Lethbridge's Faculty of Education. She teaches courses to undergraduate and graduate students in the areas of the language arts, reading, writing, and gender. Previously, Dr. Bright taught elementary school for ten years. She is the author of *Writing Instruction in the Intermediate Grades: What Is Said, What Is Done, What Is Understood* (1995); *Write from the Start: Writers Workshop in the Primary Grades* (2001); *Write through the Grades: Teaching Writing in Secondary Schools* (2007); the co-author of *From Your Child's Teacher: Helping a Child Learn to Read, Write and Speak* (1998); and has written numerous articles on learning to read and write. Her work has appeared in the *Journal of Reading Education, Canadian Children,* the *Canadian Journal of English Language Arts, Alberta English, The Writing Teacher, English Quarterly,* and the *Journal of Teacher Education.*

Sean Wiebe is Assistant Professor of Language and Literacy at the University of Prince Edward Island (www.upei.ca/education/wiebe). Formerly, he has worked as a principal in Calgary and a high school English teacher in Vancouver. His papers and poetry appear in a variety of journals and book chapters in the areas of the arts, teacher education, and curriculum studies. Recent work has appeared or is forthcoming in *The Journal of Educational Thought, The Canadian Journal of Education,* and *In Education.*

Shelley Stagg Peterson is a former elementary classroom teacher in Alberta and once was Assistant Professor at Ohio State University. Shelley now teaches, conducts research, and writes articles and books about writing instruction, assessment, and children's literature at OISE/University of Toronto. She has recently published *Teaching with Graphic Novels in Grades 4–12 Classrooms* and an edited collection with David Booth and Carol Jupiter called *Books, Media and the Internet: Children's Literature for Today's Classrooms.*

Susan E. Elliott-Johns is currently Assistant Professor at Nipissing University. She teaches courses in the pre-service teaching program in Language Arts and Literacy, courses that are specifically designed for teacher candidates preparing to teach at Junior/Intermediate levels. These courses emphasize a social constructivist approach to teaching and learning and encourage understandings of the new conditions of making meaning in the 21st century. Prior to joining the faculty at Nipissing, Susan had a long and successful career in public education as a teacher (K–8), literacy consultant, teacher educator, and elementary school administrator. She has provided leadership in numerous workshops, conference presentations, additional qualifications courses (AQ), and publications for teachers, administrators, and other teacher educators in Canada, the United States and Australia. Current research interests include pre-service and in-service teacher education, the self-study of teacher education practices (S-STEP).

Susan Walsh taught junior and senior high English Language Arts in Alberta and currently teaches secondary English Language Arts/Literacy courses at the B.Ed. and graduate levels in the Faculty of Education at Mount Saint Vincent University in Nova Scotia. She works with language from a feminist, poststructuralist perspective. Creative non-fiction writing and the arts are integral to her research.

Tammy Iftody is currently the Myer Horowitz postdoctoral scholar at the Centre for Research for Teacher Education and Development at the University of Alberta. Her ongoing research program seeks new ways to understand the evolution of "New Literacy" practices as mediated by popular cultural forms in online fan communities. This work is framed by interdisciplinary interests in studies of mind and consciousness, poststructural theories of language and subjectivity, and conceptions of knowing, learning, and teaching informed by complexity thinking. In collaboration with Davis and Sumara, she has contributed to several book chapters and articles that explore the theoretical relationship between contemporary understandings of consciousness and various popular forms of literary experience.

Tim Ludwig is author of "At Risk Life," http://atrisklife.blogspot.com, and a Grade 12 student. Tim was a member of the Ontario Minister of Education's Student Voice Panel. He gave a talk at the 2010 TEDxOntarioEd Event entitled, "What teachers need to hear from an 'at-risk student'."

Valerie Mulholland is Assistant Professor, Language and Literacy Education, in the Secondary Program of the Faculty of Education, University of Regina. Formerly a high school English teacher, her research interests include autobiography in teacher education, language and power, rural education, and postcolonial theory. She works extensively in the field with pre-service and in-service English teachers and their students.

Veronica Gaylie is a writer from Vancouver and a professor at University of British Columbia. Her writing has appeared in magazines and literary journals around the world. Her latest book is called *Roots and Research in Urban School Gardens* (2011, Peter Lang).

Introduction

By Kedrick James

A Classroom Scenario

"Under a cold and desolate star," begins the teacher from the front of the classroom, "our troubled protagonist is slipping from consciousness." The pause that follows is long enough to make the students feel a twinge of foreboding.

"Must stay awake," the teacher continues, "must stay . . . awa—" trailing off, the teacher's head sinks down, jerking slightly a few times for effect.

Suddenly breaking out of character, the teacher looks up at the class. "Our hero, Gilgamesh, has crossed over the river that separates the world of the living from the land of the dead. He's bet the Boatman, Utnapishtim, he can stay awake for *7 days*! If he does, he gets to return to the land of the living with his beloved and recently deceased friend."

The teacher lavishes in the increasing expectation—the unravelling of a tale, an epic fate. "But if he loses?" The question lingers in the air.

Good, the teacher thinks, their curiosity has been sparked.

"Has anybody ever felt that sleepy?" Hands shoot up, while a few of the more outspoken students make a pretend snoring sound.

The teacher reflects for a moment—that was a lot of new words. The teacher goes to the board and picks up the marker, writing *Gilgamesh, Utnapishtim*.

"Let's say it together, *gil-GA-mesh*. Of course, nobody knows *exactly* how the names were spoken because this is a Sumerian myth from one of the earliest civilizations. It was recorded on clay tablets in an alphabet called *cuneiform*. It was inscribed nearly five thousand years ago by an exorcist-priest named *Sin-leqi-unninni*."

The teacher walks around the room, passing out images of the cuneiform tablets photocopied from a book in the school's library (Gardner & Maier, 1984). Knowing the facts aren't really useful to these students, the teacher adds, "you know, this history is interesting but you don't need to know it to enjoy the story because the storyline, that is, the mythical narratives of Gilgamesh and his friend, are timeless. Around the world people still tell variations of this story, even today!"

Returning to the front of the class, the teacher tries to get the students a little more engaged. "The story treats the heroes as real people, but their feats are *super* human." The teacher strikes a dramatic pose, hands on hips—a superman pose, and, speaking like a radio announcer, declares, "*they are the embodiment of the desire to achieve greatness.*"

After the class titters for a moment, the teacher relaxes and continues with the lesson. "In myths, characters have superhuman abilities, but human values and emotions. Can you think of any mythical characters?"

Students call out answers: "X-men?" one of them says. "Transformers?" says another.

"Right, yes," the teacher responds. "They can be mutants, animals, machines—*anything* can be a dignitary of the mythic imagination." Turning to the board, the teacher writes the words "mythic narratives." The students know by now to be taking notes, but the teacher reminds them just the same by writing out the key words.

"Characters in myths, mythic characters. They're what are called *archetypes,* meaning they represent human characteristics that are universal, or shared by everyone, but they don't have to actually *be* human. Many mythic archetypes are personified, as animals or even plants. Sometimes it's the other way around, and characters in myths can represent elements, like wind or thunder. These personified characters are used to tell stories, that is, to tell narratives,"—as the word is spoken, the teacher taps it on the board—"that can speak across all time and all places on earth."

The teacher stops writing. "Let's look closer at this word archetype. *Arch*-type. An *arch* is something that spans an area"—drawing an arch on the board—"and everything under the arch is one type. When we say 'arch villain' for example, we mean the most extreme kind of villain, the apex of the arch"—circling the top point of the arch—"of a type of character. So, archetypes are ways that people personalize a general human trait or role in society. Let's consider what some of these roles and character types might be . . . suggestions?"

As the students make suggestions, they're recorded one by one on the board: *hero, enemy, mother, father, ruler, friend, betrayer, lover.* Taking out a list of archetypes by Carl Jung (which had been photocopied onto a transparency before class), the teacher switches on the old, analogue projector.

While the students are copying down the various archetypes, the teacher flips through a binder of transparencies (all neatly separated with pastel-coloured cardstock dividers), retrieving one created only a week ago: a sketch in pen of Gilgamesh in the land of the dead. In the process of preparing this Grade 9 mythology unit (happily, because for years the teacher had been a bit of a mytho-holic), and after having completed rereading two translations of the *Epic of Gilgamesh* (the second time to gloss important sections of the text), a moment of inspiration had taken hold, and the teacher had drawn the image that the story conjured.

Now, with a primed audience, this is the perfect time to show it.

"Where was I," the teacher asks, getting their attention, "ah, yes, the bet with the boatman." Making sure first that the students were finished copying, the teacher swaps transparencies on the overhead. The students murmur a bit, clearly amused by the idea of a teacher showing them a homemade drawing, and intrigued by the boatman looking like a big beetle in an apron.

"Why is there a big bug in the drawing?" one of them asks.

The teacher explains with a few gestures that the boatman is a beetle who floats on his belly as he pulls the coffin-shaped canoe across the river. "Creative interpretation" the teacher says with a little shrug. "It was supposed to be a scarab but I can't draw very well . . . the beetle boatman is delivering a meal to Gilgamesh, one meal a day for seven days. If the meals are not eaten then Gilgamesh loses the bet and goes home alone."

"Can you guess who wins the bet? Hands up those who think the hero wins . . . okay, now hands up those who think it's the beetle." The teacher sings a line of lyric, to no one in particular: "It's been a haaard daaay's niiight, and I've been sleepin' - like a lo-o-og."

Good—we've done some scaffolding of *prediction,* engaging their imagination about what's to follow in the plot.

The teacher stops for a moment to fill out the automated form for attendance.

"So let's read this epic poem. It's about a mythic hero. He's two-thirds god, one-third human, and rejected the love of the goddess Ishtar who got so angry she sent the bull of heaven down to kill him and his closest friend, Enkidu—his BFF!" A few of the students giggle a little.

"After the heroes kill the bull," the teacher continues, "Ishtar, enraged, smites Enkidu with a mortal illness. That's the reason why Gilgamesh travelled across the land of darkness that was guarded by the scorpion gates, across the river of death—so that he could save Enkidu, even from death itself!"

Seeing that the time is right, the teacher picks up a stack of photocopies from the desk with Pritchard's translation (Pritchard, 1958, was selected for the economy of pages and more age-appropriate word choice in the lovemaking scene), and hands them out to the students.

While they read, the teacher reviews the notes on the first two pages and then, getting their attention, says, "let's look at this text more closely for a minute here. Do you notice the unusual punctuation? What does it mean?"

Jeanne, always quick to volunteer, puts up her hand and says, "those mean there are words missing from the original."

"Excellent, Jeanne," responds the teacher, "sometimes whole lines are gone, or sometimes just a word, a letter here and there. But *I* find it makes the story even better, because those are the gaps where imagination can fill the text with wonder. The breaks are magical!"

The teacher shows them the picture of the tablets again. "But let's also look at the *way* the poem tells its story, its mythic narrative. It sounds like the writer is speaking directly to you. Those sentences start with verbs, not subjects: *behold* the outer wall, it says. *Peer* inside the inner wall, *seize* upon the threshold. All of those are imperatives, command sentences. The subject isn't stated, but it's you,"— pointing at the students—"you are the subject! The writer is telling *you* to behold, to peer, to seize. Like a tour guide, the writer is right there next to you, entering the inner temple, the sanctum of the great Mesopotamian city Uruk."

While speaking the teacher writes these new, unfamiliar vocabulary words on the board—so fast, in fact, that a piece of chalk goes flying. Picking up a new piece, the teacher pauses for a moment, and then begins to draw a picture. First the outer walls, then the inner walls, and then the circular sanctum of the city—finally, the image is complete with the great city gates where the story's narrative begins. Using the drawing as a bridge, the teacher begins an exercise.

"We are being introduced to an ancient world, but what would happen if we were to bring our tour guide back home?" the teacher asks. "Let's imitate the first few lines. Everyone take out a piece of paper and write the word *behold,* and then something you might see outside your home. Next, write the word *peer* and refer to something you'd find *inside* your home. Last, write the word *seize* followed by something you really treasure. You have one minute! Go!"

After a minute of furious scribbling, the teacher numbers the students off as one, two, and three.

"We will read this as a poem out loud, beginning with Arseth at the front and snaking along the rows to Jeanne. Stand up, and read loudly as you proclaim this strange civilization to me, your guide." They begin.

"Behold the apartment parking lot, with white parallel lines," says the first.

"Peer inside the keyhole that breaks all my keys," announces the second.

"Seize the Nintendo Wii that rumbles in your hand," declares the third, and so on down the rows. The success of the instant poem surprises the students and the class laughs throughout, enjoying the irony of giving a bombastic, mythic narrative tone to ordinary things and surprised by the range of different objects people chose to mythologize.

At the end, they all clap enthusiastically and then sit back down, ready to read more.

Planning to Teach English?

Let's leave the teacher and students in the classroom scenario and, stepping back, consider what has gone into planning this sort of lesson. A single day in a teacher's life could fill an entire novel, and maybe there *would* be more pedagogical novels if teachers had the time and energy to write it all down. But time is never abundant in a working teacher's life. There is always more preparation, more gathering resources, more marking, more meetings with parents and staff members, and most of all, more life to be lived.

This book offers advice that will be most beneficial while planning and designing English curriculum for Canadian classrooms. We intentionally avoid providing actual lesson plans because every lesson is contingent on the content and the context in which it is delivered, and reflects the teacher's own knowledge and creative input. Nonetheless, the advice collected in this book suggests the kinds of issues and concerns that professional English teachers ought to be paying attention to when they are busily preparing to teach. This introduction speaks to the planning process, and, when used in concert with the advice provided by the contributing authors, should enable novice and experienced teachers to develop compelling and exciting instructional materials, ready to launch English classes on profound learning adventures.

When planning lessons—and, by extension, planning units of study—the most valuable asset is a personal fascination with and ongoing learning about the topic. During the planning stage, teachers consolidate their knowledge on a particular subject and in so doing begin a new learning cycle, providing needed intellectual direction and momentum for the course. Teachers, in this sense, are model learners, enthused, and their enthusiasm can be especially infectious when their planning has emphasized and prepared for modelling active student participation in the learning process using all the means, modalities, and media available. Moreover, thinking critically about curriculum planning means being sensitive to diversity not only within the student body, but also within the materials that provide a ground for the pedagogical opportunities teachers create. It also means being sensitive to creating the kinds of meaningful activities and projects that will boost language fluency and literacy levels while liberating each student's learning process so that, in the end, they may satiate their thirst for knowledge and expression independently.

The process of curriculum planning involves exploring pedagogical options within the given practical and professional constraints (Ur, 1996). Practical constraints include the length of each period and length of the unit, the relative difficulty and complexity of the texts, genres, or themes to be studied, the availability of resources, class size considerations, variable levels of literacy and motivation, relevance to previously acquired knowledge, and so on. Professional constraints pertain to curriculum mandates and prescribed learning outcomes, standardized testing schedules, and issues of professional conduct. Between these two sets of constraints there is much room for creative and innovative curriculum planning, which is essential to prevent course contents from becoming stale and irrelevant; to this end, educators are constantly planning and exploring new pedagogical options, doing the vital work of curriculum renewal.

The authors of this book argue that, as teachers, we must engage in the kinds of planning and instruction that draw responsibly on the contemporary world around us. A remarkable feature of the Canadian educational landscape is its diversity; wide ranging cultural backgrounds, skills, beliefs, and kinds of knowledge give this country a richness that makes teaching in Canada particularly rewarding. All educators are entrusted with making sure we nurture this diversity, not only by being broadly representative in our choices of classroom materials but also by finding ways to extend upon students' understanding of print texts. These ways include incorporating a variety of media and literacies into the students' tasks; building productive relationships by providing opportunities to study and work in groups; and adding more-than-a-dash of creativity to their expressive undertakings.

If not already prescribed by a sponsoring teacher, the first critical task is to choose the texts and topics to be studied. Once decisions have been made regarding the primary focus of a unit, it's time to start doing what the students are going to do. If the students are going to read a novel, then the teacher should read the novel; if they are going to write a sonnet, the teacher should try one, and so on—that much is *common* sense. It is hard to teach what you don't know or haven't tried; it's even harder to predict where students might struggle with a task, and it's particularly hard to evaluate their performance if you don't already know what the challenges are. By challenging oneself to do anything that is expected of the students, a teacher is able to assess the educational value of assignments and, as a consequence, will create an example of the work to share—a ready-made teaching resource. When teachers share their own attempts at assignments, they demystify the learning process—mastery of the given task isn't something that teachers (or anyone else) acquires easily (Gallagher, 2006).

There is a difference, however, in the way teachers engage with their chosen course materials when they are in the midst of planning curriculum. As teachers reread, review, re-hear, and rehearse the specific texts they plan to teach, they also use *uncommon* sense—they study texts from a teacher's point of view, thinking all the while about how they will make that resource meaningful and accessible for a given grade level or cohort of students. Typically, this stage of planning results in copious notes which focus on topics of interest, potential related resources, close analysis of selections that can be used for language study, ideas for possible assignments and projects, test questions, inter-textual asides and ruminations, connections to other subject areas, definitions of new or difficult vocabulary, and anything else that might be a useful observation or contextual information to share (Woodward, 2001). Some teachers choose to make notes directly in the margins of the focal text(s) by photocopying selections that will be included with lesson plans. Although professionally glossed texts are helpful, a personal gloss—one that the teacher-as-curriculum-planner has written with particular themes and learning outcomes in mind—is the most useful. Critical engagement with the curriculum resources helps the teacher prepare, predict difficulties, generate meaningful activities, develop clear evaluations based on explicit content analysis, and communicate personally meaningful connections as a model of what students will be expected to do. This preparatory work inspires and brings forth the personal reveries and scholarly insights that a direct engagement with the text makes possible.

Furthermore, a personal gloss takes into account the kinds of activities and products of learning that the unit has been designed to incorporate. Hence, whether responding to graphic novels using drama, viewing documentaries with the goal of creating one, animating concrete poetry and fabricating word sculptures, or practising research essays by studying exemplars and going on field trips, a personal gloss will provide the relevant points of pedagogical departure and provide detailed account of what students will need to know in order to demonstrate their understanding and attain the learning objectives. Exploring possible resources by reading or viewing as broadly as possible, choosing and glossing course texts, thinking of interesting projects, collecting supplies and teaching aids, and adding deliberate personal twists and insight into instruction is all part of the continuous preparation and planning processes that professional teachers engage in.

If one looks in a teacher's daily planner, there may only be a few lines and photocopied handouts to go with it. Chances are the teacher has taught this subject and text before and will do it largely from memory. But without preparation in advance, teaching will never be easy and can be very awkward. Lesson plans such as those created for the purposes of teacher education programs or classroom observation tend to go into much greater detail and are primarily a way of helping teacher candidates understand what they ought to be focusing on during their preparations. It should be remembered that great lesson plans don't guarantee good teaching, and great teachers don't always make the best lesson plans. Professional teachers, however, are always planning, collecting resources, and strategizing how to improve on their practices in order to deepen the intellectual, physical, and emotional lives of their students.

Plans, though, can also get in the way when they are so scripted that there is no room for diversion or for students' knowledge to be expressed, no room for student interest and excitement to guide the learning process, no room to adapt in case unusual circumstances arise. Juggling course objectives, covering content, doing prepared activities, and giving students an opportunity to lead the learning process requires a certain amount of spontaneity, improvisation, and in-the-moment adjustments to promote curiosity—all the while shepherding learning processes and redirecting discussions and activities toward specific goals. A lesson plan should outline the process of inspiring curiosity and direct efforts toward the presumed outcomes while retaining sufficient flexibility to accommodate for student input. We teach to the students, not to the plans. Their learning needs, once they become apparent, are paramount.

Formulating Lesson Plans

Lesson plans condense the consolidated insights gained through curriculum planning into a quick reference format. When the lesson is underway, there is insufficient time to review lengthy notes and, while lengthier summaries of the content of a lesson can always be appended for review *prior* to teaching a class, the plans themselves serve only as a reference. Plans are best used to make sure the lesson is on pace, that activities are properly introduced and conducted, that necessary resources have been prepared, and the main learning objectives are being met. They also provide a basis to ensure that multiple classes taking the same course receive the same information and learning opportunities. The critical preparatory work for teachers creating lesson plans is the careful analysis of the work they plan to teach and the analysis of texts so that they can help students see the connection between the text and its purpose. Teachers must show how to connect a particular use of language with the bigger issues that it addresses, and how texts achieve various purposes through layered representations of individuals, events, and contexts—these details need to be carefully discerned beforehand in order to be comprehensively taught and critically understood in the classroom. The creative preparatory work of the teacher is to find the kinds of activities, resources, and projects that will allow students the maximum freedom to express their understanding in ways that are innovative and bring about deeper understanding and insight in the process.

One of the keys to success as a teacher is the ability to craft engaging lessons that captivate the students' interest and creativity. When the class is heading off in an unpredicted direction or the course seems to be running off the rails and getting bogged down in details, lesson planning is essential to getting matters back on track. Because of this, professional teachers are planning all the time, reviewing their plans in light of the given class and context of instruction. For the first few years of a professional career in teaching, there are few more valuable skills to possess than the ability to research, collect resources, formulate activities, and finally plan and deliver lessons that bring words and ideas to life, truly making students want to learn. These skills are also the primary point of evaluation that demonstrate teaching preparedness to those who have not actually witnessed a teacher's teaching, which will include most if not all persons involved in hiring for teaching positions.

During preparation and planning, teachers deliberate on many issues related to nurturing a respectful, active learning environment while maintaining consistent progress toward broader educational objectives: lesson plans provide structure for those deliberations (Butt, 2008). Just as there is no single, best method for teaching, likewise there is no single, best format of a lesson plan. There are many templates and planning outlines used by Canadian teachers, and many more readily available online. Before writing a large number of lesson plans, first find the format that works best for you, the one that offers all the relevant information at a glance. Try delivering the lesson to a friend or to the mirror and see if you can reference the plan without losing concentration or connection with your audience. This way, lesson plan formats can be modified to better suit one's own teaching style. Discussion topics should be incorporated in condensed, point form, and elaborated, if required, as appendices to the lesson for review prior to class time. We recognize that in some teacher education programs, templates are provided that teacher candidates are expected to follow. However, over time, even these will benefit from modifications to suit personal instructional purposes. The box below, *Typical Components of Lesson Plans,* provides a non-exhaustive list of the features from lesson plan templates and may be treated as a checklist of items that may require attention and preparation for effective teaching to take place.

Typical Components of Lesson Plans

Header information:

- Subject and grade(s) the lesson is intended for
- Unit name and position in sequence
- Author (your name/s)

(Continued)

Typical Components of Lesson Plans, *continued*

Body text:

- Title of lesson
- Approximate required time for the lesson
- Prescribed outcomes
- Pedagogical methods (including differentiated modes of instruction)
- Rationale (educational intentions and objectives of the lesson)
- List of materials (resources needed to teach the class and do the activities)

Columns or tables:

- Hook, set induction, or introductory strategy (to tantalize curiosity)
- Key topics
- Sequence of resources (including audio or video time code or page references)
- Lecture notes (point form)
- Discussion questions
- Detailed activities (including instructions, arrangement of students, required resources, types of assessment, time allotted, potential risks)
- Topics for review (from current or prior lessons)
- Homework to be assigned

Appendices:

- Lecture notes
- Evaluation instruments (such as quizzes, tests, worksheets, etc. to be done as an activity during class time).
- Answer keys
- Instructions for take home projects or assignments
- Selections of glossed text for use in modelling close analysis
- Instructional resources (physical hard copy of related teaching aids, e.g. transparencies, photocopies, sample passages for study, etc.)
- Bibliographic references and web links

Every lesson is a new opportunity to approach learning objectives, and one of the most important concerns for anyone developing lesson plans for adolescent students is how to engage students in active learning. It is important to always read, view, and listen broadly, as well as maintain pedagogical attention to what can serve as a text to enhance students' learning of the topic of the lesson. Just as important, though, is inventing, discovering, and borrowing compelling activities that support not only the learning of content but also the mastering of language—the enhancement of many kinds of literacies covering the spectrum of communicative skills student will bring with them to class, from knowing how to program computers to touching hearts through the performance of a poem.

As such, activities form the basis of how time is spent in and out of the classroom and, although that is self-evident, teachers are always at risk of slipping into routines that fail to engage or inspire their students. Middle and secondary school students need to learn with *all* their senses, and be both physically and mentally present to be attentive. They need to learn actively by *doing,* in addition to simply watching, listening, and taking notes. They also benefit from collaborative problem solving and group involvement. As Crowhurst (1994) argues, constructivist theories of learning call for students to be actively engaged in the construction and construal of meaning across the curriculum. Although some "teacher talk" is inevitable in order to direct learning toward common goals, after a short time of continuous lecturing, the students' interest, excitement, and engagement with learning wane. If, however, a variety of textual or audio/visual resources are introduced, students are given ample opportunity to respond by engaging in discussion, and they further scaffold their learning with activities, this downturn of attention can be easily avoided.

Successful activities can be recycled in other units of study and even across grades. This makes pedagogical activities modular, requiring only a change in content and a varying of the degree of difficulty while retaining the basic procedural aspects. Activities comprise the building blocks of lessons and units of instruction, and provide the learning scaffold for reaching complex learning objectives. The same activity can be modified to suit each discrete instance of its use. Quick activities that engage students physically with language, especially in groups, are invigorating and can be used to regain focus when classroom dynamics are an issue. If the language being used supports the conceptual and linguistic aims of the lesson, then the pedagogical benefits are doubled. In addition, once students are familiar with the activity, they can engage with it more quickly and confidently, taking less class time to set up or explain. The activity becomes a step toward meeting the learning objectives that the class looks forward to taking.

Planning Activities with Multiple Literacies

An important shift in the field of literacy occurs when we consider a broad variety of ways in which people acquire, store, and share knowledge (Willinsky, 1990). This expansion of the way we understand reading and writing provides room for ever-evolving forms of expression. When being literate means more than solely having the ability to read and write with letters, literacy education can be extended to all the ways we learn, live, and act meaningfully. To broaden the foundations of learning to include more ways that people make meaning and construct identity requires the kinds of curriculum design that embrace multiple literacies in the learning activities prepared for students (Alvermann et al., 2006). If we consider the wide variety of suggested teaching strategies this book contains, we have a resounding call for diversified instructional practices that include, but extend far beyond, listening to lectures and taking notes for the next test.

Combining literacies in the formulation of activities and assignments can be a useful method of designing curriculum. For example, while reading a Canadian novel, research historical documents (informational literacy) to create archival photo journals (visual and design literacy), and then animate them online (digital literacy) with fictional narration that analyzes characters (social literacy) according to the clothing worn in the photos (fashion and cultural literacy), with a corresponding soundtrack (musical and emotional literacy). Diversified instruction critically and creatively enhances and builds on how students *already* learn from and make sense of their world. It is also a good way to connect planning to the needs of a particular group of students and to invite students to be part of the planning of their own instruction.

Activities bridge the objectives of the lesson and the students' prior knowledge and understanding. Activities also create the opportunity for collaborative learning and collective productivity. They encourage the development of personal relations and put emphasis on students as active participants in the curriculum design, while also instilling the incentive for teacher-teacher collaborations (DiPardo, 1999). Creating curriculum with multiple literacies distributes understanding and places a level of dependence on non teacher-centred knowledge (DiPardo, 2005). When prior contact with students is possible, curriculum design can involve the students and planning can be a shared process of trial and reflection. Individual activities and multi-part, unit-long, collaborative final projects can be designed to suit the predominant interests and skills students bring with them to the classroom, with the teacher providing the contextual framework and educational guidance (Gross, 1997). When students are given the opportunity to demonstrate expertise and take on the role of the teacher, their commitment to learning increases, giving ample rationale to plan for differentiated instructional practices (Birdyshaw & Hoffman, 2009). Keeping in mind that no two people learn exactly alike, it is important to diversify the types of activities in order to reach students with diverse learning styles. Students bring their own ways of knowing into the classroom environment, and these can be drawn on to deepen their learning in an English lesson context.

Pacing of activities is also very important to teachers learning their craft. The most common problem for beginning teachers is predicting how long an activity will take. Good activities have a kind of minimum length of time and can be expanded gainfully if time permits. Timing needs to account for reluctance and resistance, or for additional explanation when unusual challenges are being put forth. When activities are particularly complex and insufficient time is allotted, students can wind up resenting unrealistic expectations. For this reason, it is always advisable to try the given task out prior to assigning it: doing so makes the teacher aware of both the sequence and the difficulty of the various tasks involved, and provides direct experience and, if applicable, a sample product—very useful in modelling and demonstrating how the activity should be done and what a possible end-product might look like. This gives a realistic sense of the material and temporal requirements, as well as the basis upon which student performance at the task can be evaluated (Gronlund, 2004). Every activity requires some explicit directives and resources to be handy, keeping in mind that getting underway might take longer than expected until the activities become part of classroom routine. Diversifying learning activities is never a waste of time, however, and can be greatly beneficial to maintaining the instructional momentum, students' physical attention, and the cognitive engagement of the class with well prepared and sensibly paced activities.

Lesson planning should be done with a sense of the larger learning cycles at play, beginnings, middles, and ends that become augmented beginnings and take on more depth as teacher-student relationships deepen. These bring about a comprehensible unity and direction to instruction, activity to activity and lesson to lesson, culminating in a recognizable, measurable achievement of the objectives of a unit—even of a course (Haynes, 2010). Knowing what goes into lesson plans alerts curriculum planners to the kinds of resources they should be busily gathering as they conceive, contemplate, and construct units of instruction. Dividing up lessons of a unit can largely be based on the available resources collected for study and activities prepared in the process of developing a unit. Planning is as much about collecting and creating classroom materials as it is about pondering the bigger picture. Sometimes, a single, robust resource connected with an engaging activity is all that is required for a lesson to successfully achieve its objectives. Resources that support good lesson plans include all the selected texts, notes, and related teaching materials for instruction; resources required to complete planned activities; discussion questions and assignment specifications; evaluation criteria (if relevant); and a list of key points to review. Somewhere on the lesson plan it is useful to leave space for reflective comments so that when the unit, lesson, or activity is used again, the teacher can quickly review how it played out in the classroom and what needs to be adapted or removed to improve the learning experience.

Although this process may seem like a lot of preparation and gathering of heterogeneous resources, English teachers can productively draw from the world around them—good teaching resources are everywhere. Critical effort expended finding interesting materials that are relevant to students' lives is generally rewarded with higher levels of student engagement (Maxwell & Meiser, 1997). But teachers need look no further than the students themselves; just as they are able to lead and demonstrate expertise in learning tasks, the students can also engage in finding useful resources and deciding on supplemental texts (which they might then analyze and respond to). Collaborative planning situates learning within the context of a localized, lived curriculum connecting to students' common knowledge, experience, and understanding. Doing so also supports the many facets of Canadian culture worthy of critical appraisal, celebration, and recognition, and establishes the students' coursework as relevant to their role as citizens. This makes connecting with the specific communities that feed into the local school population a priority, joining students' in-school and out-of-school learning—a process fundamental in maintaining the relevance of English education in Canadian classrooms and, more generally, its relevance to how students live their lives (Brunn, 2010). Keeping in mind the need to build up lesson resources and activities during the preparation and planning process, we will now consider how to construct a coherent series of lessons into a unified and realizable unit plan.

Unit Planning

Maxwell and Meiser (1997) introduce the opportunity to design curriculum for the English classroom in laudatory tones, proclaiming that "preparing to be an English language arts teacher means deciding what to teach and how to teach it. What's more, one of the most satisfying and pleasurable parts of teaching is the development of units" (p. 85). Unit planning elaborates on the basic components underlying effective lesson plans by orchestrating individual lessons into coherent units. The organizing principle of a unit might focus on specific topics, texts, particular media, themes, current or student-oriented issues, passions, and areas of teacher expertise. Longer units lasting several weeks might integrate aspects of language study, reading and writing practice, larger project-based activities, community-led workshops, or self-directed inquiries that continue over the course of a term or school year. Concerning what can go into a lesson or course, Woodward (2001, p. 74) offers the following general areas for consideration: classes and people, language patterns, language skills, combinations, literature, culture, study skills, and other related subjects. Most of these are self-explanatory, but it's worth noting that by "combinations," Woodward (2001, p. 96) means the "nesting of smaller units inside bigger units," and, additionally, "different types of units." By way of illustration, she comments that *discourse analysis* when combined with *understanding group dynamics* "can be not only nested inside but also mapped onto other units" (Woodward, 2001, p. 96). Combinations allow multiple learning objectives to be incorporated into the same unit, even the same lesson. Thematic combinations also allow for multiple media, different literacies, multiple modalities, and many means of expression to be woven together with an aggregate purpose that gives impetus to the larger learning cycles.

While in some instances the purpose of unit planning is solely to address comprehension of course texts or completion of sections in a textbook, the students can benefit greatly from classroom opportunities to delve creatively into producing unique artifacts that demonstrate and apply their understanding, knowledge, and skills. Final projects that bring together course content give students the opportunity to reflect broadly and deeply on their learning throughout the unit as a whole (Zook, 2001). Furthermore, students take ownership and share responsibility for the learning process when they take pride in their projects. For a period of time, the classroom dynamic becomes a buzzing hive of creative activity, critical discussions, presentations, and speakers—all directed toward the end-goal of creating a finished product within which students have had the chance to adopt different roles and to share their expertise and competencies. At times, once the preliminary instructional work has been done and the pedagogical points have been made, the teacher can allow the students to lead the learning and can step back, being there mainly to provide pedagogical support, logistical help, and on-going, salient feedback.

Unit organization harnesses a series of coordinated learning opportunities that build upon one another and culminate in an assignment or project that allows students to broadly demonstrate their understanding. In many instances, this opportunity for highly reflective and productive learning is limited to the use of summative tests or essay questions, which lack the advantage of collective learning and coordinating the manifold aptitudes of students. Moreover, a final essay for summative evaluation should include many preliminary stages of explicit teaching, creative practice, self-directed inquiry, and revision—indeed, the whole writing process should be spread out across the sequence of lessons with frequent discussion of individual work and feedback on achievement, giving all students support in their efforts to succeed. In such a unit plan, the final essay would be a *finale*! To draw a salient analogy, if one were to write a symphony, it would be important to introduce motifs, build on the listeners' expectations, excite and subdue the emotions from movement to movement—here faster, there slower, accentuating the different instruments in the orchestra—finally building to a climax or denouement where all the pieces come together to achieve the full desired effect. This is not unlike composing a unit plan. To achieve a cohesive unit, two new concepts are added to those discussed in the previous section on lesson planning, namely scope and sequence.

Scope and sequence can be understood quite literally. Scoping involves the breadth of material to be covered in the unit, but it also involves clearly seeing the targeted learning objectives of the unit. While the unit may be organized around completing the reading of a work of literature, a selection of related texts, a chapter of a textbook, and so on, the scoping of a unit more effectively focuses on a final result of learning: the point at which objectives can be met. This may take the form of a completed project, assignment, essay, chapbook, performance, portfolio, or any other means of demonstrating enhanced facility with language, literacies, and content-based knowledge—providing also a substantive basis for evaluation (Hlebowitsh, 2005). All other unit assignments are then sequenced to prepare students for that summative demonstration of their learning. By providing routine assessment and evaluation over the course of the unit, the teacher and students are able to monitor their success at meeting unit objectives. Giving students the opportunity to apply their learning across a variety of modalities and media as well as giving feedback necessary to assess progress is critical for both students and teachers, but for differing reasons.

For students, having timely feedback on how their performance on the course-related tasks is meeting learning objectives and grade expectations helps to focus future efforts on areas where improvement will be beneficial, and can be a basic ingredient of motivation by acknowledging the merit of their efforts. From a teacher's perspective, regular assessment and evaluation enables strategic, individualized goals to be set in the pedagogical relationship and provides an understanding of which objectives are being met and which might require extra instructional effort and time. These exigencies of instructional emphasis typically vary from student to student, class to class, and unit to unit, even when the students are fairly homogeneous in terms of their backgrounds and attitudes. Therefore, ongoing assessment is an important feature of all unit planning and course delivery. Evaluation should not be left until the end of the unit, at which time it is too late for students to adjust their study habits and fine tune their comprehension of the instructional materials to suit the academic context. Woodward (2001) suggests that evaluation take place at critical junctures between the beginning, middle, and end of a unit. Furthermore, every activity undertaken by students offers assessment opportunities, whether evaluated for marks (summative assessment), or done for the pleasure of it (formative assessment); combining both critical and creative endeavours as the basis for assignments that scaffold toward a final product of evaluation makes learning an engaging, teleological process for the teacher and the students.

When a curriculum planner has conceived a final project, they can begin to scope and sequence individual lessons with a clear goal in mind, drawing together all the various strands of learning and instruction that must be undertaken leading up to it. Writing out the criteria of evaluation, the expectations, tests, rubrics, and so on, and then sequencing backwards from the last class to the first, is one way to give a planning unity and direction. Once evaluative criteria are established, the planner knows what needs to be explicitly taught throughout the course and insures that crucial information is not missed and that later assignments do not become unrealistic expectations owing to time constraints. These criteria for successful completion likewise give clarity to learning objectives prioritized in the unit and can be shared with students from the outset of instruction. Starting a unit with a general statement about key topics and objectives, as well as the ways in which learning will be demonstrated and evaluation will take place, prepares both teacher and student for what is to come. Further, it helps the teacher to maintain progress throughout the course without strangling creativity, spontaneity, and curiosity by having individual lesson plans become too fixed or unimaginative.

When the scope of learning and ways of demonstrating it have been predicted, and the strategic sequencing of lessons and activities supporting those outcomes is complete, the unifying principles underlying the planned curriculum and motivating the instructional design should be apparent. These principles should be purposefully stated in the prefatory materials of the unit plan. A prosaic introduction explaining these points will give anyone reviewing the unit plan a very clear sense of what will take place and how it figures within the development of critically astute and creatively engaged students. There is no endpoint to education. Rather, there is a spiralling complexity, cycles that begin as others come to completion: no single unit of instruction can teach us everything we need to know about a subject. Nonetheless, a primary goal of pedagogical planning is to create meaningful cycles of learning that continuously feed into one another and eventually become self-starting, self-directing, and self-perpetuating. While the particular course materials, objectives, activities, resources, final projects, and evaluative criteria vary from unit to unit, all these preparations are necessary if the unit is going to give each student equal opportunity to excel and integrate their knowledge. In the best of cases, students will integrate their knowledge not only to obtain high grades, but to learn how to best live their lives.

Conclusion

It is a conceit to suggest that just because someone can speak and write English, they can teach it as a school subject, for this inherited capacity only accounts for a small portion of what an English teacher must know and do in terms of their work with students who are studying language and developing as critical thinkers and creative individuals. Because there is no level playing field among diverse student aptitudes and interests in the classroom, attention to individual progress in language and literacy is a constant concern of the English classroom. Whatever direction your students take in life, they need to be good communicators and inquirers. If an English teacher can facilitate communicative confidence and fluency, and can help them develop a critical understanding of how meaning is construed in various kinds of texts, the benefits of careful preparation and context-sensitive instructional design transfer to all walks of life. Teachers can make an enormous difference in the lives of students, their communities, the success of the school, and even the nation overall. Planning captivating lessons and units is what makes teaching English worthwhile—undoubtedly one of the most challenging and rewarding professions. The intent of this book is to suggest the many points of departure that can help teachers to realize this goal.

* * *

When the students have finished snickering over how Enkidu is "civilized" by a temple priestess, after they've enjoyed the fight scene that ends in friendship's embrace, the teacher announces that they will finish reading this mythic narrative poem for homework. "We'll begin the next class by analyzing the concept of the heroic journey, which in this case ends less magnificently than it begins."

Sarah asks, "Doesn't that make the bug the hero of this story?"

"No," responds the teacher.

"Why not?" she shoots back.

"Well, because heroes, they come from the land of the living, even if one parent happens to be a god, heroes are born here on earth. . ." The students look puzzled, expecting a more satisfying response. ". . . Because the hero has to be willing to make the ultimate sacrifice for something or someone they believe in. They have to be willing to give their life to save something else from destruction. Things that are already in the land of the dead cannot go on the hero's journey."

A sudden mood of incredulity enters the classroom. "There are lots of dead heroes!" Suzannah exclaims.

"Yes," the teacher responds, "but are there any that became heroes after they died? The gods in mythology are not heroes—they're immortals. By definition, they can't die. Remember how Gilgamesh is introduced, he's two-thirds divine, one-third mortal, and very human. Let's keep on the lookout for other threes that appear in the text. The number might be a clue to some deeper, symbolic meanings embedded in this ancient text."

The teacher smiles as they begin flipping back through the photocopied handout.

"Now, before we worry about the heroes of the *living* dead"—taking a couple lurching steps, arms up as if a zombie—"let's ask an easier question, namely, are there any *non*-human heroes?"

Now the floodgates open: What about the Lion King? What about Nemo from *Finding Nemo*? Wall-E isn't human!

Ideas are spilling forth from everyone in the room. Momentarily, the classroom becomes loud as the students shout out their examples, trying to outdo one another. The excitement in the room palpably increases. The teacher notes that most of the examples are from animated Hollywood movies with a few pop culture references thrown in. While they are calling out their answers, the teacher busily writes their examples on the blackboard under the heading "Non-Human Heroes / Protagonists."

The teacher decides to swing the discussion to non-human heroes in books. The students had recently read *Animal Farm* by Orwell; the teacher is surprised, after mentioning the book, to learn they had forgotten about it. Soon, though, the board is filling up with an array of non-human heroes.

Halting the discussion for a moment to keep the lesson on track, the teacher says to the class, "sometimes non-human characters are used to tell stories that teach humans moral lessons, like Aesop's fables do, stories like The Tortoise and the Hare."

Jay, a First Nations student, usually quite quiet, speaks up. "My people tell stories about animal spirits. They're not always good guys, some like to play practical jokes on people, like Crow and Coyote do."

"Excellent examples, Jay," says the teacher and, seizing the teachable moment, fishes a copy of Yahgulanaas' graphic novel *Red: A Haida Manga* out of the desk—a book that was going to be introduced soon anyways as their final project for the unit.

"Let's take a minute here to talk about what we are going to do for the next three weeks. As I mentioned last week, we're going to be studying mythology from around the world. At the end of our mythology unit, you're going to invent, write, and illustrate a contemporary Canadian myth. Once we have illustrated our stories, we will post them on the school's website so you can share them with your family and friends."

The teacher then picks up a pile of photocopied handouts that give detailed instructions for the final assignment and hands them to the students. The students are then organized into groups of three in order to compare and contrast their familiar heroes—what they do that's heroic, and what their faults and failings are.

When they've finished discussing their examples, the teacher asks them to take out a piece of paper and write a paragraph about a heroic deed that they, or someone they might know, performed. The teacher checks the clock, giving a little extra time because the students are still writing—the follow-up discussion about the *Epic of Gilgamesh* will have to wait until the next class.

"Your writing won't be graded, but you will get a mark for completion, so remember to write your name on it and pass your papers forward."

Satisfied that they'll get some reward for their effort, the students pass their paragraphs to the front. With a quick review of the lesson plan, the teacher notes that several points about the hero's journey have not yet been covered. The teacher highlights them on the page as a reminder to incorporate them into the next lesson.

"To recap, myths help us strive to better ourselves by giving us examples of overcoming adversity, with superhuman feats as models for our own actions and perseverance. They also help us to imagine what we cannot possibly learn from our human senses."

The teacher pauses for a moment before continuing. "Science also produces stories that explain worlds beyond our sensory perception, and these stories slake our thirst for knowledge—but they don't help us to understand the human values embedded in our knowledge the way myths do. Myths help us to imagine the inconceivable, to pass on wisdom through countless generations."

Then, as several hands are raised to salute a new round of questions, the bell rings and the students hurriedly gather their things and rush to the hallway.

The teacher jots a few notes on how the class went, puts a star beside the collaborative poem activity, and then transfers the notes that did not get mentioned to the subsequent lesson plan. After snapping the day's plans and resource materials into the Mythology 9 binder, the teacher begins erasing the board as the grade 11 students begin to walk in the door for the next class.

When the school day is finally over and the last student with questions about an assignment has left the classroom, the teacher closes the door and takes out the responses written by the grade 9s earlier that day. While reading the responses, the teacher is careful to note not only whether the students have grasped the concept of the mythic hero, but also the individual differences in their written work. Some students are still struggling with conjugating verbs, while others write as if they are speaking to a friend with slang expressions like "the hero fights many battles, and gets to keep the gold *and stuff.*" Underlining both the problems and the particularly well-used words and phrases allows the teacher to refer to these writing issues in the feedback. The feedback is hard to keep to only a sentence or two, but given that this is for assessment, not evaluation, the teacher keeps it to a few points, commenting equally if possible on the positive and detracting aspects of the student's response.

After responding to each one, a check is placed in the mark book under a column with the date and name of the assignment. A note beside individual checkmarks reminds the teacher of individual language issues that were noticed and should be routinely assessed. If necessary, some individual language practice will help the student overcome problems. If the problem appears for many students, that aspect of language study can always be a focus during a later class when they do a close reading of an assigned text. Once the students have had a chance to note the language feature in question through close reading, they will practise using it properly, in their own writing, as they prepare to write their own heroic myths. Then, their mastery of that feature of written language can be added to the evaluation criteria for the final project of the unit.

Finally done for the day, the teacher closes the mark book, sets up the next day's lesson resources, turns off the lights, locks the door and, brushing off chalk dust, heads home.

References

Alvermann, D. E., Hinchman, K. A., Moore, D. W., Phelps, S. F. and Waff, D. R. (Eds.) (2006). *Reconceptualizing the literacies in adolescent' lives, 2nd ed.* Mahwah, NJ: Lawrence Erlbaum Associates.

Birdyshaw, D. and Hoffman, L. (2009). How can content area teachers differentiate instruction for their students to improve student learning? In J. Lewis (Ed.) *Essential questions in adolescent literacy: Teachers and researchers describe what works in classrooms* (pp. 237–261). New York: The Guilford Press.

Brunn, P. (2010). *The lesson planning handbook: Essential strategies that inspire student thinking and learning*. New York and Toronto: Scholastic.

Butt, G. (2008). *Lesson planning, 3rd ed.* London and New York: Continuum.

Crowhurst, M. (1994). *Language and learning across the curriculum.* Scarborough, ON: Allyn & Bacon Canada.

DiPardo, A. (1999). *Teaching in common: Challenges to joint work in classrooms and schools.* New York: Teachers College Press.

DiPardo, A. (2005). Teacher professionalism and the rise of "multiple literacies": How to describe our specialized knowledge. In J. Flood (Ed.) *Methods of research on teaching the English language arts: The methodology chapters of the handbook of research on teaching the English language arts, 2nd ed.* (pp. 23–42). Mahwah, NJ: Erlbaum Associates.

Gallagher, K. (2006). *Teaching adolescent writers.* Portland, ME: Stenhouse Publishers.

Gardner, J. and Maier, J. (Trans.) (1984). *Gilgamesh: Translated from the Sin-leqi-unninni version.* New York: Random House Books

Gronlund, N. E. (2004). *Writing instructional objectives for teaching and assessment, 7th ed.* Upper Saddle River, NJ: Pearson.

Haynes, A. (2010). *The complete guide to lesson planning and preparation.* London and New York: Continuum.

Hlebowitsh, P. S. (2005). *Designing the school curriculum.* Boston, MA: Pearson Education.

Maxwell, R. J. & Meiser, M. J. (1997). *Teaching English in middle and secondary schools, 2nd ed.* Upper Saddle River, NJ: Merrill, Prentice Hall.

Pritchard, J. B. (Ed.). (1958). *The ancient Near East, Volume 1: An anthology of texts and pictures.* Princeton, NJ: Princeton University Press.

Ur, P. (1996). *A course in language teaching: Practice and theory.* Cambridge, UK: Cambridge University Press.

Willinsky, J. (1990). *The new literacy: Redefining reading and writing in the schools.* London and New York: Routledge.

Woodward, T. (2001). *Planning lessons and courses: Designing sequences of work for the language classroom.* Cambridge, UK: Cambridge University Press.

Yahgulanaas, M. N. (2010). *Red: A Haida manga.* Vancouver, BC: Douglas & Macintyre.

Zook, K. B. (2001). *Instructional design for classroom teaching and learning.* Boston, MA: Houghton Mifflin Company.

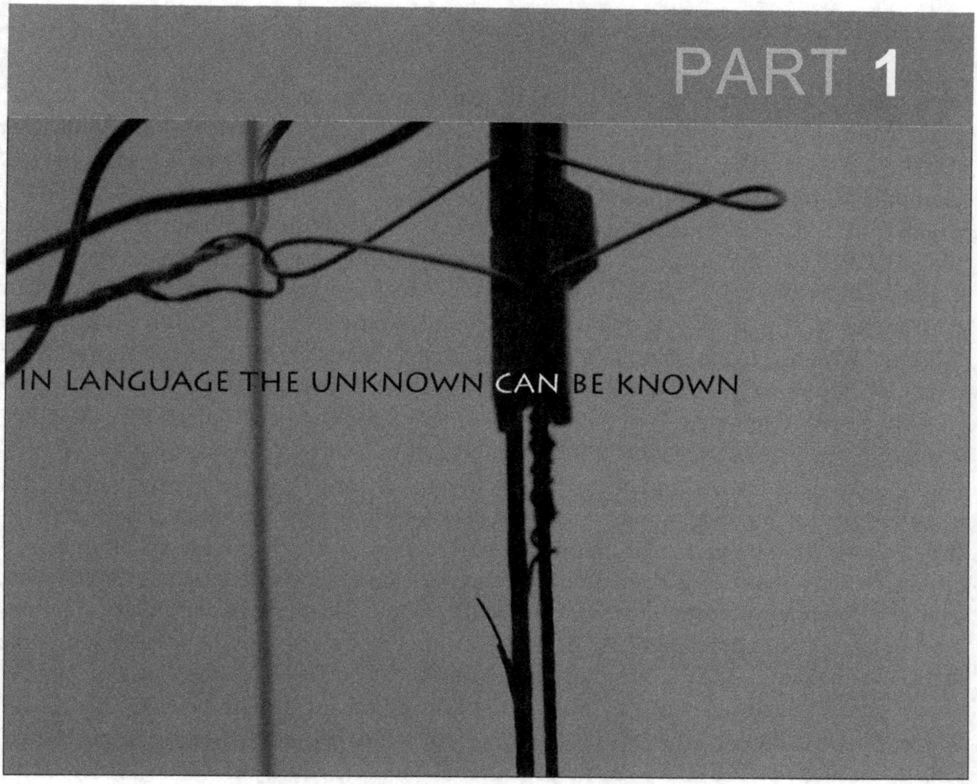

Including Diverse Learners

By Teresa M. Dobson, University of British Columbia

Diversity among learners may exist along many lines, including ethnicity, language, socio-economic status, religion, gender, sexual orientation, learning style, learning ability, and others. Kahn and Hillwig (2010) observe that, in contemplating the question of diversity in classrooms, people tend to think foremost of differences that may be outwardly discernible such as ethnicity, sex, or language use; and yet, in classroom environments "it is important that when we refer to diverse learners the term broadens to include students' individual learning and communication styles, abilities, disabilities, proficiencies, and talents" (p. 64). That is to say, even a group of students appearing to share many things in common are likely to be diverse in their learning preferences and abilities.

It's worth contemplating further the latter types of diversity named by Kahn and Hillwig. Learner "abilities" and "disabilities," to use their terminology, may include categories such as "gifted" or "learning disordered" (LD). The sorting of learners into such categories tends to occur through measurement against a societal norm. For example, Kronenberger and Dunn (2003) define "learning disorder," which encompasses a wide range of subtypes, as "significant deficits in learning relative to expectations based on the individual's age and intellectual ability, which cannot be completely explained by environment or other psychologic symptoms" (p. 941). The phrase "learning styles," on the other hand, tends to denote individual approaches to learning. There is much literature outlining different taxonomies of learning styles or approaches (e.g., Gregorc, 1982; Kolb, 1984; Fleming & Mills, 1992; Gardner, 1983, 1999; Honey & Mumford, 2006). Pashler, McDaniel, Rohrer, and Bjork (2008) propose that "most learning-styles taxonomies are 'type' theories: That is, they classify people into supposedly distinct groups" (p. 107). For example, Gardner's theory of "Multiple Intelligences" (Gardner, 1983, 1999), which is popular in North American educational contexts, suggests that learners have different aptitudes: "visual-spatial" learners may be highly aware of their environments, "linguistic" learners may excel on verbal tasks, and so on. Fleming and Mills's "VARK" theory similarly proposes that learners have different dispositions: visual, auditory, read/write, and kinesthetic (Fleming & Mills, 1992).

While such approaches are helpful in keeping educators mindful of the individual learning preferences of students, it is also important to bear in mind that they have limitations. Gauging a learner's ability or disability in relation to societal expectations, for instance, is questionable insofar as societal norms are never static, but rather are constructed over time by particular groups of people. An individual who fares well in a society that values book learning may not fare as well in a society that values apprenticed, hands-on learning of crafts or trades. As well, grouping learners in particular categories may discourage examination of the diversity *within* those categories, or recognition of the fact that a learner may fit descriptors for multiple categories (as is the case for "twice-exceptional" students, defined as those who fit the definition of both "gifted" and "LD" due to "high potential or ability concurrent with the experience of learning problems" [Dix & Schafer, p. 153]). As Pashler, McDaniel, Rohrer, and Bjork (2008) observe, the "assumption that people actually cluster into distinct groups" is one that may be challenged (p. 107).

Ultimately, in trying to account for diversity, it is somewhat ironic that the dominant approach is to classify. Such classification makes it all too easy to fall into the trap of "essentialism"—the view that particular groups of people, whether identified on the basis of learning ability, style, ethnicity, sex, or language, have "essential" characteristics and might therefore be treated similarly (e.g., my students of a particular ethnicity are bound to enjoy this book because the protagonist is of the same ethnicity). Again, such an approach fails to take account of the inevitable diversity within categories. In the end, it seems the best we can do is to accept that no system of classification is infallible because all learners are unique. Perhaps the greatest challenge for teachers in any educational setting, and particularly in educational settings with high student-to-instructor ratios, will be recognizing and meeting the distinct needs of individual learners.

Diversity in Multicultural and Multilingual Settings

Globally, Canada has a reputation for multiculturalism and multilingualism. The extent of this reputation was made clear to me not long ago when I was meeting with colleagues in the Department of English Language Education at Bahir Dar University in Ethiopia. Like Canada, Ethiopia is a country of vast linguistic and ethnic diversity. Although reported figures vary between sources, Wedekind (2002) identified 99 languages spoken as "mother tongues," and Bloor and Tamrat (1996) have offered a figure of "more than 90 different 'ethnic groups'" (p. 323). Over 80 ethnic groups were identified in the 2007 Census (Central Statistical Agency of Ethiopia, 2008). On the day of my meeting, Ato Zelalem Gefnef, an Ethiopian scholar in the area of multilingual education aware of

Canada's linguistic diversity and language policies, was eager to share experiences of the challenges facing educators in multilingual contexts. Together with a group of colleagues from Canada and Ethiopia, we considered a number of important questions for educators in both countries.

These questions included the following: How does knowing particular languages empower individuals? How does one settle on a language of instruction in a country of vast linguistic and ethnic diversity? Should the language of instruction in schools be a country's "official" language, even if the majority of people do not speak that language? (Ethiopia's "official" language, for example, is Amharic, although the Amharic people comprise only about a quarter of the population [Central Statistical Agency of Ethiopia, 2008].) Or should the language of instruction be one that will empower youth within and beyond the local context? (English, for example, is recognized within and beyond Ethiopia as a *lingua franca*—that is, a language of intercommunication between people speaking different languages.) Or should the language of instruction be decided regionally, perhaps being the predominant language spoken in any given region? That is, should children have the right to education in their first language even if it is not an "official" language of the country? How would one manage such a multilingual education system? Were it possible, what would implementing such a multilingual education system mean for national identity? If a "nation" is an "aggregate of communities and individuals united by factors such as common descent, language, culture, history, or occupation of the same territory" ("Nation," n.d.), and if language and culture are inextricably linked (e.g., Joseph, 2004), then might using different languages of instruction in different regions across a nation begin to undo the very fabric of that nation? What is the role of language in defining nation and what is the role of education in nation building? Ultimately, and here we come back to a question raised earlier, is it possible to balance the diverse needs and goals of individual learners with the broader needs and goals of society?

Individuals aiming to teach English language arts in any context would do well to consider such issues, and this is particularly important in countries with a history of colonialism such as Canada. Contemplating the question of language and nation building, for instance, Mullaney (2010) remarks on the way in which language, literature, and the field of English literary studies itself are integrally linked to imperialism:

> The emergence of the academic study of English as a distinct discipline coincides with the expansion of Empire in the nineteenth century and the need, on the part of the colonizer, to find a common language through which to rule and unite the spaces of Empire. In this, language is an instrument of conquest and literature its repertoire. The subsequent privileging of English, its institutionalizing as the language of Empire, suggests that Empire and the development and study of English literature were mutually constitutive of each other. (pp. 33–34)

In Canada, where nineteenth-century colonization coincided with the development of public education, the language of instruction remains the language of the colonizer (be it English or French), and the school literary canon has long reflected the veracity of Mullaney's assessment. Even as that canon has expanded to include diverse texts from "world literature," those texts are necessarily read in the *lingua franca,* English, and this has implications for their interpretation.

Similar to Ethiopia, Canada is an ethnically and linguistically diverse country. It is worth taking a moment to detail the extent of that diversity. According to Statistics Canada, "more than 200 different ethnic origins were reported in the 2006 Census," and "an estimated 5 068 100 individuals were members of the visible minority population" (Statistics Canada, 2006a). The country is multilingual: 58 percent of the population report English as their mother tongue, 22 percent report French, and 20 percent report a range of languages other than English or French (Statistics Canada, 2006b; see Table 1). The breakdown of linguistic diversity, however, varies greatly from region to region, with Toronto emerging as most linguistically diverse in 2006 (nearly half the population of Toronto reported a "non-official" language as their mother tongue).

Table 1 **Reported "Mother Tongue" for All of Canada and for Five Census Metropolitan Areas**

The data is drawn from the "Community Profiles" section of the 2006 Census (Statistics Canada, 2006b). Percentage figures are rounded to the nearest whole number. Multiple answers (i.e., the answers of individuals reporting more than one mother tongue) are not reflected in this data.

	English	French	Non-official Languages	Total Responses
Canada	58%	22%	20%	30 848 270
Edmonton	77%	2%	21%	1 024 820
Halifax	91%	3%	6%	369 455
Montreal	12%	65%	23%	3 588 520
Toronto	54%	1%	45%	5 072 075
Vancouver	57%	1%	42%	2 097 960

At the time of the writing of this book, the Canadian 2011 Census was complete and data analysis under way; therefore, a more current accounting of Canada's linguistic diversity should be available shortly. Initial published findings from the 2011 Census indicate that Canada's population has grown more rapidly (6 percent between 2006 and 2011) than that of the other economically privileged countries collectively known as the "Group of Eight" (G8) and is presently just about 33.5 million (Statistics Canada, 2011). We also know that the "growth has been driven mainly by migratory increase" (Statistics Canada, 2011). Further, Citizenship and Immigration Canada (2012) reports that between 2001 and 2010 the top three "source countries" for new Canadians have been the People's Republic of China, the Philippines, and India—by a wide margin. Notably, of the top 10 source countries listed in the past 10 years, only two are English speaking (Citizenship and Immigration Canada, 2012). In consideration of these facts about population growth and trends in global migration, we can anticipate increased linguistic and ethnic diversity in future years; indeed, in "Census Metropolitan Areas" such as Toronto and Vancouver, the number of "non-official" language speakers may in short order outnumber the number of "official" language speakers.

How might teachers of English language arts be called on to respond to these cultural changes in the classroom? Casbon, Schimer, and Twiss (1997) observe that different cultures have unique epistemologies, or knowledge frameworks, and that educators in diverse contexts need to remain attuned to such differences. This research group also points to the work of psychology researchers Sue and Sue (1990), who, "in examining barriers to effective cross-cultural counselling . . . have found differences in culture-bound values; in verbal, emotional, and behavioural expressiveness; in cause-and-effect orientation; and in patterns of communication" (Casbon, Schimer, & Twiss, 1997, p. 602). Such differences, they note, may lead "to misunderstanding between culturally different populations" (p. 602). Silence, for example, may be misinterpreted as hostility, a compliment may be misconstrued as an attempt at manipulation, and so on.

It is important, as well, to recognize the unique nature of Canadian multilingualism. I began this section by remarking on the similarities between two multilingual countries, Ethiopia and Canada. And yet, for all their similarities in terms of linguistic diversity, there is an important difference. Historically, there has been little immigration to Ethiopia: attempts at colonization were largely unsuccessful, and the bulk of its languages, including its "official" language, are Indigenous (the history is complicated and beyond the scope of this text; suffice it to say, a period of Italian occupation and claims to an empire including Ethiopia tend not to be viewed as colonization [e.g., Colburn, 1991, p. 579]). On the contrary, as reported above, there has been a great deal of immigration to Canada and, notably, most of its languages (including its two "official" languages) are imported. Canada is known for its inclusive language policies: Part I of the Canadian Constitution Act, the Charter of Rights and Freedoms, guarantees minority language educational rights to French-speaking communities outside Quebec (Section 23, Canadian Charter of Rights and Freedoms, 1982). This document, however, historically has protected only the language rights of two groups of colonists, English and French; it has not protected the rights of other language groups, most notably the rights of Indigenous peoples who occupied the geographic region now known as Canada in the first instance.

Norris (2007) notes that across Canada there are "some 50 or more individual languages belonging to 11 Aboriginal language families" in use; unfortunately, "over the past 100 years or more, at least ten once-flourishing languages have become extinct" (p. 19). Educators cannot ignore the fact that Canadian education and language policies have played a key role in what can only be described as the genocide—the deliberate and systematic destruction—of Canadian Aboriginal peoples over an extended period of colonization (Robinson & Quinney, 1985). Nor can the effects of this language loss be underestimated. As Norris notes, "These languages reflect distinctive histories, cultures and identities linked to family, community, the land and traditional knowledge. For many First Nations, Inuit and Métis people, these languages are at the very core of their identity" (p. 19).

Canada's linguistic and ethnic diversity, therefore, is highly complex. The constituent groups of our multilingual population include Indigenous peoples, immigrants, migrants, and refugees. Teachers of English language arts at all levels need to be sensitive to the needs of English as a Second Language (ESL) or English as an Additional Language (EAL) learners and need to find ways of integrating these learners in their classrooms. The question of what sort of English is privileged is also paramount. Census data reveals that many Canadians speak multiple languages in their homes and that some, when asked to state their mother tongue, name more than one language, likely because they cannot distinguish which they learned first (Statistics Canada, 2006b). In scenarios where English is learned alongside other languages, hybrid or variant dialects may emerge. Many "blend-names" have been coined for such variants, such as "Chinglish," "Frenglish" or "franglais," "Gerlish," "Japlish," "Swenglish," or "Taglish" (McArthur, 1998, p. 14).

As McArthur notes, these do not refer strictly to hybridization, but to unique "kinds of English spoken by people from particular backgrounds" (p. 14). Many aspiring teachers are surprised to learn that it is not uncommon for children born and raised in Canada to come to school with English as a Second Language or English as a Second Dialect (ESD)—the latter meaning they know a dialect of English but need to be taught whichever variant of Standard English (SE) is in use in a particular region (e.g., Epstein & Xu, 2003). Entries that follow in Part 1 by Lynne Wiltse, Jan Hare, Lee Gunderson, Susan Walsh, Erika Hasebe-Ludt, and Janette Hughes and Allyson Eamer take up some of the issues I have touched on in the preceding discussion, offering practical suggestions for classroom teachers.

Gender and Sexual Diversity

Meyer (2010) observes that schools "play a key role in teaching and reinforcing the dominant values of culture and this holds especially true in areas of gender and sexuality" (p. 3). Citing Blaise (2005) and Renold (2000), she notes, "From the first day they enter pre-school or kindergarten, children are identified by their sex on registration forms, referred to as 'boys and girls,' and their gender is consistently practiced and reinforced through stories, free play, and interactions with their teachers and their peers" (Meyer, 2010). Meyer provides a useful literature review in which she outlines some reasons it is important to become knowledgeable about issues related to gender and sexual diversity, including the following: 1) young people who do not conform to dominant notions of heterosexual masculinity and femininity (for example, boys who are not athletic and girls who are) may become victims of bullying; 2) students who are ostracized and isolated may suffer in their mental and physical well-being; 3) issues of equity need to be addressed to ensure equal opportunity for success; 4) it is vital to create an inclusive and supportive learning environment for all (Meyer, pp. 4–6). With regard to this last item, Canadian English language arts educator John Guiney Yallop (2002, 2004, 2007) argues that it is also important to be aware of and teach about social justice for bisexual, gay, lesbian, queer, transgender, transsexual, and/or two-spirited people. Notably, social justice values are applicable in consideration of all areas of diversity discussed herein. As van Rensburg (2004) writes, drawing on the early work of Iris Marion Young (1990), the goal of social justice is "the full participation and inclusion of everyone in the major institutions of society, and the socially supported opportunity for all to develop and exercise their capacities and realize their choices" (p. 1). Entries by John Guiney Yallop as well as Kathy Hibbert, Danika Barber, and Tim Ludwig address some of these issues in greater detail.

The problem of achievement and gender has also been a topic of concern in Canada and globally for many years. Corbeil (2003), who reviewed trends in Canadian education among learners from three linguistic groups (francophone, anglophone, and allophone) from 1971 to 2001, writes:

> In 1971, the gap between university educated men and women aged 25 to 34 was considerable. Among all three linguistic groups, men were at least twice as likely as women to have a university degree. . . . By 1991, the number of 25- to 34-year-old women with university degrees had caught up with the number of men in all three language groups and by 2001 they had surpassed them. (p. 11)

In 2001, Corbeil notes that young women were also "less likely to have not yet graduated from high school than young men" (p. 9). More recently, the Canadian Council on Learning (2009) reported that between 2003 and 2006, PISA (Programme for International Student Assessment) results in Canada showed a similar shift: in 2003, boys outperformed girls in math and science, but by 2006 there were no differences on the combined science scale. Where there *is* a marked difference in achievement is in the area of reading. A strong female reading advantage has been observed in 57 countries participating in PISA testing, including Canada, for many years. Possible reasons suggested for the difference are test bias (Lietz, 2006) and attitudes and behaviours (e.g., girls do more out-of-school reading) (Gambell & Hunter, 2000). In this volume, entries by Roberta Hammett, Meredith Cherland, Douglas Gosse, and Kathy Sanford examine the question of gender and English language arts learning, including the complex matter of sex differences in achievement.

References

Blaise, M. (2005). *Playing it straight! Uncovering gender discourses in the early childhood classroom.* New York: Routledge Press.

Bloor, T. & Tamrat, W. (1996). Issues in Ethiopian language policy and education. *Journal of Multilingual and Multicultural Development* 17(5), 321–338.

Canadian Charter of Rights and Freedoms. (1982). Part I of the Constitution Act, 1982, RSC 1985, app. II, no. 44.

Canadian Council on Learning. (2009). *Why boys don't like to read: Gender differences in reading achievement.* http://www.ccl-cca.ca/pdfs/LessonsInLearning/02_18_09-E.pdf (accessed March 2, 2012).

Casbon, J., Schirmer, B. R., & Twiss, L. (1997). Diverse learners in the classroom. *The Reading Teacher* 50(7), 602–604.

Central Statistical Agency of Ethiopia. (2008). *Population and housing census 2007.* Addis Ababa, Ethiopia: Federal Democratic Republic of Ethiopia Population Census Commission. http:// www.csa.gov.et (accessed March 2, 2012).

Citizenship and Immigration Canada. (2012). *Canada: Permanent residents by source country.* http://www.cic.gc.ca/english/resources/statistics/facts2010/permanent/10.asp (accessed March 2, 2012).

Colburn, F. D. (1991). The People's Democratic Republic of Ethiopia: Masking and unmasking tragedy. *World Politics* 43(4), 570–587.

Corbeil, J. P. (2003). 30 years of education: Canada's language groups. *Canadian Social Trends* 71, 8–12.

Dix, J. & Schafer, S. (2005). From paradox to performance: Practical strategies for identifying and teaching gifted/LD students. In K. Johnsen & J. Kendrick (Eds.), *Teaching gifted students with disabilities* (pp. 153–160). Waco, TX: Prufrock Press.

Epstein, R. I. & Xu, L. X. J. (2003). *Roots and wings: Teaching English as a second dialect to Aboriginal students, a review of the literature.* Saskatoon, SK: University of Saskatchewan.

Fleming, N. D. & Mills, C. (1992). Not another inventory, rather a catalyst for reflection. *To Improve the Academy* 11, 137–155.

Gambell, T. & Hunter, D. (2000). Surveying gender differences in Canadian school literacy. *Journal of Curriculum Studies* 32, 689–719.

Gardner, H. (1983). *Frames of mind: The theory of multiple intelligences.* New York: Basic Books.

———. (1999). *Intelligence reframed: Multiple intelligences for the 21st century.* New York: Basic Books.

Gregorc, A. F. (1982). *Gregorc style delineator: Development, technical and administration manual.* Columbia, CT: Gregorc Associates.

Guiney Yallop, J. J. (2002). Experiencing school: Stories from gays. In V. Sunnari, J. Kangasvuo, & M. Heikkinen (Eds.), *Gendered and sexualised violence in educational environments* (pp. 243–249). Oulu, Finland: University of Oulu and Femina Borealis.

———. (2004). Gay and out in secondary school: One youth's story. In J. McNinch & M. Cronin (Eds.), *I could not speak my heart: Education and social justice for gay and lesbian youth* (pp. 29–42). Regina, SK: Canadian Plains Research Center.

———. (2007). Surviving the pain and widening the circle: Celebrating lesbian and gay pride week in an elementary classroom. In I. Killoran & K. Pendleton Jimenez (Eds.), *"Unleashing the unpopular": Talking about sexual orientation and gender diversity in education.* Olney, MD: Association for Childhood Education International.

Honey, P. & Mumford, A. (2006). *The learning styles questionnaire 80-item version.* Maidenhead, UK: Peter Honey Publications.

Joseph, J. (2004). *Language and identity: National, ethnic, religious.* New York: Palgrave Macmillan.

Kahn, A. & Hillwig, P. (2010). Addressing today's diverse learners. *Journal of Psychological Issues in Organizational Culture* 1(2), 64–70.

Kolb, D. (1984). *Experiential learning: Experience as the source of learning and development.* Englewood Cliffs, NJ: Prentice-Hall.

Kronenberger, W. G. & Dunn, D. W. (2003). Learning disorders. *Neurologic Clinics* 21(4), 941–952.

Lietz, P. (2006). A meta-analysis of gender differences in reading achievement at the secondary school level. *Studies in Educational Evaluation* 32, 317–344.

McArthur, T. (1998). *The English languages.* Cambridge, United Kingdom: Cambridge University Press.

Meyer, E. (2010) *Gender and sexual diversity in schools.* New York: Springer.

Mullaney, J. (2010). *Postcolonial literatures in context.* London: Continuum International Publishing.

"Nation." OED Online. December 2011. Oxford University Press. http://oed.com/viewdictionaryentry/Entry/125285 (accessed March 2, 2012).

Norris, M. J. (2007). Aboriginal languages in Canada: Emerging trends and perspectives on second language acquisition. *Canadian Social Trends* 83, 19–27.

Pashler, H., McDaniel, M., Rohrer, D., & Bjork, R. (2008). Learning styles: Concepts and evidence. *Psychological Science in the Public Interest* 9(3), 105–119.

Renold, E. (2000). Coming out: Gender (hetero)sexuality and the primary school. *Gender and Education* 12(3), 309–326.

Robinson, E. & Quinney, H. B. (1985). *The infested blanket: Canada's constitution, genocide of Indian nations*. Winnipeg, MB: Queenston House Pub.

Statistics Canada. (2006a). *Canada Census 2006: Ethnic origin and visible minorities.* http://www12.statcan.ca/census-recensement/2006/rt-td/eth-eng.cfm (accessed March 2, 2012).

———. (2006b). *2006 community profiles*. http://www12.statcan.gc.ca/census-recensement/2006/dp-pd/prof/92-591/index.cfm (accessed March 2, 2012).

———. (2011). *The Canadian population in 2011: Population counts and growth census 2011.* http://www12.statcan.gc.ca/census-recensement/2011/as-sa/98-310-x/98-310-x2011001-eng.cfm (accessed March 2, 2012).

Sue, D. W. & Sue, D. (1990). *Counselling the culturally different: Theory and practice*. New York: Wiley University Press.

van Rensburg, W. (2004). Social justice. *Education as Change* 8(1), 1–2.

Wedekind, K. (2002). Updating linguistic maps. *SIL Electronic Survey Reports 2002-061*. SIL International. http://www.sil.org/silesr/2002/SILESR2002-061.pdf (accessed March 2, 2012).

Young, I. M. (1990). *Justice and the politics difference.* Princeton, NJ: Princeton University Press.

SECTION 1

Indigeneity

Why Is It Important to Consider Cultural Diversity in Relation to Text Selection?

By Lynne Wiltse, University of Alberta

"Children need books that are mirrors in which they can see and learn about themselves, and books that are windows open to the rest of the world" (Aldana, 2009, p. 1). This comment, made by Patsy Aldana, President of the Canadian Coalition for School Libraries, encapsulates for me the two main reasons why it is important to consider cultural diversity in relation to text selection. As an avid reader since childhood, I knew first-hand about the second point in Aldana's claim that, in the words of Mary Napoli, literature can "allow readers to imagine beyond the boundaries of their own environment to broaden their vision of self and their world" (Napoli, 2007, p. 55). Also, as much of the literature I read as a child reflected my white, middle-class background and experiences, I had taken Aldana's first point for granted. It was not until my first teaching job in a small, predominantly Aboriginal community in the Cariboo-Chilcotin region of British Columbia 30 years ago that I came to understand the importance of the first part of Aldana's statement. Johnston (2010) explains that it is "important to be able to recognize ourselves in a book, particularly if we, as readers, are from a culture that has been marginalized or previously unrecognized in literary texts in the west" (p. 135).

Johnston's comment describes well the grade 7 and 8 students who sat before me in my first English language arts class. I was encouraged to see that one book on the prescribed reading list, *Boss of the Namko Drive: A Story from Cariboo Country* (St. Pierre, 1965), was actually set in the local area and featured two "Indian cowboys" as main characters. However, much to my chagrin, this book served to further marginalize Aboriginal culture, as can be seen from the following select examples from the text: "Anatole was slow to understand things and, in fact, . . . stupid" (p. 62); "Never trust Siwashes near booze, I tell ya. It don't act on them like a white man" (p. 66). That the main character tried to defend the Indian cowboys, or that these characters helped to save the cattle drive in the end, did not seem to matter—the damage was done.

Thirty years later, the good news is that there is a range of suitable literature that I could use with a similar class of students. In addition to increased publication of literary texts by authors of Aboriginal heritage, there has also been an upsurge in texts authored by immigrant and first-generation Canadians. This increase of multicultural texts in the publishing industry reflects the increased cultural diversity in Canadian society. While these texts have the potential to be used as resources to address questions of historical injustices and inequities in Canadian society, many English language arts teachers are still uncomfortable in making changes to their selection of primarily American and British canonized texts (Bainbridge, Carbonaro, & Green, 2005; Johnston, 2010; Ward, 2010). These circumstances emphasize the need to continue the work of diversifying the selection of literature.

In the 30 years since my first teaching job, Canada's population has changed dramatically with more than 200 different ethnic origins reported in the online report "Canada's Ethnocultural Mosaic, 2006 Census" (Statistics Canada, 2008). Bainbridge (2010) notes that if current population trends continue, "Canada's visible minority population will continue to grow much more quickly than the non-visible minority population" (p. 97). The significance of this is that if teachers do not consider cultural diversity in relation to text selection, an increasing number of students will not recognize themselves in the Western literary canon.

A case in point is the culturally and linguistically diverse grade 9 class in which I conducted my doctoral study. For the most part, the teacher chose books that are considered to have "stood the test of time" (Johnston, 2010, p. 133), including a number that I read in secondary school 30 years earlier—for example, *The Pearl* (Steinbeck, 1976) and the short story "The Most Dangerous Game" (Connell, 1981).[1] Given that approximately 75 percent of the students in the inner-city school were Asian immigrants or refugees (Cambodian, Vietnamese, and Chinese), these choices were of particular concern. I wondered if texts such as *The Clay Marble* (Ho, 1991), the story about a Cambodian family separated by the war, or *Tales from Gold Mountain* (Yee, 1990), a short story collection about Chinese immigrants to Canada, might have better engaged the students in that class by providing "cultural affirmation . . . through exposure to main protagonists that share the same culture as the reader" (Loh, 2009, p. 293).

As a graduate student at the University of Alberta, I worked on a research project in which Loh's point about cultural affirmation was further reinforced. Two grade 7 classes in a culturally diverse inner-city school were supplied with a contemporary set of multicultural picture books and novels. As a research assistant, I interviewed a number of the

1 These two texts were first published in 1947 and 1924, respectively.

grade 7 students about their preferences after they had read the books. In a chapter entitled "Sites of discovery and discomfort: Reading and teaching multicultural literature," Johnston (2000) discusses the study results. A number of research participants chose books featuring characters from the same ethnic background as themselves. For example, Kari, one of the students I interviewed whose family came from Vietnam, chose *Rainbow People* by Laurence Yep (1989)—a collection of Chinese folktales told by immigrant workers—"because," as she said, "I'm sort of Oriental, too" (p. 140).[2] She also chose Paul Yee's *Ghost Train* (1996), a historical account of the dangers Chinese immigrants faced in building Canada's railways, because, as she said, aspects of the book "reminded me of things I do at home, like the incense" (p. 140). Johnston (2010) reminds us that this type of recognition may be more complicated than it first appears. For teachers who are wondering whether they should choose books that somehow "represent" the cultural backgrounds of their students, Johnston explains that good multicultural literature can provide "this sense of familiarity when the characters and setting are outside our own familiar milieu" (p. 135).[3] On this note, many students in the study chose books because they could relate in ways other than culture to the characters' lives and experiences (for example, stories of immigration, loss, and being a newcomer).

Another set of examples can be found in a recent research project in which six Canadian scholars explored pre-service teachers' responses to issues of identity and representation in contemporary multicultural Canadian picture books.[4] As part of the study, the pre-service teachers were asked to select a book from a collection of more than 70 multicultural picture books, which they would then use as the basis to plan and teach a lesson. Geneva, an Aboriginal student teacher, chose *Two Pairs of Shoes* (Sanderson, 1990), a story about an Aboriginal girl who receives two pairs of shoes for her birthday—a patent leather pair she had been coveting and a pair of beaded handmade moccasins from her grandmother who tells her that she must learn when and how to wear each pair. In the following interview excerpt, Geneva, who was adopted by a white family at age three weeks, describes her strong personal connection to the book:

> I made that choice because that's what I feel like my life was. The way I grew up is I always had the patent leather shoes and everything I needed. But, when I met my First Nations family when I was fourteen I started learning about moccasins and tanning, moose meat drying and smoking fish. And, that was very difficult for me because by that time all my cousins had been doing that for many years, so I was made fun of, called a red apple, white on the inside, red on the outside.

As part of the lesson she taught, Geneva brought in artifacts from her Aboriginal heritage to share with her students. The following excerpt provides an example as to the "sense of familiarity" that multicultural literature can provide:

---

2 All research participants have been given pseudonyms.

3 As a detailed description of the literary merit of multicultural literature is beyond the scope of this paper, please see Johnston (2010) or Rochman (1993) for further information. In addition, Bainbridge (2010) provides a set of questions that teachers can use to evaluate multicultural literature.

4 The research project was a Social Sciences and Humanities Research Council (SSHRC) funded study, *Pre-service Teachers' Perspectives on Canadian Identity and Their Understandings of Ideology in Multicultural Picture Books.* Co-investigators were I. Johnston (Principal Investigator), J. Bainbridge, A. Burke, M. C. Courtland, R. Hammett, T. Strong-Wilson, A. Ward, and L. Wiltse.

> There was one boy whose eyes lit up when I brought my baby basket, beaded earrings and deerskin vest. He was so excited to tell me that his step-mom has one of those baskets, and could he bring it. He was so proud that he could contribute something to the lesson. And, other students talked about their cultural backgrounds, like Indo-Canadian students. So, this lesson was important, not just in the First Nations component, but in having students explore their identity.

While Geneva's experience is illustrative of the significance of cultural affirmation, responses to Aboriginal literature from other students in this study demonstrated that "from cross-cultural perspectives, exposure to literary texts about other cultures allows for the imagination of a world where self exists in relation to other" (Loh, 2009, p. 293). Karina, a student teacher of European heritage, chose *Shi-Shi-Etko* (Campbell, 2005), a story of the last few days of an Aboriginal girl's life at home with her family before leaving for residential school.

> I chose *Shi-Shi-Etko* because I found it very surprising that the first time I learned about residential school was when I was in university . . . I really wanted to make sure that my grade 7 students had the opportunity to learn about this topic sooner. Before I taught my lesson, I spoke with my boyfriend, who had never heard of residential schools. It was interesting to use this book to enlighten him on the subject, and he said that it started to change some of his negative perceptions of First Nations People.

Comparable responses were expressed by a number of the non-Aboriginal research participants to *This Land Is My Land,* Littlechild's (1993) autobiographical account of the struggles his family endured over several generations:

> As a young child, I often chose to read historical settings, and I romanticized First Nations culture. I was unaware that there was a difference between then and now. But, when I decided to get into the field of education, I realized I'm likely going to teach in a small community with First Nations students . . . I knew I had to fill in the blanks. So, with this project, I gravitated towards the books with First Nations content, like *This Land is My Land*. I think Littlechild's book has a place in the classroom—let's talk about it with our students now.

In contemporary Canada, cross-cultural understanding between Aboriginal and non-Aboriginal people is crucial if we hope to settle peacefully ongoing issues such as land claims; multicultural literature has the potential to play a role in this process.

Not only is there increased cultural diversity in Canadian classrooms, we also live and teach in an increasingly global world. Loh (2009) makes the point that "in this age of globalization, . . . one needs to understand difference and complexity within and beyond the locality of one's physical neighbourhood" (p. 287). In this regard, Yandell (2008) draws on teaching experiences to offer examples of how the literature read in the classroom "can contribute towards students' understanding of and engagement with the wider world" (p. 25). In previous times, Beverly Naidoo's *Journey to Jo'burg* (1985) taught students about apartheid in South Africa, while more recently *A Little Piece of Ground* (Laird & Nimr, 2003) is teaching students about the impact of occupation on Palestinians. Literary texts such as these serve as open spaces to begin conversations about past, present, and future world events.

In closing, it is important to emphasize that the use of multicultural literature in the classroom must be "accompanied with appropriate pedagogy where discussion and critical reading is encouraged" (Loh, 2009, p. 291). While research shows that talking about books in general promotes students' comprehension of texts (Evans, 2009;

Nystrand, 2006; Wiltse, 2005, 2006), the reading of multicultural literature in particular must be "coupled with dialogic instruction within a safe classroom context" (Glazier & Seo, 2005, p. 686). I am not proud that I cringed in silence as my first students saw themselves portrayed in a derogatory manner in a mandatory class novel. As beginning teachers now have improved access to culturally relevant texts, my story need not be repeated.

References

Campbell, N. (2005). *Shi-shi-etko.* (K. La Fave, Illustr.). Toronto, ON: Groundwood Books.

Connell, R. (1981). The most dangerous game. In John E. Warriner (Ed.), *Short stories: Characters in conflict.* Orlando, FL: Harcourt Brace Jovanovich.

Evans, J. (2009). *Talking beyond the page: Reading and responding to picturebooks.* New York and London: Routledge.

Ho, M. (1991). *The clay marble.* New York: Farrar, Strauss & Giroux.

Laird, E. & Nimr, S. (2003). *A little piece of ground.* London: Macmillan.

Littlechild, G. (1993). *This land is my land.* San Francisco: Children's Book Press.

Naidoo, B. (1985). *Journey to Jo'burg: A South African story.* London: Longman.

St. Pierre, P. (1965). *Boss of the Namko drive: A story from Cariboo country.* Toronto, ON: The Ryerson Press.

Sanderson, E. (1990). *Two pairs of shoes.* (D. Beyer, Illustr.). Winnipeg, MB: Pemmican Publications Inc.

Steinbeck, J. (1976). *The pearl.* Harmondsworth, United Kingdom: Penguin Books.

Yee, P. (1989). *Tales from gold mountain.* Toronto, ON: Douglas & McIntyre.

Yee, P. (1996). *Ghost train.* Illustrated by H. Chan. Toronto, ON: Groundwood Books.

Yep, L. (1989). *Rainbow people.* New York: HarperTrophy.

Additional Resources

Aldana, P. (2009). Canadian Society of Children's Authors, Illustrators and Performers. News Release, June 17.

Bainbridge, J. (2010). Canadian multicultural picture books for young adolescents. In M. C. Courtland & T. Gambell (Eds.), *Literature, media & multiliteracies in adolescent language arts* (pp. 79–102). Vancouver, BC: Pacific Educational Press.

Bainbridge, J., Carbonaro, M., & Green, N. (2005). Canadian children's literature: An Alberta survey. *Alberta Journal of Educational Research* 51(4), 311–327.

Glazier, J. & Seo, J. (2005). Multicultural literature and discussion as mirror and window? *Journal of Adolescent and Adult Literacy* 48, 686–700.

Johnston, I. (2000). Sites of discovery and discomfort: Reading and teaching multicultural literature. In B. Barrell & R. Hammett (Eds.), *Advocating change: Contemporary issues in subject English* (pp. 136–146). Toronto, ON: Irwin Publishing.

Johnston, I. (2010). Multicultural novels for the Canadian classroom. In M. C. Courtland & T. Gambell (Eds.), *Literature, media & multiliteracies in adolescent language arts* (pp. 133–152). Vancouver, BC: Pacific Educational Press.

Loh, C. (2009). Reading the world: Reconceptualizing reading multicultural literature in the English language arts classroom in a global world. *Changing English* 16(3), 287–299.

Napoli, M. (2007). Opening children's eyes to the world in which they live: One book at a time—A conversation with Deborah Ellis. *Journal of Children's Literature* 22(1), 22–27.

Nystrand, M. (2006). Research on the role of classroom discourse as it affects reading comprehension. *Research in the Teaching of English* 40, 392–412.

Rochman, H. (1993). *Against borders: Promoting books for a multicultural world.* Chicago: American Library Association.

Statistics Canada. (2008). *Canada's Ethnocultural Mosaic, 2006 Census.* Ottawa, ON: Minister of Industry. http://www12.statcan.ca/census-recensement/2006/as-sa/97-562/index-eng.cfm (accessed January 3, 2012).

Ward, A. (2010). Talk in the middle years literature classroom. In M. C. Courtland & T. Gambell (Eds.), *Literature, media & multiliteracies in adolescent language arts* (pp. 57–78). Vancouver, BC: Pacific Educational Press.

Wiltse, L. (2005). *Cultural diversity and discourse practices in grade 9.* Edmonton, AB: Qual Institute Press.

Wiltse, L. (2006). "Like pulling teeth": Oral discourse practices in a culturally and linguistically diverse language arts classroom. *Canadian Modern Language Review* 63(2), 199–223.

Yandell, J. (2008). Exploring multicultural literature: The text, the classroom and the world outside. *Changing English* 15(1), 25–40.

What Can I Learn about Indigenous Story-Telling Traditions That I Might Apply to the Teaching of Graphic Novels Written by Indigenous Authors?

By Jan Hare, University of British Columbia

Indigenous scholars and educators repeatedly call for the inclusion of Indigenous knowledge and pedagogies in schooling as a means to improve educational outcomes for Indigenous learners, while at the same time enhancing the learning opportunities for all students. Indigenous knowledge represents the local and culturally specific knowledge of a people—a knowledge that is dynamic, accumulative, and adapting over time (Battiste, 2005). It encompasses the beliefs, cultural values, and practices that, to members of Indigenous communities like me, shape how we make sense of our world. Meaning and identity are constructed through our relationships to place, territory, and the natural world (Hare, 2011). We see knowledge as holistic; we look for how concepts can be connected and related as a means to understanding them (rather than fragmenting those ideas). The foundations of our understanding of how to live in the world are similarly centred on our extended family, community, and ancestral relations.

Indigenous knowledge is expressed through learning processes that are intergenerational, land-based, experiential, and closely tied to the narrative tradition of storytelling. Since Indigenous peoples did not possess a written tradition prior to colonization, the oral tradition was the primary method by which knowledge and wisdom were preserved and shared across the generations. As Pueblo writer Simon Ortiz (1992) points out, "the oral tradition is the consciousness of the people" (p. 7). Indigenous histories, beliefs, and ways of living were once communicated through a set of social practices that centred on storytelling. Storytelling described for children how things came to be, provided lessons about how they might conduct themselves, and taught them about the nature and place of the world around them. A creation story would tell Anishinaabe children that their world originated on the back of a turtle, while Haida children might learn how their people originally came out of a clamshell, coaxed from their protective cover by Raven. Trickster, a common cultural figure and a shape-shifter to Aboriginal peoples, may provide children with important life lessons. It is through the misdeeds and antics of Coyote's wanderings somewhere in the interior of British Columbia, through Wesjeesak making his way over the Great Plains, through Nanabozhoo's lumberings about northern Ontario, or through Gooslap venturing across the Maritimes that, as Aboriginal people, we learn how to navigate our way culturally in the world. There are, of course, also sacred or personal stories, perhaps told at certain times of the year or told only by certain members of the community. These stories possess their own unique spiritual dimensions of place and time.

Cherokee scholar, writer, and gifted storyteller Thomas King (2005) demonstrates in his book *The Truth About Stories: A Native Narrative* the fundamental differences between Aboriginal and non-Aboriginal storytelling regarding themes, structure, and narrative strategies. More importantly, his multimodal presentations of the oral tradition (e.g., lecture, radio acting, and screen writing) have "[kept] this kind of literature well alive by adapting, developing and enriching it, rather than trying to preserve it as if it were a relic" (Gilbert, 2006, n.p.). Graphic novels are foremost among the other new and exciting multimodal representations of Aboriginal oral tradition by means of new stories and new forms now finding their way into the secondary school classroom. While graphic novels have had a long history, it is only recently that we are seeing an increase in graphic novels written and illustrated by Indigenous people.

The Healthy Aboriginal Network (www.thehealthyaboriginal.net) has produced a series of graphic novels that deal with Aboriginal youth issues such as diabetes prevention, avoiding gang life, staying in school, and the prevalence of youth suicide. Little Spirit Bear Productions produces a graphic novel series called *Rabbit and Bear Paws.* Set in the 1750s of colonized North America, these stories depict two brothers, Rabbit and Bear Paws, living by their traditional teachings and engaging in humorous adventures (www.rabbitandbearpaws.com). Others include *500 Years of Resistance* by Kwakwaka'wakw writer Gord Hill and *Trickster: Native American Tales,* a compilation of 21 tales about Trickster written and illustrated by various Native American storytellers. To support educators' understanding of Indigenous oral storytelling and enhance their ability to use such texts in a classroom context, I will describe two such graphic novels (written by Indigenous writers) in more depth. It is my intention to provide teachers with "models of reading and analysis [rather] than merely to offer interpretations of particular texts" (Bradford, 2007, p. 226) so that they may deepen their students' understanding of Indigenous knowledge and histories while broadening their own perspectives on the graphic novel.

The first graphic novel under consideration is *Red: A Haida Manga* by Michael Nicoll Yahgulanaas, a Haida writer and artist. This tale, originally an oral story, is depicted by Yahgulanaas in 108 illustrations (with some written text). The graphics bring together traditional Haida design elements (e.g., ovoids, U-shapes) and colours (e.g., red and black) in combination with the conventions of Japanese manga (e.g., mini-flashbacks, perspective, speed lines). The story is about a young Haida boy named Red whose village has been raided and whose sister has been taken captive. For years his anger builds. When word reaches his village that his sister has been seen, Red sets out both to find and bring her back, and to visit revenge upon her captors—despite the warnings from his people. He depletes the local resources of the village, trading them for weapons to use in his quest. The negative consequences of his all-consuming desire for vengeance are acted out on his sister in her new life and, ultimately, upon himself as well.

The second text is by Swampy Cree writer David Robertson, who has written a four-part graphic-novel series entitled *7 Generations*. Over the course of these novellas (each about 30 pages in length), we learn about the challenges of a young Cree youth, Edwin, who is struggling to come to terms with his identity and the meaning of life. In each novella, Edwin's own life struggles are juxtaposed against those of Aboriginal peoples in Canada and, in particular, his own Cree ancestors. Through a series of flashbacks, the author links the past to the present. *Stone,* the first novella, finds Edwin attempting suicide. His distraught mother tells her son that he has much to live for and that, though the past should not be an excuse for the present, "our past has shaped us all, you, me" (Robertson & Henderson, 2010, p. 4). Telling him a story, Edwin's mother takes him back to the beginning of the nineteenth century where Stone, a young warrior, finds peace within himself and his place among his own people after avenging his brother's death. Hearing Stone's journey of hope and healing provides Edwin with the strength to begin his own healing quest. These events bridge into the second novella, *Scars* (2010), where readers learn that Edwin's pain is rooted in the loss of his father (who no longer lives with Edwin and his mother). In *Scars,* Edwin's mother tells a story that takes him back to 1870, a time when the Plains Cree were afflicted with a plague of smallpox. A Cree boy not unlike Edwin, witnessing his family die from the disease, embarks on a journey to find another village and another home. Hearing this story gives Edwin the courage to address his own emotional scars.

The distance between Edwin and his father is explored in the third part of Robertson's series, *Ends/Begins* (2010). Edwin's father situates his own childhood within the story of the very dark history of residential schooling, revealing the intergenerational consequences that live on in generations of our young Aboriginal people from the family trauma and the abuse suffered at these schools. In the concluding novella, *The Pact* (2011), Edwin's father, James, attempts to heal from the wounds of residential schooling. He recounts how his fear and pain had been causing such family turmoil for Edwin and Edwin's mother that he chose to leave them both and turn to alcohol as a way to cope. The series comes full circle as James and Edwin make a pact to move forward and heal from their pasts, recognizing that "what happened to you doesn't define you. You define you. We are not our yesterday, we are our today, our tomorrow" (Robertson & Henderson, 2011, p. 28).

The narrative structures within each of these graphic novels reflect those found in the Aboriginal oral tradition. Aboriginal stories can often emphasize circular patterns in a narrative, yielding a structure within which stories may conclude where they began, employ repeated themes across their narrative, or remain unresolved in their conclusion (Eder, 2007). Often, one may find stories nested within stories, or stories added to each other, one simply piled on the other (Gunn Allen, 1986). Sometimes, they never come to a complete resolution at all. Stories within an Indigenous knowledge framework will not always take the linear form common in Western stories. In linear narratives one can expect to find a clearly delineated beginning, middle, climax, and ending, often with a hero who overcomes a central conflict in the final moments. Rather, Aboriginal stories, rooted in an oral tradition, often have lessons that occur throughout.

We can see an example of this story-within-a-story structure in *Red: A Haida Manga.* While perhaps not evident to many readers (and maybe even confusing to others), the 108 panels communicate more than a simple progression of narrative events. Placed all together in a specific layout, the panels combine to form a four-metre-long mural consisting of traditional Haida form lines and thematic elements, intended to be read and interpreted by the viewer. In an overleaf, Yahgulanaas challenges the reader to rip the pages out of their binding and, by following the layout provided in the overleaf, reconstruct and interpret his form-line mural (a visual of which has also been included in the book). Further troubling a reader's simple interpretation of this graphic narrative are the form lines within each of the panels. Each panel displays non-uniform, curving, thick black lines. This feature breaks with the tradition of graphic novels as described by Eisner (1985) and McCloud (1993), who suggest that, as a graphic novel's narrative moves from scene to scene, linearity itself defines the panel as a unit of meaning. While we may expect a narrative to be a solid linear thread, Yahgulanaas' use of form lines challenges this notion.

How one story can inform another within the Aboriginal storytelling tradition is readily apparent in Robertson's *7 Generations*. The present is situated in the past as Edwin connects to his ancestors through stories told to him by his parents. Edwin changes how he sees himself as he hears the historical narratives of his ancestor Stone in book one, White Cloud in book two, and his own father in books three and four. The graphic format and organization of panels allows the reader to move back and forth between Edwin and his ancestors, visually depicting a story unfolding within another and even, at times, depicting how these stories parallel one another. The historical narratives told by Edwin's parents show how Indigenous knowledge can be passed on across the generations through story.

Another feature that may be observed in the Aboriginal storytelling tradition is the importance of a connection to the spiritual world. Indigenous notions of spirituality acknowledge the centrality of a person's relationships to the natural, material, and ancestral worlds. An Indigenous worldview recognizes that spiritual experiences are on equal ground with other knowledge and can manifest in the physical world through ceremony, vision quests, or dreams (Canadian Council on Learning, 2009). An example of this spiritual engagement in storytelling is Steve Saunderson's graphic novel *Darkness Calls.* Cree-Métis scholar Deanna Reder (2010) positions this novel as a sacred story featuring the Cree trickster Wesakecak. In her analysis, Reder suggests that four specific Cree values are revealed in this story. In *Darkness Calls,* a young man named Kyle, under the pressures of bullying and frustrations with school, contemplates suicide. One of the four values Reder finds in this comic is that conflict must be faced not just in the physical realm but also in the metaphysical realm. Kyle must face the metaphorical monster of Wihtiko, who is known to take over the spirit of others. Kyle summons the courage to lash out at Wihtiko, chasing him away. Reder tells us that, "Although his show of courage and strength could be dismissed as self-assurance, in the context of *Darkness Calls,* it is a spiritual epiphany" (p. 188).

In his oral story adaptation *Red: A Haida Manga,* Yahgulanaas also pulls us into the spiritual realm at several points. At the outset of the story, the Elders of the village tell Red he isn't a child anymore and that he must start to become aware of the world both outside him and inside him. He is sent off on a vision quest. As he sleeps in the woods, figures swirl and shift about him, at one point calling out, "Hello, little one" (p. 15). Interestingly, and perhaps deliberately, the vision is not described in detail for the reader. In many Aboriginal cultures, the vision quest is a rite of passage into adulthood, often taking the form of a quest for growth through spiritual awareness (as is the case for Red). Further, the theme of transformation, central to the characterization of the supernatural within Northwest Coast stories, is played out continually in this graphic novel. To make his way into the hostile village of Laanaas to find his sister, Red quickly transforms into a green-looking figure, becoming a totem on one of the village house posts. He returns to his physical self once the village is quiet. Yahgulanaas' style of illustration brings many of the motifs of Northwest Coast culture to life as he develops them in unexpected and challenging ways.

The spiritual realm is just as much a source of knowledge in the *7 Generations* series. Robertson's historical characters, Stone and White Cloud, rely on visions and dreams to ensure their survival. Following Edwin's suicide attempt, his mother turns to their family history where we first meet Stone, for whom the first book is named. This is the moment when we meet the first of Edwin's ancestors, role models for him who also embark on a vision quest. Stone's visions reveal glimpses of what is to come, depicted with an eagle centred in the panel. The eagle is recognized as a symbol of strength among Aboriginal peoples. As his vision quest is coming to a close, Stone stumbles across a special piece of stone, which he makes into an amulet to wear. He is told that this sacred object is to remind him of his journey. The sacred amulet reappears in book two where it has been passed on to Stone's children, all of whom suffer during the smallpox epidemic. White Cloud is the only child of this family and of the entire village to survive the deadly disease. While searching for any of his people who may have also lived through the deadly illness, he collapses from exhaustion near a river. Stone comes to his son in a dream, urging him to find his strength and carry on. When White Cloud awakes, he puts on the amulet and continues his journey. The story then shifts to the present where Edwin's mother passes on that same amulet, thereby giving Edwin courage to move ahead. She tells him that "it has the power of our culture within it. It will help you on your journey of healing" (*Scars,* p. 26). In both of these two books, the power of visions to warn, heal, and guide depict how a deeper understanding of the world can be gained from such sacred knowledge. The amulet, passing through the generations, is an artifact and a symbol of the culture, linking the physical with the spiritual world, the past with the present, and reality with fiction.

We are reminded by Stolo scholar and storyteller Jo-ann Archibald (2008) of the diversity of Indigenous cultures and of the different genres, purposes, protocols, and ways of making meaning in her book *Indigenous Storywork: Educating the Heart, Mind, Body and Spirit.* She tells us that the power of Indigenous stories to educate lies in our own ability to make physical, spiritual, and emotional connections to a story. For example, when she describes her own process of connecting physically to a particular story, she reports having "reflected on behaviours and actions of [hers] that needed changing or needed to be practiced more" (p. 93). From her storywork, we can come to see Indigenous storytelling as more than just being able to interpret texts. These stories are intended to take hold of our lives, teaching us how to live. The graphic novels discussed above follow this tradition of Indigenous storytelling. Red learns the personal and communal price of vengeance, and Edwin learns how our histories shape who we become. For the audience of these texts, however, the stories unfold once again—this time within a reader's experience of the world and what he or she is able to take from the stories. This brings me back to a phrase repeated in each of the five Massey Lectures that form Thomas King's *The Truth About Stories: A Native Narrative*. He concludes, at the end of each lecture, "Don't say in the years to come that you would have lived your life differently if only you had heard this story. You've heard it now." King, like Archibald, reminds us that stories carry with them social and moral responsibilities.

From the graphic novels *Red: A Haida Manga* and *7 Generations,* we see how Indigenous storytelling traditions are different from non-Indigenous ones. Students need to become familiar with story expectations of Indigenous literatures in order to make meaning from these texts. Teachers also need to familiarize themselves with the cultures and traditions of Indigenous peoples in order to share these texts respectfully. "Indigenous texts deserve to be read in light of cultures in which they are produced, and with due attention to their difference from Western texts, rather than from within the assumptions of Western culture and textual practices" (Bradford, 2007, p. 227).

References

Archibald, J. (2008). *Indigenous storywork. Educating the heart, mind, body, and spirit.* Vancouver, BC: University of British Columbia Press.

Battiste, M. (2005). Indigenous knowledge: Foundations for First Nations. *World Indigenous Nations Higher Education Consortium – WINHEC Journal.* Retrieved from http://www.win-hec.org/docs/pdfs/Journal/Marie%20Battiste%20copy.pdf

Bradford, C. (2007). *Unsettling narratives. Postcolonial readings of children's literature.* Waterloo, ON: Wilfrid Laurier University Press.

Canadian Council on Learning. (2009). *The state of Aboriginal learning in Canada: A holistic approach to measuring success.* Ottawa, ON: Government of Canada.

Eder, D. (2007). Bringing Navajo storytelling practices into schools: The importance of maintaining cultural integrity. *Anthropology & Education Quarterly* 38(3), 278–296.

Eisner, W. (1985). *Comics and sequential art.* Tamarac, FL: Poorhouse Press.

Gilbert, T. (2006). Written orality in Thomas King's short fiction. *Journal of the Short Story in English* 47, 97–109.

Gunn Allen, P. (1986). *The sacred hoop: Recovering the feminine in American Indian traditions.* Boston, MA: Beacon Press.

Hare, J. (2011). Learning from Indigenous knowledge in education. In D. Long & O. P. Dickenson (Eds.), *Visions of the heart, 3rd Edition* (pp. 91–112). Toronto, ON: Oxford University Press.

King, T. (2005). *The truth about stories. A Native narrative.* Minneapolis, MS: University of Minnesota Press.

McCloud, S. (1993). *Understanding comics: The invisible art.* New York: HarperCollins Publishing.

Ortiz, S. (1992). *Woven stone.* Tucson, AZ: University of Arizona Press.

Reder, D. (2010). Sacred stories in comic book form: A Cree reading of Darkness Calls. In D. Reder & L. M. Morra (Eds.), *Troubling tricksters: Revisioning critical conversations* (pp. 177–191). Waterloo, ON: Wilfrid Laurier University Press.

Robertson, D. A. & Henderson, S. B. (2010). *Ends/begins. 7 generations*: 3. Winnipeg, MB: High Water Press.

———. (2010). *Scars. 7 generations*: 2. Winnipeg, MB: High Water Press.

———. (2010). *Stone. 7 generations*: 1. Winnipeg, MB: High Water Press.

———. (2011). *The pact. 7 generations*: 4. Winnipeg, MB: High Water Press.

Yuhuglanaas, M. N. (2009). *Red: A Haida manga.* Vancouver, BC: Douglas & McIntyre.

What Is Aboriginal English, and What Do Teachers Need to Know about Students Who Speak Aboriginal English?

By Lynne Wiltse, University of Alberta

Thirty years ago, I arrived for my first teaching job in a small, remote, predominantly Aboriginal community in the Cariboo-Chilcotin region of British Columbia. Having recently received my teacher certification, I could hardly wait to begin my new position. The day I arrived, a group of curious children from the nearby reserve came to welcome me at the duplex that I would be sharing with the new principal and his wife. The children asked me a few questions, and then chatted among themselves. They referred to the new principal as *he* and *him*. Then, I heard one of the children referring to me as *him* and to the principal's wife in the same way. Surprised and confused, I wondered what was happening. They had been calling me "Miss Wiltse"; why were they referring to me as *him*? It is with shame that I recall thinking, "What is the matter with these kids? What have I got myself in for here?" In fact, nothing was wrong with these children who soon would become my students: they were speaking a dialect of English known variously as "Aboriginal," "Indian," "Indigenous," or "First Nations" English. The lack of understanding was mine in that I knew nothing about the dialect; my teacher education program had not prepared me for linguistic and cultural diversity of this nature.

Fifteen years later, as a graduate student, I drew on my teaching experiences in three Aboriginal communities to complete my master's thesis on Aboriginal language loss and revival (Wiltse, 1995). The following excerpt featured prominently in my thesis. It also brought back powerful memories and regrets of that first teaching anecdote:

> As in many Indigenous languages, Cree classifies things according to whether they are animate or inanimate, and not according to a gender that is masculine, feminine, or neuter as in English. Thus Cree students learning English will frequently use *he* when they mean *she*. (Heit & Blair, 1993, p. 119)

The authors explain that many Cree students speak a full-fledged dialect of English that is a result of the influence of the Indigenous language or mother tongue upon the English language. There was a perfectly logical explanation for my students' language use. Although they spoke Carrier (a Northern Athabaskan language of the central interior region of British Columbia) rather than Cree, the classification example still applied. Thirty years later, as a teacher educator, I am thankful to have the opportunity to write on the topic of Aboriginal English for teacher candidates and new teachers. My intention is to answer, in brief, the following questions. Firstly, what is Aboriginal English? Secondly, what do teachers need to know about students who speak this dialect? However, terminology poses various challenges in writing about these dialectical varieties of English. Although for the most part I use the term Aboriginal English, I will make reference as well to the terms "Indigenous," "First Nations," or "Indian" English depending on the context and, most importantly, the source to which I am referring. In this regard, the date and place of publication are significant factors. For example, as language use has changed over the years, the term "Indian English" is less often used in Canada, in part because the term "Indian" is contested in this context but still used in the United States. In terms of region, "Aboriginal" English is the term used in Australia, whereas in Canada, the non-standard variety is referred to variously as "Aboriginal," "First Nations," or "Indigenous" English.

Any discussion of Aboriginal English must be situated within an explanation of the more general term, dialect. Dialect refers to any given variety of a language shared by a group of speakers. Dialects are variations of a single language, exhibiting varying degrees of differences in the areas of pronunciation, grammar, vocabulary, and discourse patterns. Dialects reflect regional and social distinctions, and can also reflect the influences of people's mother tongue (as in my introductory example). Canadian Aboriginal English dialects have their origins within an overall context of colonization; they developed as features of the Aboriginal languages merged with the English of the colonizers (Ball & Bernhardt, 2008). Tragically, many Aboriginal languages have been lost or are currently endangered due to the legacy of colonization and residential schools. These same languages have shaped the linguistic characteristics of Aboriginal English dialects. (For a more detailed description of this process, see Wiltse [in press].)

Linguists argue that all dialects of English are legitimate, systematic, and rule-governed and that no dialect is inherently superior to another (Baugh, 1983; Labov, 1970). At the same time, Trudgill (1994) claims that there is no doubt that the "dialect of English which has the highest social status is the dialect which is widely known as Standard English" (p. 5). In North America, Standard English (SE) is the variety of English that carries the most prestige (Crystal, 1995). Standard English is considered to be the language of the workplace, the dialect usually taught in schools, and the variety of English considered essential to social mobility (Speicher & Bielanski, 2000). Other varieties of English are referred to as non-standard dialects or "Englishes"; hundreds of different Englishes are spoken around the world. Prejudice and discrimination are associated with all aspects of non-standard dialects. As Wolfram and Christian (1989) explain, "language prejudices seem more resistant to change than other kinds of prejudice. Members of the majority culture who would be quite willing to accept equality in other social and educational areas may continue to reject the legitimacy of a dialect difference" (p. 19).

On this note, it is difficult to overestimate the significance of teachers' attitudes and beliefs about students' language. Stubbs (2002) argues that a child's language may be a disadvantage in her or his educational progress not because the language in itself is deficient, but because it is different and, consequently, *deemed* deficient. Teachers sometimes regard difference in a student's language as evidence of language deficiency or as an intellectual disability. For example, although the distinctive characteristics of spoken Aboriginal English (or other non-standard dialects) are dialectal differences, students whose community language patterns are different from those of the mainstream community have often been diagnosed as having disorders of various types. In her research into English-dialect-speaking Aboriginal students, Sterzuk (2008) found a disproportionate representation of First Nations and Métis students in remedial language and speech programs in Saskatchewan schools. Similarly, Ball and Bernhardt (2008) suggest that First Nations children may be "disproportionately diagnosed with speech-language impairments, which in turn may stem in part from misrepresentations of features of children's home English dialects as evidence of speech-language deficits or delays" (p. 570). In order for students to receive appropriate treatment and teaching, speech-language pathologists and educators need to be able to differentiate language difference from language impairment.

There is general agreement that students need competency in Standard English to function effectively in school and in other settings, especially since students who do not have access to Standard English are less likely to succeed economically (Adger, Wolfram, & Christian, 2007; Leap, 1993; Delpit, 2002; Speicher & Bielanski, 2000). However, teachers need to recognize that Aboriginal students also require proficiency in the dialect of their home community because "dialects are important linguistic markers of Indigenous identity and solidarity" (Ball & Bernhardt, 2008, p. 573). Until recently, educational programs have focused on teaching Standard English to Aboriginal students as a primary dialect. The goal of current programs is to add Standard English as a *second* dialect to students' repertoire of linguistic varieties rather than to replace or eliminate the home dialect (Epstein & Xu, 2003); contemporary programs take an additive approach. For Aboriginal students whose home language is a non-standard variety of English, English as a Second Dialect (ESD) programming alongside instruction in Standard English would be the appropriate choice (Ball, 2009). Fadden and LaFrance (2010) explain that if teachers are unaware of the linguistic legitimacy of an Aboriginal English dialect, they may be unlikely to encourage its use. It is therefore crucial for teachers to understand that being fluent in Aboriginal English does not prevent speakers from acquiring fluency in Standard English. Maintaining the home dialect of English will not interfere with students' acquisition of Standard English. Tollefson (2007) should prove informative on this topic. Tollefson's article discusses studies which show evidence that the use of stigmatized varieties of English in language programs has a positive effect on the acquisition of English communicative competency, as well as on students' participation, performance on standardized tests, and overall academic achievement.

To date, the majority of Canadian ESD programs focus on younger students. There is, however, an ongoing need for programming focused on older Aboriginal students. For educators interested in using what is referred to as a "bi-dialectal" approach with middle and secondary school students, there are promising models in the literature to look to for guidance: Lee (2004) describes an apprenticeship project with secondary school students who are speakers of African American Vernacular English (AAVE); Davis, Bazzi, Cho,

Ishida, and Soria (2005) report on a school program that promotes the use of Hawai'i Creole English in conjunction with Standard English for academic purposes; and Malcolm (2001) discusses a bi-dialectal approach that incorporates both a community's Aboriginal dialect and Standard Australian English.

In closing, I would like to draw attention to an additional reason why teachers should encourage Aboriginal English in the classroom: these dialects may play a crucial role in efforts to revive endangered Aboriginal languages. As mentioned, given that Aboriginal dialects echo aspects of endangered languages, fluency in these dialects "can provide speakers who want to learn or re-learn an ancestral language an easier point of entry" (Ball & Bernhardt, 2008, p. 575). For many Aboriginal youth, especially those who live in urban centres, Aboriginal English is the only ancestral-related language that they know. Given the role that education has played in the loss of Aboriginal languages, I believe that, as educators, we should do what we can to foster their revival.

Not all Aboriginal students speak a dialect of English other than Standard English; however, with the growing Aboriginal population in Canada, prospective and new teachers are increasingly likely to encounter Aboriginal English speakers in their classrooms. The misunderstandings and mistakes that resulted from my not knowing that my first students were speaking Aboriginal English haunt me still. Fortunately, more knowledge is available on this topic now than 30 years ago when I began my teaching career. Unfortunately, there has been little change in terms of this information reaching pre-service and practising teachers. My hope is that we will begin to bridge this gap.

References

Adger, C., Wolfram, W., & Christian, D. (2007). *Dialects in schools and communities* (2nd ed.). Mahwah, NJ: Lawrence Erlbaum.

Ball, J. (2009). Supporting young Indigenous children's language development in Canada: A review of research on needs and promising practices. *Canadian Modern Language Review* 66(1), 19–47.

Ball, J. & Bernhardt. B. (2008). First Nations English dialects in Canada: Implications for speech-language pathology. *Clinical Linguistics and Phonetics* 22, 570–588.

Baugh, J. (1983). *Black street speech: Its history, structure, and survival.* Austin, TX: University of Texas Press.

Crystal, D. (1995). *The Cambridge encyclopedia of language.* Cambridge, United Kingdom: Cambridge University Press.

Davis, K., Bazzi, S., Cho, H., Ishida, M., & Soria, J. (2005). It's our Kuleana*:* A critical participatory approach to language-minority education. In L. Pease-Alvarez & S. Schecter (Eds.), *Teaching and community: Contributions of situated and participatory approaches to educational innovation* (pp. 3–25). Mahwah, NJ: Lawrence Erlbaum Associates.

Delpit, L. (2002). Introduction. In L. Delpit & J. Kilgour Dowdy (Eds.), *The skin that we speak: Thoughts on language and culture in the classroom.* New York: The New Press.

Epstein, R. & Xu, L. (2003). *Roots and wings: Teaching English as a second dialect to Aboriginal students—A review of the literature.* Retrieved from ERIC database (ED476389).

Fadden, L. & LaFrance, J. (2010). Advancing Aboriginal English. *Canadian Journal of Native Education* 32, 143–155.

Heit, M. & Blair, H. (1993). Language needs and characteristics of Saskatchewan Indian and Métis students: Implications for educators. In S. Morris, K. McLeod, & M. Danesi (Eds.), *Aboriginal languages and education: The Canadian experience* (pp. 103–128). Oakville, ON: Mosaic.

Labov, W. (1970). *The study of nonstandard English.* Urbana, IL: National Council of Teachers of English.

Leap, W. (1993). *American Indian English.* Salt Lake City, UT: University of Utah Press.

Lee, C. (2004). Double voiced discourse: African American vernacular English as a resource in cultural modeling classrooms. In A. Ball & S. Freedman (Eds.), *Bakhtinian perspectives on language, literacy and learning* (pp. 129–147). Cambridge, United Kingdom: Cambridge University Press.

Malcolm, I. (2001). Two-way English and the bicultural experience. In B. Moore (Ed.), *Who's centric now?: The present state of post-colonial Englishes* (pp. 219–240). New York: Oxford University Press.

Speicher, B. & Bielanski, J. (2000). Critical thoughts on teaching Standard English. *Curriculum Inquiry* 30(2), 147–169.

Sterzuk, A. (2008). Whose English counts? Indigenous English in Saskatchewan schools. *McGill Journal of Education/Revue des sciences de l'éducation de McGill* 43(1), 9–19.

Stubbs, M. (2002). Some basic sociolinguistic concepts. In L. Delpit & J. Kilgour Dowdy (Eds.), *The skin that we speak: Thoughts on language and culture in the classroom* (pp. 63–85). New York: The New Press.

Tollefson, J. (2007). Ideology, language varieties, and ELT. In J. Cummins & C. Davison (Eds.), *International handbook of English language teaching.* Vol. 15 (pp. 25–36). New York: Springer.

Trudgill, P. (1994). *Dialects.* London: Routledge.

Wiltse, L. (1995). *The river flows both ways: Native language loss and revival.* Unpublished master's thesis. Edmonton, AB: University of Alberta.

Wiltse, L. (in press). "But my students all speak English": Ethical research issues of Aboriginal English. *TESL Canada Journal.*

Wolfram, W. & Christian, D. (1989). *Dialect and education: Issues and answers.* Englewood Cliffs, NJ: Prentice Hall Regents.

Multilingualism

I Teach Secondary School, so Why Should I Care about ESL?

By Lee Gunderson, University of British Columbia

The term English as a Second Language (ESL) has been employed for decades to identify individuals who speak a language other than English at home (Gunderson, 2007, 2008a, 2008b, 2009; Gunderson, D'Silva, & Murphy Odo, 2011). ESL misrepresents some individuals included in the category who are fluent with multiple languages before acquiring English (Gunderson, 2007, 2008a, 2008b, 2009); therefore, English as an Additional Language (EAL) has been adopted in some jurisdictions such as British Columbia. Internationally, the term English to Speakers of Other Languages (ESOL) has been used generally since the 1960s (Gunderson, 2007, 2008a, 2008b, 2009). Over the last decade the term English Language Learner (ELL) has been adopted in the United States (Gunderson, 2007, 2008a, 2008b, 2009). No label can accommodate the range of English language learners one is likely to encounter in a classroom. As I have noted elsewhere, such labels are problematic because they tend to mask "significant underlying differences" among learners and this can have serious consequences (Gunderson, 2008, p. 186). The term ESL is used in this entry because it is commonly used in practice.

The Growing ESL Population

The number of people who speak a language other than English in English-speaking countries continues to increase. Canada in particular is a highly multilingual country, as reported in the introduction to Part 1. Projections are that the number of people who speak a language other than English will continue to grow (Gunderson, 2009). It is clear that if one is going to teach in a middle or secondary school anywhere in North America, one will have ESL students in one's classroom. How a teacher interacts with these students will have consequences for the teacher, the students, and the learning of academic content (Gunderson, 2004).

English Ability and Academic Content

A common error is to assume that ESL students' intelligence and understanding of academic content are directly related to their English ability (Gunderson, 2007). This is not the case. Indeed, many non-English speakers are, of course, brilliant mathematicians, poets, writers, chemists, philosophers, or scientists. The difficulty is not that they are lacking in talent or insight; rather, it is that that they cannot demonstrate their talents or express their insights in the language of instruction. In working with such students, teachers need to be aware of a few features of English language acquisition by ESL speakers.

It is generally accepted that there are two broad categories of English ability. The first, Basic Interpersonal Communicative Skill (BICS), is the ability to communicate orally with others in English in a face-to-face manner (Cummins, 1979a, 1979b, 1983, 1984, 2000; Cummins & Swain, 1986) and it appears to take two to three years on average for students to learn. The second, Cognitive Academic Language Proficiency (CALP), is the kind of English language ability required for a learner to read and comprehend a textbook (Cummins, 1979a, 1981, 2000; Cummins & Swain, 1986) and it requires on average about five to seven years to develop. It is the kind of English required to comprehend what one hears—a prerequisite to learning from an academic lecture. Difficulty arises when teachers and parents make false positive assumptions about a learner's knowledge of academic language use (or CALP) because the student has competency in BICS (Gunderson, 2006). Students who have acquired BICS are certainly able to communicate orally. Often, they are quite fluent. The difficulty is that they may not have attained yet a sufficiently high level of proficiency in CALP. Parents may assume such students no longer need ESL classes, and even the teachers themselves may be convinced that such students should be able to read and comprehend. This is not always the case. As a consequence, even students who have strong academic backgrounds in their first languages (L1s) may fail their academic classes because they cannot understand the English of classrooms or textbooks. Knowledge of ESL students' English ability is vital. An instructor's ESL students should be able to comprehend the material the instructor presents and the texts they are asked to read. Unfortunately, a student's oral English may give an instructor a false impression of the actual ability the student has to comprehend academic language. I would like to share a quick way to assess students' abilities to comprehend written text that, incidentally, can also be informative with students who are native English speakers.

The Quick Content Comprehension Measure

It is clear that a major difficulty for secondary school teachers is that they often have 120 to 220 students a day and, as a consequence, have little time to assess students' reading ability relative to their textbooks. In consideration of this problem, I have developed an easy measure that I have tested in various studies (Gunderson, 2009). Although the measure is a simple tool, my studies have suggested that it is quite reliable.

The Quick Content Comprehension Measure is easy to construct, administer, and score. Review the textbook you are using and select a section of approximately 250 words, usually from about the middle of the book. The section should be fairly complete as a passage. Reproduce the selection, including any graphics, and give it to students. Ask them to read the text and highlight any words they believe would be difficult for students in the class to understand. (When I first developed the measure, students were asked to highlight any words that they *personally* would have trouble understanding. This approach did not work well because the students were hesitant to indicate they had problems.) The following is a rough or fuzzy indicator of students' content comprehension:

Highlighted words:
0–10 highlighted words per hundred words = Independent
11–19 highlighted words per hundred = Instructional
20 or more highlighted words per hundred = Frustration

"Independent" level indicates that students should have no difficulty comprehending material in the textbook. "Instructional" level indicates that students will need your help, usually with the special vocabulary in the text. Even with your help, those at the "Frustration" level will not comprehend the material in the textbook. Students should not have trouble with function words such as *have, of,* and *were,* so these should not be highlighted. If they are, this is a signal that the students must focus on BICS and that they are not ready for your academic text or for your class.

Comprehensible Input

The Quick Content Comprehension Measure helps to identify whether the material in a textbook is comprehensible to students. If it is not, there is a problem. If the measure suggests a large number of students are reading at frustration level, you might benefit from seeking help from an experienced ESL instructor. If the measure suggests that a large number of students are reading at an instructional or independent level, the task is to make the lessons as comprehensible as possible. Krashen's (1982) notion of "comprehensible input" is important to the interpretation of this measurement tool.[5] Learners must be able to understand something if they are to learn new content. Krashen argued that learning success depends on the provision of comprehensible input. To make lessons more comprehensible, try supporting language learners with informative graphic organizers and visual aids. Search the Internet for books using "content area reading" as a search string for help in scaffolding content area texts for ESL students. There are other

5 Piaget (1973) referred to the notion of "moderate novelty" and Vygotsky (1962) coined the term "Zone of Proximal Development," both of which are similar to Krashen's notion (1982).

ways to help students that do not involve making changes in teaching methods, but they may require changing attitudes about the use of languages other than English in classrooms.

First Languages

Many teachers object to any language other than English being used in the classroom because they believe it will interfere with students' learning of English. My research suggests the opposite (Gunderson, 2009). The use of bilingual dictionaries allows students to access new English vocabulary through their first languages. Electronic bilingual dictionaries also have the capacity to provide English pronunciations. Peers, moreover, can become "bilingual buddies": other students who have acquired CALP and who are able to translate vocabulary and concepts. One reason these approaches are not used more frequently is because they are not promoted enough by teachers who may have received inadequate training in how to support ESL learners. They are valuable resources that help make content comprehensible. They do not interfere with the learning of English or the learning of academic content (Gunderson, 2008b, 2009).

Conclusion

Secondary school ESL students face multiple tasks and difficulties in school. In addition, they must adjust to a new country and society. In many cases, they have left their friends and face growing up in a society where a different language is spoken. For all of these reasons, these adolescents may struggle as they grow into adults.

As a school teacher there are many reasons why you should care about ESL students. Some reasons are pragmatic; others are noble. Professional self-preservation requires that you understand the complexities of ESL students because their numbers are growing rapidly across the continent and in every English-speaking country in the world. A bottom-line professional concern on the part of many teachers is *test scores*. Without the provision of teaching and learning that involves thoughtful, comprehensible input, ESL students will, in fact, lower overall class test scores.

More importantly, teachers should care about ESL students because the promise of Canadian schools is inclusion. ESL students make up a significant portion of middle and secondary school populations. Part of being a teacher is a dedication to equity, equal opportunity, and social justice. This dedication requires a commitment to all students, including ESL students, with special skills, needs, and talents. Secondary and middle school teachers are overworked and face extremely complex teaching and learning environments. Hopefully, the brief contents of this entry have helped to answer the question, "Why should I care about ESL?"

References

Cummins, J. (1979a). Cognitive/academic language proficiency, linguistic interdependence, the optimum age question and some other matters. *Working papers on bilingualism* 19, 175–205.

Cummins, J. (1979b). Linguistic interdependence and the educational development of bilingual children. *Review of Educational Research* 49, 222–251.

Cummins, J. (1981). Age on arrival and immigrant second language learning in Canada: A reassessment. *Applied Linguistics* 2, 132–149.

Cummins, J. (1983). Language proficiency and academic achievement. In J. W. Oller (Ed.), *Issues in language testing research* (pp. 108–129). Rowley, MA: Newbury House.

Cummins, J. (1984). *Bilingualism and special education: Issues in assessment and pedagogy.* Clevedon, United Kingdom: Multilingual Matters.

Cummins, J. (2000). *Language, power and pedagogy*. Toronto, ON: Multilingual Matters.

Cummins, J. & Swain, M. (1986). Linguistic interdependence: A central principle of bilingual education. In *Bilingualism in education* (pp. 80–95). New York: Longman.

Gunderson, L. (1986). ESL students and content reading. *TESL Canada Journal* 4, 49–53.

Gunderson, L. (2004). The language, literacy, achievement, and social consequences of English-only programs for immigrant students. In J. Hoffman & D. Schallert (Eds.), *The NRC Yearbook* (pp. 1–27). Milwaukee, WI: National Reading Conference.

Gunderson, L. (2006). But she speaks English. In R. T. Jimenez & V. O. Pang (Eds.), *Race, ethnicity, and education* (pp. 1–27). Westport, CT: Praeger.

Gunderson, L. (2007). *English-only instruction and immigrant students in secondary school: A critical examination.* Mahwah, NJ: Lawrence Erlbaum Associates.

Gunderson, L. (November 2008a). The state of the art of secondary ESL teaching and learning. *Journal of Adolescent and Adult Literacy* 52 (3), pp. 184–188.

Gunderson, L. (2008b). Bilingual education. In S. Mathison & W. Ross (Eds.), *Battleground schools* (pp. 57–64). Westport, CN: Greenwood Press.

Gunderson, L. (2009). *ESL (ELL) literacy instruction: A guidebook to theory and practice.* New York: Routledge.

Gunderson, L., D'Silva, R., & Murphy Odo, D. (2011). Second language literacy. In E. Hinkel (Ed.), *Handbook of research in second language teaching and learning (2nd edition)* (pp. 472–487). New York: Routledge.

Krashen, S. (1982). *Principles and practice in second language acquisition.* New York: Pergamon.

Piaget, J. (1973). *Memory and intelligence.* New York: BasicBooks.

Vygotsky, L. S. (1962). *Thought and language.* Cambridge, MA: MIT Press.

What Does It Mean to Problematize Language as We Teach "English"?

By Susan Walsh, Mount Saint Vincent University

What does it mean to problematize language as we teach "English"? The language we use to speak, listen, read, and write with students in our English or language arts classes cannot be taken for granted. Language is not neutral; it's not a simple transport system for preconceived thought. Instead, it is constitutive—it *shapes* its speakers, their ways of being and knowing in the world. This insight hit home for me when I worked with First

Nations people as a research assistant on a Dene language revitalization project.[6] In listening to the Elders talk about their language, I realized more clearly that some things that could be said in Dene simply could not be said in English. Thus, people for whom Dene is a first language have a different orientation to living in the world than those for whom English is a first language. (For interested readers, the notion of linguistic and cultural relativism implied by this statement was first introduced by Sapir [1949] and Whorf [1941].) I also understood better that being forced to speak English through decades of residential schooling meant a loss of culture and identity. As Shelton (2007) says, speaking a dominant language involves the "[implicit acceptance] of the politics, ideologies, racial tenets and economic values of [the] dominant group" (p. 61). (See First Nations writers Battiste and Henderson [2000] for a discussion about the differences between the Eurocentric worldview held in the English language and the worldview held in their Indigenous languages.) As a young, white, beginning teacher in rural Alberta in the late 1970s, I know that I did not even once consider how language shapes being and knowing. My focus then was teaching literature and writing, and helping my students (a relatively homogeneous group, at least in terms of race and religion) improve their skill with a particular form of English, the one that was acceptable at school. I did not consider the ways that language, identity, and culture are intertwined, nor did I think that I was reproducing a particular set of values and beliefs by insisting on a "school" English. My view of language was narrow and singular, rather than multiple and inclusive.

In working to problematize language—that is, to make it less of an invisible topic in the classroom—three related ideas have been helpful to me over the years. First, as noted above, language is integral to identity and culture: it shapes our being, what we can think, and what we can know. Second, languages have multiple forms, not all of which are valued equally. Consider, for example, the experience of an immigrant child from Singapore for whom English is a first language but who is told she has an "accent," an African-Canadian teenager whose speech patterns do not match those of the teacher, or a person raised in rural Newfoundland who moves to Calgary. Third, language operates in relation to identity markers such as race, ethnicity, and gender as a means through which power relations are reproduced. My research with female teachers who have immigrated to Atlantic Canada[7] has underlined the gender–language relationship for me (see Walsh, 2008). One woman from India connected race and language when she noted, "[Canadians] do not see you beyond your English proficiency. They do not see what you can offer. But they see what you cannot offer, and they just reject you. It is different for white people." Another person in the study, a white European woman, noted that her proficiency with French and her European accent made it possible for her to be accepted in the Canadian context. She acknowledged how her language and skin colour worked together to position her more favourably than the women of colour in the research group.

As secondary school English teachers, we cannot ignore the importance of the three ideas outlined above. Dei and Lordan (2006) ask, "What are the sites in our schools to

6 The research project was a Community-University Research Alliance (CURA) between people of the Cold Lake First Nations Reserve in Alberta and University of Alberta professors, linguist Sally Rice and educator Heather Blair (funded by the Social Sciences and Humanities Research Council of Canada).

7 Our research took place in the Maritime provinces. Susan Walsh and Susan Brigham were the investigators (funded by the Social Sciences and Humanities Research Council of Canada).

nurture multiple languages? Why is it that when some students speak certain forms of dialects or languages that they are told that this is not the place for it? They should be speaking the dominant language" (p. 37). In Canada, at present, we should not assume that students speak English at home. The 2006 Census data indicates that immigration levels in Canada are at their highest in 75 years (Corbeil & Blaser, 2007). Truly, people speak many different languages across the country.[8] Further, the *forms* of English that people speak vary too: they vary among and within English-speaking countries as well as in places that are not officially English speaking but wherein English has been adopted as, for example, the language of commerce. The fastest-growing groups of English speakers in the world are those for whom it is an additional language (Canagarajah, 2007; see Jenkins, 2006, regarding the distinctions among World Englishes, English as a *lingua franca,* English as a foreign language, and so forth). As teachers, then, we are faced with a multiplicity of languages and also an array of Englishes. This situation affords a rich opportunity to explore issues of difference and equity, and also to practise respect. How might we do so?

Baker (2002), a secondary school English teacher in Boston, writes about a long-term project for engaging students in explicit language study, a project she calls "trilingualism." She distinguishes three forms of English that are relevant to her students: home, academic (school), and professional (job-related) English. Students begin with documenting their home Englishes and then compare each other's grammar, speech patterns, vocabulary, and so forth. She notes that "the validation of their home language . . . allows them to feel comfortable with language study in general" (p. 56). They then engage with role-playing in different situations and examine the different possible language choices they might make in different contexts. This activity, Baker contends, leads to further (motivated) learning about academic and/or professional Englishes. Through the trilingualism project, students are empowered to make conscious language choices in different situations. They can explore Standard English and become proficient with it knowing that their home language is respected and acknowledged and that it has a place in the classroom. They are also encouraged to be critical and curious through asking questions about why particular forms of language are valued differently in different contexts. Such language study could easily extend beyond what Baker outlines, perhaps to inquiry about accents: which accent is the norm against which all other accents are measured, and which accents are valued or not valued in certain contexts? Why? Another extension might be an investigation of peer group languages, song lyrics, or text messaging. I recommend the edited volume in which Baker's essay appears (Delpit & Dowdy, 2002) because it contains many useful pieces about various Englishes in the school context (including African American Vernacular English and the home Englishes of students from varying socio-economic groups).

I have also found Canagarajah's (2004, 2007) work in the area of English as an Additional Language to be instructive in terms of moving from a singular view of language (i.e., the importance of Standard English), like the view I had at the start of my career, to one that is more inclusive and respectful. His research foregrounds the ways in which multilingual people negotiate different languages as they interact with others in social contexts. He emphasizes, moreover, how such speakers draw on their first language's

---

8 Canadian Press (2007) provides an interactive map of Canada that indicates the languages spoken in different cities and regions.

resources as they continually develop and refine their communicative strategies. He maintains that teaching language in the current context of global migration is about "developing . . . a readiness to engage with a repertoire of [language] codes" in order to "shuttle between communities" (2007, p. 934). In light of this, he urges language teachers to rethink assessment in terms of "one's ability to negotiate . . . complex communicative needs" in different contexts and to "develop instruments that are sensitive to performance and pragmatics" (p. 934). I see Canagarajah's work as connected to Baker's above. Both are concerned with broadening our understandings about language, attending to difference, and underlining multiplicity rather than singularity. For me, this is an exciting opportunity, as well as a responsibility, to engage (with) my students in issues of diversity and equity.

References

Baker, J. (2002). Trilingualism. In L. Delpit & J. Dowdy (Eds.), *The skin that we speak: Thoughts on language and culture in the classroom* (pp. 50–61). New York: The New Press.

Battiste, M. & Henderson, J. (2000). The importance of language for Indigenous knowledge. In *Protecting Indigenous knowledge and heritage* (pp. 73–85). Saskatoon SK: Purich Publishing Ltd.

Canadian Press. (2007). 2006 Census Release: Immigration and mother tongue. http://www.cbc.ca/news/interactives/cp-census-immigration/index.html (accessed September 5, 2010).

Canagarajah, S. (2004). Language rights and postmodern conditions. *Journal of Language, Identity, and Education* 3(2), 140–145.

Canagarajah, S. (2007). Lingua franca English, multilingual communities, and language acquisition. *Modern Language Journal* 91, 923–939.

Corbeil, J. P. & Blaser, C. (2007). The evolving linguistic portrait: 2006 census findings (Demography Division, Statistics Canada). Catalogue # 97-555-XIE (December 4). http://www12.statcan.ca/english/census06/analysis/language/index.cfm (accessed September 5, 2010).

Dei, G. S. & Lordan, M. (2006). Language, linguistic discrimination, and polyvocality. In N. Amin & G. S. Dei (Eds.), *The poetics of anti-racism* (pp. 31–42). Halifax, NS: Fernwood.

Delpit, L. & Dowdy, J. (Eds.). (2002). *The skin that we speak: Thoughts on language and culture in the classroom.* New York: The New Press.

Jenkins, J. (2006). Current perspectives on teaching world Englishes and English as a *lingua franca. TESOL Quarterly* 40(1), 157–181.

Sapir, E. (1949). *Selected Writings of Edward Sapir in language, culture, and personality.* (Ed. D. G. Mandelbaum). Berkeley, CA: University of California Press.

Shelton, L. (2007). Importing Canagarajah's global English theories. *English Teaching: Practice and Critique* 6(2), 58–71.

Walsh, S. (2008). Listening to difference in the teaching of "English": Insights from internationally educated teachers. *Changing English: An International Journal of English Teaching* 15(4), 397–405.

Whorf, B. L. (1941). The relation of habitual thought and behaviour to language. In L. Spier (Ed.), *Language, cultural, and personality: Essays in memory of Edward Sapir*. Salt Lake City: University of Utah Press.

How Can Life Writing be an Effective Approach and Teaching Strategy with English Language Learners from Mixed Linguistic and Racial/Cultural Backgrounds?

By Erika Hasebe-Ludt, University of Lethbridge

(Not So) Simple Recipes: Life Writing in the Mixed Cosmos of Canadian Language Classrooms

> There is a simple recipe for making rice. My father taught it to me when I was a child. Back then I used to sit on the kitchen counter watching him, how he sifted the grains in his hands, sure and quick, removing pieces of dirt or sand, tiny imperfections. . . . Sometimes I still dream my father, his bare feet flat against the floor, standing in the middle of the kitchen.
>
> —Madeleine Thien, from *Simple Recipes*

How can life writing be an effective approach and teaching strategy with English language learners from mixed linguistic and racial/cultural backgrounds? In response to this question, I offer you a small taste of the large body of literature that reflects Canada's linguistically and racially mixed population and migration history. I also invite you, dear reader, to sample a few morsels from writings by contemporary Canadian authors of diverse ancestries—Aboriginal, Japanese, Vietnamese, Chinese, Anglo European, among others—along with samples of "recipes" I use as starters for creative writing in my language arts and curriculum studies classes. In these turbulent times, teachers' and students' lives are deeply affected by the past and present migration movements that have resulted in new socio-cultural and economic stratifications and material cultures around the globe (Smith, 2006). More radically and more richly than ever, classrooms have become cosmopolitan linguistic and cultural sites where "complicated conversations" (Pinar, 2009) about literacies in relation to private and public narratives are taking place. And in the wake of these shifting, globalized currents and transnational borders, teachers and students in local Canadian classrooms need to become effective multimodal agents in shaping and reshaping their own and others' identities and literacies in the places they live, study, and work (Chambers, 2003, 2006). So here I have prepared a modest menu of strategies to provoke this kind of agency, through creative non-fiction in the form of life writing.

In my undergraduate and graduate teacher education courses, we often begin with the titles or "names" of stories to acknowledge that "to say the name is to begin the story" (Christensen, 2000, p. iii). This also creates openings for sharing personal and public narratives. After listening to and viewing excerpts from a variety of genres (e.g., fiction, film, audio, auto/biography, personal essay, poetry, memoir), students write their own naming stories, using prompts from the excerpts and freewriting exercises based on techniques by Natalie Goldberg (2007), Julia Cameron (1992), Carol Bly (2001), and others. I write along with my students. We use lines such as: "You probably won't be Melody when you read this. I'm wondering what Paulie will change your name to . . ." (Robinson, 2006, p. 3); "I wonder if the old man had reflected upon his own failed dreams in naming me . . ." (Choy, 1999, p. 17); "we ponder the meaning of 'kiimooch ka shinikashooyen/the secret of your name . . .' in Cree, and in English" (Bouchard, 2010).

As the Kenyan poet Micere Mugo proclaimed, "Writing can be a lifeline" (as cited in Christensen, 2000, p. 6), and I believe that life writing is a uniquely sturdy one for those whose life circumstances, family histories, and racial ancestries have been marginalized or silenced. Natalie Goldberg (2007) reminds us that writing is the act of reaching across the abyss of isolation to share and reflect with "an old friend from far away" (p. xix). As a teacher, I have learned that life writing is indeed a potent way to connect with both the familiar and the (e)strange(d) parts of one's self and of others who are part of our pedagogical lifeworlds. Life writing can provide each of us with insights about *who we are* in relation to *where is here,* addressing Northrop Frye's questions about Canadian identity (see Chambers, 1999). It can also show us how to live with *what is here,* where *here* is a ground saturated with identities both Indigenous and foreign, from *here* and *elsewhere.* Bearing in mind John Ralston Saul's (2008, p. 3) affirmation that "we are a métis civilization," it is important for students to see themselves as part of this "métissage" (Hasebe-Ludt, Chambers, & Leggo, 2009) and of the legacies of a colonial past. Life writing is one way to not forget "the scandals of an epoch," in Hélène Cixous' (1997) words. In Canada, these include the centuries-long colonization of Aboriginal peoples and ongoing attempts to eradicate their rich histories and languages, as well as the discrimination against immigrant languages and cultures (Coelho, 2003). To draw attention to and to counteract these persistent realities in this seemingly successful multicultural mosaic, I encourage all my students to learn other languages, to write in more than English, and to use their mother tongues—Blackfoot, Michif, Punjabi, Mandarin, and many more—along with English. For learners of English as a new language or in a new dialect, autobiographical writing in their mother tongue, even with only a partial proficiency, makes a home for the "other tongues," stirring up a savoury mix of words and worlds in our English-dominated classrooms (Santa Ana, 2004). It saddens me that many of the languages from Canada's rich Aboriginal and immigrant history seem so remote to second, third, or fourth generation students. However, when they discover the sound and sense of a mother tongue by using it in their own writing, new lifeworlds (re)emerge for many of them.

Life writing in poetic form, in particular, provides openings for students with mother tongues other than English to begin a dialogue with the still foreign and frozen landscape of English language and culture. We use poetry by writers such as Bruce Hunter (2010), who writes about "What my students teach me" and "What I know about Gerald." These poems are examples of an insightful and artful mix of literature, life writing, and pedagogy. From these lines, students can begin writing their own lines about where they come from, what they know, and what they may never know: how they "name the world" (Atwell, 2006). Students who perceive themselves as strangers in a new place—and are treated that way by others—are able to connect with life writing that names linguistic and cultural fractures through first-person experiences (Yoshimoto, 2008; Xiong, 1997).

As readers, listeners, and writers, students also learn about the pain of first language loss. They start to (re)acquaint themselves with a linguistic and racial heritage that may have been silenced or suppressed in their own family's English-only conversations (Feuer, 2008; Kouritzin, 2006). With each story, I am moved anew by the particular and universal truths that reside in these narratives, and I too enter into the conversations with different genealogies and generations. Thus life writing becomes a dialogical restorative act, reclaiming one's own familial history, and rehabilitating part of this country's and the larger world's lost linguistic and cultural traditions. Through sharing life writing in the classroom (and the reading of exemplary texts by authors like those whom Noah Richler [2006] encounters in his illuminative literary atlas of Canada), students also become more cognizant of others' histories as part of the multi-layered migration movements into and across this nation. Writing and teaching stories about particular homes and landscapes helps students understand how they have been shaped by the landscapes of loss (Clifford & Friesen, 2006) and the languages of grief (Kogawa, 1981; Lee, 2002) buried beneath the official histories bound by the curriculum texts.

As an immigrant and a non-native speaker of English myself, my own life writing is an integral part of my pedagogy: I take my students with me on my remembered journey as an immigrant from post–World War II Germany and open my life with my Canadian Japanese family to them. We ponder how these kinds of sojourns inform teaching and learning about the places one immigrates to as well as about the places one emigrated from (Hasebe-Ludt, 2003, 2004, 2009). When students listen to this kind of life writing, whether my own or those of other authors I write with (Hasebe-Ludt, Chambers, Leggo, & Oberg, 2008), they become more aware of their own tangled webs of worldly relations. In these texts, opened as communal offerings among writers and teachers, visceral knowledge about teaching and learning starts to resonate among individual human beings and places. Together, we practise timed freewriting exercises—"writing off the page" (Goldberg, 1986/2005) from lines that resonate with students from the written and audiovisual texts we read and view together from writers like Thomas King (2000) and Eden Robinson (2000). For many students, a new consciousness arises about who they are in relation to the place from which they come. As Cynthia Chambers (2006) tells us, the connections we have to places are profound pedagogical spaces: "The land is the best teacher I have ever had," she reminds us when quoting Blackfoot Elder Narcisse Blood. And J. Edward Chamberlin (2003) warns us that if we don't know the land and we don't know the stories, we don't know ourselves.

The names you are given, the ones you choose for yourself and others—including the names of the land you live on—are bearers of truths. Life writing challenges you, in Al Purdy's (2001) poetic words, to "say the names, say the names/and listen to yourself/an echo in the mountains," in many languages, Indigenous and from other lands, in pedagogically and ecologically responsive ways. Life writing challenges you to address where you live and how you live with yourself and with your daily rhythms and relations in your home, writing about things like fathers cooking rice (Thien, 2001), mothers making tabouli (Crate, 2001), *kokums* baking bannock (Loewen, 1993), in kitchens, camps, and classrooms. In this storied cosmos of earth and sky, home and not-home, life writing invites you to dwell and dig in the mixed terra of this biocultural ecology (Dunlop, 2009), to confront and compost the geographic rifts (Miki, 2001), landscapes of loss, and books of longing (Cohen, 2006) that created this nation's artful "quilt of belonging" (Weaver, 2006). Life writing can heal the ground you tremble on and the heart you hurt with, to restore and re-story our mixed—métis—common ground. In creating one's own original literature in this community of writers and readers, writing individually and collaboratively, working intertextually and interpretively with earlier texts and new ones, students come to understand life writing and teaching as political acts. By braiding local stories into global contexts inside and outside schools, writers and readers open up to the truths that these stories tell. I firmly believe that this kind of truth-telling is necessary in order to name and rename the world we live in, to repair its fragmented, broken parts, and to bring us face to face with our own beautiful and imperfect humanity: "The truth about stories is that that's all we are" (King, 2003, p. 2). Life writing is one way of telling truths and making curricula, classrooms, schools, and societies more inclusive, more art- and heart-full, and more mindful, embodied, and inspirited (Archibald, 2008).

I am inspired by teachers like Shanna Hagens (2010), who engages in life writing with her students about where they live and learn in a rural, northern Aboriginal Dene community. And I am inspired by Perry Buchan (2009), Marguerite Leahy (2009), and Favour Simoongwe (2010), who work with their students' life stories alongside their own in the multi-literate urban Vancouver and Calgary sites where they teach and live. I hope that you, dear reader, together with your students, will be equally inspired to listen to yourself, to your students, and to the mountains and plains in your own place. With this entry, I want to give you the courage to write your own stories, to say the sometimes difficult names, to recall the simple and not-so-simple recipes from your home, and to respond to Roy Miki's (2001, p. 56) poetic question: "are geographic/rifts compost/in family trees?" This kind of memory work—this kind of literature—is creating the fertile humus of the new biocultural literacies of our times. Here, on this métis ground, we are superbly positioned to braid the potent mixed languages and the visceral cosmopolitan narratives of the literary commons of all our relations.

References

Archibald, J. (2008). *Indigenous storywork: Educating the heart, mind, body, and spirit.* Vancouver, BC: UBC Press.

Atwell, N. (2006). *Naming the world: A year of poems and lessons.* Toronto, ON: Pearson Canada.

Bly, C. (2001). *Beyond the writers' workshop: New ways to write creative nonfiction.* New York: Anchor Books.

Bouchard, D., Weber, D. J., & Arcand, J. (2010). *The secret of your name/Kiimooch ka shinikashooyen.* Markham, ON: Red Deer Press.

Buchan, P. (2009). *How life works.* Unpublished major paper, University of British Columbia, Vancouver, BC.

Cameron, J. (1992). *The artist's way: A spiritual guide to higher creativity.* New York: Jeremy P. Tarcher.

Chamberlin, J. E. (2003). *If this is your land, where are your stories?: Finding common ground.* Toronto, ON: Alfred A. Knopf.

Chambers, C. (1999). A topography for Canadian curriculum theory. *Canadian Journal of Education* 24(2), 137–150.

Chambers, C. (2003). "As Canadian as possible under the circumstances": A view of contemporary Canadian curriculum discourses in Canada. In W. F. Pinar (Ed.), *International handbook of curriculum research* (pp. 221–252). Mahwah, NJ: Lawrence Erlbaum.

Chambers, C. (2006). "The land is the best teacher I ever had": Places as pedagogy for precarious times. *JCT: Journal of Curriculum Theorizing* 22(3), 27–37.

Choy, W. (1999). *Paper shadows: A Chinatown childhood.* Toronto, ON: Penguin Canada.

Christensen, L. (2000). *Reading, writing, and rising up: Teaching about social justice and the written word.* Milwaukee, WI: Rethinking Schools.

Cixous, H. & Calle-Gruber, M. (1997). *Hélène Cixous rootprints: Memory and life writing* (Prenowitz, Trans.). New York: Routledge.

Clifford, P. & Friesen, S. (2006). Landscapes of loss: The original difficulty of reading. In D. Jardine, P. Clifford, & S. Friesen (Eds.), *Back to the basics of teaching and learning: Rethinking the world together* (pp. 179–192). New York: Routledge.

Cohen, L. (2006). *Book of longing*. Toronto, ON: McClelland & Stewart.

Coehlo, E. (2003). *Adding English: A guide to teaching in multilingual classrooms.* Toronto, ON: Pippin Publishing.

Crate, J. (2001). *Foreign homes.* London, ON: Brick Books.

Dunlop, R. (2009). Primer: Alphabet for the new republic. In M. McKenzie, P. Hart, H. Bai, & B. Jickling (Eds.), *Fields of green: Restorying culture, environment, and education* (pp. 11–63). Cresskill, NJ: Hampton Press.

Feidt, M. (Director & Producer). (2006). *Tangled up in Bob: Searching for Bob Dylan: A Minnesota story.* Santa Fe, NM: Feido Films.

Feuer, A. (2008). *Who does this language belong to?: Personal narratives of language claim and identity*. Charlotte, NC: Information Age Publishing.

Goldberg, N. (2007). *Old friend from far away: The practice of writing memoir.* New York: Free Press/Simon & Schuster.

Goldberg, N. (1986/2005). *Writing down the bones: Freeing the writer within.* Boston, MA: Shambhala Publications.

Hagens, S. (2010). *Teaching in the Taiga: Learning to live where I am.* Unpublished master's thesis, University of Victoria, Victoria, BC.

Hasebe-Ludt, E. (2003). By the Oldman River I remembered. In E. Hasebe-Ludt & W. Hurren (Eds.), *Curriculum intertext: Place/language/pedagogy* (pp. 149–147). New York: Peter Lang.

Hasebe-Ludt, E. (2004). We talked freely of many things: Writing home/away from home. In A. L. Cole, L. Neilsen, J. G. Knowles, & T. C. Luciani (Eds.), *Provoked by art: Theorizing arts-informed research* (pp. 203–213). Big Tancook Island, NS: Backalong Books.

Hasebe-Ludt, E. (2009). Writing lives, writing worlds: Literacy as autobiographical and cosmopolitan text. In P. Lewis & J. Tupper (Eds.), *Challenges bequeathed: Taking up the challenges of Dwayne Huebner* (pp. 25–38). Rotterdam/Taipei: Sense Publishers.

Hasebe-Ludt, E., Chambers, C. M., & Leggo, C. (2009). *Life writing and literary métissage as an ethos for our times*. New York: Peter Lang.

Hasebe-Ludt, E., Chambers, C., Leggo, C., & Oberg, A. (2008). Embracing the world, with all our relations: Métissage as an artful braiding. In S. Springgay, R. L. Irwin, C. Leggo, & P. Gouzuasis (Eds.), *Being with a/r/tography* (pp. 58–67). Rotterdam: Sense Publishers.

Hunter, B. (2010). *Two o'clock creek: Poems new and selected.* Fernie, BC: Oolichan Books.

King, T. (2000). *Truth and Bright Water.* Toronto, ON: Harper Perennial Canada.

King, T. (2003). *The truth about stories: A Native narrative*. Toronto, ON: House of Anansi Press.

Kogawa, J. (1981). *Obasan.* Toronto, ON: Lester & Orpen Dennys.

Kouritzin, S. (2006, Winter). Songs from taboo tongues: Experiencing first language loss. *Language and Literacy: A Canadian Educational Journal* 8(1), 1–28. Available at: http://www.langandlit.ualberta.ca/archivesDate.html (accessed January 2, 2012).

Leahy, M. (2009). *Possibilities of visual texts: An urban teacher's learning vine.* Unpublished major paper, University of British Columbia, Vancouver, BC.

Lee, N. (2002). *Dead girls.* Toronto: McClelland & Stewart.

Loewen, I. (1993). *My kokum called today.* Winnipeg, MB: Pemmican Publications.

Miki, R. (2001). *Surrender.* Toronto: The Mercury Press.

Pinar, W. F. (2009). *The worldliness of a cosmopolitan education: Passionate lives in public service.* New York: Routledge.

Purdy, A. (2001). *Say the names/Pronuncia nomi.* Toronto: McArthur & Company.

Richler, N. (2006). *This is my country, what's yours?: A literary atlas of Canada.* Toronto: McClelland & Stewart.

Robinson, E. (2000). *Monkey Beach.* Toronto: Random House of Canada.

Robinson, E. (2006). *Blood sports.* Toronto: McClelland & Stewart.

Santa Ana, O. (2004). *Tongue-tied: The lives of multilingual children in public education.* Lanham, MD: Rowman & Littlefield.

Saul, J. R. (2008). *A fair country: Telling truths about Canada.* Toronto: Viking Canada.

Simoongwe, F. (2010). *Living in a culture of change: An inquiry into the learning experiences of new Sudanese students in Calgary schools.* Unpublished master's thesis, University of Lethbridge, Lethbridge, AB.

Smith, D. G. (2006). *Trying to teach in a season of great untruth: Globalization, empire, and the crises of pedagogy.* Rotterdam: Sense Publishers.

Thien, M. (2001). *Simple recipes.* Toronto: McClelland & Stewart.

Weaver, J. (2006). *The quilt of belonging: Stitching together the stories of a nation.* Toronto: Maple Tree Press.

Yoshimoto, M. (2008). *Second language learning and identity: Cracking metaphors in ideological and poetic discourse in the third space.* Amherst, NY: Cambria Press.

Xiong, G. (1997). *The yellow pear.* Vancouver, BC: Arsenal Pulp Press.

How Does the Use of Digital Media Benefit Adolescent English Language Learners in the English Classroom?

By Janette Hughes and Allyson Eamer, University of Ontario Institute of Technology

Toronto, Montreal, and Vancouver are the cities of choice for nearly two-thirds of all immigrants who arrive in Canada (Frideres, 2006). Educators in large urban schools typically find themselves striving to fill in the gaps created by budget shortfalls to meet the linguistic, social, settlement, and educational needs of immigrant students. In such a context, every teacher becomes an English as a Second Language (ESL) teacher and has a role in implementing strategies for use with English language learners (ELLs). Such strategies should help to increase students' sense of belonging and ownership with respect to the school culture, the broader school community, and the English language. Norton Peirce (1995) has written about the conceptualization of the "legitimate" English speaker. Legitimacy is often associated with birthright (being born in a country where English is the official language), having a physical appearance that corresponds with a western European ancestry, and near-fluent proficiency. (Many ESL teachers, in fact, who are not native speakers of English often encounter this sort of prejudice from students and their parents who would prefer to learn from someone who "looks like the English language *belongs* to them.") The process of acquiring Standard English has implications for identity negotiation and, thereby, access to powerful social networks that undoubtedly play a role in a student's educational achievement and satisfaction levels.

Our research reported in this entry explores how digital media, personal narratives, poetry, identity, performance, and English language learning come together through multimodal expression. The ability of multimodality to supersede limitations on students imposed by the kinds of language skills required for traditional print-based narratives makes multimodality highly effective for facilitating a sense of autonomy and agency over the English language learner's own story. For many students, especially those from developing nations, this empowerment serves to address, in part, some of the inequities they experience with respect to claims of legitimacy as Canadians and as English speakers, as well as inequities with respect to accessing information through English-language-based communication technologies. This project positions the English language learners as storytellers of personal learning and growth, and offers them opportunities to experience a "narrative reconstruction" as they reflect on their lives, their learning, their interests, their past experiences, and their goals for the future (Hull, 2003, p. 232).

The Study

The English language learners were drawn from two different schools in the Greater Toronto Area. In one school, the study was conducted with students in an ESL "reception class." Reception classes at each grade level are offered in some Toronto schools with large immigrant populations. Newly arrived students start off in a very small and intensive age-appropriate class taught by qualified ESL teachers. As their English skills improve, the students "graduate" to regular classes at that same grade level. Students in a junior ESL reception class were invited to create digital "stories" in which they would document their experiences of immigrating to Canada with images, music, text, and, in some cases, an audio (narration) track. In another school, more advanced English language learners were drawn from an intermediate English language arts classroom and invited to create digital poetry and to join it with images and music. In the reception class, several introductory lessons took place in which discussions and corresponding mini-tasks occurred on the theme of dynamic identity (for example, "we are always changing and growing" and "we can feel at home in two languages, two countries"). In the English language arts classroom, the lessons were on the theme of poetry writing (using a "where-I'm-from" focus to provide an opportunity for students to voice things that concerned them and to identify links between themselves and their community).

Some of the students from the reception class, particularly those who had been in displacement camps and had been waiting to emigrate, had minimal computer experience and did not know, for example, how to conduct Internet searches, create folders, or save files. In these cases, a significant amount of time was spent providing small-group instruction on basic computer skills. Students found images and music online, collected these artifacts in a folder, and then pieced them together to support a storyline or a poem. Some chose to juxtapose elements of their identities, lives, activities, and environments while others chose to focus almost exclusively on their lives in their countries of origin. Students were invited to narrate their story or poem in English, in their first language, or through a combination of both languages. Some students elected to refrain from voice-over narration altogether and used onscreen text to elaborate their stories. All students were invited to choose a soundtrack for their projects. Choices included theme songs from South Asian movies, well-known songs from their countries of origin, North American pop songs, theme songs from North American TV shows, and computer-generated music.

Students were then invited to share (perform) their digital stories and poems with teachers, peers, and parents. Examples of the students' work can be found at http://faculty.uoit.ca/hughes/clip1.html and http://faculty.uoit.ca/eamer/Language_Projects.html. Participation in this project resulted in empowerment of many kinds for the students, including membership in the following communities: English Speakers, Writers/Poets/Artists, Digital-Literates and New Canadians.

Why Use Digital Media?

The argument for a pedagogy that takes into account not only traditional print and oral literacies but also visual and multimodal representations has been well established in the literature (Cope & Kalantzis, 2000; Kress, 2003; Cummins, Brown, & Sayers, 2007). Unlike oral or solely print-based stories, digital stories potentially enhance the power of narrative to negotiate identity as digital stories can be "told" with minimal language proficiency and can be easily broadcast, creating a stronger sense of audience and performance. Poetry is immensely powerful for English language learners because they do not require a high level of proficiency in English to produce expressive pieces, and they can move fairly easily between English and their first language with the support of teachers and peers. Digital media facilitate the convergence of multiple modes in one medium, which, in turn, fosters the strengths of diverse learners.

The act of telling a story is an act of constructing meaning and an image can be a powerful tool in the process of identity construction. Photographic images, furthermore, can shape and inform personal narratives. Furman (2005) explains that when telling stories of events that have occurred in our lives, we base our narrative on a series of snapshot-like memories we have of that experience. We attempt to sequence and link the snapshots chronologically and to fill in the gaps between them so as to create a coherent, fully developed narrative. Likewise, music, a prominent symbol of community membership and identification, can play an important role in the construction of a digital story or poem. The playlists on an adolescent's digital music player can signal the social, cultural, and linguistic communities with which he or she identifies.

Why Use Narratives and Poetry?

Furman (2005) presents the case that identity is relational, dynamic, fluid, and always under construction. She argues that, although the migrant narrative is necessarily one of loss and estrangement, it is also one of possibility because the migrant has agency in shaping a new, hybrid identity. Moreover, she explains that for youth who generally had little or no power with regard to their displacement, narrating their migration is an especially empowering, albeit complex, process. For such children and teens, constructing their migration stories provides agency where none was originally experienced. Immigrants live in a contradictory space resulting from the dominant group's construction of them as both "other" and "acceptable" simultaneously. In order to qualify as a "real Canadian," immigrants have to suppress, conceal, or replace their authentic selves with a Canadian identity. By telling their own stories as narrative prose or through poetry, and by including images and music, students are able to resist being confined by these binaries and can negotiate their own hybrid identities.

Why Focus on Identity?

A number of researchers (Cummins, Bismilla, Chow, Cohen, Giampapa, Leoni, Sandhu, & Sastri, 2005) have analyzed migrant students' accounts of their immigration experiences and found that the students exhibited a sense of agency with respect to constructing a dual identity that served their needs in a complex and challenging environment. Toohey (2000) and Harklau (2000) are among many researchers who have studied the role of schools in ascribing identities to immigrant students. School identities are constructed based on the teachers' perceptions of a student's physical presentation as well as his or her academic, social, and communicative competence. Other school-ascribed identities encourage students to define themselves according to the hardships they have overcome and the level of gratitude they express at beginning a new life in Canada. Nostalgia for the homeland can be interpreted as a lack of gratitude and an unwillingness to acculturate or contribute to the new country. Without the language skills to negotiate their own identities, students are at risk of conforming to an identity ascribed to them by their teachers and school administrators.

Why Does Performance Matter?

When students are given opportunities to share their "identity texts" with peers, family, teachers, and the general public through media, they are likely to make gains in self-confidence, self-esteem, and a sense of "community belonging" through the positive feedback they receive (Cummins, Brown, & Sayers, 2007). Performance assumes an audience and, although texts created using new media are not always posted on the Internet, they are more likely to be. Composing stories and poetry in digital environments such as blogs or YouTube places student work more directly on the public stage, moving it beyond an audience of one (the teacher) and making it accessible to a wider audience (Hughes, 2008). The work English language learners did in crafting the digital narratives for this project suggests that: (1) the *students-as-storytellers* focus increased the students' estimation of the importance of skills needed to communicate or perform in different semiotic modes with wider audiences; and (2) the digital-narrative process provided

English language learners with the means to explore and communicate the process of hybrid identity negotiation.

Norton Peirce (1995) argues that "it is through language that a person negotiates a sense of self within and across different sites . . . and that it is through language that a person gains access to—or is denied access to—powerful social networks" (p. 13). We would argue that multimedia tools are another viable means to accomplish this end.

Suggested Resources

Multimedia projects for English teachers:

Literacy Narratives

Scott, J. B. (1997). The literacy narrative as production pedagogy in the composition classroom. *TETYC* May, 108–117.

Webquests

Sox, A. & Rubenstein-Ávila, E. (2009). WebQuests for English-Language Learners: Essential elements for design. *Journal of Adolescent & Adult Literacy* 53(1), 38–48.

Visual Arts in the English Classroom: Manga

Andazola, M. (2009). Drawn into Manga. *Albuquerque Journal,* November 8. http://www.abqjournal.com/lifestyles/08215054lifestyles11-08-09.htm (accessed January 2, 2012).

Story Re-telling Using Digital Media

Re-writing Goldilocks: Emerging Transliteracies (Heather Lotherington)

http://schools.tdsb.on.ca/joyce/main/goldilocks/index.htm

Collaborative Writing with Bilingual Student Authors

The Title's Tale (Allyson Eamer)

http://faculty.uoit.ca/eamer/Language_Multilingual.html

Dual Language Book Bags

Dual Language Showcase at Thornwood Public School

http://schools.peelschools.org/1363/pages/dual.aspx

References

Cummins, J., Bismilla, V., Chow, P., Cohen, S., Giampapa, F., Leoni, L., Sandhu, P., & Sastri, P. (2005). Affirming identity in multilingual classrooms. *Educational Leadership* 63(1), 38–43.

Cummins, J., Brown, K., & Sayers, D. (2007). *Literacy, technology, and diversity: Teaching for success in changing times*. Boston, MS: Pearson Education.

Cope, B. & Kalantzis, M. (Eds.). (2000). *Multiliteracies: Literacy learning and the design of social futures.* London and New York: Routledge/Falmer.

Frideres, J. S. (2006). Cities and immigrant integration: The future of second- and third-tier centres. *Our Diverse Cities* 2, 3–8.

Furman, F. (2005). The long road home: Migratory experience and the construction of the self. *Journal of Prevention and Intervention in the Community* 30(1/2), 91–116.

Harklau, L. (2000). From the "good kids" to the "worst": Representations of English language learners across educational settings. *TESOL Quarterly* 34(1), 35–67.

Hughes, J. (2008). The "Screen-Size" Art: Using Digital Media to Perform Poetry. *English in Education* 42(2), 148–164.

Hughes, J. & Eamer, A. (2010). *Media(ting) identities: Digital identity projects in an ESL classroom.* Paper presented at the annual CSSE conference, Carleton University, Ottawa, ON.

Hull, G. A. (2003). At last: Youth culture and digital media: New literacies for new times. *Research in the Teaching of English* 38(2), 229–233.

Kress, G. (2003). *Literacy in the New Media Age.* London: Routledge.

Norton Peirce, B. (1995). Social identity, investment, and language learning. *TESOL Quarterly* 29(1), 9–31.

Toohey, K. (2000). *Learning English at school: Identity, social relations and classroom practice.* Clevedon, United Kingdom: Multilingual Matters.

SECTION 3

Gender and Sexuality

What's the Connection between Gender and Literacy?

By Roberta F. Hammett, Memorial University of Newfoundland

Several times in my career as a secondary school English teacher and later as an educator of individuals training to be intermediate-secondary English teachers I have engaged in exploring the connections between gender and literacy. During the 1970s and '80s, educational institutions (along with many other public institutions) became increasingly aware of and paid greater attention to gender-equity issues. This was encouraged by the Report of the Royal Commission on the Status of Women (released in 1970), the subsequent establishment of the committees on the status of women in Ottawa and across Canada, and the United Nations declaration of 1975 to be the International Women's Year. This change was evidenced in schools and school systems by the efforts of educators and administrators to eliminate gender bias in education, particularly in relation to the administration of programs, through inclusive language, non-sexist textbooks, and an equitable representation of women in administrative leadership positions.

With regard to inclusive language, it fell to English teachers—as individuals, that is, since there were no official policies on inclusive language in most provinces at the time—to teach inclusive terms. These included discussions on how to solve the "Pronoun Puzzle" (Ontario Women's Directorate, p. 6), the use of gender-neutral terms for officials (e.g., "police officer" instead of "policeman"), and practical activities such as adding "or Madam" to "Dear Sir" in business letters. In my classroom, I used a publication of the Ontario Women's Directorate (1992) titled *Words That Count Women Out/In*, although not without protest from some students and their parents. Nevertheless, 83 percent of undergraduate university students surveyed in 1991 considered it important to use nonsexist language, even though only 33 percent of them had actually received instruction not to use masculine-exclusive nouns like "mankind" and "chairman" (Kennedy, 1993, p. 229).

Another concern for gender and literacy surfaced about the same time in relation to gender-biased content of school texts and curricula. Formal and informal studies were conducted on sex-role stereotyping in textbooks and the gender ratios of the authors and main characters in novels and anthologies. During the late 1980s and early 1990s, several provinces instituted guidelines to screen out bias and inequality of representation in the selection of textbooks. Unfortunately, economic realities and other considerations often assured that there was less change in what was taught than intended by policy-makers. (See Coulter [1996] for a full discussion of gender issues in schools and policies.)

By the mid-1990s, several important publications had put gender back in the news and on the educational agenda: *How Schools Shortchange Girls* (AAUW, 1992), *Failing at Fairness* (Sadker & Sadker, 1994), *School Girls* (Orenstein, 1994), and *Reviving Ophelia* (Pipher, 1994). These books, and much scholarly research, raised awareness of inequalities in school and society, resulting in policies to make math, science, and technology more "girl-friendly" within educational contexts.

The gender-literacy connection that has received the most media hype recently arises from what some commentators characterized as a "moral panic" when provincial, national, and international literacy tests revealed that boys as a group scored lower than girls (e.g., Hammett & Sanford, 2008b). There are echoes of the previous concerns for girls in this panic. Several researchers point out the boys' turn (or "boy turn") aspect of the debate, emphasizing the continuity of educators' concerns over gender-exclusionary educational practices, as well as the grounding of the recent critiques in enrolment and test scores—just as it was with girls in math and sciences (see Weaver-Hightower, 2003). Beginning in the late 1990s, some critics' readings of students' scores on the Programme for International Student Assessment (PISA) and a raft of other literacy tests caused concern because, as a group, boys were achieving lower scores than girls. News media worldwide reported that boys don't like to read, lag behind girls in reading scores, see reading as a feminine activity, prefer particular kinds of reading material when they do read, reject the feminization of schools (due to the lack of male teachers and thus male role models), and so on. A number of studies were funded by concerned provincial and state governments in Australia, Canada, New Zealand, United Kingdom, and the United States to explore the "problem," so construed, and to suggest "solutions." The solutions ranged from providing male role models (e.g., sports figures) who read as reading buddies, buying books with boy-friendly themes and genres, changing early reading instruction to more traditional forms (like phonics), and creating "boys only" classes because boys, some studies claimed, learn differently from girls by nature (Hammett & Sanford, 2008). Many of these solutions have not been supported by evidence in subsequent research. (See Sokal et al. [2008] on the putative importance of male teachers; see Moss [2007] on the presumption that all boys will respond alike to particular selections of reading materials.)

Competing analyses and research studies of this "failing boys" phenomenon have emphasized such "quick fixes" or biological determinism less and other approaches more. Weaver-Hightower (2003) provides a list of the etiologies of research on the "boy turn" as uncovered through an extensive literature review (pp. 473–478). Weaver-Hightower's findings on the origin of these studies include popular rhetorical books and articles that fuelled the "moral panic" discussed above and the resulting backlash against feminist social theory (e.g., by the descriptions in such works of boys as disadvantaged and schools as feminized), theoretically oriented works that examine societal constructions of masculinity and strive to provide nuanced understandings of gender and processes of gender construction, practice-oriented publications that describe school and classroom interventions, and feminist responses that critique the "boy turn" in various ways (Weaver-Hightower, 2003, p. 474). These etiologies problematize a straightforward acceptance of the "failing boys" phenomenon. A more nuanced account is needed.

While rejecting generalizations about boys and asking, in effect, "Which boys?" (Martino, 2008), teachers may still respond to parental concerns and their own observations when they see that children of either gender are not engaged in successful literacy learning. Such responses should bring issues of race and class back into focus (for such differences in PISA scores are largely ignored due to the emphasis on the success of "boys" as a category), ensuring that all students receive effective literacy instruction within anti-essentialist frameworks. Thus, a variety of instructional practices, texts, and contexts is likely to be most effective; for example, an inclusive curriculum and education that honours multiple ways of knowing (including Aboriginal and other cultural experiences, values, and practices), respects multiple intelligences, or employs multimodal texts that include a range of possibilities for student response. Digital technologies offer both boys and girls a wide variety of authentic literacy practices that engage them and prepare them for twenty-first-century contexts (Hammett & Toope, 2010).

At the same time, teachers might engage with students, as Harper (2007) and Dutro (2008) suggest, in examinations of essentialized representations of femininity and masculinity. Texts and reading practices have been gendered within a society that normalizes particularly narrow conceptions of masculinity and femininity, in oppositional ways. This lays out rigid constructions or performances of gender identities—at least, in public settings. Dutro (2008) describes, in several publications, her research with African-American fifth graders, which explored the relationships between gender, interests, and reading practices; one of the investigations asked: "What happens when boys are required to read books that are highly gendered as *girls' books*?" (p. 76). Dutro observed reactions to and activities associated with "literature circle" activities (e.g., Daniels, 1994) while reading the *American Girl* series, and she and the classroom teacher discussed with the students such concepts as "reifying traditional notions of masculinity," "social risks of crossing gender boundaries," (p. 80), and "rethink[ing] some of their [the fifth-grade students] own assumptions about what texts they could and would engage with" in the safe space of the classroom (p. 83).

Similarly, Harper (2007) advocates critical literacy activities that include analyzing constructions and performances of masculinity and femininity in popular young adult novels with female protagonists. Harper's descriptions of different performances of masculinity and femininity (cross-dressing, unconventional characters, and situations of rigid policing or social regulation of gendered performance) are instructive. The outcome of such in-class analyses is likely to be a broadening of the students' understandings of masculinity and femininity beyond the inflexible binaries that are most familiar in popular culture. As canonical texts persist in classrooms, studies of boy-dominated novels (*Lord of the Flies, The Outsiders*) and other texts (such as many of Shakespeare's plays, or *To Kill a Mockingbird*) could be similarly undertaken. As Harper points out, "Other aspects of social difference (race, age, class, ethnicity) need to be considered in the portrayals of masculinity" (p. 527).

Such gender work in classrooms is often difficult. Both boys and girls often have a vested interest in status quo gender relations, find stereotypes acceptable (Young, 2000), and see critical media literacy as a threat to works of popular culture that give them pleasure. Citing Bronwyn Davies, Young (2000) notes: "It was difficult for the boys to see through their own power base and not translate the critique of hegemonic masculinity into a criticism of themselves" (p. 317). Literacy work entails foregrounding the ideologies, discourses, and literacy practices that frame and mediate our readings of all texts.

Schools now are challenged to use digital technologies and the resources of Web 2.0 to engage all students with multimodal texts, composing and critiquing digital movies, blogs, glogs (interactive online posters), podcasts, and animations. Departments of Education are adding graphic novels to lists of authorized texts. Teachers are urged to engage all students and use diverse learning activities to engage a variety of literacies and intelligences. Learners may use a wide variety of movie-making and animation software to combine visual, aural, gestural, and linguistic signs to design statements or responses for selected purposes and audiences (Hammett & Toope, 2010). Both girls and boys respond creatively and enthusiastically to invitations to use digital tools and resources to compose multimodal works (Hammett, this volume).

Teachers are likely, in the future, to be challenged to negotiate emerging issues of gender but are also likely to be called upon to respond to race, class, ethnic, and queer identities. As with gender, resisting narrow, normative conceptions and embracing inclusive practices and critical literacies will support teachers as they strive toward social justice in schools.

References

American Association of University Women. (1992). *How schools shortchange girls.* New York: Marlowe.

Coulter, R. P. (1996). Gender equity and schooling: Linking research and policy, *Canadian Journal of Education* 21(4), 433–452.

Daniels, H. (1994). *Literature circles: Voice and choice in the student–centered classroom.* Portland, ME: Stenhouse.

Dutro, E. (2008). Boys reading *American Girls*: What's at stake in debates about what boys won't read. In R. F. Hammett & K. Sanford (Eds.), *Boys and girls and the myths of literacies and learning* (pp. 69–90). Toronto, ON: Canadian Scholars Press.

Hammett, R. F. & Sanford, K. (Eds.), (2008). *Boys and girls and the myths of literacies and learning.* Toronto, ON: Canadian Scholars Press Inc.

Hammett, R. F. & Sanford, K. (2008b). Introduction: Reading the myths and the panic In R. F. Hammett & K. Sanford (Eds.), *Boys, girls, and the myths of literacies and learning* (pp. 1–12). Toronto, ON: Canadian Scholars Press Inc.

Hammett, R. F. & Toope, D. (2010). New literacies and digital technologies: Exploring possibilities within the context of English language arts curriculum. In M. C. Courtland & T. Gambell (Eds.), *Young adolescents meet literature: Intersections for learning* (2nd ed, pp. 305–331). Vancouver, BC: Pacific Educational Press.

Harper, H. (2007). Studying masculinity(ies) in books about girls, *Canadian Journal of Education* 30(2), 508–530.

Kennedy, D. (1993). Nonsexist language: A progress report, *Canadian Journal of Education* 18(3), 223–238.

Martino, W. (2008). The politics and crisis of boys' literacy: Beyond essentialist mindsets and the boy-friendly curriculum. In R. F. Hammett & K. Sanford (Eds.) *Boys, girls and the myths of literacies and learning* (pp. 91–114). Toronto, ON: Canada's Scholars' Press.

Moss, G. (2007). *Literacy and gender: Researching texts, contexts and readers.* London: Routledge.

Ontario Women's Directorate. (1992). *Words that count women out/in.* Toronto, ON: Women's Directorate.

Orenstein, P. (1994). *School girls: Young women, self-esteem, and the confidence gap.* New York: Anchor Books.

Pipher, M. (1994). *Reviving Ophelia: Saving the selves of adolescent girls.* New York: Grosset/Putnam.

Sadker, M. & Sadker, D. (1994). *Failing at fairness: How our schools cheat girls.* New York: Touchstone.

Sokal, L. & Katz, H. (2008). Effects of technology and male teachers on boys' reading. *The Australian Journal of Education* 52(1), 80–93.

Weaver-Hightower, M. (2003, Winter). The "boy turn" in research on gender and education. *Review of Educational Research* 73(4), 471–498.

Young, J. P. (2000). Boy talk: Critical literacy and masculinities. *Reading Research Quarterly* 35(3), 312–337.

How Is the Reading of Popular Fiction Implicated in the Construction of Gender?

By Meredith Cherland, University of Regina

What's an English teacher to do with the fact that the *Twilight* novels by Stephenie Meyer are now the most popular teen-girl novels of all time? The success of the *Twilight* novels certainly says something about teen girls' continuing interest in heterosexual romance. It may also speak to thoughtful teachers about how teens *become* the gendered people they are, male or female, straight or gay. Popular fiction and all the other forms of popular culture teens enjoy have a contribution to make to the construction of identity.

The theory behind that assertion begins with a question: How do we become the people we are? Much of the Western world has been shaped by Enlightenment philosophy that proposes that people are born with a rational *self*; that there is one Truth, one reality that we all experience in the same way; and that language is a transparent medium, a window on reality. Poststructuralism offers a contrasting philosophy. It views language as the site where realities are created. It proposes a *subjectivity* instead of a self, an awareness of one's being that is formed in interaction with discourses. While the term *discourse* has many contemporary meanings, in poststructural theory the word *discourse* refers to patterns of language that reflect assumptions about the world and that structure social reality (Mills, 1997). Discourses provide competing ways of giving meaning to the world. Institutions like the law, the political system, the church, the family, and the media all provide cultural discourses (Weedon, 1992), ways of speaking about the world which assume certain beliefs about how the world works. It is in interaction with these discourses that people construct their subjectivities, their beliefs about themselves. Popular fiction is one type of cultural artifact that provides some of the discourses teens interact with as they construct themselves as gendered people (see, for example, St. Pierre, 2000, for more on poststructural theory in education).

The Enlightenment beliefs that so many take for granted as "common sense" require dualistic thinking. They rely on binaries, sets of two terms in which one concept or category (usually the first) is valued more highly than the other. They assume that *male* and *female* are opposite categories that exclude each other, like good and evil, mind and body, or rational and irrational. Teachers need to engage young people in challenging dualistic thinking, in questioning what seems normal and natural, and in thinking through the uncertainty and ambiguity that follows. By asking how identities are constructed, authorized and excluded, young people may come to see that the world is constructed, and can change (Kumashiro, 2009).

Poststructuralism does not view gender as a simple and exclusive binary; nor does it view gender as a collection of cultural stories about being male and female (like Cinderella, the dangerous sirens of *The Odyssey,* or the cruel and hostile hero of a Norman Mailer novel). Instead, poststructuralism sees gender as a social construction formed in interaction with the discourses encountered in daily life. Judith Butler (1999), for example, envisions gender as a matrix, a complicated structure influenced by many factors and expressed in many different forms. Butler argues that discussions of gender should complicate the male/female binary by including the range of gendered identities enacted today (gay, lesbian, bisexual, transgendered, queer, and questioning).

Why *should* English teachers concern themselves with popular fiction and work to help teens unsettle and disrupt gender binaries? Because thinking in terms of gender binaries and stereotypical stories is dangerous and unjust. It makes social hierarchies and gendered oppression seem inevitable. Binaries justify the suppression of gendered identities that are not strictly male or female, and this can produce violence and suffering. The plight of Canada's missing Indigenous women, homophobia, suicide, and violence against girls and women are all justified by belief in a gender binary that must not be questioned. Popular fiction, especially that which is mass-marketed for teens, does little to challenge the gender binaries and storylines of the Enlightenment, or to encourage teens to ask questions about who they think they are.

How can English teachers help? My approach is to make the work of troubling the gender binary part of teaching students to read critically, to challenge and to question what they read. I begin with teacher-led activities such as a presentation for the entire class explaining two contrasting theories and philosophies of the world (Enlightenment humanism and poststructuralism). I focus on two useful terms: "binaries" and "cultural storylines." I illustrate the terms with examples from the *Harry Potter* novels, works of popular fiction that many students have read (see Cherland, 2009, for more about how this can be done). I then demonstrate how a reader might critique a work of popular culture by looking for binaries and cultural storylines that deserve to be disrupted and unsettled. I read and think aloud for students as I demonstrate this particular way of reading critically.

I then have the students engage in critical reading by asking them to select a novel, film, music video, or video game *they do not like* and explain in their dialogue journals, double-entry journals, or response logs *why* they do not like it. (It is important that they choose something they do not like. It just isn't as much fun to question and challenge and deconstruct something you love and enjoy.) Ask students to point out any binaries they find in the work they are analyzing and any storylines they encounter, especially any that concern gender, race, or social class.

I suggest writing back to students in their dialogue journals or response journals. This gives teachers the opportunity to encourage students in their efforts to apply new ideas. It allows teachers to mentor students as they identify and question binaries of gender, race, and class in the storylines. Teachers may respond to what each student has written, taking the one-on-one opportunity to demonstrate new ways of thinking about language and gender. This will be time-consuming work for the teacher, but invaluable for students' learning.

Individual activities could follow. For example, some students might prefer the safety and privacy of a "reading response log" that the teacher does *not* see. Teachers could check and give credit for the response logs, but refrain from reading them. Students could later choose ideas from their response logs to use as writing topics, or use the logs to support large group discussions. "Contrapuntal readings" (suggested by Said, 1993, and by Singh and Greenlaw, 1998) might also prove useful in disrupting traditional humanist common sense. This approach involves juxtaposing two texts, such as *To Kill a Mockingbird* and *The Color Purple.* While both these texts are about the same group of people living at the same historical moment, the first is grounded in the gendered and racial assumptions of the Enlightenment, and the second challenges those assumptions. As students read, they could compare the characters in the two texts, noting the language, images, and binary discourses that create them as different.

Alternatively, Ursula Kelly's (1997) photography assignment is a useful approach. Students are asked to bring a photograph of themselves taken in early childhood. Have them write a short autobiography using the memories the photograph inspires and the discourses it invokes. What is there in the photograph that speaks to the creation of gender identity? The teacher may wish to demonstrate the process using a childhood photograph of her own. This is an opportunity for students to reflect upon how they personally became the gendered people they are.

Assignments are only one way in which a teacher can help students trouble the gender binary and understand the complexities of the cultural discourses that inform their identities. I also advise encouraging students to read (and perhaps write) fan fiction, modelled after fan fiction available online that is often produced by teens responding to works of popular fiction. The *Harry Potter* novels, the *Twilight* novels, and many other works of popular fiction each have a *fandom,* a large international community of readers, viewers, and writers united by their interest in a particular literary work or author. Fandoms connect through websites, fan fiction, podcasts, and fan art to celebrate a work of fiction and to extend it by producing new discourses. In particular, fan fiction creates new characters, new events, and new interpretations of a story. Fan fiction ought to be of special interest to literacy teachers. It creates new storylines and new subject positions for the characters in popular fiction. Sometimes it creates new relationships between characters by, for example, challenging the binary of love and hate, or writing homosexual relationships into the fictional worlds.

Fan fiction may reimagine traditional ways of thinking and seeing. Writing fan fiction is challenging, intellectual work. It requires the ability to read and write critically, against the grain, and to think beyond what we already know. These are abilities we should foster in everyone. If literacy teachers open their classroom doors to these kinds of creative intellectual endeavours without making the mistake of appropriating fan fiction or popular culture for school curricula (see Alvermann, Moon, & Hagood, 1999), they might help young people come to a better understanding of how to use literacy to disrupt gender hierarchies and act for equality and justice.

References

Alvermann, D. E., Moon, J. S., & Hagood, M. C. (1999). *Popular culture in the classroom: Teaching and researching critical media literacy.* Newark, DE: International Reading Association.

Butler, J. (1999). *Gender trouble: Feminism and the subversion of identity* (10th anniversary edition). New York: Routledge.

Cherland, M. R. (2009). Harry's girls: Harry Potter and the discourses of gender. *Journal of Adolescent and Adult Literacy* 52(4), 273–282.

Kelly, U. (1997) *Schooling desire: Literacy, cultural politics, and pedagogy.* New York: Routledge.

Kumashiro, K. K. (2009). *Against common sense: Teaching and learning toward social justice, revised edition.* New York: Routledge Falmer.

Mills, S. (1997). *Discourse.* London: Routledge.

Said, E. (1993). *Culture and imperialism.* New York: Vintage Books.

Singh, M. G. & Greenlaw, J. (1998). Postcolonial theory in the literature classroom: Contrapuntal readings. *Theory Into Practice* 37(3), 193–202.

St. Pierre, E. A. (2000). Poststructural feminism in education: An overview. *Qualitative Studies in Education,* 13(5), 477–515.

Weedon, C. (1992). *Feminist practice and poststructural theory.* Oxford, United Kingdom: Blackwell.

How Could We Approach Teaching Fiction to Boys and Explore Types of Masculinities?

By Douglas Gosse, Nipissing University

Male Identities and Sexualities in *Jackytar*, a Canadian Educational Novel

There is considerable discussion about how to use fictional resources such as plays, short stories, comics, poetry, or novels to motivate boys' learning and engagement in secondary schools. The move to examine both boys' literacies and innovative ways of teaching them stems from mounting numbers of studies and statistics that compare boys' achievements in and satisfaction with school to those of girls. A look at the research paints a bleak picture. Boys consistently score lower than girls on many areas of standardized testing (Bleach, 1998; Staff, 2009). They have greater literacy problems (Rich, 2010) and show evidence of disenfranchisement by both dropping out of school in greater numbers and accounting for the most suspensions (Zheng, 2009). They are more often victims of assault. Worse, they commit suicide in far greater numbers than girls (Dorais & Lajeunesse, 2004).

Some recommend the creation of more interactive and kinesthetic activities for boys (Blair & Sanford, 2003; Rich, 2010; Staff, 2004) or the hiring of more male role models as teachers (Bernard, Hill, Falter, & Wilson, 2004; Gosse, 2009). However, we must simultaneously move beyond such solutions to address the deeper challenges of enduring and restrictive gender stereotypes linked to male identities and sexualities. My notion of *androgenogogy* is the art and science of effectively teaching males (Gosse, 2010a) and has the analysis of male sexualities at its core. In this entry, I introduce an androgenogogy approach that challenges negative masculine stereotypes that have been linked to hegemonic masculinities and the negative perceptions of male sexual identities. This approach employs my educational novel *Jackytar* (Gosse, 2005a) and its complement, *Breaking Silences & Exploring Masculinities: A Critical Supplement to the Novel Jackytar* (Gosse, 2008).

Male Identities, Sexualities, and Fiction

There are few positive male role models in popular culture who encourage reading (Staff, 2004); many male characters depicted in movies and on television are brutish, clownish, and violent. Indeed, Geoffrey Canada (1998) claims:

> Our beliefs about maleness, the mythology that surrounds being male, has led many boys to ruin. The image of the male as strong is mixed with the image of the male as violent. Male as virile gets confused with male as promiscuous. Male as adventurous equals male as reckless. Male as intelligent gets mixed with male as arrogant, racist, and sexist. . . . We must all spend more time trying to understand what happens to boys—and how we can help shape them into better men. (p. 13)

This phenomenon led me to develop an educational novel for secondary school students that challenges both the ways boys are socialized and the oppressive male stereotypes that undergird that socialization. I specifically wrote *Jackytar,* a *Bildungsroman* or "coming-of-age" story, to delve into evolving concepts of masculinities, power, and privilege (Ruffolo, 2008). It is written for secondary school and undergraduate university courses. A *Bildungsroman* traces a protagonist's journey toward greater self-awareness and a critical understanding of society (Kontje, 1993). The main character, Alex Murphy, is minoritized in more than one way: he is a "jackytar" or Newfoundlander of mixed Aboriginal and European extraction; he is also gay and at odds with his family's and society's expectations of what it is to be a man, a teacher, a son, a brother, and a lover. Cools (2008), referring to *Jackytar*, asserts that manhood is a precarious position which boys and men must constantly earn and re-earn. Through this novel, I wanted to investigate this phenomenon that is everywhere and yet largely ignored.

I endeavour to broaden, through the medium of fiction, what Pollack (1998) terms the "Boy Code." Pollock argues that boys, despite confident exteriors, hide feelings of loneliness, isolation, depression, and thoughts of suicide. Boys frequently do less well in school than they could and often have trouble with drugs, friends, and self-esteem. Outdated gender stereotypes push boys to conform to this "Boy Code," concealing themselves behind masks of independence. People still treat boys as "little men," raising them through a toughening process. In *Real Boys*, Pollack argues that the "Boy Code" has four imperatives (1998, pp. 23–25):

A) "The Sturdy Oak"—males should be stoic, stable, independent, and never show weakness. Boys are not allowed to share pain or grief openly.

B) "The Big Wheel"—boys are pressured to achieve status, dominance, and power, to avoid shame at all costs. Boys must act cool at all costs, to appear in control even when they are not.

C) "No Sissy Stuff"—boys are taught to inhibit expression of feelings or urges mistakenly seen as "feminine," such as warmth, dependence, and empathy. Boys are encouraged to shut out these feelings and be self-reliant. When boys do express so-called "feminine" feelings or behaviours, they are often regulated with ridicule, taunts, and threats, incorporating misogynist and homophobic elements.

D) "Give 'em Hell"— this is embodied by popular culture action heroes, as well as athletes in many violent sports, such as hockey, wrestling, and football, and leads boys to believe that they should act macho, even violent, and to engage in risky behaviours that could injure themselves or others.

When critiquing *Jackytar* for the *Globe and Mail*, Wiersema (2006) says, "Murphy's discovery of his own voice, as a writer and a man, is at the heart of *Jackytar*, and makes for a moving and involving story." In *Jackytar*, I illustrate for readers the restrictions of the "Boy Code" and of hegemonic masculinities through flashbacks, narrative, and poetry. The roles of heterosexism and homophobia in the policing of boys are implicitly and explicitly explored in the text through characters who self-identify as either straight or gay. For example, the relationship of Alex and his straight brother comes into play. The reader realizes how Alex's brother, Bruce, once a star athlete, has led a life of disappointment and unrealized aspirations. Since he is also homophobic, Bruce lacks the support of Alex whom he has ostracized. Of note, in *Jackytar* I created a "Misandrous Queer List"[9] to contribute to an analysis of masculinity. It proposes a number of tenets that build on Pollock's "Boy Code" (Gosse, 2005b), of which the following are a selection (the novel has 30):

1) I cannot walk down the street holding hands with another male, even in the gay neighbourhood, without the threat of sneering remarks or violence from strangers.
2) I am not allowed to marry another male in many provinces and states and countries; civil unions are not the same.

---

9 Misandry may be defined as the fear and contempt of qualities associated with males, while queer denotes a way of exploring texts that has race, class, gender, sexual orientation, disability, geographical location, and language and culture—all through the lens of sexualities—at its core.

3) Literature for children rarely reflects my lifestyle by containing same-sex partnerships. The characters are almost all white, anyway.
4) Straight men are afraid to be alone with me because they may be perceived as gay, or fear that I might make a pass at them.
5) As a teacher, I am vulnerable to accusations of being a pedophile. Likewise as a father.
6) As a man, if I act "effeminate" or display so-called feminine traits such as caring, compassion, and gentleness, I risk being punished. These traits are human, not feminine.
7) I am expected to be competitive with members of my sex and only to confide in a female mate. Therefore, I am permitted few if any intimate friends of either sex.
8) When I report assault or abuse, whether sexual, physical, or verbal, there are few if any social services available to me other than those which treat me as a potential criminal. Especially if I am not white. And/or from a low social class. And English isn't my native tongue.
9) I have a far greater chance of being imprisoned than any female. Especially if I am not white. And/or from a low social class.
10) I have less chance of attending university than many women—at least, many of the white, middle-class women. Especially if I am not white. And/or from a low social class.

Contemplation of complex male identities that are closely linked to taboo and feared sexualities has led me to develop the added notions of: (1) *androgenophobia,* the prevalent societal conviction that maleness, the male body, and male sexualities are somehow unclean, perverse, and menacing; and (2) *erastephobia,* a pervasive expectation and fear of impending pedophilia by males in general (Gosse, forthcoming). It is my conviction that as educators, not only do we need to reform our school system to account for these prejudices, but we need to educate secondary school students—as well as teacher candidates, teachers, and educational administrators—about the ramifications of limiting societal expectations for boys and men (Calabrese, 2010; Doyle, 2010; Gosse, 2010b; Staff, 2010). Such limitations are detrimental to everyone.

Ultimately, I suggest that we engage in affirmative-action plans to hire more male teachers to act as positive role models for passionate male learning. These male role models must be diverse and demonstrate multiple masculinities, including what is currently considered "effeminate." What are so often considered "feminine" qualities are actually human qualities—like caring, compassion, and empathy—that we can show young men through fiction. The educational novel *Jackytar* (Gosse, 2005a) and *Breaking Silences & Exploring Masculinities: A Critical Supplement to the Novel Jackytar* (Gosse, 2008) can help in this regard. The latter text contains essays on father-and-son relations (Giesler, 2008), confronting rigid social expectations for boys and men (Heasley, 2008), and facing life with integrity (Lander & Nahon, 2008); it may be productively used to achieve these ends (Gosse, 2006). We need to challenge commonplace, accepted notions of patriarchy and male power to expose how males also suffer in society, how males also experience limitations. This comes to the fore in the analysis of sexualities and masculinities.

References

Bernard, J.-L., Hill, D., Falter, P., & Wilson, W. D. (2004). *Narrowing the gender gap: Attracting men to teaching*. Toronto, ON: Ontario College of Teachers.

Blair, H. & Sanford, K. (2003). *Rethinking literacy for boys*. Paper presented at the International Conference on Language, Education & Diversity. http://www.education.ualberta.ca/boysandliteracy/publications.html

Bleach, K. (Ed.). (1998). *Raising boys' achievement in schools*. Oakhill, United Kingdom: Trentham Books.

Calabrese, M. (2010). Study looks at shortage of male teachers in younger grades. *North Bay Nugget,* October 25. http://www.nugget.ca/ArticleDisplay.aspx?e=2815572 (accessed January 2, 2012).

Canada, G. (1998). *Reaching up for manhood: Transforming the lives of boys in America*. Boston, MA: Beacon Press.

Cools, J. (2008). The quest for manhood and the limitations of masculinity. In D. Gosse (Ed.), *Breaking silences & exploring masculinities: A critical supplement to the novel* Jackytar (pp. 33–42). St. John's, NL: Breakwater Books.

Dorais, M., & Lajeunesse, S. (2004). *Dead boys can't dance: Sexual orientation, masculinity, and suicide* (P. Tremblay, Trans.). Montreal, Kingston, London, Ithaca: McGill-Queen's University Press.

Doyle, G. (Host) (2010). Why aren't more young men becoming teachers? An interview with Douglas Gosse. Radio broadcast. Kitchener, Ontario, ON: 570 News.

Giesler, M. (2008). Out of the shadows of the paternal closet: *Jackytar* as a tool to recover the invisibility of the father. In D. Gosse (Ed.), *Breaking silences & exploring masculinities: A critical supplement to the novel* Jackytar (pp. 23–32). St. John's, NL: Breakwater Books.

Gosse, D. (2005a). *Jackytar: A novel.* St. John's, NL: Jesperson Publishing.

Gosse, D. (2005b). A Misandrous Queer List. In *Jackytar* (pp. 122–125). St. John's, NL: Jesperson Publishing.

Gosse, D. (2006). Arts-based educational research and *Jackytar,* the Canadian queer *Bildungsroman. Journal of Curriculum and Pedagogy* 3(1), 9–14.

Gosse, D. (2009, Oct. 14–16). *Race, sexual orientation, culture and male teacher role models: Will any teacher do as long as they are good?* Paper presented at the Edge Conference 2009, Inspiration and Innovation in Teaching and Teacher Education, St. John's, NL.

Gosse, D. (2010a, March 26). *Androgenogogy: Examining the complexities of men teaching boys.* Paper presented at the American Men's Studies Association Annual Conference, Beyond Borders: Masculinities and Margins XVIII, Georgia State University, Atlanta, GA.

Gosse, D. (2010b, May 29). *Androgenophobia and erastephobia: Regulation of 'dangerous' sexualities of male primary teachers in Ontario/Androgénophobie et érastéphobie: la régulation des sexualités «dangereuses» d'enseignants de sexe masculin au primaire en Ontario.* Paper presented at the XXXVIIIth Annual Conference, Canadian Society for the Study of Education, Concordia University, Montreal, QC.

Gosse, D. (forthcoming). Androgenophobia and erastephobia: Fear of male sexualities in the workplace of primary/junior teachers in Ontario. In M. E. Harrison & P. W. Schnarrs (Eds.),

Beyond borders: Masculinities and margins. The 17th Annual American Men's Studies Conference proceedings (pp. 224–252). Harriman, TN: Men's Studies Press.

Gosse, D. (Ed.). (2008). *Breaking silences & exploring masculinities: A critical supplement to the novel Jackytar.* St. John's, NL: Breakwater Books.

Heasley, R. (2008). Negotiating masculinity, sexuality, and identity in the context of community. In D. Gosse (Ed.), *Breaking silences & exploring masculinities: A critical supplement to the novel* Jackytar (pp. 13–22). St. John's, NL: Breakwater Books.

Kontje, T. C. (1993). *The German* Bildungsroman*: History of a national genre* (1st ed.). Columbia, SC: Camden House.

Lander, N., & Nahon, D. (2008). Nine days in the life of Alex Murphy: A journey of integrity. In D. Gosse (Ed.), *Breaking silences & exploring masculinities: A critical supplement to the novel* Jackytar (pp. 43–51). St. John's, NL: Breakwater Books.

Pollack, W. (1998). *Real boys: Rescuing our sons from the myth of boyhood.* New York: Random House.

Rich, S. (2010). Developing multiple literacies. *Nipissing University Review* 16(1), 8.

Ruffolo, D. (2008). Queer theory: A novel approach. In D. Gosse (Ed.), *Breaking silences & exploring masculinities: A critical supplement to the novel* Jackytar (pp. 61–72). St. John's, NL: Breakwater Books.

Staff. (2004). *Me read? No way! A practical guide to improving boys' literacy skills*: Toronto, ON: Ontario Ministry of Education.

Staff. (2009). How male and female students perform in Toronto District School Board (TDSB) Schools: Report to the Boys' Education Steering Committee. PowerPoint format. http://www.silverview.ca/Documents/trustee_documents/Equally%20Prepared%20For%20Life.ppt (accessed January 2, 2012).

Staff. (2010, October 22). Study: Canada needs more male primary school teachers, Have to deal with prestige and possible abuse issues. *News1130.* http://www.news1130.com/news/local/article/118804--study-canada-needs-more-male-primary-school-teachers (accessed January 3, 2012).

Wiersema, R. (2006). Small presses, big ambition. *The Globe and Mail,* March 11, D14.

Zheng, S. (December 2009). *2006 Student Census: Correlations of school experience with student demographics and achievement.* Toronto: Organizational Development/Research and Information Services (TDSB).

What Are the Benefits and Challenges of Teaching about Social Justice for Bisexual, Gay, Lesbian, Queer, Transgender, Transsexual, and/or Two-Spirited People?

By John J. Guiney Yallop, Acadia University

We begin by talking. In their stunning book, the editors of *"Unleashing the Unpopular": Talking about Sexual Orientation and Gender Diversity in Education,* Isabel Killoran and Karleen Pendleton Jiménez (2007), introduce us to Canadian students, parents, teachers, and teacher educators who are all, in their own ways, educating themselves, each other, and their readers about social justice issues for those whose sexual orientation and/or gender identity differs from the majority. The key word for me in the title of Killoran and Pendleton Jiménez's book is "talking." What is often lacking in Canadian classrooms is just that, *talking*: Canadian classrooms are frequently places of silence when it comes to sexual orientation and gender identity. As educators, we have a responsibility to open spaces for conversation, to open conversations, to break the silences that fill students' and sometimes teachers' and parents' experiences of school. In my own work as teacher (Guiney, 2000, 2002a, 2002b, 2002c; Guiney et al., 2001; Guiney Yallop, 2007), as graduate student (Guiney, 2002d; Guiney Yallop, 2004, 2005, 2008), as teacher educator (Guiney Yallop, forthcoming; Wiebe & Guiney Yallop, 2010), and as parent (Guiney Yallop, 2009), I have sought to create spaces and opportunities for learning about ourselves and about each other. Sometimes, what prevents conversations from even starting is our own fear. While the fear we experience is often justified because of the harassment and discrimination social justice educators themselves encounter, we need to push beyond our fears if we are to grow as individuals and create caring communities. When our fear causes us to participate in the silence, students, particularly marginalized students, interpret our action or inaction as a betrayal of the trust they put in us.

We also begin by listening. In another must-read book for educators, *I Could Not Speak My Heart: Education and Social Justice for Gay and Lesbian Youth,* James McNinch and Mary Cronin (2004) bring us the voices of individuals who are, finally, able to speak. They speak because McNinch and Cronin, and hopefully their readers, are listening. We need to listen to those voices, to the stories of the individuals who find their way into the pages McNinch and Cronin offer to us. How will students know that we are listening? We let them know. We remind them again and again that we are listening to them. We apologize for the times we fail; we will sometimes fail. As well, a small dose of empathy can go a long way. We have only to recall times when we, ourselves, have not been listened to, not been heard, not been included, or have felt unsafe. In many cases, we will need to multiply the intensity of that experience many times if we are to come close to the marginalization of individuals who feel unable to speak their heart because of the biphobia, homophobia, and transphobia that surrounds them. We may assume that we have created safe learning environments (a concept that is problematic in itself), but unless we are able to state explicitly what we have done and what we are doing to create those environments, then students have every right, and perhaps every need, to doubt us.

So, what *are* the benefits and challenges of teaching about social justice for bisexual, gay, lesbian, queer, transgender, transsexual, and/or two-spirited people? Like any good educational experience, we need to discover for ourselves what the benefits and challenges are for each of us individually. As an offering of my own sometimes joyful and sometimes painful learning, I can tell a short story about the benefits and challenges I have experienced.

In one grade 6 class I was teaching, a boy spoke up after we completed a week-long unit on Pride Week. He knew gay people existed, he told me and his classmates, but he thought they were off somewhere else. He didn't know that gay people were around other people, he informed us, and he certainly didn't think a gay person could be his teacher. He told me that he was glad that he was in my class. I call that experience a benefit, and many other benefits were spread throughout my teaching career. Just days before this young man shared his reflections with us, I was summoned to the principal's office and asked to give the principal and vice-principal an outline of my plans for the Pride Week unit. As well, a guest speaker arriving to talk to the class, a lesbian educator with her partner and child, was called aside to a separate room and asked by the principal what she would be saying to the students. I saw those actions by administration as challenges; many other challenges, some far worse, were also spread throughout my teaching career.

Perhaps the greatest challenge for me, however, has been finding allies, sometimes because they weren't there, but sometimes because I didn't cultivate the practice of finding them. A colleague once advised me to find more allies for social justice work in education. I dismissed his advice because I thought I could do it myself. In one sense, I was right: as the story of the student above shows, and as would many other untold stories, I did, I believe, make a difference in the lives of my students regardless of their sexual orientation or gender identity. There was little to no institutional support, however, and sometimes no visible collegial support for what I was doing. While some colleagues rallied around me and the work I was doing, systemic homophobia and institutional ignorance put up many barriers. The cost to my emotional and physical health was huge. I left teaching in order to stay well. This cost to a person's emotional and physical health is also why many students have left school, and why social justice work regarding sexual orientation and gender diversity issues is so crucial.

Teachers who wish to take up issues of social justice for bisexual, gay, lesbian, queer, transgender, transsexual, and/or two-spirited people and who are looking for resources will find an extensive and current list on the Egale Canada website (www.egale.ca). After clicking on the link to mygsa.ca, visitors to this site are then asked to select resources for youth, educators, or parents. In the educators section, one finds classroom resources including lesson plans, books, movies, and new items. The books are divided into preschool to grade 4, grades 5 to 8, and grades 9 to 12. Each book listed includes a brief description. Despite that description, it is always wise to pre-read and pre-view materials before using them in the classroom. The site also has resource guides and forums where issues in education regarding bisexual, gay, lesbian, queer, transgender, transsexual, and two-spirited people are discussed. While the forum does not appear to be used much, it is a source of additional current information. And, finally, do talk to your colleagues, your supervisors, your students, and the parents of your students. Get support and advice for your work. Sometimes you will need to lead; sometimes you will need to let yourself be led. Whether leading or following, be guided by the principles of social justice and you will be what many of us strive to be—a good educator.

References

Guiney, J. J. (2000). Equity for all: Reflections from an educator. *The Rainbow Classroom* 6(1), 11–13.

Guiney, J. J., Bonnick, C., Millington, S., Mohla, A., Mohla, R., & Routledge, A. (2001). Lesbian and gay pride week in an elementary classroom. *ETFO VOICE*, 21–24.

Guiney, J. J. (2002a). Experiencing school: Stories from gays. In V. Sunnari, J. Kangasvuo & M. Heikkinen (Eds.), *Gendered and sexualised violence in educational environments* (pp. 243–249). Oulu, Finland: University of Oulu and Femina Borealis.

Guiney, J. J. (2002b). Lesbian and gay pride week. *GALE Force* 12(6), 1.

Guiney, J. J. (2002c). Using picture books to address homophobia and heterosexism. *Outside In...*, Spring, 22–24.

Guiney, J. J. (2002d). *School life for gays: A critical study through story.* Unpublished Master of Education research project. Brock University, St. Catharines, ON.

Guiney Yallop, J. (2004). Gay and out in secondary school: One youth's story. In J. McNinch & M. Cronin (Eds.), *I could not speak my heart: Education and social justice for gay and lesbian youth* (pp. 29–42). Regina, SK: Canadian Plains Research Center.

Guiney Yallop, J. J. (2005). Exploring an emotional landscape: Becoming a researcher by reawakening the poet. *Brock Education* 14(2), 132–144.

Guiney Yallop, J. J. (2007). Surviving the pain and widening the circle: Celebrating lesbian and gay pride week in an elementary classroom. In I. Killoran & K. Pendleton Jimenez (Eds.), *"Unleashing the unpopular": Talking about sexual orientation and gender diversity in education* (pp. 111–116). Olney, MD: Association for Childhood Education International.

Guiney Yallop, J. J. (2008). *OUT of place: A poetic journey through the emotional landscape of a gay person's identities within/without communities.* Unpublished doctoral dissertation. The University of Western Ontario, London, ON.

Guiney Yallop, J. J. (2009). My daughter is going to school: How a queer Catholic is learning again to pray. In M. Prendergast, C. Leggo, & P. Sameshima. (Eds.). *Poetic inquiry: Vibrant voices in the social sciences* (pp. 219–228). Rotterdam, Netherlands: Sense Publishers.

Guiney Yallop, J. J. (forthcoming). *Of place and memory: A poetic journey.*

Killoran, I. & Pendleton Jiménez, K. (Eds.). (2007). *"Unleashing the unpopular": Talking about sexual orientation and gender diversity in education* (pp. 111–116). Olney, MD: Association for Childhood Education International.

McNinch, J. & Cronin, M. (Eds.). (2004). *I could not speak my heart: Education and social justice for gay and lesbian youth.* Regina, SK: Canadian Plains Research Center.

Wiebe, S. & Guiney Yallop, J. J. (2010). Ways of being in teaching: Conversing paths to meaning. *Canadian Journal of Education* 33(1), 177–198.

How Can Youth Explore Their Gendered Identities through New Literacies?

By Kathy Sanford, University of Victoria

To understand the possibility of new literacies with/in digital worlds is to acknowledge the "constellation of literacy activities" (Black & Steinkuehler, 2009) afforded through and inherent in digital media. Jenkins (2006) describes this phenomenon as "convergence culture":

> [C]onvergence represents a paradigm shift—a move from medium-specific content toward content that flows across multiple media channels, toward the increased interdependence of communication systems, toward multiple ways of accessing media content, and toward ever more complex relations between top-down corporate media and bottom-up participatory culture. (p. 243)

Many youth are active participants in convergence culture, a part of the "active and circular" (Jenkins, 2006) shifting of roles individuals take in the consumption and creation of media content in this multi-directional media flow. Youth who participate in convergence culture are experiencing forms of literacy that challenge traditional notions of consuming text, thus destabilizing ways of (in)forming gendered, racial, and socio-cultural identity. Adolescents and young adults are in particularly dynamic transitory spaces of becoming (Buckingham, 2008), and their literacy activities inform and transform how they make sense of their identities, their performance, and the ways they work in the world.[10] In the fluidity of convergence culture, youth have the opportunity to play with identity, to perform multiple roles, and to present or "try on" multiple identities. Buckingham (2008) explains how digital media environments create opportunities for young people to explore the complexities of adolescence and identity formation:

> [Digital media] has produced new styles of playful learning . . . and is creating new competencies or forms of 'literacy,' which require and produce new intellectual powers, and even 'more complex brain structures.' It provides new ways of forming identity, and hence new forms of personhood; and by offering communication with different aspects of the self, it enables young people to relate to the world and to others in more powerful ways. (p. 14)

As educators and adults guiding the next generations as they immerse in and emerge from multiple, complex, digital communities, we have an opportunity to make apparent this cultural convergence, engage in critical discussions about digital media and content, and build relationships with young (gendered) individuals who are involved in a multiplicity of ways in a range of texts and new literacies (including books, magazines, websites, blogs, Facebook, YouTube, and video games).

The playful learning that digital media affords takes many forms involving multiple expressions informing identity, one of the most significant being gender. Of particular interest here is how this playful learning with/in digital worlds offers opportunity for youth and educators to investigate issues of gender through dialogue and exploration by engaging with differently gendered characters in differently gendered situations. Gender, although ubiquitous in our society, is seldom explicitly considered for its significant influence on our identity development. The term "gender" is most often used synonymously with "biological sex," which provides us with one of two choices (excepting transsexual individuals by birth or choice): male or female. However, as de Lauretis (1987) notes, gender is "not a property of bodies or something originally existent in human beings . . . it is the product and process of various social technologies, institutional discourses, epistemologies, and critical practices, as well as practices of daily life" (p. 23). As a social construction, gender offers multiple options for individuals to choose as they shape and reshape their gendered identities. Why then, we wonder, are students' conceptions of gendered nuances limited through offering only narrow descriptions of "boys" and "girls" not acknowledging the complex convergences of gender—of abilities, interests, desires, and appearances.

Research surrounding boys' academic success in school literacies has led us to realize that many youth, boys and girls, are succeeding in a wide array of alternative, complex, and sophisticated literacies that are often not addressed in traditional school language and

10 Which is not to say that people at every stage of life aren't continuously developing a sense of identity, informed by literacy practices—we all are. However, I focus here on adolescence, wherein the ups and downs are heightened physiologically by hormonal change and by new school structures (e.g., secondary school and university).

literacy classes. The low test scores and resistant behaviours often associated with males as an essentialized group are reflective of a much larger issue involving gender roles; hegemonic masculine values and behaviours are being explicitly and implicitly taught to boys and girls. This happens through the expectations and opportunities offered students (Sanford, 2006), through materials selected for them (Brozo, 2006), and through perspectives shared by means of actions and comments, modelled as acceptable ways of being. Consequently, boys and girls often identify traditional school literacies, such as novels, short stories, and poetry as a "feminine" means of communication and representation. Meanwhile, boys are expected to be hands-on learners, needing activities and the building of things as their ways of being in the world. Researchers using a gendered lens to explore youths' literacy practices have found that boys and girls are practising their literacy skills through comic books, graphic novels, and digital texts such as cell phone texts, chat rooms, websites, and video games (Newkirk, 2002; Sanford & Blair, 2004; Wilhelm & Smith, 2002). Their literacy practices significantly shape how they construct their identities, and pedagogical attention to diverse digital multimodal texts can afford them opportunities to explore their gendered selves in relation to others.

As educators, it seems we often want to categorize the ways in which boys and girls learn in hope of prescribing antidotal learning activities. To buy into the apparent "gender divide" (Hayes, 2007) of digital literacies and/or gaming in particular is to ignore the complex ways in which people from all genders interact with digital literacies. Walkerdine (2007) advances a relational approach to understanding issues of gender with/in multimedia, wherein profoundly gendered behaviours and characters (still) exist but can be challenged, discussed, critiqued, and "tried on" (see also Hayes, 2007) as some youth are already doing through engagement with diverse media representations.

The literacy aspects of alternative texts are often undervalued in school because they are seen as mass culture (i.e., cultural practices produced for the general public) (Hong Xu, Sawyer Perkins, & Zunich, 2005). However, scholars have observed sophisticated learning and literacies taking place when students transact with alternative literacies. Reading non-linear, multi-layered, intertextual texts and reading images or other semiotic sign systems are just some of the literacy skills being practised with these alternative texts.

In video games and in other digital spaces, youth are navigating perpetual stereotypical images of women and men, many of which display fantastical representations of hyper-masculinity and femininity (Walkerdine, 2007). These stereotypes are challenged, however, by digital texts that both allow for avatar creation and manipulation (as described below) and advance women as heroic protagonists.

Observing avatar creation in the introduction of a video game seems a moment of research significance to us as educational researchers, and yet is an exercise of normalcy and simple strategy to the teenage participants with whom we work. The young men and women who play and discuss video games with us create virtual people or characters to represent themselves in online virtual worlds, or MMORPGs (Massively Multiplayer Online Role-Playing Games). As they are constantly playing with strategies to gain expertise, they try on differently gendered characters, observing responses from other players from both within the game play and outside (as players communicate over microphones or instant messaging). Players pick and choose what physical and personality characteristics and qualities they want to perform in virtual space.

Not only do youth perform via avatars, they also demonstrate through their "constellation of literacy practices" (Black & Steinkuehler, 2009) the possibility of opening up to multiple ways of defining gender identity through reading and responding to online blogs and forums written by people all around the world. These kinds of online interactions "disrup[t] the existing set of power relations between adult authority and youth voice" (Ito, Davidson, Jenkins, Lee, Eisenberg, & Weiss, 2008, p. viii), empowering users to try out ideas and questions in online spaces.

Providing in-depth and sophisticated exploration of issues relating to gendered literacies enables educators to resist popularly circulated myths of "boys' literacies" and "girls' literacies." We become able to provide choices based on more than a limited understanding of our students' needs and interests in relation to literacy development, thereby broadening the opportunities that are open to them and possibly even their perspectives on the world. Exploring the genderedness of characters and situations through a variety of multimodal texts, including video games, blogs, and other digital media, offers glimpses of other worlds. Through those glimpses students may come to know themselves and to recognize possibilities that allow for broader and more nuanced conceptions of gender and literacy.

References

Black, R. W., & Steinkuehler, C. (2009). Literacy in virtual worlds. In L. Christenbury, R. Bomer, & P. Smagorinsky (Eds.), Handbook of adolescent literacy research (pp. 271–286). New York: Guilford.

Blair, H. & Sanford, K. (2004). Morphing literacy: Boys reshaping their school-based literacy practices. *Language Arts* 81(6), 452–460.

Brozo, W. (2006). Bridges to literacy for boys. *Educational Leadership*, September, 71–74.

Buckingham, D. (2008). Introducing identity. In D. Buckingham (Ed.), *Youth, Identity, and Digital Media* (pp. 1–24). Cambridge, MA: MIT Press.

De Lauretis, T. (1987). *Technologies of gender*. Bloomington, IN: Indiana University Press.

Hayes, E. (2007). Gendered identities at play: Case studies of two women playing "Morrowind." *Games and Culture* 2(1), 23–48.

Hong Xu, S., Sawyer Perkins, R., & Zunich, L. (2005). *Trading cards to comic strips. Popular culture texts and literacy learning in grades k-8.* Newark, DE: International Reading Association.

Ito, M., Davidson, C., Jenkins, H., Lee, C., Eisenberg, M., & Weiss, J. (2008). Foreword. In W. L. Bennett (Ed.), *Civic life online: Learning how digital media can engage youth* (pp. vii–ix). Cambridge, MA: MIT Press.

Jenkins, H. (2006). *Convergence culture*. New York: New York UP.

Newkirk, T. (2002). *Misreading masculinities: Boys, literacy, and popular culture.* Portsmouth, NH: Heinemann.

Sanford, K. (2006). Gendered literacy experiences: The effects of expectation and opportunity for boys' and girls' learning. *Journal of Adolescent and Adult Literacy* 49(4), 302–316.

Smith, M. & Wilhelm, J. (2002). *Reading don't fix no Chevys: Literacy in the lives of young men.* Portsmouth, NH: Heinemann.

Walkerdine, V. (2007). Children, gender, video games: Towards a relational approach to multimedia. New York: Palgrave.

PART 2

Engaging Diverse Knowledge Frameworks

By Teresa M. Dobson, University of British Columbia

Graff (2007) notes that in English-speaking countries the study of literature as an academic discipline is relatively new. Until the later decades of the nineteenth century, "the idea had hardly arisen that the literature of one's own language needed to be taught in formal classes instead of being enjoyed as part of the normal experience of the community" (p. 19). The rise of literary studies in English, as established in the introduction to Part 1, was strongly associated with imperialism: defining a canon of "great works" for teaching within and beyond England played an important role in facilitating the transmission of the English language, presumably used within these canonical writings in an exemplary fashion, as well as the transmission of English culture and values to colonies around the globe (e.g., Mullaney, 2010). The study of such literary classics at the time was deemed particularly important for "cultivated gentlemen" of the empire (Graff, 2007, p. 20). Graff cites Carl Becker on the goal of education in the late nineteenth century: "the end desired was the disciplined and informed mind; but a mind disciplined to conformity and informed with nothing that a patriotic, Christian and clubable gentleman had better not know" (p. 21). Such attitudes, although perhaps somewhat tempered, have persisted in English literature studies for much of the discipline's history. As Bolter (2001) observes, "In the 19th and 20th centuries, when the canon of literature was often taken as the definition of a liberal education, the goal was to give everyone the experience of reading the same texts—Shakespeare, Milton, Dickens, and so on" (p. 11).

Although Canadian curricula in the English language arts extend beyond the study of literature—often being formulated as a series of activities within which learners are envisioned in pairings of receptive and productive modes (e.g., reading and writing, listening and speaking, viewing and producing)—in practice, literature studies dominates in secondary English language arts classrooms. The work of scholars such as Graff, Mullaney, and Bolter serves to remind English educators that literature studies is strongly rooted in a particular knowledge framework. Although changes in the technologies for knowledge diffusion through the last century, the breakdown of the imperial ethos, globalization, shifts in literary theory, social justice movements within education that emphasize inclusivity, and other similar changes have worked to modify the aims of, as well as methods and content in, English language arts classes, the roots of the discipline are still evident. As Margaret Mackey notes in her contribution later in this section, a few key literary genres in print—the novel, short fiction, poetry, and drama—have long been the focus of English language arts classrooms in Canadian middle and secondary schools. Further, the literary canon has been remarkably stable. In spite of the fact that teachers in Canada generally have much autonomy in making text selections, a series of texts considered to be exemplars of "great literature" appear on course syllabi again and again, with *Romeo and Juliet* topping the list (Mackey, Vermeer, Storie, & Deblois, 2012; Altmann, Johnston, & Mackey, 1999). Likewise, the dominant forms of text-production students undertake in Canadian schools appear to be remarkably conventional. In a study of school writing practices, for example, Peterson and McClay (2010) observe that in upper elementary and middle school classrooms "across the country, teachers assigned primarily print-based compositions" (n.p.).

The contributors in Part 2 speak to the importance of thinking beyond traditional knowledge frameworks. This critique applies particularly to frameworks that are tied to a Western, print-based knowledge economy that in the English language arts has tended to privilege the written expression of language (e.g., alphabetic text) over other forms of knowledge diffusion, such as visual art, dramatic performance, music, and so on. This perspective is important because Canada is, as demonstrated in Part 1, an ethnically diverse country wherein many knowledge frameworks are at play. Moreover, it is important because we are situated in a remarkable historical moment when new technologies for knowledge mobilization are influencing the ways in which humans orient to knowledge. For appreciating the import of the latter, it is worth contemplating the communications history leading up to this moment.

For 500 years, print has been the primary vehicle for knowledge diffusion in English-speaking countries. On the European continent, the Gutenberg Bible was the first major printed monograph (ca. 1454); not long after, William Caxton published the first English printed book in 1476, a translation from French of *The Recuyell of the Histories of Troye* (Eisenstein, 1979). Eisenstein (1979) notes that in the period from 1460 to 1480, printing presses went from a rare technology to a common one in Europe, and that the consequent rise of print initiated a series of communications and cultural transformations—among them standardization of written forms to accommodate the process of printing and the physical properties of the book. For example, printers played the key role in standardizing spelling within European languages.

Some (e.g., Chandler, 1995) have rightly criticized Eisenstein for "technological determinism"—that is, falling into the trap of imagining that technology determines human practices as opposed to recognizing that there is always a reciprocal relation between humans and the technology they invent. (Shifts in human practices may lead to technological innovation, and technological innovation may in turn influence shifts in social practices, but one side never acts unilaterally on the other.) Chandler's criticism is valid; nevertheless, Eisenstein makes some important observations about how print has contributed to the modification of reading and writing practices while facilitating the rise of particular genres over the last half millennium.

It is clear, for example, that print technology enabled the rise of the novel, which displaced other genres (e.g., poetry and the sermon) as the pinnacle of literary art. Notably, the conventional novel is a form that has no oral antecedent, is text-intensive, generally written to be read in a linear fashion (from beginning to end), and often devoid of images. As such, we might call the novel "monomodal" (relying on one mode of communication). Monomodal, linear forms have been the mainstay of the literary canon in middle and secondary schools for many years. As Kress and van Leeuwen (2001) observe,

> For some time now, there has been, in Western culture, a distinct preference for monomodality. The most highly valued genres of writing (literary novels, academic treatises, official documents and reports, etc.) came entirely without illustration, and had graphically uniform, dense pages of print. (p. 1)

Even in cases where the printed text is a script for multimodality, as with drama, a key focus in schools has been (and to some extent continues to be) understanding the words *as written*. For example, a debate I have often heard among English language arts educators concerns whether a film or stage performance of a given drama should be scheduled prior to, during, or after the reading of the text. In such debates, the "prior to" option tends to be viewed as a way of engaging student interest in the text; the "during" option as a way of encouraging continued interest in the text; and the "after" option as a way of ensuring the performance does not colour students' reading of the text, by precluding the imagination of anything other than a particular director's interpretation. Significantly, each argument positions performance as an aid to understanding written text; that is, performance is not viewed as an end in itself. This is somewhat ironic given that in practice—in the theatre or film world among artists and audiences—the text (script) functions purely as an aid to performance.

In middle and secondary English language arts classrooms, as the above discussion suggests, the focus for many years was on literacy in a singular sense: "The quality, condition, or state of being literate; the ability to read and write" ("Literacy," n.d.). Literacy scholars began to seriously question this singular notion of literacy in the latter part of the twentieth century. Dobson and Willinsky (2009) summarize some of the critical sentiment as follows:

> Graff (1979) . . . argued that it is not appropriate to characterize literacy as a discrete property that individuals possess or lack in varying degrees; rather, literacy should be viewed as a set of complex characteristics and processes that influence and are influenced by social context and personal circumstance. Street (1984) likewise advocated for viewing literacy as a social

> practice rather than as acquisition and employment of a particular skill set, an approach that came to be known as the New Literacy Studies (Gee, 1991; Street, 1995). . . . Drawing on and expanding this tradition, the New London Group (1996) introduced the term multiliteracies with a view to accounting not only for the cultural and linguistic diversity of increasingly globalized societies and the plurality of texts that are exchanged in this context but also for the "burgeoning variety of text forms associated with information and multimedia technologies" (p. 61). (Dobson & Willinsky, 2009, p. 297)

The last half of this quotation addresses a crucial point about literacy: a key emphasis of the New London Group (1996) has been distinguishing their notion of "multiliteracies" (attendance to diverse knowledge frameworks and modes of representation) from what they term "mere literacy" (a focus on letters). To teach from a "multiliteracies" perspective, therefore, is to introduce multiple modes of representation—text, image, sound, and so on—and in so doing to more properly acknowledge the full range of modalities with which youth engage beyond the classroom. As Siegel (2006) observes, this is not a particularly new idea: "Despite the claim that multimodality is new on the literacy scene, children have always engaged in what are now multimodal literacy practices" (p. 65). Nevertheless, the concept still needs to be emphasized in middle and secondary classrooms, where the range of text types studied tends to diminish, as we have seen. If the mandate of English language arts teachers is preparing students to make meaning of the language cues they will encounter in their lifetimes beyond the classroom—and I would argue this is the case—then a multiliteracies perspective is imperative.

One impetus for this marked shift in perspective—the shift from *literacy* to *multiliteracies*—has been the rise of screen media and digital media in particular through the latter part of the twentieth century. Much early response to the rise of digital media enumerated the differences between print and digital media and either sounded alarms or played fanfares: digital media would destroy literacy and erode the practice of careful reading (e.g., Birkerts, 1994) *or* enable a more student-centred, collaborative, stimulating, and satisfying model of learning (e.g., Landow, 1997; Tapscott, 1998). In the meantime, a number of literacy scholars claimed that "electronic and printed texts are qualitatively different" (Reinking, McKenna, Labbo, & Kieffer, 1998, xxiv), iterating those qualitative differences as follows:

> Digitized text entails much more than the translation of printed documents into binary electronic form. Electronic text possesses important features not shared with its print counterpart: (a) It is interactive in the literal sense, inviting the reader to impose organizations and compose responses; (b) it can accommodate textual supports (electronic scaffolds) for poor or developing readers; (c) it invites and often requires nonlinear strategies; (d) it can incorporate multimedia components; and (e) it is fluid rather than fixed. (p. 1)

Elsewhere I have cautioned against applying such notions uncritically (Dobson, 2006; Dobson & Willinsky, 2009, p. 290). None of the features Reinking and his colleagues outline are, in fact, exclusive to electronic text. Any saunter through a children's bookstore, or browsing of a newspaper and magazine rack, or examination of textbooks in the natural and social sciences will reveal that print can accommodate multiple modes: image, word, texture, and even three-dimensionality (as in the case of pop-up books). Print can also accommodate multiple reading paths, as evidenced in newspapers, magazines, essay collections, academic text with extensive footnoting, and so on. Anyone who has consulted an encyclopedia or dictionary or recipe book, or flipped through a morning paper, or used an index to locate pertinent information about a topic in a collection of essays will recognize that some print texts are not intended to be read from front to back. Further, there are examples of literary texts that encourage multiple reading paths: some collections of poetry or short fiction may be pursued "out of order" and there are many examples of children's literature with multiple reading paths. In the picture book *Black and White,* for example, Macaulay (1990) tells four stories simultaneously. Each of these stories occupies a quadrant of successive double-page spreads and, at times, there is textual interaction between the stories, enabling multiple reading paths. Ultimately, "it may be argued that books more successfully enable 'random access' than their computer-based counterparts, for readers may commence print texts at any point and establish links therein indefinitely" (Dobson & Willinsky, 2009, p. 290).

It seems that arguments such as those proposed by Reinking and his colleagues arise in part as a result of the failure to acknowledge the full range of genres in both print and electronic media. Thinking back to the earlier discussion of which forms of text are most often read in English language arts classrooms, this shortsightedness is perhaps not surprising. Surveys of the books commonly assigned in middle and secondary school suggest that when English language arts educators of students beyond the early elementary years think of "reading" they may well be envisioning only one form: sustained, continuous, silent reading of longer texts such as fiction, plays, and perhaps essays. To be sure, electronic texts with many links and multiple media may differ from such texts, but this is as likely to be a question of genre as it is a matter of how the media themselves differ. Novels differ from popular magazines as well, after all, and it is possible to read a literary novel on a computer or e-reading device and skim the *National Enquirer* in print. Ultimately, each medium can accommodate monomodal text forms and each can accommodate multimodal text forms; each can accommodate texts that encourage a singular reading path and each can accommodate texts that encourage multiple reading paths. This is not to say that the nature of multimodality is the same. At the moment, print perhaps better accommodates tactile interaction (as is the case with children's books containing fabric inserts or flaps), while digital media better accommodates sound and moving image. What is most important for educators to bear in mind is that "great divide" theories, which set up binaries between categories and fail to recognize any continuity or opportunity for hybridity, are rarely helpful. This is particularly the case in considering such vast categories as print and digital media, as well as the diverse practices of engaging and producing knowledge within those spaces. What is clear is that present-day learners invariably encounter multiple genres in both digital and print knowledge environments. It is not for educators to judge which genre or environment is better; it is for educators to determine how students might best be prepared to understand and interpret such diverse forms.

The entries in Part 2 take up some of the issues discussed above, focusing particularly on the importance of inviting students to engage with multimodal texts, print or digital. Kathy Hibbert, Danika Barker, and Tim Ludwig consider how employing multiliteracies pedagogies in classroom settings might engage students with diverse learning needs. Margaret Mackey writes of why it is important for English language arts teachers to be aware and make use of students' out-of-school exposure to multiple kinds of texts. Teresa Dobson asks how reading emergent genres such as electronic literature might benefit students. Deborah Begoray writes of the importance of attending to visual literacy. Linda Coles and Barrie Barrell likewise attend to visual literacy, focusing on the merit of engaging students in activities that involve "transmediation" between different modes of representation. Jeff Park argues for the inclusion of graphic novels in middle and secondary classrooms. Kathy Sanford and Liz Merkel remark on the complex literacy skills supported by and developed in the context of video game play. Finally, John Willinsky takes up a key question that is often glossed in discussions of digital media in the classroom: namely, what do teachers and students need to know about intellectual property as they engage with and construct knowledge employing online resources?

References

Altmann, A. E., Johnston, I. & Mackey, M. (1999). Romeo and Juliet rule: The stability of the grade 10 language arts canon. *Alberta English* 37(2), 17–24.

Birkerts, S. (1994). *The Gutenberg elegies: The fate of reading in an electronic age*. New York: Fawcett Columbine.

Bolter, J. D. (1996). Remediation. *Configurations* 4(3), 311–358.

———. (2001). *Writing space: The computer, hypertext, and the remediation of print*. Hillsdale, NJ: Lawrence Erlbaum.

Chandler, D. (1995). Technological or media determinism. http://www.aber.ac.uk/media/Documents/tecdet/(accessed March 8, 2012).

Dobson, T. M. (2006). From text to textoid? Reading and writing post-typography. Paper presented at the Canadian Society for Studies in Education Annual Meeting, York, ON, 27–30 May.

Dobson, T. M. & Willinsky, J. (2009). Digital literacy. In D. Olson & N. Torrance (Eds.), *Cambridge handbook of literacy* (pp. 286–312). Cambridge, United Kingdom: Cambridge University Press.

Eisenstein, E. L. (1979). *The printing press as an agent of change: Communications and cultural transformations in early-modern Europe*. Cambridge, United Kingdom: Cambridge University Press.

Gee, J. P. (1991). What is literacy? In C. Mitchell & K. Weiler (Eds.), *Rewriting literacy: Culture and the discourse of the other* (pp. 1–11). New York: Bergin and Garvey.

Graff, H. (1979). *The literacy myth: Literacy and social structure in the nineteenth-century city.* New York and London: Academic Press.

Graff, G. (2007). *Professing literature: An institutional history* (20th anniversary edition). Chicago, IL: University of Chicago Press.

Kress, G. & van Leeuwen, T. (2001). *Multimodal discourse: The modes and media of contemporary communication.* Oxford, United Kingdom: Oxford University Press.

Landow, G. P. (1997). *Hypertext 2.0: The convergence of contemporary critical theory and technology* (Revised ed.). Baltimore, MD: Johns Hopkins University Press.

"Literacy." (n.d.). OED online. December 2011. Oxford University Press. http://oed.com/view/Entry/109054 (accessed March 9, 2012).

Macaulay, D. (1990). *Black and white.* New York: Houghton Mifflin Company.

Mackey, M., Vermeer, L., Storie, D., & Deblois, E. (2012). The constancy of the school "canon": A survey of texts used in grade 10 English language arts in 2006 and 1996. *Language and Literacy* 14(1), 26–58.

Mullaney, J. (2010). *Postcolonial literatures in context.* London: Continuum International Publishing.

New London Group. (1996). A pedagogy of multiliteracies: Designing social futures. *Harvard Educational Review* 66(1), 60–92.

Peterson, S. S. & McClay, J. (2010). Assessing and providing feedback for student writing in Canadian classrooms. *Assessing Writing* 15(2), 86–99.

Reinking, D., McKenna, M. C., Labbo, L. D., & Kieffer, R. D. (Eds.) (1998). *Handbook of literacy and technology: Transformations in a post-typographic world transforming texts.* Mahway, NJ: Lawrence Erlbaum.

Siegel, M. (2006). Rereading the signs: Multimodal transformations in the field of literacy education. *Language Arts 84*(1), 65–77.

Street, B. (1984). *Literacy in theory and practice.* Cambridge, United Kingdom: Cambridge University Press.

———. (1995). *Social literacies: Critical approaches to literacy development, ethnography, and education.* London: Longman.

Tapscott, D. (1998). *Growing up digital. The rise of the net generation.* New York: McGraw Hill.

Willinsky, J. (1990). *The new literacy: Redefining reading and writing in the schools.* New York: Routledge.

SECTION 1

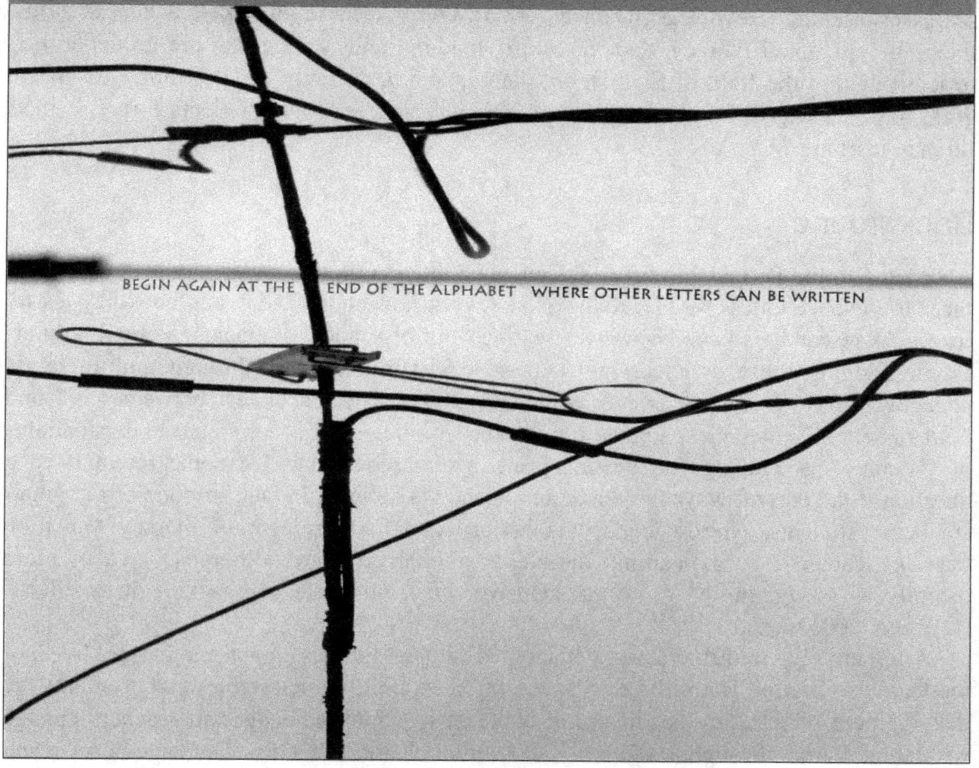

Mixing Media

How Must Our Approach to Teaching Adolescent Literature Change in Order to Engage the Complex Needs of At-Risk Students?

By Kathy Hibbert, University of Western Ontario, Danika Barker, Thames Valley District School Board of St. Thomas, Ontario, and Tim Ludwig, grade 12 student

"At-risk" students *need* "risk-taking" teachers. In this entry, I engage Tim Ludwig (a 17-year-old "at-risk" student) and Danika Barker (an innovative, risk-taking secondary school English teacher) to consider how new approaches to teaching adolescent literature can engage the complex needs of at-risk students. We met at a TEDxOntarioEd event[1] and found synergy in our diverse talks about what motivates us. Our shared enthusiasm toward disrupting a cycle that perpetuates thinking about learners solely in terms of deficits, diagnoses, and remediation has led us to look more closely at multiliteracies pedagogies and how they may provide an approach that moves educators away from

1 TEDxOntarioEd: http://www.mrhazzard.com/tedx/

pathologizing practices (Shields, Bishop, & Mazawi, 2005) and toward pedagogies that are asset-oriented (Heydon & Iannacci, 2008). Our goal is to provoke teachers to adjust their "beliefs about literacy, text, literature, reading, and writing that are grounded historically within the field of English and language arts teaching and learning" (O'Brien, 2003, n.p.) in ways that create inviting, engaging spaces where students thrive in their literacy learning.

Background

According to the Partnership for 21st Century Schools (2004), "today's education system faces irrelevance unless we bridge the gap between how students live and how they learn" (p. 5). As researchers have been investigating "out-of-school" literacies, a growing interest in bridging those practices and experiences within schools through multiliteracies pedagogies has emerged (Cope & Kalantzis, 2009). The disconnect between "in" and "out-of-school" literacies, coupled with the privileging of dominant understandings of "literacy" as reading and writing print in classrooms, has led some researchers to question if the current ways in which competency is defined, in fact, exclude or marginalize some students. Narrow conceptualizations and measurement of literacy "position 'at risk' learners . . . as learning disabled, minimally literate, alliterate[,] . . . or more recently as 'struggling'[,] . . . unresponsive, lazy, obstinate and lacking in intellect" (O'Brien, 2001, n.p.).

Alternatively, multiliteracies pedagogies situate literacy practices in the lives of the learners (Barton, Hamilton & Ivanic, 2000). A multiliteracies approach promotes the development of teaching and learning contexts in which students and teachers engage with their world through a diversity of communications media, language forms, and cultures. In this way, students can access and participate in literacy events that support their personal meaning-making processes while they continue to learn new ways of designing and working with text that "ensure that all students benefit from learning in ways that allow them to participate fully in public, community and economic life" (New London Group, 2000, p. 9).

Cummins, Carder, and Gallagher (2004) argue that the default options for what is considered "normal" embed a number of assumptions and practices that limit full participation. Multiliteracies pedagogies compel us to rethink traditional approaches to teaching and learning:

Multiliteracies Pedagogies

- construct an image of the learner as intelligent, imaginative, and linguistically talented; individual differences in these traits do not diminish the potential of each learner to shine in specific ways
- acknowledge and build on the cultural and linguistic capital (prior knowledge) of students and communities
- aim explicitly to promote cognitive engagement and identity investment on the part of students

(Continued)

Multiliteracies Pedagogies, *continued*

- enable students to construct knowledge, create literature and art, and act on social realities through dialogue and critical inquiry
- employ a variety of technological tools to support students' construction of knowledge, literature, and art and their presentation of this intellectual work to multiple audiences through the creation of identity texts

(Adapted from Cummins, Carder & Gallagher, 2004, p. 13)

Risky Business

In a multiliteracies context, educators must learn to navigate the competing discourses of new literacies within a comparatively narrow context in which adherence to traditional forms of print literacy that comprise the foundation of institutional accountability practices continue to be monitored and scrutinized. They must learn to harness what some view to be disruptive technologies in powerful ways that reposition students and teachers as creators of multiple texts in ways that further meaning-making rather than as consumers of multiple texts. For some educators, it may feel safer to stick with what they mistakenly believe to be "tried and true." Carroll, De Luise, and Howard (2009) have suggested that for teachers, a multiliteracies approach might appear "risky"

> due, in part, to the fact that [educators] don't yet know how to incorporate the tools and the products of adolescents' out-of-school worlds into our comfort zones—the in-school worlds in which we still hold power and set standards. (p. 96)

However, as I will relate below, Tim's experience begs us to ask the question, "If teachers took more risks, might that temper the 'at-risk' behaviours we see in our students?"

Tim's Story

Tim candidly refers to himself as "every teacher's nightmare." For him, sitting silently in rows all day taking notes, reading independently, or working alone on assignments is a "de-motivator." He craves social interaction and movement. He comments:

> School and I don't always fit so well. I feel like I am in a box—like a prison. I like to express my opinion, but sometimes that gets me into trouble. After I gave the TEDxOntarioEd talk, I started a blog, "At Risk Life"[2] so I can keep sharing tips for teachers to help kids in future generations. I am "at risk" of not getting enough credits to graduate. I have failed the literacy test[3] twice now, so I am in a "Student Success"[4] program which I like because there is more freedom and respect.

---

2 http://atrisklife.blogspot.com/

3 Ontario Secondary Literacy School Test: http://www.edu.gov.on.ca/eng/document/brochure/osslt/

4 Student Success/Learning to 18 program: http://www.edu.gov.on.ca/eng/parents/studentsuccess.html

He wants teachers to know that he is intelligent, and that he even enjoys reading:

> Some of the books that we read (*The Outsiders, Crabbe*) were pretty good because they were about kids my age and how they survived in different situations. I like when I can relate to what is going on in a story. The thing I enjoyed the most in my English class was debating. We had to work hard on making arguments to convince people to vote for our perspective. That was fun, and I like expressing my opinion. I wish we could talk about what we read more often.

Outside of school, Tim pursues his interests on the internet and in the "great outdoors." For example, he knows a lot about different species of fish, and argues "We should understand as much as we can about fish because of the problems with global warming and pollution and what that is doing to them."

Danika's Story

Danika thinks a lot about the world for which she is preparing her students. She positions herself as a "co-learner," and is excited about the potential that Web 2.0 technologies have to offer. She likes to draw on the tools with which her students are engaging outside of her classroom and to build on them. She explores options that have allowed her to create a safe environment within the virtual world by setting up a private social network called "Ning"[5] for her class. This allows her to select features such as blogging, audio, music, and images. These tools have allowed the class to build an online community:

> The students developed profile pages with pictures and texts to represent themselves. We began with a virtual 'role play' based on a class text, but I needed to go beyond the lower-level thinking that these first efforts involved. I decided to provide more opportunities for my students to work collaboratively to make meaning from the text. I combined the collaborative discussion features of Ning with the blogging features. The students blogged about topics that inspired them, engaged in dialogue with their peers and took more interest in writing responses to what they read because they had a difference sense of audience and purpose beyond just writing for "the teacher." Eventually they started interacting on their own—even if they hadn't come to school that day they were online. We ended up expanding our community to work with a class at another school. This type of activity seemed to validate what they do in their lives, building on it so that they could grow in their ability to access and produce information in multiple environments.

Danika makes sure that she offers choice and diversity of literature based on her students' reading levels and what is important in their lives. Learning in Danika's class focuses on relationships and "big ideas," acknowledging that not everyone approaches literacy in the same way. Engaging students with texts that they thoroughly enjoy makes it possible to scaffold them into the more complex texts, and helps them transfer the learning to other areas of their lives.

When All Else Fails, Look at the Student!

The organizational structures that govern our current system of progressing through predefined grades are, as Gary Stager (2010) has pointed out, "the only places where we sort

---

5 Ning: http://www.ning.com/

people by their manufacturing date" (n.p.). When we are accountable to the students first, allowing their interest and diversity to inform text selection and decisions that govern how they will spend their time with those texts, we see their intellect and creativity emerge. Engaging in literacy practices through social networking provides a sense of purpose, audience, and opportunity to extend community, express ideas and opinions in more meaningful ways, and rework emerging identities (Lewis, Leander, & Wang, 2008). Approaching curricular planning from a "Yours, Mine, and Ours" framework (Rich, 2001) honours the place of traditional "didactic" teaching, but also opens up spaces for students to share ownership for their individual learning and for the development of their collaborative learning community. It's worth the risk!

References

Barton, D., Hamilton, M., & Ivanic, R. (Eds.). (2000). *Situated literacies: Reading and writing in context*. London: Routledge.

Carroll, P., De Luise, R., & Howard, T. (2009). Best literacy practices for secondary English Language Arts classrooms. In S. Parris, D. Fisher, & K. Headly (Eds.), *Adolescent literacy, field tested: Effective solutions for every classroom* (pp. 94–105). Chicago, IL: International Reading Association.

Cope, M. & Kalantzis, M. (2009). *"Multiliteracies": New literacies, new learning.* http://newlearningonline.com/~newlearn/wp-content/uploads/2009/03/m-litspaper13apr08.pdf (accessed July 3, 2010).

Cummins, J., Carder, M., & Gallagher, E. (2004). Technology, diversity and literacy: Planning for multiliteracies instruction. Presentation given to the ECIS Conference, Nice, France. http:// www.marymountrome.org/ecis/ARTICOLI/preconf/ecis.nice2004.pdf (accessed January 8, 2010).

Heydon, R. & Iannacci, L. (2008). *Early childhood curricula and the de-pathologizing of childhood.* Toronto, ON: University of Toronto Press.

Lewis, C., Leander, K., & Wang, X. (2008). Digital literacies. In B. J. Guzzetti (Ed.), *Literacy for the new millennium: Adolescent literacy* (pp. 207–222). Westport, CT: Praeger.

New London Group. (2000). A pedagogy of multiliteracies: Designing social futures. In B. Cope & M. Kalantzis (Eds), *Multiliteracies: literacy learning and the design of social futures* (pp. 9–39). New York: Routledge.

O'Brien, D. (2001). "At-risk" adolescents: Redefining competence through the multilieracies of intermediality, visual arts and representation. *Reading Online,* 4(11). http:// www.readingonline.org/newliteracies/lit_index.asp?HREF=/newliteracies/obrien/index.html (accessed April 3, 2008).

O'Brien, D. (2003, March). Juxtaposing traditional and intermedial literacies to redefine the competence of struggling adolescents. *Reading Online* 6(7). http://www.readingonline.org/ newliteracies/lit_index.asp?HREF=obrien2/ (accessed April 3, 2008).

Partnership for 21st Century Skills. (2004). *Learning for the 21st Century* (p. 5). www.21stcenturyskills.org/images/stories/otherdocs/P21_Report.pdf (accessed May 1, 2008).

Rich, S. (1998). *Reading for meaning in the elementary school.* Toronto, ON: Nelson

Shields, C. M., Bishop, R., & Mazawi, A. E. (2005). *Pathologizing practices: The impact of deficit thinking on education.* New York: Peter Lang.

Stager, G. The only places where we sort people by their manufacturing date. Twitter post. http://twitter.com (accessed March 6, 2010).

How Can Teachers Best Make Use of Students' Out-of-School Exposure to Multiple Kinds of Texts?

By Margaret Mackey, University of Alberta

The singular novel, short story, and poem have long been the focus of the English classroom. A recent survey of materials used in grade 10 English classrooms in the public schools of a western Canadian city in 2006 (Mackey, Vermeer, Storie, & DeBlois, 2012) revealed a very strong bias towards print, with film being the only serious alternative. Out of 753 titles recorded, the following genre breakdown was reported:

Print	537
Video/DVD	191
Audio recording	11
Digital/Web/Database	10
Undetermined	3
Artwork	1

The balance between traditional and new forms is conveyed differently through a graphic representation of percentages:

FIGURE 1 Survey of Genres Taught in English Classrooms

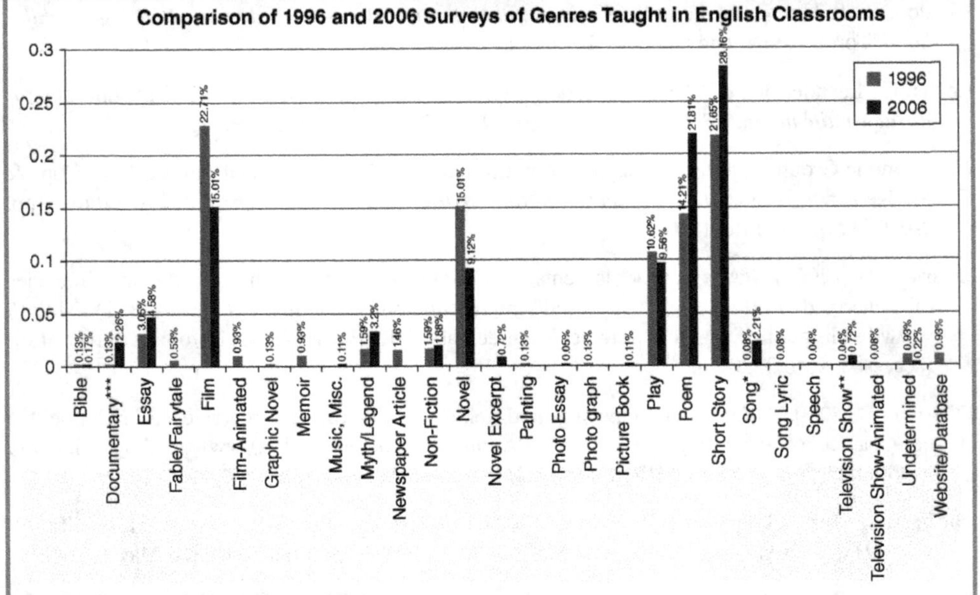

Source: Copyright © 2012 Margaret Mackey

The five main formats are short story, poems, film, plays and novels—just as they were 10 years earlier in a parallel survey (Altmann, Johnston, & Mackey, 1998, 1999).

The orthodox and traditional nature of these classroom materials is very clear. How do they compare with the multimedia lives of students outside school? More importantly, how should teachers reflect on the contrast?

Today's students spend their out-of-school lives connecting with stories and information in multiple formats. A story may begin its existence as a book, a movie, or a video game, but its narrative life often continues in a variety of other formats. Some of these are officially produced by the story's original authors or their authorized successors, while others are created by fans, critics, or parodists. Information similarly has become much more open to mutation; in cases such as Wikipedia, readers can alter what they read in order to improve it (though, of course, their new information can also be changed by others).

More and more commonly, stories are told in multiple formats. Henry Jenkins defines a "transmedia" universe where no single version of a narrative tells the complete story:

> Increasingly, we inhabit a world of transmedia story-telling, one which depends less on each individual work being self-sufficient than on each work contributing to a larger narrative economy . . . with story information communicated through books, film, television, comics, and other media, each doing what it does best, each a relatively autonomous experience, but the richest understanding of the story world coming to those who follow the narrative across the various channels. (Jenkins, 2004, p. 124)

Acknowledging this development, the Producers Guild of America approved a new credit: "Transmedia Producer." They explain the idea of transmedia as follows:

> A Transmedia Narrative project or franchise must consist of three (or more) narrative storylines existing within the same fictional universe on any of the following platforms: Film, Television, Short Film, Broadband, Publishing, Comics, Animation, Mobile, Special Venues, DVD/Blu-ray/CD-ROM, Narrative Commercial and Marketing rollouts, and other technologies that may or may not currently exist. These narrative extensions are NOT the same as repurposing material from one platform to be cut or repurposed to different platforms. (http://www.producersguild.org/?page=coc_nm#transmedia, accessed February 15, 2012)

It is easy to think that such digital refinements have little to do with the kind of print literature that is valued in the classrooms described above. As Lyle Skains points out,

> Print literature as an entertainment genre is still feeling its way into the digital world. Film has shifted to DVD, music to MP3, photography to compact flash cards, and communications to mobile phones, but print narratives are still largely delivered via books and magazines, or through e-readers, such as Amazon's Kindle, that merely reproduce the print text in digital format. (2010, p. 96)

But Skains goes on argue that change, when it does comes to print literature, may be very swift:

> It is conceivable that digital stories will be accepted into a literary canon within one generation; film and television texts, internet sites and interactive games have already achieved that level of acceptance among teenagers. Younger audiences have no difficulties with the multi-track discontinuous narratives offered in electronic texts and ludic environments, having grown up with the multiple influences of television and online interactivity. (2010, p. 99)

An ever-increasing number of signs (particularly the rapidly escalating sales of e-reading devices) suggest that the kind of shift Skains is describing is well on its way. Young readers themselves are precipitating certain kinds of multiplicity with their online discussion sites and fan fiction forums. Further, certain forms of published print stories for young readers are already mutating. Take, for example, the young adult novel *Cathy's Book* (Stewart, Weisman, & Brigg, 2006). The hardback book told a fantasy story of Cathy's out-of-time romance by means of standard printed and bound pages that were lavishly illustrated but also supplemented by a plastic pouch of physical "clues" to the mystery (such as a phone number on a napkin, a torn-up family photograph, and so forth). Readers could call the phone numbers given in the book and reach in-character voice-mails; they could also pursue the character of Cathy on her MySpace page. A later edition of a portion of the story appeared as an iPhone app that includes live web and phone links. This book is definitely pushing past the limits of its bound pages.

Publishers are beginning to experiment more broadly with multiple routes to storytelling. One interesting example comes from the Subutai Corporation, which has introduced the Personal Ubiquitous Literature Platform (PULP), a "social book platform." Authors Neal Stephenson and Greg Bear spearheaded a collective serial novel called *The Mongoliad*. As of February 2012, they were describing their enterprise in the following terms on their official website:

> We publish chapters every so often (about weekly), and every chapter has associated discussions and other ways for readers to interact with each other and with us. Sometimes we'll also have graphics to share as well, or movies, or music. There is a user-editable 'Pedia with information about Foreworld-related topics, general-purpose user forums, and soon we hope to have easy ways for people to contribute their own stories, art, and music to our shared Foreworld experience. (http://mongoliad.com/faq, accessed February 15, 2012)

Not every long-time reader will be comfortable with a story that mutates instead of staying put on the page. Younger readers, however, may find this kind of mutable text world more familiar and interesting than the kinds of classics they meet in their classrooms. Many of today's readers think of texts in the kinds of contexts summarized by this complex diagram, with its many cross-connections:

FIGURE 2 Relationships Among Mutable Texts

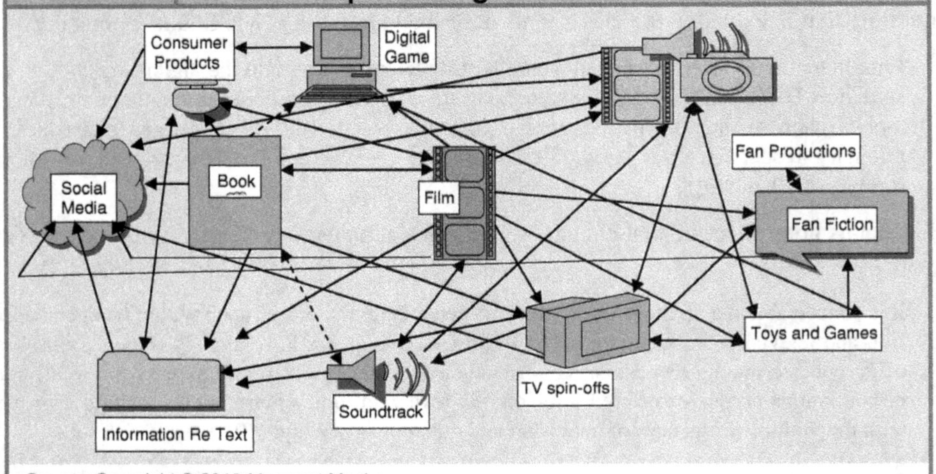

Source: Copyright © 2012 Margaret Mackey

The fluidity and interconnectedness of contemporary recreational culture contrasts and conflicts significantly with the idea of developing respect for the great singular texts of our culture. Many people—not just teachers—would agree on the importance of teaching a classic such as *Romeo and Juliet,* the top play being taught in those western Canadian grade 10 classes both in 1996 and in 2006. But treating *Romeo and Juliet* as a monument may be counterproductive; teachers need to find ways to make it significant to students whose approach to their own texts is flexible and contingent.

To make meaningful connections between the virtues and values of the contemporary textual world and the classroom, teachers should first of all find ways of understanding and (probably more importantly) respecting the possibilities of that world. They should consider how important it is to make room inside the classroom for what children know in their daily lives. Anne Haas Dyson expresses this priority in terms of preventing loss as much as adding value:

> Even very young school children . . . have acquired varied sorts of knowledge and know-how about literacy use from their participation in social practices in and out of school. Given this resource potential, how are children's compositional actions informed by the perceived parameters of school literacy practices? What are the consequences for how their meaning making is made officially visible? What aspects of their meaning making—indeed, what practices—are sidelined or even lost to the official world (but not to the unofficial one)? (2008, p. 120)

But preventing loss is only part of the story. What subtleties and nuances can young people learn to express when they have a variety of media options at their disposal? How can a story be enhanced through multiple incarnations and additions?

The preponderance of old media in those surveys from western Canada suggests that schools may be lagging when it comes to taking note of the creative and critical potential built into the worlds created through multiple texts. Inertia is a systemic issue in large educational organizations, not just in Canada. Gunnar Hansson, reporting on a Swedish study of close to a century's worth of student examination papers in literature, suggests that the lag time may run to decades. Writes Hansson, "It takes a long time—20, 30 or even 40 years—for a new approach in literary research to find its way into school teaching and to gain a dominant position there" (1992, p. 147).

The absence of radical change in those classrooms in the decade between 1996 and 2006—a decade in which Napster rose and fell, DVDs took over from videos, and social media took off in all their huge and unprecedented variety—suggests that teachers need to make explicit efforts to prepare themselves for an equivalent shift in the world of print literature. We do not have three or four decades to catch up. Showing the film adaptation of *Romeo and Juliet* is a worthwhile exercise but it is not enough. If we do not pay attention to the new dynamism of the digital world, we run the risk that students will simply dismiss print as the stagnant corner of the textual world where nothing interesting happens and the representative texts are fit only for schoolwork. We would all be the losers if this happens.

So how can teachers best make use of students' exposure to multiple texts? The answer (simple to write on this page but complex to achieve in the schools) is to invite that student expertise into the classroom. Everyone can benefit when different forms of knowledge and understanding are respectfully shared. Nobody knows what changes are imminent; English language arts classrooms should be one site where the revolution is welcomed—to be observed, explored, critiqued, and enjoyed.

References

Altmann, Anna, Ingrid Johnston, & Margaret Mackey. (1998). Curriculum decisions about literature in contemporary classrooms: A preliminary analysis of a survey of materials used in Edmonton grade ten English courses. *Alberta Journal of Educational Research* XLIV, 208–220.

Altmann, Anna, Ingrid Johnston, & Margaret Mackey. (1999). *Romeo and Juliet* rule: The stability of the grade 10 language arts canon. *Alberta English* 37(2), 17–24.

Dyson, Anne Haas. (2008). Staying in the (curricular) lines: Practice constraints and possibilities in childhood writing. *Written Communication* 25(1), 119–159.

Hansson, Gunnar. (1992). Readers responding: And then? *Research in the Teaching of English* 26(2), 135–148.

Jenkins, Henry. (2004). Game design as narrative architecture. In N. Wardrip-Fruin & P. Harrigan (Eds.), *First person: New media as story, performance, and game* (pp. 118–130). Cambridge, MA: MIT Press.

Mackey, Margaret, Leslie Vermeer, Dale Storie, & Elizabeth DeBlois. (2012). The constancy of the school "canon": A survey of texts used in grade 10 English language arts in 2006 and 1996. *Language and Literacy: A Canadian E-Journal* 14(1), 26–58.

Skains, R. Lyle. (2010). The shifting author-reader dynamic: Online novel communities as a bridge from print to digital literature. *Convergence: The International Journal of Research into New Media Technologies* 16(1), 95–111.

Stewart, Sean, Jordan Weisman, & Cathy Brigg. (2006). *Cathy's book.* Philadelphia, PA: Running Press Kids.

How Might Reading Emergent Genres Such as Electronic Literature Benefit Secondary and Middle School Students?

By Teresa M. Dobson, University of British Columbia

As humanities and literacy scholars have remarked through the last 20 years, digital environments for knowledge mobilization have invited us to re-examine our understandings of textuality. This re-examination of textuality has been accompanied by renewed interest in book culture in the humanities (e.g., Johns, 1998; Nunberg, 1996), and a renewed exploration of the nature of literacy in the social sciences (e.g., New London Group, 1996; Cope & Kalantzis, 2000). There has also been much hype about how digital textuality will modify literary education (e.g., Landow, 1997), and about how social media is changing basic parameters of the construction and diffusion of knowledge, motivating a shift from taxonomies to "folksonomies" of knowing (Lankshear & Knobel, 2006). However, two closely related questions about textuality remain largely unexamined in literacy and literary education circles: In what ways is digital media changing the parameters of literature itself, and how might reading emergent genres such as electronic literature benefit secondary and middle school students?

Electronic literature or "e-literature" is defined by the Electronic Literature Organization (ELO) as a class of "works with important literary aspects that take advantage of the capabilities and contexts provided by the stand-alone or networked computer"

(ELO, 2006, n.p.). E-literature includes genres such as hypertext fiction, reactive poetry, blog novels, Flash fiction and poetry, generative art, installation, code poetry, and so on. The best source for examples of e-literature is the *Electronic Literature Collection,* a two-volume collection of 120 representative works (60 per volume). The collection is openly accessible and published under a Creative Commons licence. As I have noted elsewhere, it is arguable that "some of the most innovative text experiments online—ones that truly push the boundaries of established conventions of writing, and that work to explore the particular affordances of digital media" fall within the category of e-literature (Dobson & Willinsky, 2009, p. 292). Further, students' practices of reading increasingly include and are extended by emergent genres such as e-literature. In order to enhance critical literacy in education, we should closely examine these practices and consider how we might best facilitate students' engagement with and understanding of these forms. In this entry, I will first provide a sense of the genre and then contemplate its distinctive features, discussing why it might be important for young people to engage with such literary media.

A Brief History of e-Literature

E-literature is shifting significantly from its genesis in the late 1980s and early 1990s. Older forms such as hypertext fiction (e.g., Joyce, 1987; Jackson, 1995) are largely text-intensive, and are said to derive from text-based adventure games (Bolter, 2001; Dobson & Willinsky, 2009). These works consist primarily of nodes of text (or lexia) connected by links, often in multiple ways, requiring readers to choose their own paths through the network. They are most noted for challenging the traditional Aristotelian plotline and for inviting readers to examine their assumptions about the necessity of determinacy and closure in fiction (cf. Dobson, 2002). Hayles (2007) notes, "the hypertext link is considered the distinguishing feature" (n.p.) of these earlier works, for it is the link that enables both the fragmentation of the text and the possibility of a new form of reader engagement. Commenting on the history of the genre, Hayles suggests that Shelley Jackson's *Patchwork Girl,* published in 1995, is the culminating piece of first-generation or "classical" e-literature. She also remarks that these early works have been superseded by a second-generation e-literature that makes "fuller use of the multi-modal capabilities of the Web" and de-emphasizes the link by employing a "wide variety of navigation schemes and interface metaphors" (Hayles, 2007, n.p.). A look through e-literature publishing venues such as *Dreaming Methods, Born Magazine, Poems That Go,* and the *Electronic Literature Collection* reveals that digital literary art is becoming increasingly media-intensive to the point where it has been described as a marriage of "literary arts and interactive media" (Born Magazine, 2007). Along these lines, *Born Magazine*'s motto is "art and literature, together."

Two Examples of Flash Poetry

Second-generation e-literature often employs animated image and text accompanied by sound in an effort to produce visually dynamic pieces. Two examples, both Flash poetry found in the *Electronic Literature Collection, Volume I,* will serve to give a sense of the genre. Ankerson and Sapnar's *Cruising* (Ankerson & Sapnar, 2001/2006) is a compelling poem about teenage "car cruising" (driving main streets hoping to encounter other youth with whom to join up) in small-town Wisconsin, wherein the text of the poem is imposed on a stitched-together series of black and white pictures—street scenes linked together in filmstrip fashion. This strip scrolls horizontally over the still image of a teenager applying lipstick. Mousing over the strip enables readers to control its speed, size, and direction (left or right) as they listen to the poem narrated to up-tempo folk guitar. It is possible to "catch up" with the narration and read along with the narrator; it is also possible simply to "drive" the poem while listening to the narration—one hand on the wheel (mouse or mouse pad), watching the night roll by in film frames, and, along with the speaking voice of the poem, sniffing the street for love in the hopes it might drive past in a pickup truck. The poem, being multi-layered (text, narration, image, music, and so on), begs multiple readings as reader-viewers explore various modes of engagement. The poem may be viewed online at *Poems That Go* or the *Electronic Literature Collection, Volume 1*.

The second piece of e-literature, *Girls' Day Out* (Lawrynovicz, 2006), is also published in the *Electronic Literature Collection, Volume 1*. Combining creative non-fiction and poetry, the work begins as a short prose passage that tells of two sisters who, on their vacation in Texas, hire riding horses at "Star Dust Stables"—a scrub-grass operation that allows competent riders to ride unsupervised across miles of desert-like terrain. The girls' favourite mounts are reliable, surefooted, and generally unflappable, but on one occasion, they inexplicably refuse to pass across certain areas of the pasture. They shy violently, rearing and spinning in fear at something the girls cannot discern:

> A spurt of gallop across the plateau, and then me over my horse's shoulder, the mud like a fist against my back. My sister still in the saddle, but her horse crouched back on his hocks, eyes rolling white. I catch my gelding, nearly going down beneath his hooves on the slick grass. He lunges left, right, nostrils flared so wide I can see the red deep inside them. My sister is standing in her stirrups, her horse rounded, shifting, snorting beneath her. But there is nothing to see. Only windtorn field. (Lawrynovicz, 2006)

Clicking on the prose passage reveals a found poem that emerges slowly in four parts, revealing that murder victims lie beneath the soil. In a note, the author writes that Star Dust Stables was her preferred place for riding as a girl during her family summer vacations, but was shut down when a number of women were found buried in one of the pastures. Lawrynovicz's childhood-vacation riding terrain became known locally as the "killing fields." A supplemental piece, "Shards," consists of a series of found poems generated from fragmentary phrases excerpted from dozens of newspaper articles. Clicking on the successive poems sends the letters tumbling, whirling through the air like a dust devil in the Texan scrub grass, fragments of phrases in a media storm.

Layering and Embodied Metaphor in e-Literature

In a feature commonly observed of digital media, both pieces are "composited." Compositing is a process first defined in the context of film that involves combining a number of separate elements to create an apparent whole (Manovich, 2001). To take this notion further, in this instance the two poems might be construed as appropriations or mash-ups, in that they pull together a range of media in a form of bricolage and some of this media clearly wasn't generated by the authors (for example, the fragments of text in the "Shards" section of *Girls' Day Out* are mined from newspaper articles). If the content of successful social networking spaces such as YouTube is any indication, sampling in this regard marks a significant trend in contemporary visual and literary art, as well as contemporary music. Critical engagement with such art requires a willingness to interrogate understandings of authorship, which may be viewed as a creative process that entails re-presenting fragments of other artifacts as much as generating original material. It also requires awareness of and sensitivity to the various rhetorical modes central to the art form: juxtaposition, for example, is a dominant rhetorical mode in e-literature (and mash-ups more generally), whereby the significance of one element is intensified by its positioning alongside another.

In *Cruising* and *Girls' Day Out,* the composited media fragments are layered: in the case of the former piece, the rolling film strip/text string is layered over a stationary image, and readers decide its prominence in the frame (whether it fades into the background or whether it dominates); further, the very strip itself is comprised of text layered over still images strung together. *Girls' Day Out,* in a poignant marriage of form and content, gives the impression that the poem lies beneath the surface of the prose text, waiting to be excavated like the ill-fated women of which it tells.

The artistry of these pieces in this regard brings to mind Hayles's discussion of how interactive fiction (IF), another second-generation e-literature form, can work (Hayles, 2007). IF refers to the sort of text in which the interactor (Montfort, 2003) controls a player-character and issues directives to which a program responds by displaying other text in a possible branch of the plot. Hayles observes that solving many "IF puzzles requires the user to make a leap of inference from one device to another that resembles it in function; for example, if a door and box are properly linked, opening the box also opens the door, which otherwise will not yield" (Hayles, 2007, n.p.). Such moves, she continues, "resemble the operation of literary metaphor, although here the commonality is routed not through verbal comparison of two objects but rather functional similarities combined with the player-character's actions—a kind of embodied metaphor" (n.p.).

In the case of *Cruising,* as intimated earlier, controlling the strip is a sort of embodied metaphor in that it is akin to driving the car, speeding down Main Street, listening to music and conversation at one moment, paying minimal attention to the particularity of what is passing by, and then slowing down to peer more closely at the street scenes. Something similar is true of *Girls' Day Out*: a reader's action of clicking on the prose text to reveal the poetic subtext constitutes a form of embodied metaphor whereby one becomes complicit in unearthing the horror below the surface. And when that horror is revealed, a process is set in motion: the reader watches, perhaps casually at first, but in increasing dismay as meaning emerges slowly, in four segments—one for each victim found in a particular pasture after the location of the first prompted a thorough search of the area. And notably, in this case the timing is essential to the experience of the metaphor: readers can't ingest the text as quickly as they might in another medium; instead, they come to awareness gradually, archaeologist-like, as though brushing earth from an unidentified object.

What is achieved in these texts in the way of embodied metaphor would be difficult to accomplish in another medium and constitutes a unique feature of e-literature. It demands a different form of critical viewing or reading. In certain respects, the demands of the genre might be likened to a form of literary engagement that has been described by some scholars (examining reader response to print texts) as "expressive enactment" (Kuiken, Miall, & Sikora, 2004). Kuiken, Miall, and Sikora (2004) observe that one form of expressive enactment functions like metaphor: the reader becomes so identified with some aspect of the text that a form of self-implication ensues, and boundaries become blurred between the self and a character. In other words, expressive enactment constitutes an intense form of literary engagement that is likely to disarm critical reading. Embodied metaphor in the electronic medium may or may not be experienced as intensely by readers, but it does constitute a form of complicity with what is represented that may likewise disarm attempts at critical reading. Moreover, it is important to bear in mind that embodied metaphor, as discussed earlier, is a feature of forms of e-literature that are akin to gaming spaces, such as IF. It is also the reality of immersive gameworlds, which some contest will replace literary fiction as the preferred narrative space of future generations (Ryan, 2005). As well, it is an emergent strategy of the online advertising industry. Swedish vodka giant Absolut, for example, led the trend in this direction by rolling out a series of interactive advertisements in connection with its flavoured vodka. Other corporations were quick to follow suit. A search for "interactive advertising" online will reveal a number of examples.

Critical Literacy in a Post-Typographic Age

I've attempted in this entry to point to some features of emergent digital texts using e-literature as an exemplar. First, these forms are often subversive or iconoclastic in nature, explicitly working to undermine traditional literary structures as well as understandings of authorship and originality. In regard to the latter, the creative process is often one of bricolage or appropriation and it is often collaborative (in the case of e-literature, for example, it may combine the efforts of literary and visual artists). Second, the predominance of appropriation or bricolage means that the rhetorical artistry often privileges juxtaposition over unity of effect and Aristotelian (i.e., linear) plot configurations. Third, such works often achieve their effect through implication of the reader (e.g., in the case of embodied metaphor discussed above). If we value critical literacy in education we need to examine very closely how practices of reading are extended by emergent genres such as e-literature, to include such forms in our everyday school curricula, and to consider how we might best facilitate students' engagement with and understanding of these forms.

References

Ankerson, I. & Sapnar, M. (2006). Cruising. *Electronic literature collection, volume I.* http://collection.eliterature.org/1/ (accessed March 9, 2012).

Bolter, J. D. (2001). *Writing space: The computer, hypertext, and the history of writing.* Hillsdale, NJ: Lawrence Erlbaum.

Borràs, L., Memmott, T., Raley, R., & Stefans, B. (Eds.). (2011). *Electronic literature collection, volume II.* http://collection.eliterature.org/2/ (accessed March 10, 2012).

Born Magazine. (2012). http://www.bornmagazine.com/ (accessed March 10, 2012).

Cope, B. & Kalantzis, M. (Eds.). (2000). *Multiliteracies: Literacy learning and the design of social futures.* London: Routledge.

Dobson, T. M. (2002). E(c)lect(r)ic stories. *English Quarterly* 34(4), 53–63.

Dobson, T. M. & Willinsky, J. (2009). Digital literacy. In D. Olson & N. Torrance (Eds.), *Cambridge handbook of literacy* (pp. 286–312). Cambridge, United Kingdom: Cambridge University Press.

Dreaming Methods. (n.d.). http://www.dreamingmethods.com/ (accessed March 10, 2012).

Electronic Literature Organization (ELO). (2006). About the ELO. http://www.eliterature.org/about (accessed March 9, 2012).

Epstein, M. (n.d.). Language, textuality. *A lexicon of neologisms.* Emory University. http://www.emory.edu/INTELNET/lex_language.html (accessed March 9, 2012).

Hayles, N. K. (2003). Translating media: Why we should rethink textuality. *Yale Journal of Criticism* 16(2), 263–290.

———. (2007). Electronic literature: What is it? *Electronic Literature Organization.* http://eliterature.org/pad/elp.html (accessed March 10, 2012).

Hayles, N. K., Montfort, N., Rettberg, S., & Strickland, S. (Eds.). (2006). *Electronic literature collection, volume I.* College Park, Maryland: Electronic Literature Organization. http://collection.eliterature.org/1/ (accessed March 10, 2012).

Jackson, S. (1995). *Patchwork girl: A modern monster* [Computer software]. Watertown, MA: Eastgate Systems.

Johns, A. (1998). *The nature of the book: Print and knowledge in the making.* Chicago, IL: University of Chicago Press.

Joyce, M. (1987). *Afternoon, a story.* Cambridge, MA: Eastgate Systems. Computer software.

Kuiken, D., Miall, D. S., & Sikora, S. (2004). Forms of self-implication in literary reading. *Poetics Today 25*(2), 171–203.

Landow, G. P. (1997). *Hypertext 2.0: The convergence of contemporary critical theory and technology* (Revised ed.). Baltimore, MD: Johns Hopkins University Press.

Lankshear, C. & Knobel, M. (11 April, 2006). Blogging as participation: The active sociality of a new literacy. Paper presented at the American Educational Research Association, San Francisco, CA. http://www.geocities.com/c.lankshear/bloggingparticipation.pdf (accessed March 10, 2008).

Lawrynovicz, K. (2006). Girls' day out. In N. K. Hayles, N. Montfort, S. Rettberg, & S. Strickland (Eds.), *Electronic Literature Collection, Volume One.* College Park, MD: Electronic Literature Organization. http://collection.eliterature.org/1/ (accessed March 10, 2012).

Leu, D. J., Jr. (2000). Literacy and technology: Deictic consequences for literacy education in an information age. In M. L. Kamil, P. Mosenthal, P. D. Pearson, & R. Barr (Eds.) *Handbook of Reading Research,* Volume III. Mahwah, NJ: Erlbaum.

Manovich, L. (2001) *The language of new media.* Cambridge, MA: MIT Press.

Montfort, N. (2003). *Twisty little passages: An approach to interactive fiction.* Cambridge, MA: MIT Press.

New London Group. (1996). A pedagogy of multiliteracies: Designing social futures. *Harvard Educational Review* 66(1), 60–92.

Nunberg, G. (Ed.). (1996). *The future of the book.* Berkeley, CA: University of California Press.

Poems That Go. (n.d.). http://www.poemsthatgo.com/ (accessed March 10, 2012).

Reinking, D., McKenna, M., Labbo, L., & Kieffer, R. (Eds.). (1998). *Handbook of literacy and technology: Transformations in a post-typographic world*. Mahwah, NJ: Erlbaum.

Ryan, M. (2005). Narrative and the split condition of digital textuality. *Dichtung-digital: Journal für digitale ästhetik* 5(34), n.p. http://www.brown.edu/Research/dichtung-digital/2005/1/Ryan/ (accessed May 10, 2006).

SECTION 2

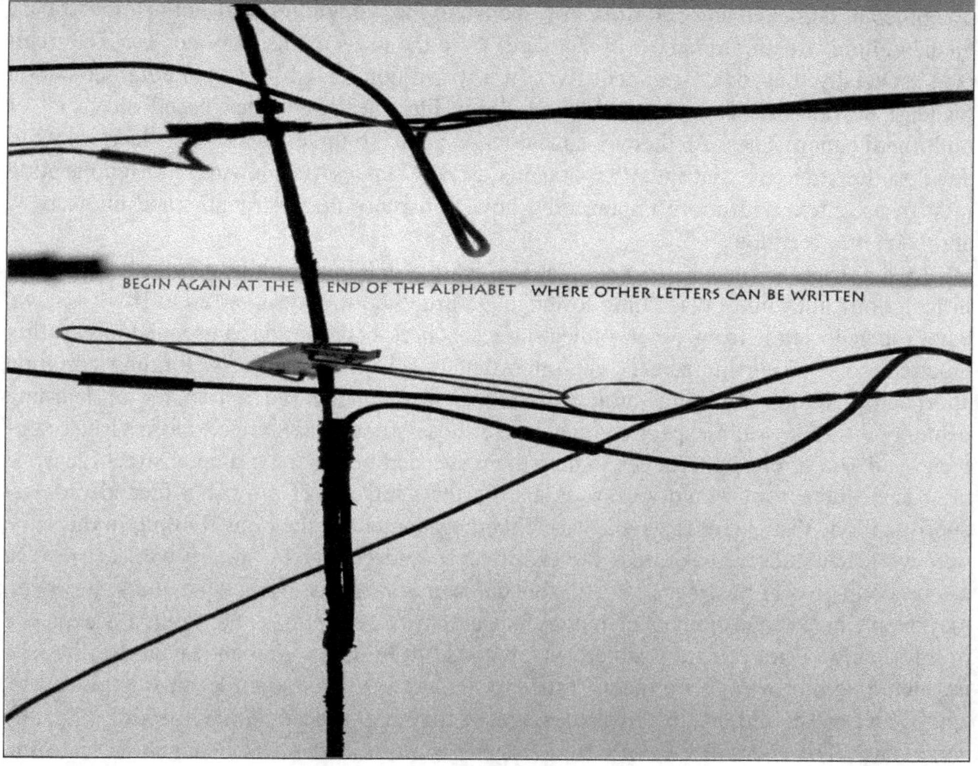

Visual Literacy

Why Should We Teach Visual Literacy?

By Deborah Begoray, University of Victoria

Visual literacies are all those based on image rather than on written text. Visual literacies are historically important. As a species, we evolved the ability to "read" facial expressions and body language, to interpret the weather, the seasons, and the movements of animals, and to judge the ripening of crops. We expressed ourselves through arts such as painting, dance, sculpture, and costuming using all manner of visual symbols. Written language is a much more recent and important addition to our communication repertoire. Nevertheless, reading and writing came to dominate the education system and, indeed, they still do. As early as the 1960s, Canadian communication theorist Marshall McLuhan was arguing that the media was actually influencing the way we think, but little of his thought made its way into the official curricula of secondary schools. In the 1980s, various scholars began to argue for a greater multiplicity of literacies in the classroom so that students might express themselves in ways more suited to their own strengths and in ways more appropriate for a greater multiplicity of messages.

By the 1990s, across the Western world, visual literacies began to appear as mandated outcomes in language arts curricula in response to the recognition that ours is now a very visual culture; we are immersed in messages from the mass media, for one. Teachers realized especially that today's student lives in a world dominated by visual communication (at least outside the school walls). These "new literacies" are often based on visual or multimedia approaches. As literacy educators, we need to understand more clearly how to develop the strengths and interests students already possess in viewing and representing in such a context and, more importantly, how to harness these strengths and interests as approaches to learning.

As language arts teachers, we are at the heart of the curricula of most schools. Most jurisdictions allot more class time to language arts than to any other area. However, we have much to learn from other subject-area teachers because viewing and representing practices, or "visual literacies," are important in all school subjects. Finding common approaches among different subject areas can also encourage a transfer of learning behaviours. This would especially encourage those students who need more visual, concrete, and kinesthetic approaches to help them succeed in understanding abstract ideas.

Visual literacy, it would appear, is also in the vanguard of a much wider ideological confrontation. Visual messages encourage the engagement of the critical mind. In the same way we teach students to discuss the significance and quality of literary works, we must also encourage a critical stance toward visual representations. Such behaviours, however, may result in the questioning of power and authority rather than the passive acceptance of information—not just from advertisers, but also from others who endeavour to persuade us, including our own governments. Students should thus be able to deconstruct, evaluate, appreciate, resist, and create visual messages if they are to become members of a healthy democracy. The alternative is to raise this generation of students to believe that if a film, cartoon, or website, for example, has been made public, it must be good and truthful—or, on the other hand, to imply that all visuals are manipulative and evil.

What Visual Literacy Should We Teach?

As literacy educators, we can build on the familiar topics of print literacy to get us started with visual literacy. For example, a close look at the most recent curricula shows us that students must be able to comprehend messages both from print sources such as poetry or essays, and from visual sources such as magazine advertisements or films. Literacy educators can use visual topics more familiar to language arts classrooms (such as graphic novels for older students like *Maus* by Art Spiegelman) to teach students how the illustrations work independently or in support of the print text.

Teachers who want to venture beyond the familiar and add to the suggestions in regional curriculum documents can pursue proposed learning outcomes in a variety of ways. Several traditions provide frameworks to guide visual literacy education. For example, both arts education (music, movement, art, drama, and film) and mass-media education (newspapers, television, and websites) offer teachers topics that include diverse systems of visual signs. Any middle, junior, or secondary school faculty includes teacher-experts in art, music, drama and, often, technology with whom English language arts teachers might consult or collaborate. Topics here might include how to analyze visuals, such as a group of films all depicting the same scene from a work of literature (e.g., *Hamlet*), how to create a role play, or how to evaluate a YouTube clip. Those lucky enough to have a teacher-librarian in residence will likely find someone skilled across these disciplinary areas. Otherwise, literacy teachers can learn from teachers in science, history, social studies, or mathematics and ask themselves how they might integrate more hands-on, visual approaches. Social studies teachers use maps and historical photographs; science teachers use specimens and conduct experiments; mathematics teachers use three-dimensional objects. Language arts teachers can bring in similar visual items to help students "see" from different perspectives.

To help students to think critically about issues of power and control, technologically mediated visual and multimedia texts are motivating and easily obtained. Texts that are obviously constructed, most often for commercial purposes, are especially appealing for middle or secondary students, not least because they lie beyond the traditional concerns of language arts classrooms and within the realm of popular culture.

How Should We Teach about Visual Literacy?

The current shift toward a more postmodern literacy, one which includes written, oral, and visual texts framed through multiple subjective perspectives, contributes to a climate favourable for re-considering traditional approaches to literacy teaching. However, this climate also challenges the status quo in many language arts classrooms. Teachers need to adopt risk-taking attitudes such as giving up some measure of control and certitude. For example, students can become the teachers when a new technology is introduced. Teachers might seek expertise beyond the school to help learners experience, understand, and create visual texts such as cartoons, films, photographs, videotapes, web sites, or forms of dance. Community members, including parents of the students themselves, can be sought for expert knowledge on drawing, orienteering, or film-making. The teacher then becomes the central hub, helping students to meet the curricular outcomes through active viewing and representing activities. Specific lesson ideas such as the following use various visual approaches to teach literacy outcomes:

- **Use actual objects students can see and handle.** For a lesson at the beginning of a unit on the novel *Three Day Road* (Joseph Boyden), students analyzing Indigenous artifacts are engaged in conversations about their knowledge of the Ojibway. They are then shown a number of artifacts, asked to look carefully at each one and to predict what their function might be. Afterwards, they write about the artifacts, describing them and explaining what they might be used for and why they thought so. These ideas are then posted with the artifacts and considered by the class. The teacher concludes by praising their ideas and revealing the actual use of each item.
- **Discuss the visual representation of abstract ideas through student-led creation activities.** (Divide major activities for creating and representing into a number of smaller activities, proceeding from whole group to small group.) The teacher begins with a print text and asks students to discuss the narrative, emphasizing the "big ideas" and considering what these ideas mean to each of the students in their own lives. The teacher then leads a whole-class discussion on how to represent these often abstract notions (such as "isolation" in *Go Ask Alice,* which might be shown by a small scrap of faint colour on a dark background, or by a single deer surrounded by a pack of wolves). Next, students are divided into smaller groups. They are asked to collect pictures, think about the visual cues in messages (such as larger size indicating more importance,

placement on the edge indicating marginal importance), arrange and re-arrange images, and make their final decisions about composition—all the while being guided by the teacher, who circulates from group to group.

- **Add visual components to text-based lessons.** Note-taking, for example, can be expanded by adding a visual component. Students are first asked to read for 10 minutes (this can be expanded depending on the capability of the group). Next, they are directed to sketch, quickly drawing something that they could "see in their mind's eye" as they read. This focuses students on the story and prepares them for later, follow-up discussions, where the sketches serve as visual notes. In this case, students need to be reminded that sketches are unfinished aids to the memory. The teacher can demonstrate this by drawing quickly on the board or overhead using stick figures, circles, and squares, or whatever demonstrates that refined art is not the goal of the lesson. Students are asked to complete their notes with five key written phrases placed around the sketch.
- **Demonstrate that all visuals are "constructed" for effect—to have a certain impact on the viewer.** First, the teacher obtains a picture from a news source with various people and background details shown. Using a cropping tool—two L-shaped borders in the case of printed images, or built-in cropping tools in image editing software such as Adobe Photoshop—the teacher shows students how to frame in various ways: to isolate a single face, for example, and then expand the view to include some or all of the background. Students are asked how the visual message changes. Is the emotional impact different if the photographer shows us only a small child smashing a window, rather than the group of adults who accompanied him or her? What if we are allowed to see just their faces and raised hands, compared to when we can also see their bodies and ragged clothing? Is it different if the background is concealed, or revealed as a famous store? What if the focus on the window reveals television sets, or if it reveals baked goods? The teacher ends by asking students to provide a written caption that will modify the message of each cropped photograph.

One way to encourage active participation in visual literacy is by instituting a plan some teachers call BDA: *before, during, after* (this works, of course, for reading and listening as well). Make sure students know what to look for *before* they begin viewing. Give them something specific to do *during* the viewing time (this activity could be visual representing or writing). Follow up *after* the viewing by discussing or expanding the representation or writing. In this way, learning goals are not lost. Finally, remember that the goal of all literacy education is to encourage critical and creative participation in communication. Visual literacy is especially well-suited to meet this goal. Integrate viewing and representing with reading, writing, speaking, and listening to reinforce learning and to help students participate actively in their literacy education and in the world beyond the classroom walls.

References

Begoray, D., Cimon, M., & Wharf Higgins, J. (2010). Lifelong learning and lifestyles: The influence of media on adolescent health literacy. In M. Caltone, (Ed.), *Handbook of Lifelong Learning Developments* (pp. 111–139). Nova Science Publishers. https://www.novapublishers.com/catalog/product_info.php?products_id=10918 (accessed January 2, 2011).

Begoray, D. (2003). Viewing and visually representing. In J. Richards & M. McKenna (Eds.), *Integrating multiple literacies in K–8 classrooms: Cases, commentaries, and practical applications* (pp. 190–209). Mahwah, NJ: Erlbaum.

Begoray, D. (2003). Sign, sign, everywhere a sign: Multiplying literacies in the pre-service language arts curriculum. In J. Worthy, D. Schallert, C. M. Fairbanks, B. Maloch, & J. V. Hoffman (Eds.), *Fifty-second National Reading Conference Yearbook* (pp. 128–138). Oak Creek, WI: National Reading Conference.

Begoray, D. (2002). Viewing and visually representing: Helping students see more clearly. *Journal of Reading Education* 28, 39–41.

Begoray, D. (2002). Visual literacy education for student teachers in Canada, Scotland and England: Motives and methods of three teacher educators. In D. Schallert, C. M. Fairbanks, J. Worthy, B. Maloch, & J. V. Hoffman (Eds.), *Fifty-first National Reading Conference Yearbook* (pp. 117–128). Oak Creek, WI: National Reading Conference.

Begoray, D. (2001). Through a class darkly: Visual literacy in English language arts classrooms. *Canadian Journal of Teacher Education* 26(2), 201–217.

Begoray, D. (2000). Seventy-plus ideas for viewing and representing (and they're not just for language arts!). *English Quarterly* 32(1/2), 30–40.

Begoray, D. & Morin, F. (2002). Multiple literacies in language arts: Sustainable teacher change through a summer institute. *Reading Online* 6(4). Online serial. http://www.readingonline.org/articles/art_index.asp?HREF=/articles/begoray (accessed January 2, 2011).

Sipe, L. & Pantaleo, S. (Eds.). (2008). *Postmodern picture books: Play, parody, and self-referentiality*. New York: Routledge.

How Can "Transmediation" Illuminate Print and Visual Literacy?

By Linda Coles & Barrie Barrell, Memorial University of Newfoundland

Visual literacy, the ability to understand and produce visual messages, is becoming increasingly significant with the ever-expanding proliferation of mass media in society. As more information and entertainment are acquired through non-print media, the ability to think critically and visually about knowledge becomes a crucial skill. "Transmediation" is a rhetorical device in which the act of translating meaning from one sign system to another, increases opportunities for engagement in generative and reflective thinking (Siegel, 1995). It is a compelling means for developing students' written and visual literacy perceptions and expressions. Modern computer applications facilitate processes that bring print and images together to create multimodal representations. Engaging in transmediation processes with written and visual texts to understand an experience or event heightens insight, understanding, and metacognitive awareness (Wilhelm, 1997). Secondary students now have the ability to combine a variety of multimodal applications to express their feelings and engagements with the world. Creative opportunities await secondary teachers and students as digital technologies are embraced for making meaning. New textual constructions require the acknowledgment of the rightful place of visual literacy within the context of the English language arts curriculum and pedagogy.

Multimodal performance artist Natasha Tsakos (2009) has a message for English language arts teachers that embraces the rightful place of visual literacy:

> There is a revolution [going on]. It's a human and technological revolution. It is motion and emotion. It's information. It's visual. It's musical. It's sensorial. It's conceptual. It's universal. It's beyond words and numbers. It's happening, the natural progression of science and art find each other to better touch and define the human experience. There is a revolution in the way that we think, in the way that we share, and the way that we express our stories, our evolution. This is a time of communication, connection, and creative collaboration. (n.p.)

To explore the importance of visual literacy within Canadian secondary English language arts curricula, we display our own work with paintings, digital images, and poetry. The rationale for this work is based on our recognition that although well-schooled in various literatures, student teachers of English language arts often arrive in Bachelor of Education programs with limited experience working pedagogically with images.

How can visual literacy enable and challenge teachers to re-conceive language study, literacy practices, and the transmission of literacy heritage and knowledge in the humanities? To answer this question we must ask some basic questions about the curriculum and visual literacy in general, and explore why and how teacher candidates might be prepared to work with students as they go about constructing, deconstructing, and interpreting new texts. As well as coming to a curricular justification for the greater inclusion of visual literacy in secondary English classrooms, we offer some of our own text constructions (an acrylic painting and a photograph with accompanying poems) to help illuminate pedagogical possibilities. Visual literacy is a contested concept; for present purposes, we use a definition of visual literacy that includes all forms of visual media used in the expressive and receptive modes of communication.

Transmediation

One rainy March morning on Newfoundland's East Coast Trail, the relentless movement of sea fog engaged me. This was a day best viewed from a cabin or the shelter offered by a car. However, I ventured along the cliff's trail, protected by the close tangle of trees before standing exposed to the wind, rain, surf and fog to take this photograph.

Photograph by Barrie Barrell Copyright © 2012 Barrie Barrell

Voices of the Cliffs*

The voices of the cliffs hang in my mind
whispered secrets lifted up on the wind
to settle and dance.

My wet chin resting on a branch feeling
the mixture of sea spray and rain and
welcomes my warm pocketed hand.

The cliffs dressed in long icicles
drop to the ebbing tide resisting foaming
advances and cutting swirling power.

I zip my coat and sink back into the forest
and follow moose tracks to an open field
and the car that sits beyond.

The above pairing of photograph and poem demonstrates the act of transmediation. For secondary students, transmediation has the power to allow them to look directly at one art form and try to capture its essence through the use of another. When successful, such an engagement encourages the audience to relate more directly with the rhetorical vividness offered by the original artwork and to come to an enhanced understanding of it. Of course, the joint work can lead to the creation of a distinctly new artifact with its own power and essence. In bringing together a photograph or painting and poetry, a third piece of work emerges that moves beyond the stand-alone photograph, painting, or poem. Together, they offer a chance to illustrate more vividly the ongoing frantic assault of the sea, fog, rain, and wind upon the cliffs and trees.

The art processes involved in constructing meanings through an acrylic painting represent an evolutionary process within (and invisibly tethered to) the context of a subject and an audience. The tension within the construction process calls for an intense engagement with the elements and principles of design: the building blocks of art creation. Learners, moreover, invent the connection between two symbolic systems, linguistic and visual, as the connection does not exist *a priori* (Siegel, 1995). The elements (line, shape, direction, size, texture, colour, and value) and the principles of design (balance, gradation, repetition, contrast, harmony, dominance, and unity) come together in particular ways for a visual work to guide the learner in constructing a particular meaning of a literary work. Similarly, poetry may guide the learner in constructing a particular meaning of a visual work by illuminating particular connections among context and building blocks.

I Must Not Talk in School†

School… waiting, quietness, suppression
waiting for the bell, waiting for recess,
in silence waiting for lunch,
waiting for others to finish a story,
waiting to be engaged

---

* "Voices of the Cliffs" by Barrie Barrell. Copyright © 2012 Barrie Barrell.

† "I Must Not Talk In School" by Barrie Barrell. Copyright © 2012 Barrie Barrell.

in silence waiting in line to read,
waiting for someone to see your raised hand.
A suppressed voice inside talks quiet whispers
The voice stirs, mobilizes, surfaces
For the unveiling…
Nobody hears? The teacher does. Caught!
Arrested, sentenced, doing time
tethered to a chalkboard
Writing lines
I must not talk, I must not talk in school
the time seems to drag on forever
When will this be over?
I must not talk in school
Mindless repetition must not talk, must not talk,
silenced, stillness, shame, languid
Folded hands…talk, talk, must not talk.

"Writing Lines", painting by Linda Coles Copyright © 2012 Linda Coles

Transmediation provides a process for exploring the juncture of art and literature. Transmediated verse goes beyond sheer description and presents itself as a transformative critical statement, illuminating the art piece in all of its fecundity. The process provides an avenue for teachers of English language arts to embrace visual literacy practices as central to communication and meaning-making, alongside the centuries-long domination of texts and words in Western culture (Mitchell, 1995).

As outlined in the Western Protocol for English Language Arts Curriculum, the Ontario English Language Arts Curriculum, and the Foundation for the Atlantic Canada English Language Arts Curriculum, schools must engage students in a range of experiences and interactions that broaden the canons of traditional education and the curriculum through embracing an expanded definition of text. This expanded notion of text takes into account the visual representations with which students interact in their personal lives and from which they construct meaning on a daily basis. For, as Peter Felten (2008) suggests, "Living in an image-rich world . . . does not mean students (or faculty and administrators) naturally possess sophisticated visual literacy skills, just as continually listening to an iPod does not teach a person to critically analyze or create music" (p. 60).

The concept of visual literacy challenges teachers to find ways to help students develop the ability to recognize, interpret, and employ the distinct grammar, syntax, pragmatics, and semantics of different visual forms. Teachers are thereby challenged to re-conceive language study, literacy practice, and the transmission of literary heritage and knowledge.

References

Atlantic Provinces Education Foundation (APEF). (1996). *English language arts foundation.* Halifax, NS: Atlantic Provinces Education Foundation. http://doc-depot.ednet.ns.ca/

Branton, B. (1999). Visual literacy literature review. http://vicu.utoronto.ca/staff/branton/litreview.html (accessed September 17, 2010).

Government of Newfoundland and Labrador. (1995). *The Foundation for the Atlantic Canada English language arts curriculum.* Department of Education, St. John's, NL: Queens Printer.

Felten, P. (2008). Visual literacy. *Change: The Magazine of Higher Learning* 40(6), 60–64.

Heinich, R., Molenda, M., Russell, J. D., & Smaldino, S. E. (1999). *Instructional media and technologies for learning* (6th ed.). Upper Saddle River, NJ: Prentice-Hall.

Kellner, D. (1998). Multiple literacies and critical pedagogy in a multicultural society. *Educational Theory* 48(1), 103–122.

Miller, L. (2010). *Make me a story: Teaching writing through digital storytelling*. Portland, ME: Stenhouse Publishers.

Mitchell, W. J. (1995). *Picture Theory: Essays on verbal and visual representation.* Chicago, IL: University of Chicago Press.

Ontario Ministry of Education. (2007a). *The Ontario curriculum, grades 9 and 10: English, 2007 (revised).* Toronto, ON: Ministry of Education. http://www.edu.gov.on.ca/eng/curriculum/secondary/english910currb.pdf (accessed April 2, 2011).

Ontario Ministry of Education. (2007b). *The Ontario curriculum, grades 11 and 12: English, 2007 (revised).* Toronto, ON: Ministry of Education. http://www.edu.gov.on.ca/eng/curriculum/secondary/english1112currb.pdf (accessed April 2, 2011).

Siegel, M. (1995). More than words: The generative power of transmediation for learning. *Canadian Journal of Education* 20(4), 455–475.

Sinatra, R. (1986). *Visual literacy connections to thinking, reading and writing.* Springfield, IL: Charles C. Thomas.

Stokes, S. (2002). Visual literacy in teaching and learning: A literature perspective. *Electronic Journal for the Integration of Technology in Education* 1(1).

Tsakos, N. (2009). Multimedia theatrical adventure. http://newparadigmdigest.com/3347/great-performance-words-of-wisdom-from-multimedia-ted-presenter/ (accessed April 1, 2011).

West, T. G. (1997). *In the mind's eye.* Amherst, NY: Prometheus Books.

Wileman, R. E. (1993). *Visual communicating.* Englewood Cliffs, NJ: Educational Technology Publications.

Wilhelm, J. (1997). *You gotta be the book: Teaching engaged and reflective reading with adolescents.* Portsmouth, NH: Heinemann.

Why Is the Teaching of Graphic Novels Important in a Modern ELA Classroom?

By Jeff Park, University of Saskatchewan

The teaching of English language arts (ELA) is far more complex than it was just a few decades ago when most language classes were divided into two sections, literature and composition, with the primary focus in the field being on reading and writing. Most curricula now recognize six strands in a modern English language arts course—reading, writing, listening, speaking, representing, and viewing—as well as acknowledge a move towards cultural studies and the integration of social justice issues in the classroom.

In conjunction with the complexity of modern English language arts classrooms, secondary students are bombarded daily with visual and aural information through movies, television, internet sites, radio, DVDs, magazines, billboards, streaming video, smart phones, and ubiquitous digital video on YouTube. Educators have a responsibility to provide students with the means to navigate through complex multimedia, especially in critical visual literacy because of the prevalence of visual media in our culture. One simple way to introduce students to visual literacy issues is to use graphic novels in the classroom.

How Can Graphic Novels Introduce Concepts of Critical Visual Literacy?

Graphic novels are an effective and relatively inexpensive means of introducing critical literacy concepts in the classroom. Graphic novels integrate visual and textual elements to create meaning for the reader, and require different teaching approaches than those used for traditional texts such as novels or short stories. The narrative sequence in graphic novels is advanced by visual and textual elements, and because of this, both teachers and students need to become literate in a "visual syntax" in order to fully engage with a graphic novel. It is not enough for teachers to simply supply the novels, hand them out, and have students read them on their own without first teaching them the skills required to engage with graphic novels. Graphic novels require a specific form of integrated literacy skill to be fully understood and teachers must be well versed in how to read and understand comics or graphic narratives before they begin to teach them. Comics and graphic novels are a merging of visual and textual information, and their meaning is constructed through the holistic and simultaneous reading of both the visual and textual elements.

What Are the Important Visual Elements and Syntax of Graphic Novels?

Reading a graphic novel is different than reading traditional text, and students need guidance on how to engage in critical meaning-making. It is important to understand that the visual elements do not simply illustrate the text; instead, the visual elements work together with the text to create meaning. A brief summation of these visual elements may be helpful for both the teacher and the students.

Will Eisner (1985), one of the first to coin the phrase *graphic novel,* maintained that comics could be defined as "sequential art." One of the primary features of graphic novels is *cartooning,* a specific kind of drawing that uses hyperbole and metaphor as dominant qualities. Cartooning uses simple, symbolic lines as a kind of "visual shorthand [to] imply . . . temporal, spatial, and emotional effects" (Wolk, 2007, p. 120). Cartooning is rarely meant to be naturalistic, and usually it only hints at realistic complexity.

Graphic novelists use a series of established conventions to convey narrative sequence and symbolic meaning. The *panel* is the basic unit of meaning in a comic and can be defined as a frame that depicts a specific scene using both text and visuals. Panels are arranged sequentially on a page. The organization of the panels on a page is central to the understanding of the graphic novel's narrative sequence since the "framing of a series of images moving through space undertakes the containment of thoughts, ideas, actions, and locations or site" (Eisner, 1985, p. 38). Each panel is usually read in sequence from left to right like traditional text but this sequence may vary according to the size and arrangement of the panels. In connection with one another, the panels offer "a jagged, staccato rhythm of unconnected moments. But closure allows us to connect these moments and mentally construct a continuous unified reality" (McCloud, 1993, p. 67).

The *border* or outline of the panel creates a framework for the action, and this feature becomes part of the apparatus for suggesting such dimensions as size, time, and significance. The space between the panels is known as the *gutter* and can be used by the cartoonist to convey shifts in time and space. Text is handled in a number of ways. Expository text is usually contained by a square frame within the panel, while dialogue is conveyed through the use of speech balloons that are assigned to a specific character. Sound effects are usually conveyed through words operating almost as pictures, employing highly stylized lettering. In general, lettering is an important component in creating meaning in a comic since the graphemic design (font size, punctuation, bold, capitals, etc.) can all influence the meaning of a comic panel.

The comic page itself should be considered a unit of meaning in graphic narratives. This is quite different from a traditional text that simply wraps around to the next page. Spiegelman (2004) maintains that "Comic pages are architectural structures—the narrative rows of panels are stories of a building" (n.p.). Most graphic novelists design each page to convey information through the visual elements and the narrative itself. McCloud (1993) suggests "Our need for a unified language of comics sends us toward the center where words and pictures are like two sides of the same coin" (p. 49). Eisner's (1985) *Comics and Sequential Art*, and McCloud's (1993) *Understanding Comics: The Invisible Art* are excellent resources for both teachers and students to gain a quick understanding of the graphic art form, and how the various visual elements are used to create meaning in a graphic novel.

How Can I Decide What Graphic Novels to Use in a Classroom?

Graphic novels are now ubiquitous in modern society, and it is not always easy to decide what is suitable in the classroom. Educators are urged to seriously vet any material to ensure quality and relevance. There are many library resources available, including the American Library Association website, to recommend suitable graphic novels for schools. The following graphic novels are briefly described in order to provide a sample of suitable materials:

- Spiegelman's (1983, 1985) *Maus*, winner of a Pulitzer Prize special award, is a biographical memoir focusing on a son's relationship with his father, a Holocaust survivor. The graphic novel is drawn in a black and white expressionistic style, reminiscent of woodblock art, and the starkness of its graphic lines works well in conjunction with the narrative. Thematically, the graphic novel explores not only the historical ramification of the Holocaust, but also issues of family tensions and relationships, and the significance of memory. The book could also be used in conjunction with a novel study of *Anne Frank: Diary of a Young Girl* to further explore the relevant historical and social contexts from a different perspective. In *Maus* (German for mouse) all the characters are depicted anthropomorphically as animals: persons of Jewish heritage are presented as mice, German nationals as cats, Polish nationals as pigs, and American nationals as dogs. Students could be asked to explore the metaphorical significance of the animal imagery and how it connects to the specific narrative, as well as to stereotypes and historical contexts.
- Jeff Smith's (2004) *Bone* series is a good resource for all ages, although probably best for middle school or junior high. The series of books (also collected in one volume) follow the adventures of the three Bones—Phoney, Smiley, and Fone—as they find themselves lost and separated in a valley. The characters originally engage in a series of fun adventures, but the narrative eventually broadens into a fairly complex epic when "evil" approaches the valley, bringing with it growing intrigue and the potential of war.
- Ho Che Anderson's (2005) *King: A Comics Biography of Martin Luther King, Jr.* uses stark black and white drawings, and in doing so emphasizes the racial tension in the narrative. When colour is introduced later in the text, the shift is both profoundly moving, and shocking.
- Marjane Satrapi's (2003, 2004) *Persepolis* is a memoir of her experiences growing up (ages 6–14) in Iran during the Islamic Revolution and the overthrow of the Shah's regime. The graphic novel is an unforgettable exploration of growing up female in the contradictory worlds of Western culture and Islamic culture, examining complex issues of family, generational gaps, culture, society, history, and gender. The graphic novel is

predominantly autobiographical, but it is also a poignant portrait of daily life under authoritative religious fundamentalism.

- Craig Thompson's (2004) coming-of-age graphic novel *Blankets* is a nearly 600-page narrative with themes of spiritual identity, alienation, first-love, and teenage angst. Thompson's use of minimal prose is impressive, yet the narrative truly comes alive with the visual aspects that allow the "reader" to actually enter the complex world of the protagonist.

Why Use Graphic Novels in the Classroom?

Graphic novels could be used as a topic for more traditional literary studies and linked to social and cultural issues, as the best graphic novels have sufficient narrative depth, character development, and complexity of plot. The visual and textual aspects of graphic novels allow for the introduction of critical visual literacies that are extremely relevant in our modern society. Educators need to constantly question what it means to be literate in today's world, and, in doing so, consider aesthetic aspects as well as functional ones. The reading of graphic novels addresses how literacy can be viewed in a multimodal framework, linking different ways of expression and ways of interpreting those expressions.

Parts of this chapter drew upon earlier research in this area (Park, 2010).

References

Anderson, H. C. (2005). *King: A comics biography of Martin Luther King, Jr.* Seattle, WA: Fantagraphics Books.

Eisner, W. (1985). *Comics and sequential art*. Tamarac, FL: Poorhouse Press.

McCloud, S. (1993). *Understanding comics: The invisible art*. New York: Kitchen Sink Press/Harper Perennial.

Park, J. (2010). Graphic novels in the modern English language arts classroom: Acknowledging the complexity of literacy. In T. Gambell & M. C. Courtland (Eds.), *Literature, media and multiliteracies in adolescent language arts* (pp. 173–188). Vancouver, BC: Pacific Educational Press.

Satrapi, M. (2003). *Persepolis: The story of a childhood*. New York: Pantheon.

Satrapi, M. (2004). *Persepolis 2: The story of a return*. New York: Pantheon.

Smith, J. (2004). *Bone: The complete cartoon epic in one volume*. Columbus, OH: Cartoon Books.

Spiegelman, A. (1983). *Maus: A survivor's tale. I: My father bleeds history*. New York: Pantheon Books.

Spiegelman, A. (1985). *Maus: A survivor's tale. II: And here my troubles began*. New York: Pantheon Books.

Spiegelman, A. (2004). *In the shadow of no towers*. New York: Pantheon Books.

Wolk, D. (2007). *Reading comics: How graphic novels work and what they mean*. Cambridge, MA: Da Capa Press.

Thompson, C. (2004). *Blankets*. Marietta, GA: Top Shelf Productions.

SECTION **3**

Digital Worlds and Opportunities

How Can Video Games Support Literacy Skills for Youth?

By Kathy Sanford and Liz Merkel, University of Victoria

Though current research recognizes that video gaming involves complex, immersive, and socially constructed learning and literacy possibilities (e.g., Gee, 2003; Gee, 2007; Squire, 2008; Sanford & Madill, 2007; Black & Steinkuehler, 2009), video games remain highly controversial in the media and are not readily accepted as a valid form of text for literacy learning. Commercial video games have provoked discomfort for some parents, educators, and news media organizations due to questionable graphics and content (e.g., themes of violence, stereotypical and problematic images), and also due to the perceived immersion of youth in digital worlds that are often unknown to older generations. Through our in-depth discussions with 15 youth over five years of research, we have been able to both recognize and begin to articulate the complex literacies in which many youth engage. We have come to believe that educators need to know about these new literacy forms and the ways youth engage with them in order to enhance contemporary school-based literacy learning.

The types of literacies involved in video gaming disrupt conventional notions of literacy that are most familiar to educators (the ability to read so-called linear, print-based texts), which, as Squire (2008) suggests, are propagated as the "*right* kinds of 'literary' texts" (p. 635, italics in original). As such, it is difficult for lifelong readers and educators of the "right kinds" of texts to imagine how video gaming might provide rich literacy opportunities for youth. We have found that the experiences of our teenage participants have enabled us, as educators and researchers, to reconceptualize our notions of literacy learning.

Black and Steinkuehler (2009) advance the metaphor of the "constellation of literacy activities" in contemporary gaming[6] to describe the multi-faceted ways in which game communities not only read but also produce, distribute, and perform texts. Similarly, we have recognized this phenomenon as "rhizomatic" (Deleuze & Guattari, 1987; Moulthrop, 1995; Sanford, Merkel, & Madill, 2011). That is, when players are engaged in a video game, they are certainly engaged in the storyline and text right in front of them. However, there is also a complex and catalytic back-story wherein players have engaged in multiple forms of on- and off-line texts and practices relating to the particular game at hand. Black and Steinkuehler (2009) categorize such related activities as follows: "in-game text based interaction"; "in-game literacy practices"; and the "out-of-game online world of fandom" (p. 277). Here we use Black and Steinkuehler's (2009) categories to describe just a glimpse of the "constellation of literacy activities" in which we have witnessed our youth participants engaging.

In-Game Text-Based Interaction

Engagement with video games enables sophisticated problem-based learning (Gee, 2007) and "reading" of a wide range of print-based, visual, and aural media—often simultaneously and rapidly in order to be successful in completing the game. A range of genres, blended fictional or non-fictional multimodal texts, and symbolism are incorporated. We have observed learners following complex story lines that change somewhat according to choices made in the game; developing their own "avatars" or characters who are designed with specific personalities and skills to fulfill roles within that game; navigating maps and symbols in order to strategize and solve problems; and reading and writing "text talk" (Black & Steinkuehler, 2009), an evolving short-form language with complex icons, symbols, abbreviations, and terminology developed for quick processing.

In-Game Literacy Practices

Formed from the in-game text-based interactions, players are navigating gaming worlds to communicate online in social groups, both orally and in instant messaging, in forming collaborative guilds and teams. In these groups, players work towards game goals, barter

---

6 Black and Steinkuehler (2009) use the example of MMO (Massively Multiplayer Online) game play to describe these literacy activities. Some examples of these games are *World of Warcraft, GuildWars,* and *Lineage.* More and more games are being developed as MMOs, and some that were previously off-line have been re-designed to have online components (e.g., *Halo*). This chapter by Black and Steinkuehler is found in the *Handbook of Adolescent Literacy Research* (Christenbury, Bomor, & Smagorinsky, Eds.) and is an excellent resource for literacy in virtual worlds.

for goods within role-play games, teach others skills and strategies, and try out new strategies as they make choices in game play.

Out-of-Game Literacy

What may surprise many educators and concerned adults is that most video game players access and contribute to a variety of complex literacy activities related to their game play in order to develop in-game expertise. We have observed youth engage in the following activities: read and write in-depth critiques of games played; research upcoming games on online forums and blog sites; research voice actors, game developers and designers of particular games; videotape their game play, review it in order to reflect on mistakes made in play, and then post clips online for other gamers; host personal blogs in order to discuss games and strategies; write movie scripts and record readings for previously completed game play; host face-to-face gaming parties and social events; and hold interesting conversations displaying expertise and social receptiveness.

When asked about the pedagogical implications for the types of literacy video games can support, we resist the urge (and popular demand) to deliver a set of rigid guidelines about how to implement video games in the classroom. We are not suggesting that our students only play *Halo* instead of reading novels in English. That is, "the task for games [and literacy] scholars is not to argue *how* games necessarily fit within traditional forms, but to better understand how games are *transforming* previous forms" (Squire, 2008, p. 642, italics in original). We observe that youth are *already* engaged in sophisticated, self-directed, and immersive literacy activities both in and out of game play. The task for teachers is to acknowledge and become informed about these literacy activities, engage in conversation with students about them, and then to creatively adjust their pedagogy to invite the "constellation of literacy activities" into classrooms. Recognizing that youth have sophisticated knowledge about a wide array of media and texts and are eager to engage in meaningful activities, we invite teachers to consider the possibilities suggested by our video game research for their own classroom practices.

We suggest that this invitation involve the following:

1. **Long-term, process-based activities:** Learners are immersed in self-managed, long-term projects/games featuring a rich storyline and complex issues to be addressed, or problems to be solved that develop progressively into a final and successful completion rather than short, one-off worksheet assignments.
2. **Multiple ways to approach activities:** Learners have choice in the issues, problems, and stories that they select and ways that they approach problem-solving; they are confident and supported in taking risks to find the most appropriate and challenging strategies rather than activities with simplistic right or wrong answers that serve to discourage risk-taking and multiple tries.
3. **Productive play** (see Pearce, 2006): Learners engage in constant tinkering, trying, and re-trying around sophisticated series of challenges and problems that increase in difficulty as learners advance towards the overarching goal (Gee, 2007). This allows students to be engaged in self-directed ways of creating and strategizing with the emphasis on *playing* with ideas and concepts to produce creative and original works, rather than working to re-produce something already existing, as in the industrial model.

4. **Multi-literacy constellations and relationships:** Learners work in multiple ways, making sense of new information and drawing on multiple literacies and forms of texts rather than within one medium; learners engage with diverse social groupings rather than being situated independent of a collective of other learners. Further, when given both choice and support, learners can both access and contribute to a learning community in ways they find meaningful to their own learning and to the knowledge of the collective.

This last point is strengthened by Squire's (2008) definition of games literacy: "Games literacy can be defined as developing expertise in designing rewarding experiences for oneself within a gameworld" (pp. 639–640). Learners who demonstrate literacy in video game play and related multiliteracies are active participants in their own learning agenda, seeking out information and developing expertise within immersive activities and texts.

Acknowledging the gameworld experiences of youth not only recognizes their interests and expertise, but also supports the aims of mandated curricula by enabling students to make meaning of the world and to prepare them to participate effectively in all aspects of society (e.g., BC Ministry of Education, 2007; Alberta Education, 2003; Ontario Ministry of Education, 2007). If students are to comprehend and respond, communicate, think critically and creatively, reflect on their thinking and learning, and develop an increasing understanding of themselves and others, then experience with the multiple literacies of video gameworlds can only enhance their abilities in all aspects of their complex lives. Rather than ignoring and dismissing the vast knowledge of literacy and new literacies that youth have gained through engagement with video games, it is imperative that teachers recognize and draw on the broad array of skills and understandings students have developed in order to re-engage them in English language arts.

References

Alberta Education. (2007). English language arts. http://education.alberta.ca/media/645805/srhelapofs.pdf (accessed January 2, 2012).

BC Ministry of Education. (2007). English language arts 8 to 12. http://www.bced.gov.bc.ca/irp/course.php?lang=en&subject=English_Language_Arts&course=English_Language_Arts_8_to_12&year=2007 (accessed January 2, 2012).

Black, R. W. & Steinkuehler, C. (2009). Literacy in virtual worlds. In L. Christenbury, R. Bomer, & P. Smagorinsky (Eds.), *Handbook of adolescent literacy research* (pp. 271–286). New York: Guilford.

Deleuze, G. & Guattari, F. (1987). *A thousand plateaus*. (B. Massumi, Trans.). Minneapolis, MN: University of Minnesota Press.

Gee, J. (2003). *What videogames have to teach us about learning and literacy*. New York: Palgrave Macmillan.

Gee, J. (2007). *Good video games and good learning*. New York: Peter Lang.

Moulthrop, S. (1995). Rhizome and resistance: Hypertext and the dreams of a new culture. In G. P. Landow (Ed.), *Hyper/Text/Theory*, (pp. 299-320). Baltimore, MD: Johns Hopkins University Press.

Ontario Ministry of Education. (2007). http://www.edu.gov.on.ca/eng/curriculum/secondary/english910currb.pdf

Pearce, C. (2006). Productive play: Game culture from the bottom up. *Games and Culture* 1(1), 17–24.

Picard, M. (2006). Machinima: Video game as art form? [Electronic version]. *Proceedings of CGSA 2006 Symposium: Authors & Canadian Games Study Association CGSA.*

Sanford, K., Merkel, L., & Madill, L. (2011). "There's no fixed course": Rhizomatic learning communities in adolescent videogaming. *Loading...,* 5(8). http://journals.sfu.ca/loading/index.php/loading/article/view/93 (accessed May 3, 2012).

Sanford, K. & Madill, L. (2007). Understanding the power of new literacies through video game play and design. *Canadian Journal of Education* 30(2), 432–455.

Squire, K. (2008). Video game literacy: A literacy of expertise. In J. Coiro, M. Knobel, C. Lankshear, & D. Leu (Eds.), *Handbook of research on new literacies* (pp. 635–669). New York: Lawrence Erlbaum Associates.

What's the Fuss about "Intellectual Property"?

By John Willinsky, Stanford University

Do Students Have Reason to Be Interested in IP?

Students encounter IP with every website they use, every video game they play, every song they download, as well as every book they read. They will enter a job market dominated by knowledge-based economies that trade in IP. Thus, anything that they can learn about IP with regard to their own rights and those of others will help to prepare them for situations in which they create, share, and trade in IP.

How Does IP Relate to Copyright Law?

In Canadian law, the expression of an idea is generally regarded as a form of IP that is protected by the Copyright Act. While IP can also take the legal form of a patent, trademark, or trade secret, in our work as teachers, IP typically takes the form of texts, including multimedia works. Whether published or unpublished, whether by Margaret Atwood or a student in class, any composition can be regarded as IP and, as such, is protected by copyright law. That is, authors have a right to control the reproduction and use of their work without having to register it, publish it, or take any other action beyond representing their ideas and experiences in words or in other media, such as a still or moving image.

What's the Point of Copyrighting IP?

It is wise to remember that copyright was not originally instituted to protect the songs of Metallica. It began in the early eighteenth century in English law "for the encouragement of learning." It was intended to protect authors and their publishers from publications of writings in pirated editions that prevented the author and original publisher from making a living. Copyright law today is also designed to protect an author's IP by preventing others from using (copying) that work without the author's permission or, potentially, payment.

How Does Copyright Work?

The Canadian Copyright Act gives the creator and his or her estate rights over a work for 50 years after the author's death. Sometimes a publisher will ask an author for a transfer of rights to the publisher before the work is published. Those who violate someone's copyright by copying the work and distributing it can be taken to court. This has happened more often in recent times with illegally downloaded music by bands such as Metallica than it has with the surreptitious copying of Canadian poetry.

How Can My Students Legally Use Copyrighted Work?

There are a number of provisions to protect the rights of students and teachers to use copyrighted work to advance their learning. First of all, the Canadian Ministers of Education pay an annual fee to Access Copyright that allows individual students as well as whole classes to use much of the print material in Canadian schools, with a portion of the fees distributed to authors and publishers. In addition, students should know that under the Fair Dealing clause of the Copyright Act in Canada, they may copy portions of a work for purposes of their own study and research. Fair Dealing also allows students who are writing about a work in a review or essay to quote from that work or show part of it (for visual works) for use in their own publication (on the Web, for example). They can also draw on others' copyrighted works to create a new work of art, as this creative right is protected within the Fair Dealing clause in the Copyright Act. However, in Canada, the "moral rights" of authors and artists protects the integrity of the work (resulting from a famous case in which the artist Michael Snow sued the Eaton Centre in Toronto for adorning his sculpture of geese with festive bows). Finally, a current legislative initiative to "modernize" Canadian copyright law includes a clause that would, if passed, allow students to creatively remix content for non-commercial purposes.

So There's Really No Danger of Violation in Schools?

It is true that the chances of running into trouble on this issue are pretty slim because of the Fair Dealing clause of the Copyright Act and the financial arrangements with Access Copyright. However, apart from the legalities of one's teaching, there are sound educational reasons for introducing the concept of IP into the classroom. Otherwise, students are missing out on learning about the value of their own intellectual work and that of others. Even as the legal terrain for IP is rapidly changing with the digital era, social movements are afoot to increase the educational and democratic qualities of our intellectual lives beyond the schools.

Are There Any Alternatives to Copyright?

Some authors or creators feel that copyright is too restrictive, impeding other people's use of their own work. These people are now able to place their work under a Creative Commons licence, which allows others to freely use the work, typically with just an acknowledgement of the original creator of the work. The advanced search functions in Google and Yahoo, for example, can be used to search for "free to share" works, and this will allow students to find pictures, music, and other resources for their projects that are not covered by Access Copyright. This is particularly helpful if the students are publishing their work on the Internet; it is also valuable insofar as it enables them to understand the alternative idea of people wanting to share their IP and contribute to a "creative commons." *Wikipedia* is a massive public works project in the production of IP that is placed under a Creative Commons licence. It serves as an excellent example of how students can contribute to IP and learn about how the concept works in shared and public ways, as well as how it may be applied to other cases such as a pop song, a commercial, or any number of private ways.

What about Work Said to Be in the Public Domain?

After the copyright on a work has expired, it enters the public domain where there are no restrictions on reprinting, posting online, or using the work. This applies, for example, to the texts of Charles Dickens and Jane Austen, texts that anyone who wants to may now legally publish (although a scholarly edition of a work, given the additional work that has gone into preparing it, may be copyright protected).

What Does IP Have to Do with the Students' Own Work?

While the economics of IP are an important aspect of today's work world, money is not the whole picture. Learning in schools is often about working with and creating intellectual properties that do not operate on a commercial basis. If one student shares a poem with the class or creates a poster that teaches others how to do something, the student has created an IP of value to others. Students can then begin to see how creating IP goes beyond just learning about something. It also has to do with working hard to communicate what has been learned to others and to communicate it well enough so that it can inspire learning and delight.

How Can Students Increase the Value of Their IP?

While all writing that a student does creates a form of IP, there are ways of increasing the value of that work as IP. Following the principles already mentioned, students can direct their learning toward creating intellectual properties that are designed to be of value to their communities. There are plenty of examples of students making and preparing materials that make a contribution to local history, environmental studies, public art and music, all of which others are able to enjoy, use, learn from, and appreciate. The students can come to realize that their learning has value as they create intellectual properties that contribute to the learning of others.

What about Student and Teacher Access to Research and Scholarship?

One area where IP has become a public issue in recent years is access to the research and scholarship produced by universities. Here a movement known as "open access" has been working to make more of this published work available to individuals outside of the universities that cannot afford to pay the subscription fees charged by academic journals. By searching on a topic with Google Scholar, teachers and advanced students can discover published scholarly work that may add to their own work. About a quarter of the research articles that are published each year are now made freely available online through open access. Although the students' use of these resources is bound to be limited, it does provide an excellent opportunity to look into quality of knowledge issues that trouble IP online.

Where Can I See This Approach to Intellectual Property in Action?

Among the many sites students have created that demonstrate the value of IP, one of the most intriguing is a wiki (http://wikimarion.org/Main_Page) on Marion, Indiana, in which students have captured and shared the history of their community. As well, Comments4Kids (http://comments4kids.wikispaces.com/) is a site that lists student blogs, inviting further commenting and engagement with their work.

What If I Wanted to Learn More about This Topic?

Among the resources available for following up on this theme is the Creative Commons site (http://creativecommons.org/), which provides a variety of ready-to-cut-and-paste types of licences for sharing IP. As for books on new approaches to IP, there is a series of academic texts by authors who have decided to make their contributions freely available online, as part of their own response to this issue:

Benkler, Yochai. (2006). *The wealth of networks: How social production transforms markets and freedom*. New Haven and London: Yale University Press. http://cyber.law.harvard.edu/wealth_of_networks/Download_PDFs_of_the_book

Boyle, James. (2008). *The public domain: Enclosing the commons of the mind*. New Haven and London: Yale University Press. http://www.thepublicdomain.org/download/

Lessig, Lawrence. (2008). *Remix: Making art and commerce thrive in the hybrid economy*. New York: Penguin. http://www.bloomsburyacademic.com/remix.htm

Willinsky, John. (2006). *The access principle: The case for open access to research and scholarship*. Cambridge, MA: MIT Press. http://mitpress.mit.edu/catalog/item/default.asp?tid=10611&ttype=2

As well, there are a number of resources for students freely available online:

Ikpeze, Chinwe H. (2009). Writing for real purpose. *Learning & Leading with Technology* 36(7), 36–37. http://www.eric.ed.gov/ERICWebPortal/contentdelivery/servlet/ERICServlet?accno=EJ839530

Imperatore, Catherine. (2009). What you need to know about Web 2.0. *Techniques: Connecting Education and Careers* 84(1), 20–23. http://www.eric.ed.gov/ERICWebPortal/contentdelivery/servlet/ERICServlet?accno=EJ829501

Much, Jocelyn. (2009). Blogging as a tool for meaningful learning for sustainability education: A review of the literature. http://mrsmuch.com/blog/wp-content/uploads/2009/05/bloggingasameaningfullearningtool.pdf

Ray, Jan. (2006). Welcome to the Blogoshere: The educational use of blogs (aka Edublogs). *Kappa Delta Pi Record* 42(4), 175–177. http://www.eric.ed.gov/ERICWebPortal/contentdelivery/servlet/ERICServlet?accno=EJ738088

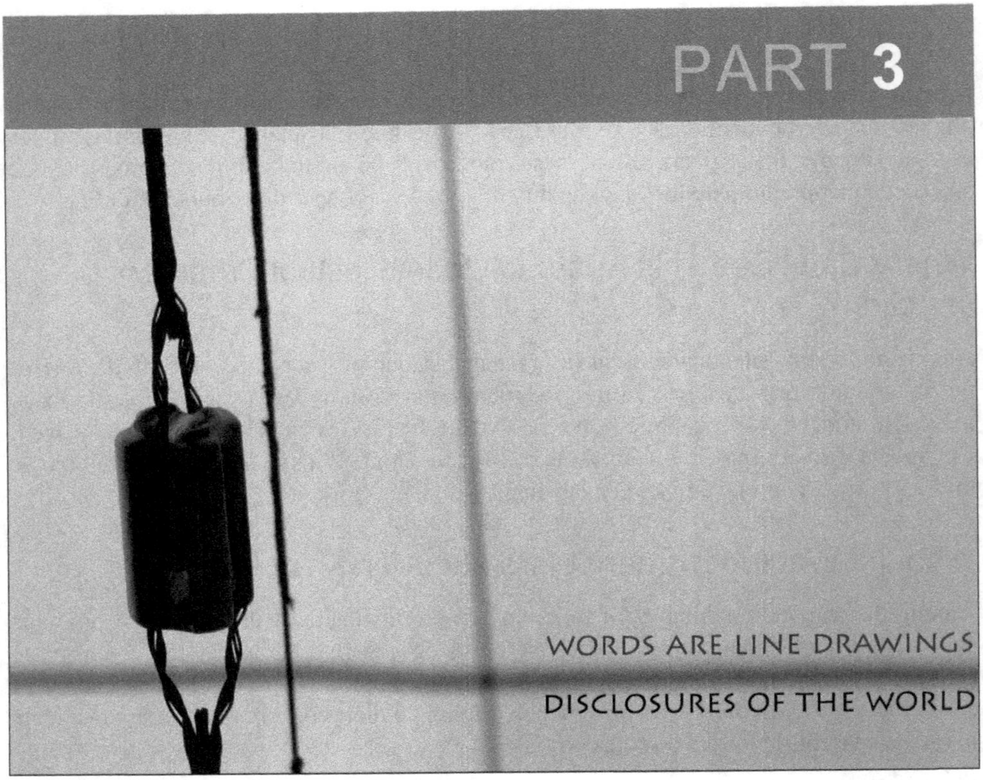

Inspiring Imagination and Creativity

By Carl Leggo, University of British Columbia

Beginning with Questions

In *Art Objects: Essays on Ecstasy and Effrontery,* Jeanette Winterson (1995) asks: "Can we afford to live imaginatively, contemplatively? Why have we submitted to a society that tries to make imagination a privilege when to each of us it comes as a birthright?" (p. 139). English language arts educators have a profound and poetic responsibility to invite and inspire imagination and creativity. Richard E. Miller (2005) asks in *Writing at the End of the World,* "Why go on teaching when everything seems to be falling apart? Why read when the world is overrun with books? Why write when there's no hope of ever gaining an audience?" (p. x). These are the kinds of questions that English language educators need to ask. We need a thoughtful rationale for the importance of our work as English teachers. Miller claims that "posing such questions aloud is not a sign of despair; it's a way to start a conversation about how and why reading, writing, and teaching the literate arts can be made to continue to matter in the twenty-first century" (p. x).

Like most English language arts teachers, I enthusiastically contend that literature is a significant means by which all of us are constructed as social beings. We develop a sense of our own identity as well as the identities of others from the images and stories of people we read about. Literature provides us with possibilities for human living and relationships. As English language arts educators, we need to ask questions such as the following: What criteria do we use when making decisions about the literature that we teach? How well-read are we in literature that is local, or contemporary, international, or canonical? Are we convinced that there are 100 Great Books of Western Culture that stand as a towering touchstone against which all literature ought to be evaluated? Do we expect students to find the "correct" meaning in a literary text? Do different readers respond differently to the same literary texts? Are some literary versions of lived experience more appropriate for reading and discussing in classrooms? These questions get at the heart of why we read literature, and why our students *should* read literature.

Reasons for Reading Literature

As readers and educators, we need to choose a wide range of literature so that we can read imaginatively, creatively interrogating the images of human beings and human life given to us in literature. Fundamentally, this allows us to create new possibilities for ways of being in the world. Because we write, read, think, talk, listen, represent, and know ourselves and others through language, literature is a significant means by which we disclose and construct our understandings of the world. When we read a text, we bring our language experiences into connection with the language of the text, with the language experiences of the writer, and with the whole cultural enterprise of literature. In these connections there is a dynamic dialogue. We learn about ourselves, we learn about others, and we learn about the world, all through words. Like Alberto Manguel (1996), English language educators need to deconstruct "the artificial dichotomy between life and reading" (p. 21). So, English educators can benefit from considering why reading literature is important. I propose six main reasons as a beginning to the conversation.

1. Reading Literature Teaches Us How to Live

Like Nancy Malone (2003), I read in order "to stay alive, to be as fully alive as I can be" (p. 32). No single activity has consumed more of my life than reading. My earliest memories include books. Malone claims that "reading helps us, helps me, to love" (2003, p. 177). So, reading is a way of living and loving in words and in the world. Malone spells out how "reading . . . is a spiritual practice" (2003, p. 3), and she invites us to "consider the influence of reading" in our lives (2003, p. 5). For Malone, reading is an ongoing search for the "'meaning of life,' a portrayal of who I am called to be" (2003, pp. 119–120). Too much of the education enterprise is focused on cognitive learning, training the mind and brain in rationalization, objectivity, argumentation, and exposition. We need a matching commitment to holistic education that acknowledges the integrity of body, mind, brain, spirit, heart, and emotions. Reading is a way of living in the world. We need to learn to read critically and interrogatively. Learning to read critically is not necessarily the same as learning to read. As readers, we are all engaged in a lifetime journey of reading critically and learning to read critically. I agree with Mark Edmundson (2004), who claims that "the test of a book lies in its power to map or transform a life" (p. 129). Literature invites us to live in words and live in the world through ongoing processes of learning and composing.

2. Reading literature teaches us to question

In *Why Read?* Edmundson (2004) claims that literature is "our best goad toward new beginnings" (p. 3). Arguing for the ways that language shapes and informs and transforms our understanding of experience and identity in what we might call the story of our lives, Edmundson calls for a liberal education that uses "books to rejuvenate, reaffirm, replenish, revise, overwhelm, replace, in some cases (alas) even help begin to generate the web of words that we're defined by" (2004, p. 31), especially because this "web of words" is "a new language" (p. 31) that can help create "a new way to live" (2004, p. 32). So, literature provides the language we need in order to grow critical, subversive, interrogative, skeptical, ironic, visionary, and even prophetic about our ways of being in the world, and about other possibilities for being in the world. Edmundson writes about the need to acknowledge our ignorance and our confusion so that we can enter into a place of learning and knowing. So much of my literary education was based on games of finding the theme. In school, I was like a tireless detective, always seeking to break the code of the text, to decipher the hidden meanings, to find the secret messages cleverly tucked away amidst the syntax. I now promote a pedagogy of questioning.

3. Reading literature teaches us to play

Like Anna Quindlen (1998), "I lived within the covers of books and those books were more real to me than any other thing in my life" (p. 4). The reader brings characters and places and stories to life. The reader breathes life into books and imagines how the characters are like real people, or how real people are like characters in books. We read books in order "to take the measure of ourselves" (Quindlen, 1998, p. 13). Like Quindlen, "in books I have travelled, not only to other worlds, but into my own. I learned who I was and who I wanted to be, what I might aspire to, and what I might dare to dream about my world and myself" (1998, p. 6).

Our reading responses are determined by the kind of people we are—our personalities, our experiences, our views, and our attitudes. Different readers will respond differently to different texts at different times in their lives, and all these possibilities of difference fire the spirit of reading as an experience of personal growth in identity and relationship. The reader brings characters and places and stories to life. The reader breathes life into books, inspires the characters, experiences, emotions, plots, settings, and themes in order to bring them to life. I object to interpretive closure. There can be no univocal, authoritative reading of a text. There is always more. I encourage a multiplicity of responses. I promote playing with texts. I celebrate the wildness of language, full of wonder.

4. Reading literature teaches us to connect with one another

Reading literature opens up possibilities for sympathy and empathy, for heart connections among readers, readers and authors, and readers and characters. Quindlen's (1998) claim that "I read because I loved it more than any other activity on earth" (p. 9) resonates with my personal experience, but as I linger with this claim, I realize that I have always had a difficult time understanding others who do not share my passion for reading. I have known almost no one else who reads as voraciously, with the same kind of vivacious, voluptuous rapture. So, as a teacher, how can I hope to inspire or instil or incite a love for literature? My love of literature seems innate—all my life I have loved books (reading, collecting, owning), but I understand that many people do not feel that way. Therefore, as an English educator, I will constantly confront the challenge of lack of interest in reading.

5. Reading literature teaches us to browse

In the contemporary culture of speed, where everybody and everything seem caught up in a frantic and frenetic pace, reading literature can slow us down and invite us to browse, to linger, to breathe, to understand how life is composed in a process or journey of experiences, choices, decisions, and contingencies. Geoffrey O'Brien (2000) writes, "I will wonder, years later, if my life would have been quite different if I had not, on such and such a day, opened a certain book to a certain page" (p. 22). This is a fascinating issue that relates to questions of identity and humanity. Who might I have become if I had been born in a different place, in a different family, in a different time? Who might I have become if I had read other books, more books, or fewer books? My autobiography is written in the circumstances of lived and living experiences that are often perceived as given, determined, preordained, predestined. O'Brien reminds us to consider how we are participants in a field of expansive existence and consciousness, unendingly spacious and timeless.

So, reading is a kind of wayfinding, a sojourning in the complex and beautiful world by attending to words. O'Brien holds out the promise, or at least the possibility, that in reading we will "find beyond the last full stop a tabula rasa where silence grows wild" (2000, p. 148). Reading is not consumption or interpretation; reading is a way of living in words with artful and heartful attention to wonder.

6. Reading literature teaches us to celebrate

By reading literature, I learn how to celebrate, how to laugh and grieve, how to acknowledge joy, and how to express a critical consciousness. To celebrate is to remember and to care and to hope. Literature invites us to live in words and to live in the world. Literature is valuable because it encourages us to ruminate on how we live, and to raise questions about values, ideas, experiences, and emotions. Literature reminds us that we are alive, and that all of us are living essentially the same human stories, over and over, even if in different places and times and contexts. When we can come to see ourselves as all living the same human stories, we can embrace the joy and pain of living and being alive. Helping our students come to this point can be the greatest challenge of an English teacher. Indeed, my own less-than-ideal experiences as a student led me to the attitudes outlined above and to a more capacious understanding of how to teach literature.

Approaches to Teaching and Reading Literature

I went to school in the 1960s when the approach to teaching literature in school classrooms was modelled on the approach to teaching literature in university classrooms. This was often called the New Critical approach. It involved a close attention to the literary text as a text. It was assumed that a literary text had a unitary meaning and that all the parts of the text worked together to illustrate and emphasize that meaning. The reader's responsibility was to name the meaning and demonstrate how the meaning was developed in the text. To this end, I read poems and stories and essays in a fat anthology and answered endless lists of comprehension questions. The main goal of reading was connected to successfully answering these inevitable questions. Only after I began to teach did I learn about the reader response approach, which promotes an understanding of reading as a creative process where a reader actively engages in a transaction with a text. According to Louise Rosenblatt (1978), "the reading of a text is an event occurring at a particular time in a particular environment at a particular moment in the life history of the reader. The transaction will involve not only the past experience but also the present state and present interests or preoccupations of the reader" (p. 20). This approach to reading literature has been popular in many classrooms for at least two decades, but it has been ignored or rejected by teachers who think that the reader response approach fails to pay sufficient attention to the complexity of a literary text. In brief, many teachers think that the reader response approach to reading only invites subjective and personal responses that ignore the many ways that a text is crafted and shaped *as* a text, as well as the social and cultural and political contexts in which texts are written and published and read. So, my aim is to promote a reader response approach to reading texts that pays careful attention to the complex dynamics of the interaction of readers and writers and texts and cultural contexts.

There is no one approach to reading literature that ought to be used all the time. While some think the New Critical approach to reading focuses too much attention on the text, some think that the reader response approach focuses too much attention on the reader. I promote a reader response approach that takes into account the many dynamics at work in reading. Indeed, reading is a productive and creative transaction with a text. The meaning does not reside in the text, and the meaning does not reside in the reader. Instead, the meaning resides in the transaction between the two. There is a kind of balance between the reader and the text. On the one hand, the reader's personality, emotions, and experiences are all called into active participation with the text. On the other hand, the text is a system of signs that helps guide the reader's response. In this way, both the subjective and the objective aspects of the reading process are married. This interrelationship is worth returning to for a moment.

The reader response approach invites readers to bring their experiences and emotions and thoughts and questions to the reading experience. Instead of trying to decode a complicated text for its sometimes hidden and obscure meaning, the readers know that they are collaborating with the text and the author to create the meaningfulness of the text. "Reading is a complex experience," writes Manguel (1996), "which involves the reader and the writer and the text in a relationship of generating meaning" (p. 39). He continues, "Reading . . . is not an automatic process of capturing a text in the way photosensitive paper captures light, but a bewildering, labyrinthine, common and yet personal process of reconstruction" (1996, p. 39). The reader does not make the meaning alone, any more than does the writer or the text. The meaning is produced as the reader and the writer and the text interact together. The reader response approach suggests that in order to foster the process of interaction, readers need literary competence and an awareness of how texts are constructed and constrained and comprehended in the larger contexts of the world of publishing, literary reviews, heritage, and teaching. Therefore, teachers should use a combination of approaches that encourages readers to make their own personal connections to literature, while also understanding the contexts of its production.

Transcending Single Approaches

Indeed, there is value in all the approaches, traditional and contemporary, to teaching literature. Literature is eminently capacious and can readily accommodate a diverse range of approaches for fostering reading, interrogating, and responding. Teachers need to teach out of their enthusiasms, and teachers and students need to approach literature with an openness to creative exploration. In *Creativity: Flow and the Psychology of Discovery and Invention,* Mihaly Csikszentmihalyi (1996) concludes that "the most important message we can learn from creative people" is "how to find purpose and enjoyment in the chaos of existence" (p. 20). He notes that the diverse creative people he and his research team interviewed "all agree that they do what they do primarily because it's fun" (1996, p. 107). Also, he notes that "the first step toward a more creative life is the cultivation of curiosity and interest, that is, the allocation of attention to things for their own sake" (1996, p. 346). English teachers need to nurture in students an ongoing experience of creative engagement with literature.

A reader brings to the reading of a poem, story, novel, essay, or drama a set of assumptions, practices, and rules regarding what these different genres are and, just as importantly, how they produce effects and how they ought to be read. This understanding comprises part of the reader's ideology about reading literature. The reader also brings to reading literature a set of values, beliefs, and views about the world, human experiences, and his or her own relationships among people. This understanding comprises part of the reader's ideology about society, culture, and history. So, readers always read out of their ideological stance—the assumptions and practices that inform their views about literature and society. In addition, a literary text is also constrained by ideology, including the rules or conventions that the text uses, as well as the views or assumptions about what is "natural" and appropriate for the culture represented in the text. The act of reading a literary text is, then, the production of meaning that occurs when the reader's ideological perspectives and the text's ideological perspectives come together. The most successful readings will occur when there is openness to new ideas, questions, and ways of interrogating or knowing the world through another's lived experience.

Our readings will be polyvalent, tension-filled, and tentative, not the stuff of a neat and tidy classroom experience. Reading is, then, always a process—ongoing, flexible, changing. I encourage students to be skeptical, critical, and creative in their responses. We never read the same text twice. My goal as a teacher is always to open up the experience of reading so that it is filled with fun, insight, and enthusiasm for living in creative ways. We need to understand that the reading of literature is connected to our living in the world, part of a dynamic process of growth, and we need to communicate our readings to one another. Our readings will be diverse, tentative, transformative; our readings will be full of the energy at the heart of pedagogy that seeks a living with wellness in the world by living creatively in words.

It is very important, then, to keep this in mind: as there are many reasons for teaching literature, there are also many approaches to teaching literature. I have taught literature in many different ways. I have promoted approaches informed by New Critical textual analysis, reader response, cultural criticism, cultural heritage, cultural literacy, postmodernism, deconstruction, semiotics, feminism, and Marxism. What counts is engaging with texts so that they stay with us. In the literature classroom, we need to focus on the texts, on the ways we respond to the texts, and on the ways that our conversations together open up possibilities for meaning-making. In my own approach to teaching literature, I seek to promote an understanding of reading as a way of growing, being, and living in the world. In order to promote literacy, we need to learn to read literature critically, interrogatively, and creatively. (Learning to read critically, it's worth noting, is not necessarily the same as learning to read. I do not expect young children to read with the critical insight of adolescents or adults, but, in my experience, I also know that young children can be encouraged and supported in reading critically, and I know that many adolescents and adults do *not* read critically.) As readers, we are all engaged in a lifetime journey of reading critically and learning to read critically.

Even though I have taught literature for many years, I still think that, in many ways, literature cannot be taught. Literature cannot be taught any more than beauty, truth, virtue, love, morality, wisdom, or grace can be taught. Only literary criticism can be taught, or, at least, different approaches to responding to literature. Reading literature encourages people to raise questions. As an English language arts educator, what am I attempting to do when I invite and encourage my students to read? I want my students to learn an appreciation for literature. But what does "an appreciation for literature" mean? I do not want my students to learn to appreciate *only* the literature that I appreciate, and I do not want them to learn to appreciate literature in the same ways that I appreciate literature. Besides, I frequently change in my own responses, judgments, and evaluations.

Indeed, I am finally recognizing how my early education and experiences with literature contributed to a sense of snobbery concerning what was "good" literature and what were appropriate ways of analyzing and comprehending literature. These days, I want to promote a more democratic approach to assessing the value of literature. In other words, I want to interrogate the contents of the canon of literature that is taught in schools as well as the ways that the canon is constituted. I want to question the ways that literature is read in schools, and what motivates reading practices in classrooms. I want to acknowledge that the judgments of others are their unique judgments, and not necessarily better or worse than my own. I do not want to regard a prestigious literary critic or university professor's taste in literature as representing a standard measure against which all other writing is assessed. I prefer to let people decide for themselves what they like and do not like, admire and do not admire, regard as successful and unsuccessful.

So, what *am* I going to teach in a school classroom? Certainly, many of my favourite books will be introduced. But I do not want the teacher to hold the whole authority for selecting the books that others will read, and, certainly, I do not want the responsibility for insisting that others must read the books that I like. I do not want to read boring books either, especially just because somebody has said that they are books that every well-read person ought to have read. I will decide what being a well-read person means for me personally, and I want others to decide for themselves, too. Above all else, reading literature ought to be fun.

I invite people to respond to literature in personal ways, out of their lived experiences and views of the world. My goal is to invite readers into the experience of reading literature as having relevance to their lives in the world. I seek to create wide-ranging discussions about the ideas and emotions and issues that are raised in and by literature. When readers respond personally to a story, a poem, a drama, or a novel, they are not only responding out of a self-centred interest—they are seeking to know their own experiences, but they are also seeking to know those experiences in relation to the experiences of others, and surely that seeking is at the heart of the pedagogical enterprise of English language arts education.

We need to read subjectively and personally and creatively. We are not looking for the correct answer or the correct critical analysis paper. We do not need *Coles Notes*. We do not need to mimic the critics. For so long, students of literature have been seeking to imitate the model essay in the teacher's guidebook. Instead, we need to understand that the reading of literature is connected to our living in the world, part of a dynamic process of growth, and we need to communicate our readings to one another. Our readings will be polyvalent, conflicting, tension-filled, and tentative, not the stuff of a neat and tidy classroom experience, but the energy at the heart of pedagogy that seeks living well in the world by living creatively in words. Indeed, English language arts educators need to promote *plural* readings that recognize the many contexts in which literature is written and read and discussed. Any literary text will be read differently in different times by different readers. Instead of sanctioning particular readings, we ought to open up spaces for conflicting and contested readings.

Our reading responses are determined by the kind of people we are—our personalities, experiences, views, and attitudes. What is needed most is an interrogation of the ways that we read, why we read in the ways that we do, and what other positions we can adopt in our reading. It is not enough to read a text; we need to read ourselves reading texts. We need to be self-conscious readers who ask questions about the ways we respond to texts. We never read the same text twice. We step into reading like stepping into a flowing river. Reading is always a living process.

Continuing with Questions

The authors in Part 3 promote literary engagement with imagination and creativity. They promote an expansive range of texts, and a wide range of approaches for attending to the texts. Above all, the authors in Part 3 acknowledge how reading and responding to literature is a way of being in the world. They are asking, in provocative and evocative ways: What is the hold of literature on a reader's imagination? Like Walter Brueggemann (2001), these authors seek "to recognize how singularly words, speech, language, and phrase shape consciousness and define reality" (p. 64). Brueggemann presents a compelling understanding of how political consciousness and transformative living are connected to a language and literature infused with imagination: "The evocation of an alternative reality consists at least in part in the battle for language and the legitimization of a new rhetoric" (2001, p. 18). Literary imagination is integral to interrogating lived and living experiences, and to narrating other possibilities. Literature does not seek to tell us how to live. Literature works to evoke possibilities for living. Therefore, in order to encourage creative, imaginative, and critical attention to texts, teachers can ask questions such as the following:

1. Why do we read literature?
2. Who reads literature?
3. What is the canon of literature?
4. Why has a canon been developed?
5. What criteria are used in selecting the literature read in schools?
6. What is appropriate literature for reading in classrooms?
7. Who chooses the literature read in schools?
8. What are the images of reality presented in literature?
9. How does literature help us to form and reform our conceptions of the world?

10. What is the "truth" of literature?
11. What are the multiple positions from which a text can be read?
12. How are responses evaluated and given value?
13. Is literature read for the sake of literature or for the sake of the readers?
14. How is literature connected to historical, cultural, social, and ideological contexts?
15. How can literature be read differently in different historical, cultural, social, and ideological contexts?

References

Brueggemann, W. (2001). *The prophetic imagination* (2nd ed.) Minneapolis, MN: Fortress Press.

Csikszentmihalyi, M. (1996). *Creativity: Flow and the psychology of discovery and invention.* New York: HarperCollins.

Edmundson, M. (2004). *Why read?* New York: Bloomsbury.

Malone, N. M. (2003). *Walking a literary labyrinth: A spirituality of reading.* New York: Riverhead Books.

Manguel, A. (1996). *A history of reading.* Toronto, ON: Alfred A. Knopf Canada.

Miller, R. E. (2005). *Writing at the end of the world.* Pittsburgh, PA: University of Pittsburgh Press.

O'Brien, G. (2000). *The browser's ecstasy: A meditation on reading.* New York: Counterpoint.

Quindlen, A. (1998). *How reading changed my life.* New York: Ballantine.

Rosenblatt, L. (1978). *The reader, the text, the poem.* Carbondale, IL: Southern Illinois University Press.

Winterson, J. (1995). *Art objects: Essays on ecstasy and effrontery.* Toronto, ON: Alfred A. Knopf Canada.

SECTION 1

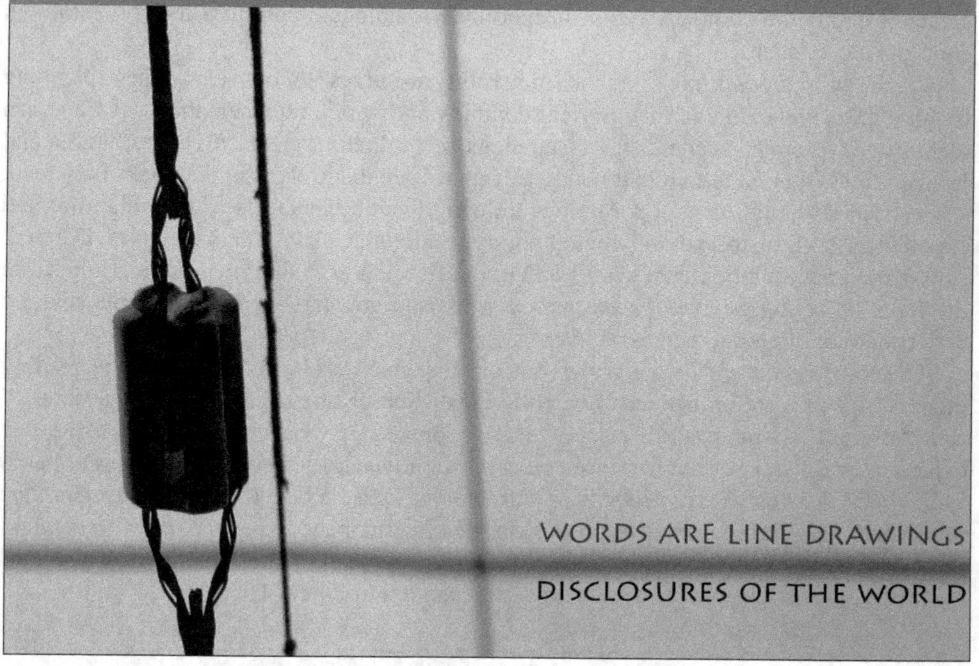

Literacies and Mind

What Are Multimodal Novel Studies and How Would They Benefit My Students? What Steps Can I Take to Create Multimodal Response-Based Novel Studies That Invite My Students' Engagement and Response?

By Mary Clare Courtland, Lakehead University

> The term multimodalities refers to the sign systems human beings use to create meaning. These include poetry, prose, expressive and performing arts, digital literacies, gestures, and media. Each discipline has particular discourses and signs which members of the discourse community use to communicate meaning.
>
> —Mary Clare Courtland (2010, p. 334)

Novel studies that are thoughtfully conceptualized have the potential to invite adolescent readers' engagement with and response to literary texts. Multimodal novel studies incorporate opportunities for literacy learning that transmediate across sign systems. Leland and Harste (1994) explain that "movement between and among communication systems provides the opportunity for new perspectives on our knowing and, hence, for the expression of an expanded range of meanings. Transmediation encourages reflection and supports learning in making new connections" (p. 340). The texts students read and those that they create promote reflection, as well as deeper understandings of and new insights into both concepts and contents.

Canadian multicultural texts are powerful resources to consider when planning multimodal novel studies. They present complex and varied representations of Canadian identity and promote readers' understandings of multiculturalism, diversity, and social justice issues. It is important that young Canadians see themselves in the books they read. As well, they should have opportunities to learn about other facets of Canadian life and experience, both historical and contemporary. Some Canadian authors such as Deborah Ellis write about international events and issues in relation to their devastating impact on the lives of young people. These texts can expand students' reading experiences and understanding of global themes and issues.

The term *reader response* grows out of Rosenblatt's (1978) theory of the reading process as a transaction between reader and text. She distinguishes between "aesthetic" and "efferent" stances. Both stances draw upon readers' background knowledge and experiences. In the aesthetic stance, readers initially engage with and interpret a text. They make intertextual connections to self, among texts, and to the world. Readers then reinterpret and represent their responses. In the efferent stance, readers attend to detail—for example, in reading content area texts or when reading literature critically. Thus, readers' purposes for reading are iterative, as depicted in Figure 1.

FIGURE 1 Reader Response Theory (Rosenblatt, 1978)

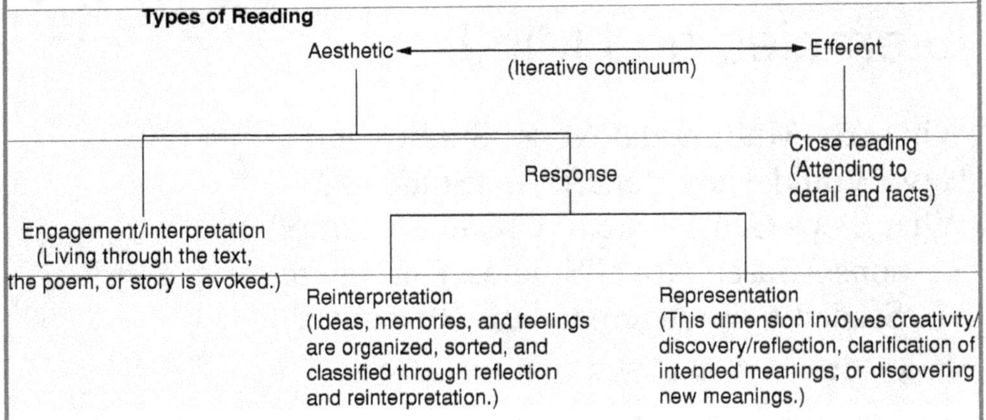

Source: From page 339 in Courtland, M. C. (2010). Integrating multimodal literacies through thematic units. In M. C. Courtland & T. J. Gambell (Eds.), *Literature, media & multiliteracies in adolescent language art* (2nd ed., p. 339). Vancouver, BC: Pacific Educational Press. Copyright © 2012 Mary Clare Courtland. Reprinted with Permission from Pacific Educational Press.

In planning multimodal novel studies, educators should also consider the role of sociocultural constructivist learning theory (Bruner, 1986; Vygotsky, 1978). Human beings construct meaning in interaction with others; they develop concepts through scaffolding imparted by more experienced mentors who themselves belong to particular discourse communities. Educators need to consider what types of scaffolding students might need in order to comprehend concepts or content.

Eisner (2002) describes dimensions of curriculum that are helpful in planning: goals, content, types of learning opportunities, organization of learning opportunities, organization of content areas (as discrete subjects or integrated studies), mode of presentation, mode of response, and assessment. Mode of presentation and mode of response are central to the creation of multimodal units. How will ideas and concepts be presented to students, or, how will they experience them? For example, will reading picture books on a related theme, viewing a film or a documentary, or playing a song best scaffold students' understanding? When we assign responses, what types of responses will mediate comprehension and promote deeper thinking and reflection, ultimately leading to new insights on the theme? All sign systems are characterized by particular tools and techniques. Will students need guidance in using the tools and techniques of a particular mode of expression to create their representations (see Courtland et al., 2006)?

The curriculum cycle may be described as having four iterative phases: planning, development, implementation, and assessment. Planning is the phase where educators' imagination and creativity come into play. Here educators paint broad brushstrokes of possibilities. It is important at this stage to conduct research, generate ideas, and collect resources. Eisner's (2002) dimensions of curriculum serve as a guide to aspects of planning that need to be addressed. Development involves making curriculum choices:

- What expectations should be selected?
- How will the novel study be organized?
- Over what period of time will it take place?
- How/when will students read the novel?
- What strategies and resources will be used?
- What multimodal components will be included (for example, print texts, picture books, films, research on the internet)?
- Will students have opportunities to read and analyze critically?
- How will students be grouped?
- What activities will promote students' ongoing engagement and interpretation? What type of final assignment(s) or project(s) will enable students to reinterpret and represent their understanding of texts?
- What assessment strategies will provide insights into students' processes and learning?

Consideration should also be given to differentiated instruction to address specific learning needs of students (Tobin, 2010). Development, then, results in a detailed plan.

In the implementation phase, the teacher and classroom community bring the plan to life. Here educators must be vigilant about monitoring students' understanding of the text and the processes in which they are engaged. Observing group talk and interactions, processes, and products all inform the teacher and enable him or her to revise the plan. At the end of every unit, it is important to allow students to showcase their completed projects to peers and to parents. They might invite parents or other classes for refreshments, organize a gallery walk, present performances, or set up booths in the class or auditorium to explain and share their work. The type of sharing will depend on the nature of the projects. If projects involve social action, students might develop workshops for peers, fundraise for a cause, or volunteer to purchase food, prepare a meal, and serve it at a shelter.

Eisner (2002) notes that evaluation should focus on the program (in this case, a novel study), the teaching, and the learning. Assessment of learning is both formative (during the implementation phase of the curriculum cycle) and summative. It should be linked to expectations. Gambell (2010) offers many options for the assessment of literacy learning. Both teachers and students should evaluate and reflect on the unit and the teaching. Students can be very astute when they are invited to comment on the strengths of a novel study and how the teaching and activities supported their learning. There are many creative ways to invite reflection. Students may reflect in a journal or online chat room, participate in a class discussion with the teacher about what they have learned, view a videotape of a performance and critique it, or write a letter to a friend or relative about the unit and their learning.

Multimodal novel studies provide teachers and students with exciting and creative opportunities for engagement and response over a sustained period of time. Transmediation across symbol systems supports students' learning. Reader response theory illuminates the nature of such engagement and response and offers teachers a framework for conceptualizing possibilities for transforming the study of literary texts. Teachers may want to consider collaborating with other instructors to develop diverse networks of expertise and to engage in dialogue that nurtures professional learning.

References

Bruner, J. (1986). *Actual minds, possible worlds*. Cambridge, MA: Harvard University Press.

Courtland, M. C. (2010). Integrating multimodal literacies through thematic units. In M. C. Courtland & T. J. Gambell (Eds.), *Literature, media & multiliteracies in adolescent language art* (2nd ed., pp. 333–359). Vancouver, BC: Pacific Educational Press.

Courtland, M. C., Niemi, S., Paddington, D., & Magnusson, R. (2006). Burning gender: Artistic responses to Ellis' (2000) *The Breadwinner* in a Grade 8 classroom. *Language and Literacy: A Canadian Educational E-journal* 8(1). Retrieved from: http://www.langandlit.ualberta.ca/.

Eisner, E. (2002). *The educational imagination: On the design and evaluation of school programs* (3rd ed.). Upper Saddle River, NJ: Pearson Education.

Gambell, T. J. (2010). Assessment for constructive learning. In M. C. Courtland & T. Gambell (Eds.), *Literature, media & multiliteracies in adolescent language arts* (pp. 385–425). Vancouver, BC: Pacific Educational Press.

Leland, C. H. & Harste, J. C. (1994). Multiple ways of knowing: Curriculum in a new key. *Language Arts* 71, 331–345.

Rosenblatt, L. (1978). *The reader, the text, the poem: The transactional theory of the literary work*. Carbondale, IL: Southern Illinois University Press.

Tobin, R. (2010). Differentiation: Respectful responses to diverse literacy learners. In M. C. Courtland & T. Gambell (Eds.), *Literature, media & multiliteracies in adolescent language arts* (pp. 361–384). Vancouver, BC: Pacific Educational Press.

Vygotsky, L. S. (1978). *Mind in society: The development of higher psychological processes*. M. Cole, V. John-Steiner, S. Scribner, & E. Souberman (Eds.). Cambridge, MA: Harvard University Press.

What Is "Participatory Consciousness" and Why Should It Matter to English Teachers?

By Dennis Sumara, University of Calgary and Tammy Iftody, University of Alberta

We all know what consciousness *feels* like, but most of us would be hard-pressed to define exactly what it *is* or how it influences our day-to-day lives as teachers and learners. One way to tease out the implications of consciousness for teaching, learning, and curriculum in English language arts (ELA) contexts is to consider some of the affordances and limitations of familiar images that are often used to describe this collective yet commonly understated human capacity. Although most of us experience consciousness as unified and coherent, consciousness is not, in fact, physically "centred" anywhere in the body. Despite this recognition, most of the metaphors and images used to represent consciousness uphold the perceived divisions between mind and body or individual and culture. Consequently, a theory of consciousness for English language arts teachers must challenge those metaphorical associations whereby the individual and isolated brain remains the primary origin of consciousness. Contemporary notions of consciousness attempt to address "participatory" rather than personalized ways of knowing and forms of knowledge.

Beyond the Spotlight of Perception

Most contemporary scientists and philosophers reject the notion of a "Cartesian theatre," or that supposed place in the brain where objects are brought into the light of consciousness for a central observer. The tendency to assume a physical centrality for consciousness remains mainly because that is how we experience conscious thought. Once commonly associated with the internalized faculties of sight and vision (or the "light" of knowledge), consciousness, contemporary theorists have suggested, is better understood in terms of a *decentralized network* of biological and cultural connections (Capra, 2002). Human consciousness is not limited to the capacities of individual brains but rather reaches its full potential in relation to others as part of a distributed cognitive/cultural network (Donald, 2001).

Consciousness Is Merely the Tip of the Iceberg

The knowledge gained through our interactions in the world is not limited to what is noticed by the conscious self but, more importantly, consists of vast amounts of information stored by the biological body without our awareness. It is this sort of embodied knowledge that gives human beings the ability to recognize certain patterns in unfamiliar contexts without necessarily being able to explain how. Such a "cognitive unconscious" is a fundamentally adaptive system that organizes and influences behaviour automatically, effortlessly, and intuitively (Epstein, 1994). Lakoff and Johnson (1999) use the metaphor of an iceberg to represent the relationship between consciousness and the cognitive unconscious. In this image, the cognitive unconscious is "the massive portion . . . that lies below the surface, below the visible tip that is consciousness" (p. 13). Most importantly, they suggest, "what lies beneath is not inert" but rather "shapes and structures all conscious thought" (Lakoff & Johnson, 1999, p. 103). The implication is that many of our preferences, habits, and assumptions are shaped *directly* by our experiences, independently of what we may or may not "want" at some conscious level.

More Than Meets the Mind's "I"

Rather than invoking the essentialist ideal of a core or "true" self around which we build our world, the capital "I" of consciousness is better described as "an index to a subjectivity that is always open to new possibilities of expression and realization" (Grumet, 1988, p. 66). This suggests that the self-as-conscious-subject is never fixed, but is in constant flux, co-evolving (in complicity) with the culture surrounding it. This is not to say that the self is never stable or coherent, but instead challenges the notion that the source of this stability is exclusively internal. In this way, maintaining a coherent sense of self is, paradoxically, not so much a project of "self-attention," as it is of attending to the many relations upon which an ongoing sense of self depends (Sumara, 2002, p. 25). More than a purely brain-based faculty, the personal feeling of consciousness, Donald (2001) and others have argued, depends almost entirely on culture for its realization. Thompson (2007) further argues that even though we may experience it as a self-contained phenomenon developed from the inside out, consciousness is instead a complex form of cognition that is shaped both by our ability to empathize and by our participation in particular cultures (or our "enculturation").

Consciousness is ever emerging and evolving, part of a lifelong process of learning how to be a subject both for oneself and for others. For example, early in life, children begin to recognize that their immediate caregivers, siblings, and peers have thoughts that are different from their own. This innate cognitive ability enables us as adults to interpret human experience by observing, imagining, and predicting what another might be thinking. Donald (2001) calls such "theorizing" about other human minds a form of "mind reading," or imaginative identification that requires the individual to attend to verbal, gestural, and contextual clues and cues in order to discern what the "other" is thinking and feeling. While mind reading is a biological capacity, it must be triggered by cultural and social experiences that compel the "reader" to elaborate his or her own consciousness by engaging in "thought experiments" about the consciousnesses of others. Our shared capacity for mind reading illustrates how literary experience and consciousness are actually co-evolving (or complicit) phenomena.

One's sense of identity (one's consciousness of self), then, depends upon an imagined empathetic identification with others—whether real or fictional. As a number of commentators have argued, one's sense of personal consciousness emerges as much from what one imagines as what one actually encounters; this process necessarily includes the kind of "imaginings" that take place through literary engagements and, more recently, in the shared spaces of the Internet (Hine, 2000; Turkle, 1995).

One could say that the process of educating and the structures of English language arts curriculum in particular are primarily concerned with affecting consciousness. We may be so bold as to suggest that English language arts curriculum and teaching are nearing a new crossroads as they face a shift in emphasis away from conceptions of individual consciousness—with their concomitant pedagogical concerns over passing on established knowledge—toward collective or participatory images of consciousness. This shift in emphasis yields a new pedagogical concern with elaborating knowledge that emerges relationally among the interactions that arise in the meeting of conscious minds.

On that count, it seems fair to say that English language arts education is on the verge of embracing an inherently participatory and therefore less individualized understanding of human consciousness. Teaching English language arts in a participatory framework becomes a matter of occasioning the conditions necessary for learners to engage in and share the kinds of discriminatory practices and interpretive exchanges that allow them to "exceed themselves" (Davis, 2004, p. 215). More colloquially, these are engagements that move the focus of learning from "me" to "we."

Identifying a "participatory culture" as one of the main conceptual challenges confronting education in the twenty-first century, Jenkins, Clinton, Purushotma, Robison, and Weigel (2007) define it as one which maintains "relatively low barriers to creative expression and civic engagement" (p. 7), a strong support for representing and sharing the products of engagement, opportunities for informal learning and apprenticeship, some degree of social commitment between participants, and a belief that individual contributions are valued by the community. The implication of flourishing participatory cultures for English language arts education is that teaching must likewise shift from a focus on the products of "individual expression" toward the conditions of "community involvement" and informal learning engagements. English education in the age of participatory culture (and participatory consciousness) creates opportunities for students to "recognize and articulate the different assumptions that guide their behavior" (p. 17) as communicators and participants in various formal and informal learning communities.

In the context of English language arts curriculum and instruction, participatory structures for engagement can provide familiar yet contextually rich opportunities for students to pause, interrogate, and reconsider the ways in which their identities are caught up in both conscious and unconscious ways of knowing. In this way, students' ongoing opportunities to "recognize and articulate the different assumptions that guide their behavior" may also be linked to a willingness to practise a kind of communal reflexiveness, which, as Britzman (2003) has suggested, itself reflects "the desire to dialogue with a range of perspectives, to see things as if they could be otherwise, and to take up, as well as encourage, the interpretive risks that learning demands" (p. 187). In this way, consciousness is no longer associated with the "light of knowledge," but rather the distributed "networks of knowing" that emerge through participation in a variety of formal and informal cultures, and through an engagement with a variety of literary and popular cultural texts.

If consciousness is an emergent property of the creative collision between cognition and culture (Donald, 2001) and not simply a brain-based or socially constructed phenomenon, how does one educate for a participatory consciousness in English language arts? Perhaps the best we can do is provide our students with meaningful opportunities to both *experience* and *articulate* empathetic identifications through "mind reading" engagements with both conventional and popular literary forms in both formal and new participatory cultures.

References

Britzman, D. (2003). *Practice makes practice: A critical study of learning to teach.* (Revised Edition) Albany, NY: State University of New York Press.

Capra, F. (2002). *The hidden connections: Integrating the biological, cognitive, and social dimensions of life into a science of sustainability.* New York: Doubleday.

Davis, B. (2004). *Inventions of teaching: A genealogy.* Mahwah, NJ: Lawrence Erlbaum.

Donald, M. (2001). *A mind so rare: The evolution of human consciousness*. New York, W.W. Norton.

Epstein, S. (1994). Integration of the cognitive and the psychodynamic unconscious. *American Psychologist* 49(8), 709–724.

Grumet, M. (1988). *Bitter milk: Women and teaching*. Amherst, MA: University of Massachusetts Press.

Hine, C. (2000). *Virtual ethnography*. London: Sage Publications.

Jenkins, H., Clinton, K., Purushotma, R., Robison, A.J., & Weigel, M. (2007). Confronting the challenges of participatory culture: media education for the 21st century. MacArthur Foundation. http://digitallearning.macfound.org/atf/cf/%7B7E45C7E0-A3E0-4B89-AC9C-E807E1B0AE4E%7D/JENKINS_WHITE_PAPER.PDF (accessed January 2, 2012).

Lakoff, G. & Johnson, M. (1999). *Philosophy in the flesh*. New York: Basic Books.

Sumara, D. (2002). *Why reading literature in school still matters: Imagination, interpretation, insight*. Mahwah, NJ: Lawrence Erlbaum Associates.

Thompson, E. (2007). *Mind in life: Biology, phenomenology, and the sciences of mind*. Cambridge and London: The Belknap Press of Harvard University Press.

Turkle, S. (1995). *Life on screen: Identity in the age of the internet*. New York: Simon & Schuster.

What Is the literary imagination?

By Kelly Young, Trent University

A working definition of the word "literary," in its broadened sense, is any representation of a story or work of art in the form of a novel, short story, poem, song, painting, sculpture, or other aesthetic form. The etymology of the word, moreover, is associated with forms of representation: "[p]ertaining to the letters of the alphabet; [c]arried on by letters; epistolary . . . [o]f painting, sculpture, etc.: that [which] depicts or represents a story" (Oxford English Dictionary [OED], 2008). "Literary" also has to do with our human capacity to "form internal images or ideas of objects and situation[s]," as well as the "power or capacity by which the mind integrates sensory data in the process of perception" (ibid). Stories, as works of art, evoke a literary imagination when their structures are used in pedagogical situations to teach and delight (Sumara, 1996).

What, then, is the role of the imagination in literary engagement? According to Maxine Greene, "the role of the imagination is not to resolve, not to point the way, not to improve. It is to awaken, to disclose the ordinarily unseen, unheard, and unexpected" (1995, p. 21). Engaging the literary imagination involves, among other things, close reading and interpretation of literary art. To hone these abilities, teachers may have students practise responding in writing and other representational forms to evoke creative thinking and theorizing, to trigger memories, to imagine events to be lived through, or to create internal feelings, images, and associations.

How Might a Secondary English Teacher Evoke the Literary Imagination?

In the secondary English classroom, reading and writing are interactive social processes. Evoking the literary imagination involves responding to literary form through conditioned reading and writing practices. Sumara (1996) writes, "to imagine, within the spaces opened up by the literary fiction, is not merely to imagine what might fill those spaces, but to imagine oneself as well" (p. 40). Literary forms can include visual forms such as paintings and sculptures. Including conditioned reading and writing practices as part of a writers' workshop can evoke the literary imagination.

A Secondary English Writers' Workshop

A writers' workshop involves a group of writers who write together and share their work both by reading aloud and through written forms such as electronic magazines (e-zines), anthologies, web logs (blogs), and so on. Setting up a writers' workshop can help students make connections between the literary imagination and the texts of short stories, poetry, drama, or novels. Over the past two decades, I have been building a collection of conditioned writing practices from my own experiences as a writer and a member of several different writing groups.

Conditioned writing practices involve the use of a particular framework that brings together a freedom of interpretation and representation within constraints that restrict the interpretation or representation of a work of art through what Davis, Sumara, and Luce-Kapler (2000) term "liberating-constraint." A "liberating-constraint" often involves following a step-by-step process whereby the circumstances surrounding a learner's engagement and experiences with a literary form (painting, poem, or novel passage) are constrained by the instructor in particular ways during the writers' workshop.

In the writers' workshop, we warm up to writing and create a safe space for sharing. For example, we agree that as a writer in the group, it is okay to lie if you want to. Spelling does not count, and you only share if you want to. Learners are encouraged not to take their pens or pencils off the page when engaging in timed-writing exercises. Other constraints or suggestions can be added for the workshop as needed. Over a period of several months, learners who are engaged in a writers' workshop can become a writing collective, and the writings of the collective can become a shared aesthetic and social practice. The following are some examples of this process and may help teachers facilitate their own writers' workshops.

Writers' Workshop Suggestions

In the library of the school, divide students into groups of four and have them copy language (words, phrases, sayings, symbols) from the walls. As a group, students review the collection and arrange and rearrange the words into a poetic form (shape, acrostic, free-form, etc.). Students are invited to share their found poems.

Using a step-by-step process, engage students in a guided writing practice about a favourite physical place. First, ask students to imagine a favourite place where they grew up, such as grandmother's porch, a cottage by the lake, or a private place they enjoyed or still enjoy. Next, ask them to write about the place, evoking all of the senses—what does it smell, look, feel, taste, and sound like? Use a timed freewriting session. Then, together as a large group, cross out function words (e.g., pronouns, articles, and conjunctions). Copy the remaining nouns, adjectives, and adverbs into a new space. Rearrange what you are left with and play with the form. Add words you took out if you wish. Finally, punctuate and title the piece. Have students consider the liberation of writing about a favourite place through freewriting, in contrast with this constraining six-step process. Then, ask students to share their work aloud.

Using the framework of a "liberating-constraint," engage students in *ekphrastic* poetics, a classical Greek form that involves an aesthetic response to a visual form. As an example, explore Don McLean's *ekphrastic* response to Vincent Van Gogh's painting, *Starry Night*. Spend time interpreting the painting. Next, play Don McLean's song "Vincent" several times with the lyrics projected for the class to see. Then, as a large group, have students copy the first stanza, leaving a space between each line. Use a timed-writing exercise in which students are given one minute to read the first line of "Vincent" and respond with whatever comes to mind. Interpretations are written down in the space between the lines of McLean's verses. Continue this for the whole stanza. Students then copy only their response lines onto another piece of paper. Finally, arrange and rearrange words, add words, punctuate, and add a title. Invite students to share work.

In the writers' workshop, all of the senses are evoked as often as possible. To stir up the sense of taste, for example, engage learners in a freewriting exercise about their first experience of having a lollipop as a child. To evoke the sense of smell, engage writers in a trip down memory lane as they peel and eat clementines. To evoke a spiritual sense, take learners outside and sit under trees. Ask students to write about their first memories of engaging with the natural world and to consider their memories of "being in nature" (Young, 2008). To evoke the sense of hearing, ask students to complete a freewriting session while listening to a favourite song. Additionally, invite students to write about a character's secret thoughts from a novel after reading a chapter aloud.

Engage learners in a reader's theatre of any book. For example, you might wish to choose Dr. Seuss' *The Lorax*. In groups, invite students to rotate through several classroom stations that 1) explore *shape poetry* spatially using words from the text; 2) rewrite the ending of the story; 3) explore ecological themes that expose ideas of capitalism, consumerism, and individualism; and 4) spend time researching the etymology of words found in *The Lorax*.

Invite students to bring in a small cultural object (jewellery, trinket, etc.) in a concealed bag. Students receive a concealed bag that is not their own. Students take the item out of the bag and write a narrative about the item by considering the five Ws (who, what, where, when, why) during a timed activity of 5 to 10 minutes. Consider what the story behind the object is and invite students to share their work and guess who owns the item.

At the end of the workshop, invite students to polish and contribute one piece of writing of their choice for a class anthology/zine. This way, the writers' workshop produces a work of art collaboratively. Celebrate the writers' workshop with a literary café wherein music and props are used to set the mood, refreshments are consumed, and guests of the students' choosing are invited (space permitting). Selections from the culminating anthology/zine can be read aloud, either by their authors or by volunteer readers.

References

Davis, B., Sumara, D., & Luce-Kapler, R. (2000). *Engaging minds: Learning and teaching in a complex world.* Mahwah, NJ: Lawrence Erlbaum Associates.

Greene, M. (1995). *Releasing the imagination: Essays on education, the arts, and social change.* San Francisco: Jossey-Bass Publishers.

"literary, adj. and n." OED Online. Oxford University Press. http://oed.com/view/Entry/109067?redirectedFrom=literary (accessed December 29, 2011).

Sumara, D. (1996). *Private readings in public: Schooling the literary imagination.* New York: Peter Lang.

Young, K. (2008). Ecological habits of mind and the literary imagination. *Educational Insights* 12(1), 1–9.

Additional Resources

Luce-Kapler, R. (1999). White chickens, wild swings, and winter nights. *Language Arts,* 76(4), 298–304.

Luce-Kapler, R., & Dobson, T. (2005). In search of a story: Reading and writing e-literature. *Reading Online,* May/June, 8(6). http://www.readingonline.org/articles/art_index.asp?HREF=luce-kapler/index.html (accessed January 2, 2012).

McLean, D. (1971). "Vincent" music lyrics. http://www.lyrics007.com/Don%20McLean%20Lyrics/Vincent%20Lyrics.html (accessed March 21, 2011).

Seuss, D. (1974). *Dr. Seuss storytime.* New York: Random House.

SECTION 2

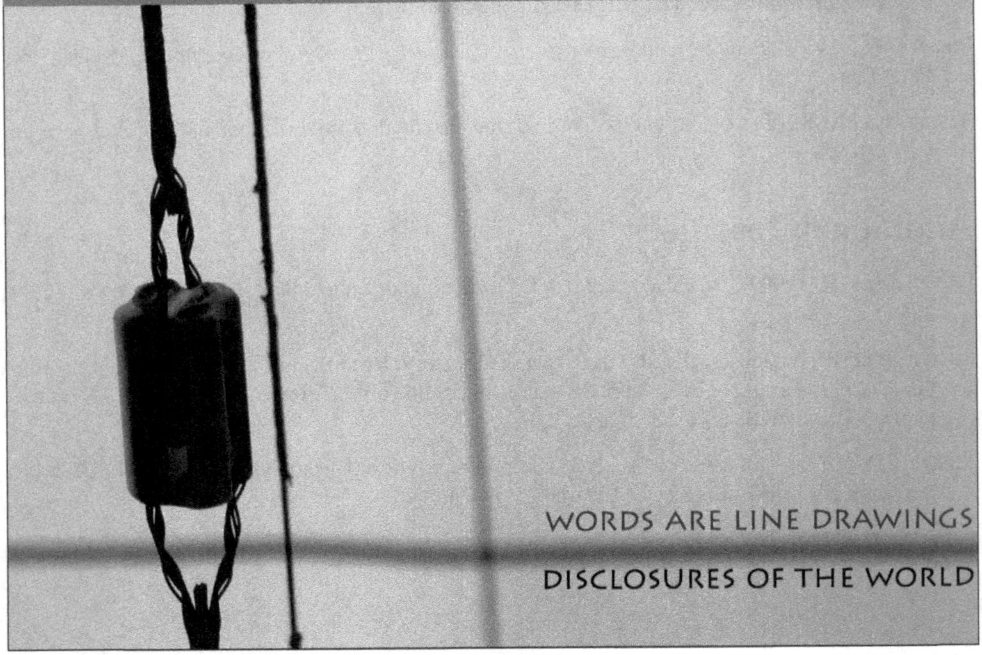

Being and Reading Canadian

Why Does Reading Canadian Literature in School Matter?

By Leah C. Fowler, University of Lethbridge

Every classroom is a country: its students explore, articulate, and live within its borders. They map its geography, learning its terrain and horizons; they organize with its laws and its culture; and they create with its music, art, humour, and curriculum of knowledge-goals. In a classroom, students both become themselves and transcend themselves, creating possibilities for future lives through language and literature.

As we read stories, we activate the part of the brain that is responsible for developing empathy. We have social and psychological experiences as we read and become aware of multiple concurrent narratives around us. We make the familiar strange, perhaps in order to see things more clearly (or as they actually are) through the lens of a Canadian author's writing. As we develop empathy and intercultural understanding through literature, we begin first by appreciating and next by supporting and defending diversity, equity, and human rights; we unlearn heartlessness and contribute to well-being and meaning in life (Fowler, 2006). We come to know our place, its topography, and how to dwell in it (Chambers, 1994). When a classroom of people read together, they begin to cultivate a cultural literacy of self and others that makes participatory citizenship possible—a process like the CBC's annual national project, *Canada Reads*.

With the participatory citizenship that an engaged secondary literature classroom offers, the curriculum is about real vision into others' ways of being as well as the solution to real, problematic issues. Students learn to commit to the inclusion of all citizens (ATA, 2010) and move toward social justice and environmental sustainability in our culturally diverse and growing country.

What Canada's writers are saying these days about life provides a sure way to engage students in relevant, meaningful thought and conversation while still attaining a school's curriculum outcomes, all while developing students' individual knowledge, skills, and attributes. For more than 30 years, I have used Canadian literature in secondary school, college, and university classrooms. Sometimes, I would invite authors to follow up with a visit. This facilitated student engagement with "real live writers" and their stories, poems, and novels. This has been among the more meaningful work in my teaching. As a professor in teacher education, I still work to connect with Canadian writers through literature, literature fairs, writers' guilds, libraries, book launches, and the actual words from one heartful mind to another. Whether Kindle or paperback, internet site or tattered, dog-eared hand-me-down novels, I issue the invitations: "Here, read this. It is amazing!" and, "Well, if you liked that book, try this one!"

First, a word about reading, schema theory, and bridging language arts to experience: ever since Louise Rosenblatt's groundbreaking work (1938, 1978), she and other researchers (Milner & Milner, 2008) have made abiding and eloquent arguments that reading literature *is* experience. Teachers demonstrate every school day that reading literature together in groups encourages compelling encounters in the psychological and social mirror. Those activities of learning build neuroplasticity of mind and elaborate cognitive schemative foundations. This is substantiated, for example, by those Positron Emission Tomography (PET) scans of the head showing that when humans are engaged in reading, the whole brain lights up! Imagination, interpretation, and insight are being developed while students are reading in public school (Sumara, 2002).

Stories reflect back to us how we navigate what is given to us: What chimney or tent or condo or barn gave us our first supportive architecture around our breath? What weather determined our clothes as we learned about the land, the people, the paths, and the stories around us? What happened, and happens, to us when we grow up? These are not trivial questions; they are related to our historical, current, and future survival (Atwood, 1972, 2008).

If a key teaching challenge is to connect students to the country in which they live together, then reading Canadian literature together and saying, "This is my country, what's yours?" (Richler, 2006) engages everybody in the room with mind and interest to focus on such questions as "Where are we?", "Why are we here?", and "What shall we do together?" Real questions like these have a way of getting and keeping both students' and teachers' attention on the learning they construct together. Reading together can mean staying together as a family of learners. This produces an environment in which learning increases in personal significance, performance on assignments and attendance improve, fewer students are "lost," and more can have a better chance at *success* in school regardless of *ability*.

Initially, I get students involved with a class novel so we have a shared text. This is useful especially with students whose first language is not English. Our oral reading is infused with liberal offerings of poets and stories. I might start a class with Shane Koyzcan's "This Is My Voice" from YouTube, the first chapter of *The Crazy Man* by

Pamela Porter (2005), or *The Book of Negroes* by Lawrence Hill (2007). On exams, I use excerpts from Canadian young adult novels or an essay by an outrageous Canadian to whom students can respond in kind. On Friday afternoons, I use interviews with authors or webquests on literature websites in Canada. I bring in the book section of the *Globe and Mail* (now handy on my iPhone). Personal copies of novels by Canadian authors are always available in the classroom library for the silent reading part of our classes (we have a running book list of *Canada Reads,* the Governor General's Literary Awards winners, and Giller and other prize titles). I bring in Canadian periodicals such as *Walrus,* or *Canadian Children's Book News,* or local and provincial magazines such as *Alberta Views* or *BC Books,* the Burlington Public Library's newest acquisitions, or titles from Newfoundland book fairs: I always choose something students are unlikely to have at home so I can enlarge their boundaries of knowledge and discourse.

I like to have "mimic your favourite author and read it" contests. We have book symposiums, literature circles, and book talks. Students write literary reviews and enter literature contests, including using blogs and presentation software (e.g. *Prezi, Smartboard, Glogster,* etc.), so students are involved in teaching others in the classroom about their favourite authors and literature choices. All the language arts are at work in this focus on Canadian literature and its writers. A favourite of mine is a Canadian Children's Literature unit in which students read and develop their visual literacy through the "dual texts" of picture books, both artistic artifacts as well as textual. I challenge my students (and myself—I do all the assignments along with them) to research children's books around a theme (first teaching a few key research skills such as using research tools or identifying figurative literary devices). The great challenge is then to create a picture book for their siblings or students in younger grades at the school. We also study historical and contemporary realism in current graphic novels; the level of interest male students particularly exhibit in this new genre is stunning. Author studies, genre studies, theme studies, or media events related to books and literature also increase interest levels in relevant curriculum that is focused on students' needs and lives (Donawa & Fowler, 2012, in press).

Award-winning Canadian young adult literature recently has blossomed to reflect the astonishing diversity and interests and lives of our students. The "normal" classroom is no longer homogenous but rich with diversity and *uncommon* ground. Sharing and shared literature provides a *common place* (Sumara, 2002) in which to dwell together in the space between (Aoki, 1986/2005). The classroom becomes a new, contemporary country with its own language, culture, literature, human rights, and responsibilities for its immigrant constituents—including the teacher. It becomes a microcosm of a realism that already exists in the world, a wonderful domain for learning and growth and possibility. As Irshad Manji (2005) said, "home is where my dignity lives." Students' dignity can develop through secondary school classroom experiences with Canadian literature, letting them arrive at the home of their own being.

References

Alberta Teachers' Association. (2010). *Here comes everyone: Teaching in the intercultural classroom.* Edmonton, AB: Alberta Teachers Association.

Aoki, T. (1986/2005). Teaching as in-dwelling between two curriculum worlds. In W. F. Pinar & R. L. Irwin (Ed.), *Curriculum in a new key: The collected works of Ted T. Aoki* (pp. 159–166). Mahwah, NJ: Lawrence Erlbaum.

Atwood, M. (1972). *Survival: A thematic guide to Canadian literature*. Toronto, ON: Anansi. [McClelland and Stewart, 1996, 2004]

———. (2008). *Payback*. Toronto, ON: House of Anansi.

Chambers, C. (1994). Looking for a home: A work in progress. *Frontiers: A Journal of Women Studies*, 15(2), 23-50.

Donawa, W. & Fowler, L. (in press for 2012). *Reading Canada: Teaching fiction in secondary schools*. Toronto, ON: Oxford University Press.

Fowler, L. (2006). *A curriculum of difficulty: Narrative research and the practice of teaching*. New York: Peter Lang.

Hill, L. (2007). *The book of Negroes*. Toronto, ON: HarperCollins.

Manji, I. (2005). *The trouble with Islam today: A wake-up call for honesty and change*. Toronto, ON: Random House.

Milner, J. & Milner, L. (2008). *Bridging English*. Upper Saddle River, NJ: Pearson.

Porter, P. (2005). *The crazy man*. Toronto, ON: Groundwood Books.

Richler, N. (2006). *This is my country, what's yours?: A literary atlas of Canada*. Toronto, ON: McClelland and Stewart.

Rosenblatt, L. (1938). *Literature as exploration*. New York: Appleton Century.

———. (1978). *The reader, the text, the poem*. Carbondale, IL: Southern Illinois University Press.

Sumara, D. (2002). *Why reading literature in school still matters: Imagination, interpretation, insight*. Mahwah, NJ: Lawrence Erlbaum.

Is Reading and Writing Fiction Still Relevant for Students in Contemporary Canadian Secondary English Classrooms?

By Valerie Mulholland, University of Regina

Yes, and I'll explain why. And so, a quote, to set the mood:

> To speak, and to write, is to assert who we are, what we think. The necessary other side is to surrender these things—to stand humbled and stunned and silent before the wild and inexplicable beauties and mysteries of being. (Hirschfield, 1993, p. 221)

To begin, I ask the reader's indulgence to accept that fiction and story are synonymous terms. Most dictionaries do. Stories, we know, can be true as in "situated in reality," or made up as in "feigned or imagined" (a phrase that Fred Stenson, 2002, used as a title for his book about the craft of fiction). Notwithstanding the fact that fiction can create a profound sense of truth, I approach the question of its relevancy with an understanding that fiction is a work of the imagination. Reading and writing fiction are interrelated actions, embedded in the most human of experiences. In Western cultures, imagination and fantasy have been aligned with the body, and information and knowledge have been aligned with the mind. However, the aesthetic experience of reading and writing exists in both the mind *and* the body. Therefore, reading and writing fiction is a place of reconciliation. Franz Wright, in "Learning to Read," ends with the lines, "Life has taught me/to understand books." Somewhat ironically, I will draw upon scholarly writing to convince you of the relevance of reading and writing fiction.

First, reading fiction provides opportunities for pleasure, for uniting the worlds that we live in through the sensual experiences that reading can provide. In her 1988 essay "Bodyreading," Madeleine Grumet calls on educators to recognize the place of the body in the reading experience. She argues for a reconciliation of the dual purposes of gaining information and aesthetic experience that motivate and constitute reading in school. Although she is addressing curriculum in the broadest sense, her focus on literacy speaks to language arts teachers today. Grumet notes, "the *bodyreading* need not be seen as a nostalgic fantasy, but as a practical necessity, the exploration of a world where we can live" (p. 132). She resists technical approaches that reduce reading to a series of steps or linear strategies, saying, "If we can wrest meaning from the grip of knowledge and return it to art, we will be able to give students something to do with texts. Reading all cultural texts must be seen as a fundamentally human activity" (p. 148). Her vibrant writing is remarkably contemporary as the following statement, which echoes current pedagogical concerns, demonstrates: "Our current concern about the distance between what we know, and how we live is mirrored in our fear that our children do not read" (p. 129). In the 20 years since Grumet's *Bitter Milk* was published, concern about students' resistance to reading has persisted. Grumet theorizes that embedded in our fear about children not reading is the fear that what *we* know, what *we* have valued, will be lost: "the symbolic inscriptions of our collective experience in the world . . . [move] away from them like an ice floe and [leave] them stranded, separated from the past and, we fear, from the future as well" (p. 129). Rather than cultivate the pleasures of reading, we respond to the fear of its loss by making reading the subject of testing. The furious distractions of large-scale assessments and measureable objectives shield students from the profits and pleasures of writing and reading fiction.

Second, reading and writing fiction provides English teachers with meaningful ways to disrupt educational rituals and conventions that otherwise may starve students of the experience of the bodyreading. In *Critical Literacy and the Aesthetic: Transforming the English Classroom,* Ray Misson and Wendy Morgan (2006), like Grumet, address the binary of mind and body as it persists conceptually in schools and is enacted in classrooms. They argue that because the body is the site of emotions and emotions are bound up with an imagination which itself drives creativity, it is the body that creates art. When we talk about the effect of a work of art, literary or otherwise (as cultural texts we could be talking about dance, visual art, music, film, television, video games, and so on), we often use phrases associating the effect with the body like "heart-warming," "bone-chilling," or "brought tears to my eyes." Fiction may be said to engage the whole person, mind and body.

As English teachers, we negotiate the spaces between binaries daily. For example, we may place emphasis on transactional writing at the expense of poetic or expressive writing. If we privilege criticism of fiction and discount the production of fiction, then we starve students of possibility. In so doing, we create a hierarchy of knowledge that advantages one way of knowing over another, one group over another, one student over another. What then happens to our responsibility to language and to contemporary ideas of equity that challenge entrenched teaching practices?

Third, reading and writing fiction is a deeply, if not essentially, human experience. Patrick Lewis's (2007) *How We Think, but Not in School: A Storied Approach to Teaching* makes the argument that all human experience can be rendered through story; it is, therefore, from stories that we learn about self, the world, and the other. Through story, we cultivate memory, imagination, and creativity, and, ultimately, enrich our experience of living. Following this narrative arc, "story" in a general sense provides the infrastructure of human culture. Furthermore, according to Lewis, creative and critical thinking follow story, not the other way around. In his explication of narrative knowing and being, Lewis cites David Carr, who writes, "Life that is not some kind of story is unthinkable—or, more precisely, unlivable" (p. 10). Without story, Lewis argues, humans would have endless, unconnected, chaotic experiences. We use stories to make sense of our being and to create meaning with others. Agency and power reside in story. Naturally, families, communities, and cultures are treasure troves of stories. They provide their members with narratives for adoption that integrate members into stories of individual life. This way of thinking is similar to Bruner's (1994) understanding of "Life as Narrative." In oral cultures, storytelling conveys values, beliefs, and knowledge. To neglect story is akin to neglecting life.

Fourth, and urgently in Canada, respect for story—for recognizing the relevance of reading and writing fiction—provides opportunities for cultural expressions and "storywork" outside of mainstream culture. Jo-Ann Archibald's (2008) *Indigenous Storywork: Educating the Heart, Mind, Body and Spirit* offers story as a source of strength and energy. Similar to Patrick Lewis, who says that teaching is storytelling, she writes that story comes alive through the telling and becomes the teacher itself. Her apprenticeship as a storyteller is an apprenticeship of learning and teaching. She uses traditional stories to honour the principles of inter-relatedness and synergy. She recognizes the duality of mind and body in writing of "the power of stories to educate the heart." These are her words:

> My appreciation for the cultural values of respect, responsibility, reciprocity, and reverence embedded in Indigenous stories did not occur until I let the Elders' teachings about storywork guide me. I did not intentionally set out to become a storyteller, but I did set out to learn more about the nature of Indigenous stories and how they could be used to produce quality education. . . . My experiential story is told to exemplify the cultural values and to introduce some issues related to story memory, letting Elders guide a learning process, learning patience, and appreciating silence. (Archibald, 2008, p. 95)

And, finally, I present a story about teaching fiction that respects oral traditions. When I was a secondary school English teacher, I often taught the Tolstoy story "How Much Land Does a Man Need?" using a "story circle" approach. Working in groups of nine, each student was assigned one section of the story to learn thoroughly enough to tell it to the group. They were not responsible for memorizing the passage word for word, but they had to demonstrate reverence by representing the details of the story faithfully and by beginning and ending the telling with language sufficiently similar to the text so as to accurately cue the speaker to follow. Finally, the students sat in a circle and told the story. It was enchanting to witness. Patience and silence are learned using this method, and a fictional refuge created in the classroom. The process of telling a story exercises and engages the mind and the body.

The last word goes to Grumet: "what reading is about, very much like writing, is bridging the gap between private and public worlds. Its purpose is not to reduce mystery to what is obvious . . . but to provide a passage between the images, impulses, and glimpses of meaning that constitute being in the world" (pp. 135–136).

References

Archibald, J. (2008). *Indigenous storywork: Educating the heart, mind, body, and spirit.* Vancouver, BC: UBC Press.

Bruner, J. (1994). Life as narrative. In A. H. Dyson & C. Genishi (Eds.). *The need for story: Cultural diversity in classroom and community*. Urbana, IL: National Council of Teachers of English.

Grumet, M. R. (1988). Bodyreading. In *Bitter milk: Women and teaching*. Amherst, MA: University of Massachusetts Press.

Hirschfield, J. (1998). *Nine gates: Entering the mind of poetry*. New York: Harper Perennial.

Lewis, P. J. (2007). *How we think, but not in school*. Rotterdam, Netherlands: Sense Publishers.

Misson, R. & Morgan, W. (2006). *Critical literacy and the aesthetic: Transforming the English classroom.* Urbana, IL: National Council of Teachers of English.

Stenson, F. (2002). *Thing feigned or imagined: A self-directed course in the craft of fiction*. Banff, AB: The Banff Centre Press.

Wright, F. (2009). Learning to read. *The New Yorker,* January 19, 70.

Who Are the Local Writers in *Your* Community?

By Jean Baird, Al Purdy A-Frame Trust and D.M.R. Bentley, University of Western Ontario

Al Purdy has been described at various times and by various writers as the "first," the "last," and the "most" Canadian poet, but for many of us, he is simply *the* Canadian poet—the poet who captured and came to personify the distinctive genius of Canada. In a creative career that began when he was serving with the Royal Canadian Air Force in Vancouver during World War II and ended with his death in 2000, he wrote with passion, commitment, and brilliant insight about almost every part of Canada and every aspect of Canadian life, past and present. No anthology of Canadian literature would be complete without such Purdy masterpieces as "The Cariboo Horses," "The Country North of Belleville," "Trees at the Arctic Circle," "Wilderness Gothic," "Lament for the Dorsets," "Roblin's Mills," and "Elegy for a Grandfather." Among Purdy's many honours were two Governor General's Awards, the Order of Ontario, and the Order of Canada.

During much of his writing life, Purdy lived and drew inspiration from the A-frame house that he and his wife Eurithe built in 1957 on the shores of Roblin Lake, near Ameliasburgh, Ontario. It was there that he wrote many of his masterpieces. It was there that he communed imaginatively with the Loyalists who settled in Prince Edward County. It was there that he discussed the past and future of Canadian literature well into the night with Milton Acorn, Margaret Laurence, Michael Ondaatje, and many other friends, including, it is rumoured, John Labatt and Johnnie Walker. In a quite literal way, Eurithe and Al Purdy's A-frame is part of the fabric of Canadian literature and Canadian culture: among the "ingredients" of its chimney, he wrote in "Place of Fire," are "limestone from an 1840 Regency house," "historic stone from the Roblin gristmill site," "anonymous stone from Norris Whitney's barnyard," and "some pickup loads from the Point Anne quarry" near Kingston. There is surely no more striking and concrete metaphor than the Purdys' A-frame house for the integration of past and present, everyday and historied, Canadian literature and the Canadian landscape that lies at the very heart of Purdy's poetry.

In 2008, the A-frame was threatened with sale and demolition; Eurithe had maintained the property for many years after Purdy's death but decided she could no longer sustain the place. If the destruction of the property were allowed to happen, not only would a unique piece of Canada's literary and cultural heritage disappear, but so, too, would a unique opportunity to preserve the A-frame as an inspiration for present and future Canadians and Canadian writers. The Al Purdy A-frame Trust was formed to raise enough funds to purchase the property, do some upgrades and run the A-frame as a writer-in-residence program, under which writers will be offered the opportunity to live and work in a space and place of inspirational literary and historic significance and resonance. Canada has not done an admirable job of preserving its literary sites.

Eric Lorenzen, a physics teacher at a Trenton, Ontario, secondary school, read about the Al Purdy A-frame project in the *National Post.* Trenton is a few kilometres from Ameliasburgh. Lorenzen had been teaching at Trenton High School for 10 years and was shocked that he didn't know that Purdy had been a student—well, a dropout, actually. In his autobiography, Purdy wrote about being a teen in Trenton, hating secondary school, and feeling comfortable only in the library. Lorenzen formed a committee of teachers and spent months guiding his recommendation through educational red tape to rename the school library the Al Purdy Library. Some of the English teachers thought they would start covering units of Purdy's poetry. The students loved it—they identified strongly with Purdy's dislike of small-town Ontario and his desire to get away. They recognized the landscapes of the poems, and the language was the language of their own world. The art teachers proposed that students create work for permanent installation in the soon-to-be-renamed library. Displays were created for the hallways, full of students' work and Purdy's books.

The tech students also wanted to get involved. Built in the late 50s, it was years before the A-frame got indoor plumbing, which meant that visitors used the outhouse and, at Purdy's insistence, signed the walls. Even after plumbing was installed, Purdy preferred the outhouse—his favourite place to think, Eurithe once said. In October 2010, the outhouse was removed. It spent the winter at Trenton High School, where students carefully removed paint, searching for the names of Margaret Laurence, Farley Mowat, Earle Birney, and others. The refurbished outhouse was returned to the property in April 2011, National Poetry Month.

On the same day, an official ceremony was held at the secondary school with Eurithe Purdy in attendance. In celebration of the Al Purdy Library, students read Purdy's poems to the assembly and read their own poems, inspired by Purdy's work. Yes, it's pretty funny, an outhouse in a school tech department. But what is more important is that these students became engaged in the literature of their own community. Purdy's work validates the rural experience, and these students developed a sense of pride in their community. Today, the students at Trenton feel a sense of ownership of the A-frame. They've read the words but they have also participated. However, you will notice that the change that happened in this secondary school came about because one teacher reached out and made an effort. Lorenzen changed the focus of the school back to the local.

If there is a shared Canadian cultural experience in secondary schools, more often than not it is *To Kill a Mockingbird* or *Catcher in the Rye,* McDonald's, Tommy Hilfiger, and Brad Pitt. Let's instead borrow from Walt Whitman. He believed that a postage stamp on which you stand is as important as any other place. For you as teachers, more importantly, the shared Canadian cultural experience is where *you* stand, where *you* live: know that place, write about it, and read about it.

Are you, as a serious teacher, also a serious reader? Are you reading local writers? Do you know who the local writers are in your community? If not, make the effort to find out. Ask your public librarian or independent bookseller about local writers they would recommend for the age range of your students. In my experience, people who work in used-book stores are also well-informed about local writers. Watch the newspaper for articles about local writers. Attend readings; they provide an excellent opportunity to hear writers and see if you think they might connect with your students. After the reading, you could approach the writer and ask, "Would you be interested in coming to my classroom?" One writer will be able to tell you about others, too.

And no matter where you live in Canada, read Al Purdy.

Example: Teaching "The Local" in British Columbia

This list is by no means meant to be comprehensive—it's a starting point. It is also deeply shaped by my own reading and my circle of writer friends, many of whom made these suggestions. All material in quotation marks is from the publishers of these books.

Burnaby

Hiromi Goto, *Half World*. "Melanie Tamaki is an outsider. Unpopular and impoverished, she is the only child of a loving but neglectful mother. She barely copes with surviving school and life. But everything changes on the day she returns home to find her mother is missing, lured back to Half World by a vile creature calling himself Mr. Glueskin. Soon Melanie embarks on an epic and darkly fantastical journey to Half World to save her mother. What she does not yet realize is that the state of the universe is at stake. . . ."

Cariboo

Sheila Watson, *The Double Hook*. "In spare, allusive prose, Sheila Watson charts the destiny of a small, tightly knit community nestled in the BC Interior. Here, among the hills of Cariboo country, men and women are caught upon the double hook of existence, unaware that the flight from danger and the search for glory are both part of the same journey. In Watson's compelling novel, cruelty and kindness, betrayal and faith shape a pattern of enduring significance."

Chinatown, Vancouver

Wayson Choy, *The Jade Peony*. "Chinatown, Vancouver, in the late 1930s and '40s provides the setting for this poignant first novel, told through the vivid and intense reminiscences of the three younger children of an immigrant family. They each experience a very different childhood, depending on age and sex, as they encounter the complexities of birth and death, love and hate, kinship and otherness. Mingling with the realities of Canada and the horror of war are the magic, ghosts, paper uncles and family secrets of Poh-Poh, or Grandmother, who is the heart and pillar of the family."

Sky Lee, *Disappearing Moon Café*. "Sometimes funny, sometimes scandalous, always riveting, this extraordinary first novel traces the lives and passionate loves of the women of the Wong family through four generations. As past sins and inborn strengths are passed on from mother to daughter to granddaughter, each generation confronts, in its own way, the same problems—isolation, racism the clash of cultures—and each evolves a little bit more."

Cyberspace

William Gibson, *Neuromancer*. "Here is the novel that started it all, launching the cyberpunk generation. With *Neuromancer,* William Gibson introduced the world to cyberspace—and science fiction has never been the same. Case was the hottest computer cowboy cruising the information superhighway—jacking his consciousness into cyberspace, soaring through tactile lattices of data and logic, rustling encoded secrets for anyone with the money to buy his skills. Then he double-crossed the wrong people, who caught up with him in a big way—and burned the talent out of his brain, micron by micron. Banished from cyberspace, trapped in the meat of his physical body, Case courted death in the high-tech underworld. Until a shadowy conspiracy offered him a second chance—and a cure—for a price. . . ."

East Vancouver

Wayde Compton, *49th Parallel Psalm*. "Compton's first poetry book: a stunning set of poems documenting the migration of blacks to Canada, specifically when the first black settlers—facing an increasingly hostile racist government—left San Francisco and travelled north to British Columbia beginning in 1858."

Ivan Coyote, *Missed Her*. "In her passionate and humourous new collection, Ivan takes readers on an intimate journey, both literal and figurative, through the experiences of her life: from her year spent in eastern Canada, to her return to the west coast, to travels in between. Whether discussing the politics of being a butch with a pet lapdog, or befriending an effeminate young man at a gay camp, or revisiting a forty-year-old heartbreak around her grandmother's kitchen, Ivan traverses love, gender and identity with a wistful, perceptive eye, and a warmth that's as embracing and powerful as Ivan herself."

Evelyn Lau, *Runaway: Diary of a Street Kid*. "A bestselling memoir, *Runaway* is a story of survival: physical, emotional and psychological. It is at times tragic, sometimes infuriating, but always honest and inspired; *Runaway* makes no apologies and offers no solutions. It is a vivid and frightening portrait of a young girl's life on the street."

George Ryga, *The Ecstasy of Rita Joe*. "Rita Joe is a Native girl who leaves the reservation for the city, only to die on skid row as a victim of white men's violence and paternalistic attitudes towards First Nations peoples. As perhaps the best-known contemporary Canadian play and a poetic drama of enormous theatrical power, *The Ecstasy of Rita Joe* had a major influence in awakening consciousness to the 'Indian problem' both in whites and Natives themselves. With a preface by Chief Dan George."

Fort St. John

G. P. Lainsbury, *Versions of North* "engages with the environment of northern British Columbia; it is the manifestation of the poet's desire to create a cosmopolitan art in a place that modernity sometimes seems to have skipped right over."

Gulf Islands

Brian Brett, *Trauma Farm: A Rebel History of Rural Life*[1] "tells a story that's poetic, passionate, practical, and frequently hilarious, providing an unforgettable portrait of one farm and of urban life's separation from the natural world, as well as a common-sense analysis of rural life."

Kamloops area

George Bowering, *Shoot.* "The true story of the notorious and murderous McLean Gang that roamed the West of the late 1870s provides the framework for an intricate and often funny chronicle of a group of cultural outcasts who belong to nothing and who meet a tragic end."

Ethel Wilson, *Swamp Angel.* "Walking out on a demoralizing second marriage, Maggie Lloyd leaves Vancouver to work at a fishing lodge in the interior of British Columbia. But the serenity of Maggie's new surroundings is soon disturbed by the irrational jealousy of the lodge-keeper's wife. Restoring her own broken spirit, Maggie must also become a healer to others. In this, she is supported by her eccentric friend, Nell Severance, whose pearl-handled revolver—the Swamp Angel—becomes Maggie's ambiguous talisman and the novel's symbolic core."

Kootenays

Fred Wah, *The Diamond Grill* is Wah's recollections of his boyhood working in his father's Chinese restaurant in Nelson. "This story of family and identity, migration and integration, culture and self-discovery is told through family history, memory, and the occasional recipe. Diamond Grill is a rich banquet where Salisbury Steak shares a menu with chicken fried rice, bird's nest soup sets the stage for Christmas plum pudding, where racism simmers behind the shiny clean surface of the action in the cafe."

Okanagan

Jeannette Armstrong, *Slash.* "*Slash* poignantly traces the struggles, pain, alienation and accounts of a young Okanagan man's search for truth and meaning in his life."

Harry Robinson, *Living by Stories* "includes a number of classic stories set in the 'mythological age' about the trickster/transformer, Coyote, and his efforts to rid the world of bad people—spatla or 'monsters,' but this new volume is more important for its presentation of historical narratives set in the more recent past. As with the mythological accounts, there is much chaos and conflict in these stories, mainly due to the arrival of new quasi-monsters—'shamas' (or Whites)—who dispossess 'Indians' of their lands and rights, impose new political and legal systems, and erect roads, rail lines, mines, farms, ranches and towns on the landscape."

---

1 Starting in 2011, The Writers' Trust Hilary Weston prize produces a teaching resource of short-listed and prize-winning non-fiction books. The first booklet in this series includes material about *Trauma Farm.* Information about the teaching resources and the resources themselves are available on the website of The Writers' Trust.

Prince George

Ken Belford, *Decompositions*. A former guide and outfitter, poet Belford writes plainly and expertly about the life of British Columbia's northern wilderness. "For much of his life, Ken Belford has lived in the north, in the pristine region of the headwaters of the Nass River. His careful (de)compositions disclose the land as a complex living organism, articulate the names of it, see the whole of it. Yet the landscape of these poems is not a matter of latitude and longitude, but that unroaded place which begins at the edge of the rancher's field, wherever that boundary is, and looks back at "civilization" with a vision and a voice that is unique and new. These poems catch their readers up in a surprising social engagement that is at once larger and other than the consumer discourse of trade and ownership."

Brian Fawcett, *Virtual Clearcut: Or, The Way Things Are in My Hometown*. "In the Bowron River valley of British Columbia, there is a logging clearcut so vast that astronauts can see it. Sixty kilometers to the northwest lies Prince George, a once-thriving city of 80,000 that has experienced an accelerating 40-year virtual clearcut that has slashed through the strata of its economic and social culture, wiping out its locally-owned businesses and industries, demoralizing its public institutions and its local politics, and creating a psychological quagmire of entertainment opportunities, consumer franchises, and dreams that won't come true. Prince George has lost its ability to control its destiny, and is losing its will to care. Author Brian Fawcett, who grew up in Prince George and has followed its steady decline, draws a troubling parallel between the shattered forests of Bowron and the gradual destruction of a town's confidence and quality of life, a wake-up call to the rest of the world. *Virtual Clearcut* is classic Fawcett: a blend of unconventional analysis, poignant vignettes, and biting humour. His concern is for the condition of good people and places hit hard by globalization, and how the globalists are harvesting so much more than mere profits from the hinterlands."

Richmond

Daphne Marlatt, *Steveston*. "A collection of poetry and photographs that reinvents the little village of Steveston, close to Vancouver, Canada—a fishing village populated at one time by mostly Japanese fishermen and their wives. [The book includes] [s]plendid black-and-white photographs of the Fraser River, the canneries and the people of Steveston."

Rockies

Howard O'Hagan, *Tay John*. "The awesome terrain of the Rocky Mountains is the setting for this extraordinary novel about a heroic man who boldly defies destiny. Tay John, a messianic halfbreed, is fated to lead his people to their Promised Land. In a rebellious act of will, he turns to the mountains to seek his own truths."

Surrey

Gurjinder Basran, *Everything Was Good-bye*. "*Everything Was Good-bye* centers around Meena, a young Indo Canadian woman growing up in the lower mainland of British Columbia and traces her life as she struggles to assert her independence in a Punjabi community. Raised by her tradition-bound widowed mother, Meena knows the freedoms of her Canadian peers can never be hers, but unlike her sisters, she is reluctant to submit to a life that is defined by a suitable marriage. Though a narrative moving between race and culture, it is ultimately a story of love, loss and self acceptance amidst shifting cultural ideals."

Ranj Dhaliwal, *Daaku*. "In the violent and ruthless world of Indo-Canadian gangs, Ruby Pandher is on his way up. A self-described daaku (Punjabi for outlaw), Ruby learns young that might, in the form of his drunken father's fists, is right and that money is easier to steal than earn. Ruby's small-time scams reveal a knack for leadership and after his first stint in youth detention, the big-timers start to notice his potential. Soon, Ruby is doing collections for Indo-Canadian drug dealers. Now 'known to police,' Ruby is drawn into a gang war just as he's trying to beat the rap on weapons charges and theft—while simultaneously organizing a jailhouse smuggling ring. On the cusp of adulthood, and surrounded by Punjabi terrorists, bikers and Indo-Canadian gangsters, Ruby is drawn like a moth to the glamour of the power, money, and drugs."

Truman Green, *A Credit to Your Race*. "A longtime resident of Surrey, Truman Green wrote *A Credit to Your Race* (1973), in which a fifteen-year-old black porter's son falls in love with, and impregnates, the white girl next door. Set in Surrey, circa 1960, *A Credit to Your Race* is a disturbing and convincing portrayal of how the full weight of Canadian racism could come to bear on a youth."

Vancouver

Irene Baird, *Waste Heritage* "is a remarkably focused, visceral, controversial and uncompromising novel that deals with the labour disputes that were front page news in Canadian newspapers in the summer of 1938. Unlike many novels of the period that offer idealized representations of Canada, *Waste Heritage* exposes a deeply hypocritical, violent and divided society."

Michael Barnholden, *Reading the Riot Act: A Brief History of Riots in Vancouver*. "Every city has its distinct history of rioting—the Rocket Richard riots in Montreal, the Christie Pits riot in Toronto, the Winnipeg and Regina riots, even the Shakespeare riots in New York where rival factions rioted over which actor was the better interpreter of Shakespeare's work. *Reading the Riot Act* is a popular history that rereads and rewrites the legacy of riots in Vancouver. The project was conceived following the city's Stanley Cup riots in 1994, when official reports and media coverage differed significantly from eyewitness accounts. Later, media reports on the APEC riots downplayed and obscured certain facets of the conflict. Seeking out sources beyond the official reports, Barnholden has compiled a record of participants and observers, allowing the 'vanquished' to have their say. Barnholden shuns the simplistic 'bad apple' explanation, and explores the deeper economic causes and effects of riots."

Helen Potrebenko, *Taxi*. "In the 1970s and '80s, Helen Potrebenko was a cherished and important Vancouver writer, well known for her early writing in *Pedestal,* Canada's first women's-liberation newspaper, and for her numerous books that included short stories, novels, poems and plays. Hers was the significant working-class urban feminist voice. She also had jokes, good ones. Modern Times, a major bookstore in San Francisco, had a big sign telling customers that if they only read one book in 1975, it should be *Taxi*!"

Jane Rule, *The Young in One Another's Arms* "is set at the end of the Vietnam War in and around a boarding house in the Kitsilano neighborhood of Vancouver. Ruth, a middle-aged woman accustomed to tragedy in her own life, cares for the young and changing boarders of her house as a mother and guide. The novel is about the building of female communities. Combining issues of race, gender, sexuality and politics, this warm, sophisticated novel celebrates the camaraderie and strength of women against a backdrop of war and tragedy."

Michael Turner, *Kingsway*. "A collection of linked poems inspired by Kingsway, Vancouver's oldest thoroughfare, which is neither a 'street' nor an 'avenue' but a 'way' of thinking—about cities, people, and different points of view. It demarcates the community of the living: a thoroughfare that is repeated in cities across the country, a world of strip malls, Chinese restaurants, and car repair shops."

Rex Weyler, *Greenpeace: How a Group of Ecologists, Journalists, and Visionaries Changed the World*. "In the late 1960s, as cultural upheaval swept the world and American war resisters flooded north, a disarmament and ecology movement took shape in the streets, pubs, and private living rooms of Vancouver, Canada. In the decade from 1969 to 1979, the loosely-knit protest group adopted the name "Greenpeace" and transformed itself from an effective, but decidedly underground, international heckler into a mobilized, global 'eco-navy.' This is their story."

Vancouver Island

Jack Hodgins, *Spit Delaney's Island*. Jack Hodgins does for small town Vancouver Island what William Faulkner did for small-town Mississippi. "The lush green forests, the pulp mills, the all-encompassing sea, and the ferries crossing to the mainland permeate this stunning collection of short fiction. Opening and closing with stories about Spit Delaney himself, the operator of Old Number One steam locomotive in the local mill, the volume travels between the harsh world of its people's reality and the comforts of their fantasies."

Why Is Telling Historical Tales in School Important?

By Linda MacKinley-Hay and Bill Hay, University of Northern British Columbia

Mapping Survival in the Twenty-First-Century Canadian Upper-Secondary Classroom

At the 2010 Winter Olympics opening ceremony held in Vancouver, Canadian poet Shane Koyczan attempted to define Canada for a global audience. He likened the country to an unfinished "story told to your friends" (2010). This apt comparison clearly alludes to Canada and its history as a narrative and one that, as Griffiths suggests in his preface to *Story of a Nation: Defining Moments in Our History,* is "not something transfixed in amber, but a story that is open to us to create and recreate in the image of the values we hold important as Canadians" (Griffiths, 2001, p. ix). Moreover, it is a story in which we must be able to identify both ourselves and our place. Factor into this the "changing face of Canada" as reflected in the twenty-first century multicultural secondary classroom (Friesen, 2010), and it becomes apparent that literary study plays a vital role in the successful integration of new Canadians. When one also considers that, as members of the human community, each student has "a life story, an inner narrative . . . which is constructed continually, unconsciously" (Sacks, 1985, p. 105), curriculum theorists and teachers must heed Cynthia Chambers' call for "new interpretive tools for understanding what it means to be Canadian" in the current multicultural climate (Chambers, 1999, p. 137).

In terms of curriculum development, turning to a new Canadian literary canon that "embraces cultural diversity as the rule rather than the norm" might be valuable (Hanson, 2010, p. 24). The incorporation into secondary literary studies of Canadian historical novels by writers such as Joy Kogawa, Michael Ondaatje, Wayson Choy, Joseph Boyden, and Lawrence Hill—writers from minority groups who are likely "the first to feel secure enough about their [own] place in Canadian society to write about their histories" (qtd. in Wyile, 2007, p. 157)—will go far to address the needs of Canadian students and ensure their "survival" in an unfamiliar context. In the absence of any unifying national narrative, not only do these writers dialogue with public history in their texts, but they also introduce considerations of class, race, ethnicity, and post-coloniality that are certain to provoke readers to search for themselves within the telling of the stories. John Berger's line from the epigraph to Ondaatje's *In the Skin of a Lion,* "Never again will a single story be told as though it were the only one," could essentially serve as the mantra of the current group of Canadian novelists whose historical fiction, instead of "unilaterally conveying an authoritative historical account to be passively consumed," "emphasizes rather than suppresses the multiplicity of viewpoints and the narrative strategies involved in constructing a plausible story about historical events" (Wyile, 2007, p. 18).

While the ultimate goal of literary study in the classroom is literacy, it is crucial to use imaginative literature such as the stories above to assist students in learning how to read and later in honing those reading and writing skills. Story serves as a means to sort out both identity and place, and when the story is a blend of fact and fiction—as in the case of the historical novel—it not only provides students with vicarious experience, but "by logical extension gives them access to cultural and historical information" (Gutteridge, 2000, p. 89).

Why, one might ask, do Canadian novelists turn to history in an age of globalization and technological change? To answer this is to understand why the historical novel addresses the needs of the diverse secondary school classroom. History, writes Rudyard Griffiths (2001, pp. viii–ix), "gives us a renewed sense of place and context" and an opportunity to "reimagine community" and connect "one's personal narrative with the story of a larger whole"—in effect, supporting the concept of community within diversity.

In addition to having achieved national and international acclaim, the novels *Obasan, In the Skin of a Lion,* and *The Jade Peony* represent the large East and South Asian migrations to Canada with their attendant difficulties; *Three Day Road* offers a First Nations perspective on the residential school system and the First Nations contribution to World War I; and *The Book of Negroes* revisits the treatment of Black Loyalists in eighteenth-century Nova Scotia. A number of these texts are already used in Canadian secondary schools and therefore developing units around such contemporary historical novels is entirely feasible.

How Should These Novels Be Taught?

A possible unit plan could feature teacher- and student-led discussion and presentations on story, Canadian history, multiculturalism, and Canadian culture. Through interactive discussion, students can become aware of others' stories and the inherent unfairness of stereotyping as well as distrusting difference. The unit proposed below is designed to allow students time to read independently, to absorb the material, and to recognize others' stories in relation to their own. Its duration will differ depending on timetable scheduling of individual schools; however, we envision 15 classes over the course of two months.

Month 1

Week 1 (two classes):

1. Introduce the Canadian historical novel and two novels within this genre you have selected for study. Selection of the novels should take into account the composition of the particular secondary class and the needs of the students involved. Students may be invited into the process of selection if there are several possibilities in the school inventory.
2. Begin by having students freewrite their own stories.
3. Invite students to share these verbally, collecting the stories afterward.
4. Discuss the differences between a "historical" account (of an event) and a fictitious account of this same event, producing examples of each and speculating about what one might learn about Canada and Canadian culture through these differing accounts.
5. Introduce two of the novels from the five recommended for this unit plan—or from the expanded list below.
6. Consider the authors' heritage and the scene or setting of each, following up with a teacher-led shared reading of at least the first chapter, thereby engaging the entire class in the venture while stopping periodically to examine aspects of the chapter such as point of view, character, tone, and potential conflict.
7. Ask each student to choose one of the two novels for reading over the first month, thereby according some autonomy over the project. The second novel will be read during the second month of the novel study.
8. Students begin their independent reading of the novel armed with journals in which they are encouraged to note their observations and make brief comments.
9. During Weeks 2, 3, and 4 (one class each week), students will participate in small, student-led group discussions on teacher-generated topics. Possible topics include the following:
   1. i. Students' initial impressions of the developing aspects of the story—character, plot, language, conflict, theme, and so on;
   2. ii. Students' findings from research conducted on historical events and characters contained in the novel;
   3. iii. Students' recognition of the multicultural aspects of the novel—cultures, differences, similarities, conflicts, prejudices, and so on.

Month 2

Weeks 5 and 6 (one class each week):

1. Students begin independent reading of the second novel, again keeping journals for noting observations and making comments.
2. Students continue participating in student-led discussions on teacher-generated topics. Possible topics might include the following:
   i. Students' consideration of aspects of good storytelling—from historical account to "good story";
   ii. Students' selection of an important scene from the novel and preparation of a dramatization with commentary.

Week 7 (three classes):

1. Students continue independent reading of second novel, again keeping a journal.
2. Groups share their findings related to the aforementioned topics.
3. The teacher leads class discussions on comparisons and contrasts in relation to the above topics.
4. Groups present scene dramatizations with commentaries, followed by teacher-led discussions.

Weeks 8 and 9 (one class each week):

1. Students complete sharing and presentations from Week 7.
2. The teacher leads discussions on important aspects of both novels.
3. The teacher introduces and presents a final writing project for the novels. Possible topics might include the following:
   i. Students revise their freewritten personal stories from Week 1;
   ii. Students select a modern public figure or incident and write a short historical story about that figure;
   iii. Students compare and contrast cultures within the two novels;
   iv. Students develop a longer composition from journal observations and commentaries;
   v. Students examine the novels for ideas about what it means to be Canadian.
4. Introduction of extended activity:

Present three additional Canadian historical novels for possible reading to be taken from the remaining recommended novels or from the following list:

River Thieves—Michael Crummey

The Trade—Fred Stenson

Icefields—Thomas Wharton

A Discovery of Strangers—Rudy Wiebe

No Great Mischief—Alistair MacLeod

The Last Crossing—Guy Vanderhaeghe

(Continued)

Month 2, *continued*

Away—Jane Urquhart
Ravensong: A Novel—Lee Maracle
Burning Water—George Bowering
George and Rue—George Elliott Clarke
Through Black Spruce—Joseph Boyden

References

Atwood, Margaret, et al. (2001). *Story of a nation: Defining moments in our history.* Toronto, ON: Doubleday.

Chambers, Cynthia. (1999). A topography for Canadian curriculum theory. *Canadian Journal of Education* 24(2), 137–150.

Friesen, Joe. (2010). Diversity: The changing face of Canada: As minority population booms, a visible majority emerges. *Globe and Mail*, March 10, A1+.

Griffiths, Rudyard. (2001). Preface. In *Story of a nation: Defining moments in our history,* Margaret Atwood et al. (pp. vii–x) Toronto, ON: Doubleday.

Gutteridge, Don. (2000). *Teaching English: Theory and practice from kindergarten to grade twelve*. Toronto, ON: James Lorimer.

Hanson, Cheri. (2010). Rebuilding the canon. *Quill & Quire,* April, pp. 24–25.

Koyczan, Shane. (2010). We are more. *Prince George Citizen,* May 13, p. 17.

Sacks, Oliver. (1985). *The man who mistook his wife for a hat, and other clinical tales*. New York: Summit.

Wyile, Herb. (2007). *Speaking in the past tense: Canadian novelists on writing historical fiction.* Waterloo, ON: Wilfrid Laurier UP.

SECTION 3

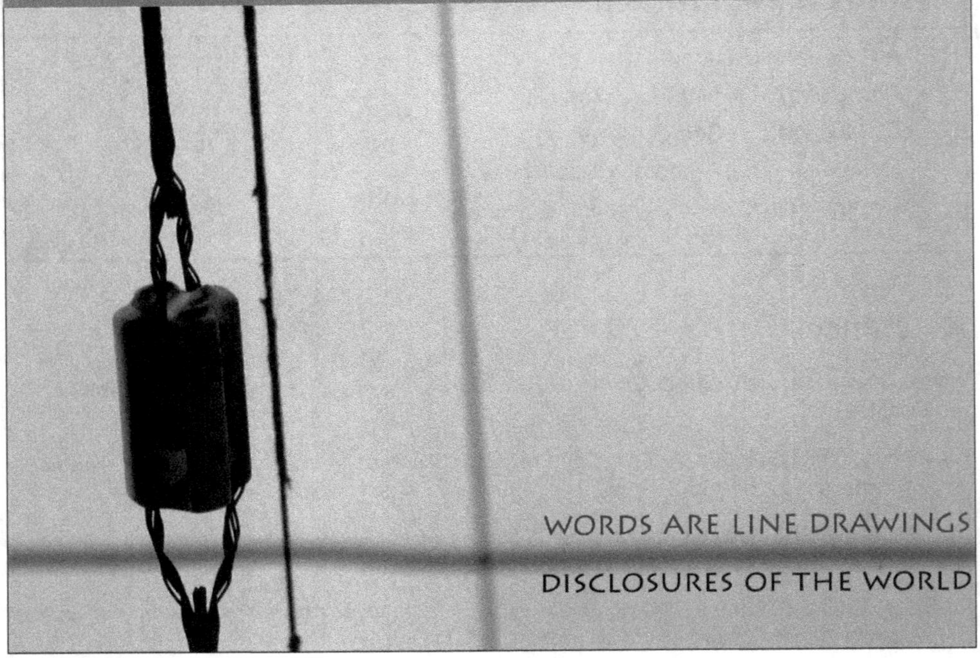

Engaging Adolescent Readers

How Can Drama and Theatre Techniques Be Used to Provide an Entry Point into Literary Study?

By George Belliveau, University of British Columbia

For most middle and secondary school English teachers, picking up a piece of literature is a cherished moment, an adventure to be undertaken. The reality is that for a number of our students, beginning a study of literature can be daunting. Imagine reading the first few pages of a Dostoyevsky novel where countless characters are introduced, or a Dickens novel in which the first sentence continues beyond the midway point of the page, or browsing through the *dramatis personae* of a Shakespearean play and seeing more than 25 characters! Fortunately, scholars and practitioners have developed strategies that can enable students to feel less intimidated and even excited about engaging with a new piece of literature. Let's consider why and how using drama-based pre-reading strategies might enrich (and possibly stimulate) a secondary student's experience with literature. To make the strategies clear, I describe a specific example using Shakespeare's *A Midsummer Night's Dream*; nonetheless, these drama-based strategies can be adapted to other literature or used to prepare students to see live theatre or cinema.

In *The Disciplined Mind,* Howard Gardner builds on his theory of multiple intelligence by proposing "entry points" to introduce learners to complex and challenging topics and works (2000, pp. 188–199). He notes the benefits of using narrative, hands-on, and aesthetic (e.g., drama) entry points to stimulate students to approach new work, to encourage curiosity and anticipation, and to appeal to diverse learners (p. 199). UK theatre scholar John Somers developed in his Applied Theatre research various approaches to initiate students' engagement, one being "compound stimulus" (2008, p. 67). Compound stimulus engages participants through the use of artifacts—usually objects, images, or letters—set within an appropriate container that suits the story or setting of the drama (p. 68). This drama-based strategy has been proven to help participants better understand motivations and rapports between characters and specific artifacts as they begin studying a new work (Somers, 2008). Building on drama education research—particularly in process drama (Bowell & Heap, 2001; O'Toole, 1992; O'Neill, 1995)—Monica Prendergast has developed (through her Belfry 101 research) initiatory activities for secondary students to help them prepare to view live theatre (2002, 2003). Prendergast's drama-based work includes using a theatre production's poster and program, set design, and character descriptions to improvise and devise scenes. Engaging with these objects and concepts allows students to predict and make connections with the play they are about to see. Such an approach has been proven to make a positive impact on students' level of engagement (Prendergast, 2001).

The sample strategies I introduce below are both informed by education and theatre scholars and build on the scholarly literature in arts education. As a former secondary school English teacher in Toronto and Victoria, I have used variations of these pre-reading approaches numerous times. Many of my teacher candidates (now teachers) have been using and adapting this drama-based work in their various classrooms.

Entering *A Midsummer Night's Dream* through Drama-Based Strategies

The following mask-making activity invites students to explore key characters and objects from *A Midsummer Night's Dream* (although it could be a different play, novel, or short story), helping them to enter the world constructed by its author (in this case, Shakespeare). To begin, you'll need various classroom resources (paper, scissors, glue, etc.) and brief descriptions of the characters, such as "**Oberon**: King of the Fairies, temperamental, quarrels with Titania over a child."

a. On a whiteboard, *project or write the character names from the play,* followed by their brief descriptions.

b. From a hat, students will each choose a small slip of paper which contains a character from *Dream* that they are asked to visually *illustrate on a mask, using colours, symbols and facial features.* This is not a visual art class and students are not expected to produce works of art. Their task is to symbolically illustrate key features of the character as given in the description.

c. Once the students have completed their masks, they are to *share their illustration in small groups,* having fellow students discover which character is illustrated on the respective masks. This encourages students to keep looking at the character descriptions on the whiteboard, *familiarizing them with the various characters and identifying relationships* and key features.

d. Once everyone has had the chance to share his or her mask in small groups, the teacher *groups the characters into their respective worlds* (e.g., Demetrius, Lysander, Helena, and Hermia join one another). The play has four distinct worlds: 1) fairies, 2) lovers, 3) mechanicals, and 4) court. By dividing these characters into groups, students are then introduced to the various groupings the play encompasses. This can be extended to overlapping some of the worlds, as they interact with one another. In having Bottom and Flute (through masks) come together, students visually see some of the relationships that unfold in the play, as well as the overlaps (e.g., Bottom entering the fairy world as Titania's lover).
e. *Students then create tableaux* within their worlds to anticipate moments from and tensions within the plot. Suggestions: 1) fairies: squabbling over a child; 2) lovers: hiding in the forest; 3) mechanicals: struggling to rehearse a play; 4) court: hosting a wedding.
f. *Introduce an object* (e.g., prop, letter, clothing) specific to each world and ask the students, in their respective worlds, to find ways to create a new tableaux incorporating the object. Offer, for instance, the lion's mane to the mechanicals, or a sack of magic herbs to the fairies.
g. *Provide one line of text* to each of the characters from the play, so the masks/characters come to life and language is introduced (e.g., *Titania: "These are the forgeries of jealousy"*).

A final note: it is important for students and teachers to place the masks (with character names) and key objects on the wall at the end of the activity. The masks become visual entry points, a gentle reminder for students as they continue their journey and study of the play (or given piece of literature). Digital images of the tableaux can also be taken as reference points.

This sequence of pre-reading activities is meant to help students enter into the world of the play and at the same time encourage them to predict and make initial connections. The use of drama-based approaches to initiate the study of literature has been supported by the work of literacy and drama scholars who suggest that predicting and finding connections increases students' ability and willingness to read and comprehend (Baldwin & Fleming, 2003; Booth, 2005; Smith & Herring, 2001; Wilhelm, 2002). Drama-based pre-texts (Bowell & Heap, 2001) invite students to imagine the world of the literature to be encountered, offering entry points and building confidence prior to studying the literary work. In *Exploring Curriculum: Performative Inquiry, Role Drama, and Learning* (2008), Lynn Fels and I ground our research in complexity and learning theories (pp. 24–30) and share how drama becomes a meaningful way to explore various content areas of the curriculum. More specifically, in chapter 4 on literature and in chapter 5 on poetry, we illustrate drama-based approaches that can be used to begin or end a literature unit. The pre- and post-reading drama strategies invite students to experientially enter the literary texts, using body and voice to explore the context, conflicts, and characters of the fictional or non-fictional world encountered within the text (Fels & Belliveau, 2008, p. 13).

It is important to consider how drama-based strategies can also become stimuli for post-reading, allowing students to reflect on their learning experience. Using, for example, the hot seat strategy (Fels & Belliveau, 2008, pp. 237–38), students can question characters or one another through role-playing, asking how they feel and what they think about certain decisions and outcomes (e.g., has Egeus changed his outlook regarding his daughter's decision to marry? Have Oberon and Titania settled their differences?).

Coming full circle, the same drama-based activities that were used as entry points to begin the literature unit can be revisited. For instance, what could be added to the *Dream* masks after studying the play? What other layers have been discovered? Do these Shakespearean characters resemble other literary characters encountered in class or outside of class? What new levels could be added to the initial tableaux (created during the pre-reading) among the characters and objects? Revisiting the initial pre-reading drama work helps students recognize the journey they took, reviewing where they began and how far they have come, essentially marking their learning. Using body and voice through drama strategies allows students to illustrate aspects of their learning that may not otherwise have been shared through reading, writing, or discussion, offering teachers another lens to assess student learning.[2]

References

Baldwin, P. & K. Fleming. (2003). *Teaching literacy through drama: Creative approaches.* London: Routledge/Falmer.

Booth, D. (2005). *Story drama: Creating stories through role playing, improvising, and reading aloud.* Markham, ON: Pembroke Publishers.

Bowell, P. & Heap, B. (2001). *Planning process drama.* London: David Fulton.

Fels, L., & G. Belliveau. (2008). *Exploring curriculum: Performative inquiry, role drama, and learning.* Vancouver, BC: Pacific Education Press.

Gardner, H. (2000). *The disciplined mind.* Penguin Books: New York.

O'Neill, C. (1995). *Drama worlds: A framework for process drama.* Portsmouth, NH: Heinemann.

O'Toole, J. (1992). *The process of drama: Negotiating art and meaning*. London: Routledge.

Prendergast, M. (2002). Belfry 101: Audience education in professional theatre. *Stage of the Art, American Alliance for Theatre and Education* 34(2), 4–8.

Prendergast, M. (2003). I, me, mine: Soliloquizing as reflective practice. *International Journal of Education and the Arts* 4(1). http://www.ijea.org/v4n1/index.html (accessed December 29, 2011).

Prendergast, M. (2001). *"Imaginative complicity": Audience education in professional theatre.* Unpublished Master's thesis, University of Victoria, Victoria, BC.

Smith, J. L. & D. J. Herring, D. (2001). *Dramatic literacy: Using drama and literature to teach middle-level content.* Portsmouth, NH: Heinemann.

Somers, J. (2008). Interactive theatre: Drama as social intervention. *Music & Arts in Action* 1(1), 61–86.

Wilhelm, J. (2002). *Action strategies for deepening comprehension*, Toronto, ON: Scholastic Professional.

---

2 See chapter 10 "A question of Evaluation" (pp. 205–219) in Fels & Belliveau (2008) for a full discussion on evaluating and assessing drama-based work.

What Are the Merits and Challenges of Reading Aloud in Class?

By Susan E. Elliott-Johns, Nipissing University

In a number of informal conversations, several middle and secondary school colleagues identified what they regard as the merits and challenges of reading aloud in contemporary classrooms. The merits included our abilities as educators to "bring print to life" in facilitating student learning. Teachers talked about using reading aloud to enable their students to hear and experience all kinds of stories, poems, and non-fiction selections to capture the mood and enjoyment of literature, and to model fluent, effective reading conducted with enthusiasm and skill (e.g., pace, modulation, and vocal expression that engages listeners). Some challenges the teachers cited included their confidence in their abilities to engage older students when reading aloud, questions around whether reading aloud is "appropriate" for older students, teachers' own scant knowledge of suitable literature, the scant availability of suitable resources, a lack of time, and a view that reading aloud is a "luxury." I hope the research, practices, and resources sampled here might encourage teachers to reconsider reading aloud as a way to further enrich and enhance classroom programs. As Philip Pullman suggested in his 1996 Carnegie Medal Acceptance Speech, "We don't need lists of rights and wrongs, tables of do's and don'ts: we need books, time, and silence. 'Thou shalt not' is soon forgotten, but 'Once upon a time' lasts forever."

While much has been researched and written to recommend reading aloud to students before formal schooling and in the early grades, the rich potential for reading aloud in middle grades and secondary levels is often overlooked. However, research has indicated that motivation, interest, and engagement are frequently enhanced when teachers read aloud—including reading aloud with older students and even "across the curriculum" (Albright, 2002; Beers, 1990; Ivey & Broaddus, 2001).

Peterson and Swartz (2008) advocate for the benefits of reading aloud in the middle and secondary years and for utilizing picture books as a resource:

> Since picture books are designed to be read aloud, children can experience literature through the ear and the eye, and perhaps be touched by the emotional quality inherent in this art form. Sometimes adults forget that students in the middle years are especially needful of hearing stories read aloud. Through modeling, the adult demonstrates the importance of reading, their attitude toward print, and the satisfaction of a story. (p. 88)

Recommending picture books suitable for older readers (ages 12 and up) and reminding educators of the increasingly sophisticated design and formatting of these books that make them appealing to an older audience, Peterson and Swartz argue that many picture books today contain controversial themes and complex issues of relevance to mature readers. Furthermore, these stories often have "universal, archetypal, or strong emotional appeal" (p. 92). For example, titles by Chris Van Allsburg, Eve Bunting, or David Bouchard all offer visually appealing books with thought-provoking, critical issues and themes in the text. While students in grade 7 and up may be reluctant to select a picture book for independent reading, shared reading experiences and interactive "read alouds" (Harvey & Goudvis, 2009) allow students to engage in reading words and pictures at the same time.

Lamenting that "we know very little about teacher read-aloud practices beyond the elementary grades," Albright and Arial (2005) surveyed three middle schools in one district and discovered that many middle school teachers (85.8 percent) were reading aloud to their students. However, teachers were also found to be placing more emphasis on instrumental purposes for reading aloud (e.g., facilitating students' learning via modelling, making challenging texts available, supporting comprehension and reinforcing content), while giving considerably less attention to reading and listening to literature selections for aesthetic reading purposes (e.g., constructing personal meaning, making connections, or creating "virtual" experiences through reading aloud).

Serafini and Giorgis (2003) outline research suggesting that reading aloud plays a role in the improvement of test scores and student achievement. As Routman (2003) comments, reading aloud is about teaching students *why* to read, and not merely *how* to read: "it's about inviting them into the world of literature and exposing them to the joys of reading" (p. 11). Serafini and Giorgis's "13 Good (Scientifically Based) Reasons to Read Aloud with Older Readers" is a useful resource for educators interested in developing their own practice in this area. Each of the "13 Reasons" reflects compelling purposes for reading aloud in middle and secondary school classrooms. For example, in "Reason #1," Serafini and Giorgis cite increases in students' background knowledge, their familiarity with various story structures, and their demonstration of competent reading strategies as contributors to both improved reading abilities and improved achievement on standardized tests. What follows is a slightly adapted version of "13 Good Reasons to Read Aloud":

1. *Reading aloud increases test scores.*
2. *Reading aloud (i.e., a wide range of text selections on a regular basis) introduces readers to new titles, authors, illustrators, genres, and text structures.*
3. *Reading aloud builds a sense of community.*
4. *Reading aloud provides opportunities for extended discussions.*
5. *Reading aloud with older readers is pleasurable.*
6. *Reading aloud connects readers with content area subjects.*
7. *Reading aloud demonstrates response strategies.*
8. *Reading aloud increases readers' interests in independent reading.*
9. *Reading aloud provides access to books that readers may not be able to experience on their own.*
10. *Reading aloud provides demonstrations of oral reading and fluency.*
11. *Reading aloud helps readers see the connection between reading in school and reading in life.*
12. *Reading aloud provides demonstrations of quality writing.*
13. *Reading aloud supports readers' development.*

(Serafini & Giorgis, 2003)

Booth (2009) recommends thinking about building communities of readers and writers in our classrooms at *all* ages and stages; he regards reading aloud as one of five "basic events" that nurture and support strategic literacy behaviours. When we read to our students "in role," listeners are assisted in constructing meaning and are likely to be more fully engaged in the experience of listening and interpreting texts. (For example, Booth suggests we might try reading aloud as a traveller, an expert, or a storyteller.) By reading aloud at every opportunity from new or familiar texts, we can share a wide variety of genres and formats with our students, narrate novels or short stories, perform poetry or plays out loud, and read interesting excerpts from content area texts to "challenge [students'] minds with ideas and constructs they may not as yet find in their own reading" (Booth, 2009, p. 70).

Digital literacies and the multiplicity of texts relevant to the literacy lives of older readers are also an essential component of contemporary classroom approaches to reading aloud. (In my own teacher education classes, digital cameras that take stills and video are now an essential tool for sharing texts and illustrations that are read aloud.) We model our own literacy habits by sharing texts we think students will enjoy. Booth describes related behaviours as part of his own literacy teaching:

> I am constantly on the lookout for texts to share with students. I clip newspaper columns, download interesting information from the Internet, search for excerpts from a novel I am enjoying, share a review of a new film, or bring in an instruction sheet from a piece of ready-to assemble furniture. I might scan a selection to use on a data-projector, tape a piece to the board, or make copies for students to read and highlight. (p. 71)

I, myself, am a proponent for reading aloud with students of *all* ages and have continued to read aloud with students throughout my career (from preschool to post-graduate levels). Principles of successful reading aloud are similar whether you are seeking to engage younger or older students. When done well, reading aloud can comprise some of the best classroom moments. Consider incorporating the following six keys to successfully reading aloud in your own developing practice:

1. *Read aloud with students every day or every class.*
2. *Select a wide range of different texts knowledgeably and carefully.*
3. *Always pre-read (i.e., read the text yourself) before sharing texts with students.*
4. *Practise developing expression, pacing, fluency, and modulation.*
5. *Teach students how to listen and how to interpret texts read aloud.*
6. *Foster appreciation for visual literacy and ongoing discussion.*

Some challenges in promoting reading aloud include a lack of quality resources available to teachers. Lists of titles do not, by themselves, develop effective practices. *The Read-Aloud Handbook* by Jim Trelease (2007) is a useful resource (now in its sixth edition), but resources that support reading aloud in classrooms and, more specifically, in the later grades, have not always been helpful. In my experience, reading aloud is not often given its due as a teaching skill that improves with practice. Trelease's handbook offers some guidance to teachers, but is primarily directed toward parents and caregivers. A resource better suited to teachers is David Bouchard's (2001) work, which includes sections focusing on families, books, and reading; teachers, students and literacy; and administrators, districts, and schools (it also includes recommended selections for reading aloud across different genres). In a companion text, Bouchard et al. (2004) suggest many annotated titles for reading aloud, divided according to age group and including a category suitable for secondary school students, "Fifteen and Up."

Last but not least, some of the best practical resources are by Laminack and Wadsworth (2006), who have indeed revolutionized the read-aloud technique. Both texts offer much food for thought in terms of building time into your lessons for reading aloud every day, across the curriculum. In addition, many resources can be found on the internet that promote a "readers' theatre" and opportunities for students to read aloud and share stories in their own voices—but select from these with care. Ensure that the scripts are not too long and that they involve only a minimal number of speaking voices. Flynn (2007) outlines a novel approach to a readers' theatre that involves students in collaborative work by having them write short, focused scripts around topics that grow out of the curriculum. Furthermore, when the scripts are rehearsed and presented in class, there are opportunities for all students to participate in solo or choral parts. Flynn writes that some secondary school teachers "have (also) shared scripts about classroom procedures, anti-bullying, memories of the school year, tolerance" and so on (2007, p. xii). Flynn's numerous examples of ways to get students motivated to read (and write) through readers' theatre (including sample scripts that can be used as models to get them writing their own) make this work another highly recommended resource for teachers.

References

Albright, L. K. (2002). Bringing the Ice Maiden to life: Engaging adolescents in learning through picture book read-alouds in content areas. *Journal of Adolescent & Adult Literacy* 45, 418–428.

Albright, L. K. & Arial, M. A. (2005). Tapping the potential of teacher read alouds in middle schools. *Adolescent & Adult Literacy, 48(7)*, 582-692.

Beers, G. K. (1990). *Choosing not to read: An ethnographic study of seventh-grade illiterate students.* Unpublished doctoral dissertation, University of Houston, TX.

Booth, D. (2009). *Whatever happened to language arts?* Markham, ON: Pembroke Publishers.

Bouchard, D. (2001). *The gift of reading: A guide for educators and parents.* Victoria, BC: Orca Book Publishers.

———. (2004). *For the love of reading: Books to build lifelong readers.* Victoria, BC: Orca Book Publishers.

Flynn, R. M. (2007). *Dramatizing the content with curriculum-based readers theatre, grades 6–12.* Newark, DE: International Reading Association.

Harvey, S. & Goudvis, A. (2009). *Strategies that work* (2nd ed.). Portsmouth, NH: Heinemann.

Laminack, L. L. & Wadsworth, R. M. (2006). *Learning under the influence of language and literature: Making the most of read alouds across the day.* Portsmouth, NH: Heinemann.

———. (2006). *Reading aloud across the curriculum: How to build bridges in language arts, math, science, and social studies.* Portsmouth, NH: Heinemann.

Ivey, G. & Broaddus, K. (2001). "Just plain reading": A survey of what makes students want to read in middle school classrooms. *Reading Research Quarterly* 36, 350–377.

Pullman, Philip. Carnegie medal acceptance speech. *Philip Pullman: His dark materials.* Random House. http://www.randomhouse.com/features/pullman/author/carnegie.php (accessed December 31, 2011).

Peterson, S. & Swartz, L. (2008). *Good books matter.* Markham, ON: Pembroke Publishers.

Routman, R. (2003). *Reading essentials: The specifics you need to teach reading well.* Portsmouth, NH: Heinemann.

Serafini, F. and Giorgis, C. (2003) *Reading aloud and beyond.* Portsmouth, NH: Heinemann.

Trelease, J. (2007). *The read-aloud handbook* (6th ed.). New York: Penguin Books.

Poetry Has Sprung to Life in the Contemporary World. How Do I Choose What Poetry to Teach?

By Lorri Neilsen Glenn, Mount Saint Vincent University

It's not difficult, because poetry is everywhere. It's how we sing our lives. You will find poetry in local spoken word performances, online groups, festival slam sessions, in audio files at poetry websites, on YouTube, on the radio, and in podcasts. In fact, the rich offerings out there may overwhelm us—we have so much from which to choose. Where are your students from? What moves them? What makes them want to sing in the streets, set their hair on fire? Are they urban or rural, are they contemplative or edgy? Do they love the sounds that words can make, do they love to tap along to a tune? Follow their lead; look for free verse, formal verse, lyric poetry, narrative or epic poetry, country songs, spoken word, rap, sound poetry, haiku—you name it—and help your students find the works that speak to them. Don't censor what they find (within reason, of course). Whatever entry point we can find we should use. Immersion in a wide range of forms and voices will not only encourage students' poetry writing (and perhaps yours), but it will stretch their poetic minds, give them a rich and diverse sense of what words can do and where we can take them, as well as where they can take us. The more poetry we are exposed to, the more discerning we become.

Poetry is from the body and from the heart and it is essential to the spirit. You may not find those words in your curriculum document. Don't worry about that. And don't worry about curriculum outcomes when you begin to teach poetry. Those will follow; trust me. How you choose poetry depends on how well you know your students. If you want them to become energized, and excited about the written word, you have to get them in the heart and in the gut. You have to meet them where they are (sometimes they may make you wince, and sometimes they will inspire you with their fine instincts).

If you begin by pulling out a list of literary terms, along with a collection of canonical poems with allusions that are obscure to contemporary audiences, you may snap the wings of poetic joy from the outset. So, where to find poetry? Call up (or sign up with) your provincial or regional writers' organization—they'll connect you with readings, websites, resources, and poets who teach. Check out resources on youngpoets.ca, an initiative sponsored by The League of Canadian Poets. Find audio files at poetryfoundation.org or poets.org (American websites). Download podcasts from the CBC (www.cbc.ca) or the Public Radio Exchange (www.prx.org). Check out the U.S. Library of Congress website Poetry 180 (www.loc.gov/poetry/180), which offers a poem for every school day of the year. Invite a local poet to your classroom. Read, read, and read. Write some poetry yourself and bring it to class. Relax and play with words.

About That Curriculum Document

Yes, let's address that issue. Learning is both simpler and more complex than what appears in a list of curricular outcomes. If we are engaged—if we are passionate and hungry about poetry and literature—we immerse ourselves. The deeper and wider the immersion, the greater the learning. I recall the year I taught a secondary school class that rallied around a collective writing and reading project. When the term was over, the students had met the outcomes even though I had not organized class lessons explicitly to meet them. Their engagement and their passion for learning stretched their reading and their confidence, and they reached the goals sideways. It's always been my practice to start with engagement: it's a sign of respect for students' interests, it's a means to create community, and it's guaranteed to sustain interest. I don't mean we pander; we need to be discriminating. But it's the difference between choosing the top-down *shoulds* over community-based *let's try this*.

I Don't Even Like Poetry. *(Or, if I like it, I feel I need to know what it means before I can teach it. I can't teach what I don't know. And don't even get me started on writing poetry—I'm not a poet.)*

Ah, but you've heard of Emily Dickinson. She said, and I'm paraphrasing, "If I feel physically as if the top of my head were taken off, I know that it is poetry." In many ways, we can't teach poetry. It is something we must experience. If we feel the hair stand up on our neck, if we are awash in emotion, if we are in love with the sound and the taste of the words, we are experiencing the poem. Experiencing a poem without talking about it or taking it apart is often enough. When we allow our students that body/mind sensation, we open them up to the beauty and music of language. Moments of lyric engagement are rare; let's cultivate them. Yes, it can be interesting and informative to look closely at a particular poem, talk about the poet's choice of words, how that metaphor works, how rhythm speaks to the tone of the poem. But let's be careful we don't pull the wings off the creature—watching it in flight can often be enough.

Meaning is a loaded word. Practising poets (check out interviews with them) are often themselves baffled about a poem's meaning. As novelist E. M. Forster (1974) once observed, "How do I know what I think until I see what I say?" As a poet, I use words to pick my way through mystery, fog, and thought as dense as wool before a poem emerges: I'd be hard-pressed to make an expository statement, either about the process or the outcome. (Along these lines, consider Louise Rosenblatt's article, "What Facts Does This Poem Teach You?") I may be writing about a prairie phenomenon, for example, but it may take on one meaning for you, and slightly another for me or for another. We may find a sweet spot where we agree, more or less, on meaning, but a good poem should leave room for the reader, too, which is why the notion of creating tests to measure students' understanding of poems baffles me.

And yet, having said all that, you—their teacher, their advocate, their guide, their inspiration—must write with them, not merely dispense assignments. As Donald Murray (2009) says, we must write badly to write well. You must write badly to write well, too, and bring your bad first draft to class. (Anne Lamott [1994] calls them "shitty first drafts.") When my teachers and mentors showed me their early drafts, I was honoured and inspired to see clumsy starts and rocky attempts. They taught me through their courage that writing is messy, that we have to let go, lose control, and let words take us somewhere. If we have ego or control issues, if we lack the confidence to be our flawed, emergent selves, we will let ourselves down and, worse, we'll model a safe compliance, a calculated tentativeness that blunts lives and learning. If we're not feeling some risk, some fear, then we're not stretching ourselves. One thing I have learned is this: when people are engaged with an idea or a process, the last thing on their mind is a grade.

Fear of judgment is rampant in education—try not to let it infect your writing or your teaching. I once offered to take the reins of a secondary English teacher's class for a day to teach poetry. She said she was exhausted, and yet she turned me down. I was puzzled until I learned she was embarrassed for me to find out what her classroom, her daybook, and her students were like. How sad, I thought.

Poetry—the reading, writing, and performance of it—calls on us to let go, to imagine, to feel, to be present and to listen. Linguists and language theorists over the last 50 years remind us that language has many dimensions: we can use language to make rules, to summarize, to theorize, to order and to control. We can also fall into language, let it fall apart on our tongue, let it take us places that light our imagination, places where there are no right answers. As I write this, I am watching a red-winged blackbird gathering materials for a nest on a small, prairie-town street. I could stop what I'm doing and look up its particular name and its species. I could track down the nest, and see if there are eggs yet. I could hover. Or I could sit here, watch the sun jump from behind clouds massive as ocean liners, listen to the blackbird going about her business, and call it—with thanks to whomever provides these moments—poetry.

References

Forster, E. M. (1974). *Aspects of the novel: And related writings*. London: E. Arnold.

Lamott, Anne. (1994). *Bird by bird: Instructions on writing and life*. New York: Pantheon.

Murray, Donald. (2009). Writing badly to write well: Searching for the instructive line. *The essential Don Murray*. Portsmouth, NH: Heinemann.

Additional Resources

CBC podcasts. Canadian Broadcasting Corporation, http://www.cbc.ca/podcasting/index.html (accessed December 28, 2011).

Poetry Foundation website. http://www.poetryfoundation.org/ (accessed December 28, 2011).

Poetry 180. Library of Congress. http://www.loc.gov/poetry/180/ (accessed December 28, 2011).

Poets.org. Academy of American Poets. http:/www.poets.org/ (accessed December 28, 2011).

Public Radio Exchange (PRX). http://www.prx.org/ (accessed December 28, 2011).

Rosenblatt, Louise. (1980). What facts does this poem teach you? *Language Arts 57*, 386–394.

Young Poets. The League of Canadian Poets. http://www.youngpoets.ca/ (accessed December 28, 2011).

What Is the Role of Poetry in Developing Ecoliterate Understandings of the Earth? The Poetry of Place/The Place of Poetry: Ecological Literacy in the English Classroom

By Veronica Gaylie, University of British Columbia

> Compose. (No ideas
> but in things) Invent!
> Saxifrage is my flower that splits
> the rocks.*

—William Carlos Williams, A Sort of Song

* By William Carlos Williams, from *The Collected Poems: Volume II, 1939-1962*, copyright ©1994 by William Carlos Williams. Reprinted by permission of New Directions Publishing Corp.

How Can Language Educators Encourage Experiential Learning, While Ensuring That the Connection between Language and Land Is Also Given Voice?

Current educational and political discourse calls for "sustainable" management of the earth's resources, even as environmentalist education theorists state that a shift in practice must be preceded by a shift in perspective that includes tangible, first-hand awareness of local environments. Val Plumwood (2002) says that the language of learning itself must change: "For the narrative itself . . . leads us to reproduce continuously the same elements of failure . . . while we seek desperately for solutions within it" (p. 6). Some believe that the current environmental crisis rests on a "prior disorder of thought" (Orr, 2004, p. 44). Okanagan Elder Mary Louie states: "The water, it's a gift of life. Our water is . . . disappearing because it's not being respected" (Blackstock, 2001, p. 4). Much of the work of environmental education now focuses on the need to develop in young people a deeper connection to the natural world. Orr questions the study of "science without love" and asks: "Why is it so hard to talk about love, the most powerful of human emotions, in relation to science, the most powerful and far reaching of human activities?" (2004, p. 44).

Where, Then, Is a Language for Teaching and Learning That Will Inspire Awe, Respect, Love, and Heartfelt Appreciation for the Natural Environment as Gift?

The processes of experiential learning outdoors bring transformative understanding in a number of ways. For example, a school garden may be valued as a garden (i.e., as soil and food), in the way it unites a community, and in the way the place itself changes the learning process. In my own experience building a campus garden and researching poetry in schools, I know that the most powerful, most transformative movements typically revolve around students' experiences in the natural environment and the poetic sharing of that experience. When students feel permitted to express their understanding of the "wild world" through their own "wild words," a deep connection is made between learner and land; it is often a connection that moves well beyond a teacher's ability to control it or contain it. In such a way of teaching and learning, both the goal and the process are focused plainly on an ethic of respect and care.

Poetry brings profound awareness to environmental learning. Yet, such understanding can be difficult to prove using standardized or traditional methods of learning and measurement. Reading a list of resources on the subject is only meant as a starting point to help contextualize such a teaching practice. Environmental learning in poetry or eco-poetic inquiry always involves setting a tone of deep care for the world combined with profound joy in experiential learning and discovery. As an English teacher, I have taken my students into creek beds, up mountainsides, and into the watersheds of British Columbia.

How Does Eco-Poetic Inquiry Take Place?

In environmental learning, nature is the teacher. To permit nature's teaching means to nurture in students an approach to the environment and learning that includes but also moves beyond a scientific awareness and even an aesthetic appreciation. When students begin to respect and honour the natural world for its own sake, they also begin to respond to the earth as if they were, in fact, a part of it. A lesson in environmental immersion might be: "Listen. What do you hear? What do you see?" A teacher in the environment learns alongside her students; she bends, weeds, and digs with them.

I usually start my eco-poetry classes in schools by asking students: Where is the *environment*? Many point out the classroom window and say: "Out there." Some say: "Up in the mountains." Others say: "In that water bottle on the window sill." The idea that "the environment" is somewhere else, always out of reach (even beyond their own bodies), is common in classrooms. Such awareness, accepted for centuries in science-based learning, allows us to theorize about the earth as if our actions do not carry consequences, as if the "environment" that is "out there" can be damaged without any intrinsic, organic changes to the system of which we are all a part.

Also, as a system itself, eco-poetic teaching and learning rarely take place in isolation. Like many environmental educators, I do not have a background in the natural sciences. I teach lessons in the garden with community gardeners or other local experts; I may sometimes co-teach a lesson on the local "bio-region" with a science teacher. In such lessons, the ultimate collaborator is nature. I tell my students: "Now we are going into nature. We are going out there. Your assignment: Take note." What takes place from that point forward is a deep sense of learner empowerment as students immerse themselves in forests, in rivers, in city parks, and abandoned lots; they return with their "field notes," journals to share their discoveries. Students in eco-poetic inquiry do not simply fulfil course-load assignments or meet standardized achievement requirements; they learn how to learn and, in their sharing, they learn how to lead.

Eco-poetry is language that both describes and embodies the earth. Teaching, learning, and research in eco-poetics has the potential to recognize our creative, emotional, and responsive selves within the world around us while viewing, with skepticism, the rational scientific perspectives that have dominated human interaction with the planet. Eco-poetry and eco-poetic learning, then, include aspects of traditional nature poetry (for example, in the close observation of nature) while recognizing the intricate, fragile systems of life and the role humans have played in changing such systems, as well as the intrinsic value of preserving the integrity of such natural systems. Teaching and learning eco-poetically depends a great deal on humility and on recognizing and honouring the limits of both nature and humans. Writing poetry outdoors with students invites a new, radical approach to language, learning, and literacy where the outcome involves a deeply situated and open-hearted authenticity, one that begins so simply: sit still in one's surroundings, and listen.

Eco-poetic learning depends on letting students learn by finding their own pathways and asking their own questions. Such a way of encountering the world, through love and through a poetic heart, can be a difficult lesson for both new and experienced teachers. However, in eco-poetic inquiry, there is no knowing the earth without learning at the level of the earth, without returning to humility/humus—to the earth itself. Poetry, and teaching and learning poetically, cultivates in students a capacity to use knowledge without harming their surroundings. Poetry teaches students how to be present to the world and to the word.

By approaching the world through careful, close observation, a poet listens and learns from a stance of deep appreciation. To invite students to describe and study their surroundings through poetry is an invitation to connect to the world, to their neighbourhoods and local bio-regions, with all of the awareness, feeling, emotion, awe, care and gentleness that poetry brings to the world.

Stories are embedded in the natural world, beyond the English classroom. The natural environment is deeply embedded in story, far beyond the science classroom. The inclusion of the poetic imagination in ecological literacy brings to life new connection between learning and land that allows students to understand deeper questions about their roles as storytellers, and as learners, in the larger world. A garden becomes a poem in the telling, and in the permission to tell.

Poetry allows students to explore the mud, water bodies, flowers, and rocks of the world in a way that embodies the world. The value of eco-poetic inquiry as a method in teaching and learning is the gentle connection made between the learner and the land itself. When students engage in such exploration, the lesson is rooted within the process of life as students discover the meaning of their local ecologies through the same methodologies they use to explore them. In eco-poetic inquiry, the process of a lesson mirrors its purpose: to cultivate a careful, close observation of the natural world. As poets have known across the centuries, it is possible, even easy, to make profound connections to the land through language in a way that leaves the lightest of footprints.

References

Blackstock, M. (2001). Water: A first nation's spiritual and ecological perspective. *B.C. Journal of Ecosystems and Management* 1, 1–14.

Orr, D. W. (2004). *Earth in mind: On education, environment and the human prospect.* Washington, DC: Island Press.

Plumwood, A. (2002). *Environmental culture: The ecological crisis of reason.* New York: Routledge.

Additional Resources

Abbs, P. (2002). *Earth songs: A resurgence anthology of contemporary eco-poetry.* Devon, UK: Green Books.

BC Ministry of Education. (2007). *Environmental learning and experience: An interdisciplinary guide for teachers.* http://www.bced.gov.bc.ca/environment_ed/ (accessed January 2, 2012).

Bryson, J. S. (Ed). (2002). *Ecopoetry: A critical introduction.* Chicago, IL: University of Utah Press.

Ecopoetry Study Packs. Resources for poetry lessons & creative writing. The Poetry Society. Arts Council of England. http://www.poetrysociety.org.uk/content/education/poetryclass/news/0608 (accessed January 2, 2012).

Gaylie, V. (2008). The garden as poem in eco-centred learning. *English Quarterly* 40(3/4), 68–72.

Gaylie, V. (2009). *The learning garden: Ecology, teaching and transformation.* New York: Peter Lang Publishing.

Gaylie, V. (2008). The poetry garden: Ecoliteracy in an urban school. *Language and Literacy* 10(2), n. pag. http://www.langandlit.ualberta.ca/Fall2008/Gaylie.pdf (accessed January 2, 2012).

Gaylie, V. (2009). What is green? Poems from inner city youth. Aboriginal Education Research Centre, University of Saskatchewan. http://aerc.usask.ca/downloads/green-poetry.pdf (accessed January 2, 2012).

Smith, G. A. & Williams, D. R. (Eds.). (1998). *Ecological education in action: On weaving education, culture and the environment.* New York: SUNY Press.

Stone, M. K., Barlow, Z., & Capra, F. (Eds.). (2005). *Ecological literacy: Educating our children for a sustainable world.* San Francisco: Sierra Club Books.

PART 4

Exploring Processes and Products of Learning

By Carl Leggo, University of British Columbia

I recently spent several days with five other Canadian writers in Whitehorse at the Yukon Writers' Festival. I read poetry in a number of public venues and worked with some students. I was interviewed by the local CBC. As part of my agenda I was scheduled for a book-signing at a local bookstore. The only person who spoke to me was a young employee of the bookstore who had been asked by a former student of mine to pick up a copy of my latest poetry book. I spent my time writing in my journal. As a poet in the world, I am almost always lonely; I am always seeking readers.

Mac's Bookstore*

In May in Whitehorse
I sat in Mac's Bookstore,

huddled behind a little table and
a stack of books, ready for signing,

---

* "Mac's Bookstore" by Carl Leggo. Copyright © 2012 Carl Leggo.

filled with just one aching question,
Who is going to walk into Mac's

on a warm Wednesday afternoon
seeking *Come-By-Chance*

about growing old in stories caught
between Atlantic and Pacific coasts?

And because I don't know what
I'm doing in Mac's Bookstore

I write in my journal,
notes for this poem perhaps:

The lonely poet sits alone
at a little table in Mac's Bookstore

exposed in Whitehorse
like a petty criminal

locked in the stock, laughing stock
for the public's gaze

surrounded by the ghosts of
Robert Service and Jack London.

I won't sell many, if any, books,
but J. K. Rowling is a billionaire.

I feel like a bear in a cage
at the zoo or the nature park.

Look, see the poet write.
See the poet pretend to write.

What is the poet writing?
A poem or a grocery list?

See the poet sad with so many
words nobody wants or needs.

Behind the counter Talia tells me she has
more copies of my book in the back

like she anticipates I will need lots more,
or is perhaps stoking my dull desire.

I see the poet, dark and feral and furtive,
in the door of the Coca-Cola cooler,

while a grim old woman sits silently
on my shoulder, like she suspects poets.

A man with a huge mustache stops by,
So, you're from Newfoundland.

I knew a Newf once, he was funny.
Are you funny? Not really, I admit.

Then Charlie shows up, and tells me
he was once taught by a teacher

I once taught, and buys a book because
she asked him to, and we begin to talk

about George Herbert and Anglicanism
and African bishoprics and gay marriage

like those are angles we can handle
without poetry's angels glaring back.

And in the dusty sunlight I stroll back
to the Westmark Hotel, glad I sold a book.

I live in the world as a poet. I spend a part of most days in reading and writing poetry, in the practice of poetry, even in the experience of poetic living. I am constantly vigilant about seeing the world with a poet's senses and heart and imagination. I didn't write poetry in school. I was long out of school when I began to write poetry. I came to poetry only in my late twenties. During a time of personal crisis, I began to write in a journal, and I began to hear a vibrant voice in my writing that I had never heard before. Then I started to write poetry, and I discovered that I had much I wanted, even needed, to say about my daily life and world. Above all, I discovered that I love to revel in the possibilities of language. Now I write poetry as a way to make sense in the world. Like Patrick Lane (2004) observes in *There Is a Season: A Memoir,* "I found my place in the world with language" (p. 169). For the past few decades I have been writing poetry as a way to know the world, as a way to be and become in the world.

As a poet I live by the maxim that the world is words. As human beings, we are born into language, and as human beings we are borne up by language. We are awash in a sea of textuality. Like a whale that moves through the oceans with its environment pressing on its sides while it, in turn, presses its shape on its environment, we move through the ocean of language, universally pervasive, pressed and pressing. In our language use, we are constantly shaped and informed and defined, and we are constantly shaping and informing and defining. We are the words we speak and write and think and hear and read. We speak and write and think and hear and read ourselves into existence.

The challenge for educators is to celebrate the ubiquity, the multiplicity, the plurality, and the wildness of language full of wonder. We weave words and in weaving words we weave our worlds. My concern is that in schools, we educators often get in the way of the processes and products of learning. We try to tame the wildness of language. We try to categorize and box and control the messiness of language. We try to reduce language to basics and essentials and rules and conventions and patterns.

Remembering Writing in School

As a writer in school, I almost always felt inadequate, not quite sure where to put commas, concerned that I did not have anything worth saying, fearful that I was not as humorous or witty or bold or eloquent as my classmates, convinced that I was inferior because I wrote slowly, ashamed that my drafts were messy and chaotic and confusing—a litter of letters sprawling over scraps of paper. I was sure everybody else wrote as if transcribing dictation from speakers inside their heads or hearts or souls or stomachs. I heard voices, too, but they were always too quiet or too loud or too contradictory, voices that drowned one another out, voices that I could never master, confusing voices that silenced my voice. And so I wrote little, and found scholastic success in memorizing facts, formulae, and definitions and transcribing them faithfully in short-answer and fill-in-the-blank tests.

As a student in school in the '50s and '60s, my experiences with writing were essentially similar from grade to grade. Most of my writing comprised written answers to questions, answers that were embedded in the prose of the textbooks and required a simple effort of excavation. Or I wrote notes, essentially the words that the teacher wrote on the blackboard or dictated. Only seldom was I invited to write where the writing was not a simple exercise of copying. Only seldom was I invited to write a story or a poem or even a composition that required a thoughtful collection and selection and inscription of thoughts instead of blatant plagiarism. But even on those infrequent occasions when I was invited to write a story or a composition, the approach that I was required to take was largely counterproductive to creative expression. I remember that the teacher always presented the class with a list of potential topics (the same innocuous and boring topics: How I Spent My Summer Vacation; Lost at Sea; My Most Frightening Experience; A Spider's Web; The Snowstorm; The Virtue of Honesty). We chose one. I do not remember students, even once, suggesting topics. The composition that I wrote was written quickly because the assignment was typically completed in one class period of 40 minutes. This meant that there was usually time for only one draft. Errors were corrected with a rubber eraser. Since compositions always had to be written in ink, the composition could look like a scuffed rug by the end of the class period. If compositions were assigned for homework, there was at least the opportunity to write a clean, neat final copy.

Writing was a very private affair. When I wrote a composition at home, I would occasionally ask a parent to read it, but not often. I did not have a sense that writers sought advice from others. I did not see writing as dialogical or communal. Instead, I almost always perceived writing as a private affair between the teacher and me. I wrote almost exclusively for the teacher who waited expectantly for my composition with the red pencil in hand. I submitted the composition to the teacher who read it, circled the mistakes, and wrote a grade as well as a word of commendation or complaint at the end: excellent work, needs improvement, very good work, shows progress. I learned, in this experience, that writing was a product that I composed for the teacher's consumption and evaluation. Worse, I learned that writing in school was always practice writing, never real writing. The only purpose for writing was learning to write. Writing in school was akin to pushing a big rock up the hill, like Sisyphus, only to see it roll back down again, only to continue the effort over and over. Not once in school did I ever write to an audience other than the teacher—not even to my classmates, unless one counts the occasional surreptitious note. Writing was not integral to our lives; writing was an activity that we engaged in because we were required to and were cajoled with promises that this kind of school writing would one day be beneficial in our lives outside school.

The approach to writing that I knew in school has been called a "product approach" because the focus was on the writing of a product for evaluation. The product approach assumes that all students write in similar ways, that all students can be treated in the same ways and be expected to perform at a similar pace, that they will have similar interests, and that they will all naturally seek to imitate a model paper. But all writers write differently and need ownership of their writing. They need to take responsibility for their writing if their writing is ever going to mean anything to them. There is no single best way to learn to write; each writer must discover what works best for him or her.

Since the early 1970s, writing instruction in schools has focused on the "writing process" model. The writing process model encourages students to understand themselves as real writers: they're invited to write about real subjects, personally relevant to them, in order to communicate with real audiences. The writing process model is organized around overlapping stages such as warming up, drafting, revising, editing, and publishing. The process approach does not compete with the product approach, and it does not preclude an emphasis on creating a well-written product. Instead of seeing the process approach as an *alternative* to the product approach, I prefer to see the process approach as the way to a good product. What is needed in the writing classroom is a balance between an emphasis on the process and an emphasis on the product.

Honouring the Wildness of Language

Richard E. Miller (2005) presents an intriguing notion of autobiographical writing that attends to how the personal and institutional are inextricably connected. He suggests that the goal of institutional autobiography is "to locate one's evolving narrative within a specific range of institutional contexts, shifting attention from the self to the nexus where the self and institution meet" (2005, p. 138). According to Miller, the questions to which a writer must attend include: "What experiences have led you to teach, study, read, and write in the ways you do? What institutional policies have promoted or inhibited your success? What shape and texture has your life in the institutions given to your dreams of release?" (2005, p. 138). Miller promotes "a pragmatic pedagogy" (2005, p. 136) that provides "students with the opportunity to speak, read, and write in a wider range of discursive contexts" than is typically available or sustained "in the culture of schooling" (2005, pp. 140–141).

I emerged from years of school and university education with a conviction that the pedagogical approach to writing I had experienced was not effective. Eventually, my writing began to emerge from a fascination with language, especially the possibilities of the alphabet. I am always enthralled with the magic of grammar, the way that words bump into one another and greet one another and acknowledge their kinship, and the way they dream together possibilities for more creative energy and activity than any one person will ever have time to explore and embrace. This is always my hope—to roam and linger in the alphabet, the dictionary: the places of syntax and semantics. According to Wallace Stegner (1988), writing is "a voyage of discovery that may discover nothing" (p. 9). He wisely recommends that "nobody can teach the geography of the undiscovered" (1988, p. 10). Instead, teachers can "encourage the will to explore, plus impress upon the inexperienced a few of the do's and don'ts of voyaging" (1988, p. 10). As an

English teacher, I always want to investigate why ordered, logical, grammatical arguments fuelled by a classical rhetorical stance are epistemologically valorized. I want to question how the alphabet has been used to construct a linear way of knowing. I am seeking ways to juggle many divergent paths of knowing, to walk down many paths at once, to walk in the maze, the labyrinth, the carnival funhouse of mirrors that lies at the end of the alphabet, in the alphabet, and beyond the alphabet.

Spelling*

in school I learned to spell words with precise correctness
but I seldom learned the sensuous spell of language

in school I learned the rules and stipulations of grammar
but I seldom learned the glamour, the alchemy of prepositions

in school I learned the conventions of syntax
but I seldom learned the lyrical resonances of connections

in school I learned to chant the teacher's dictums
but I seldom learned the enchantment of poetry

in school I learned facts, fat fatuous facts full of lies,
but I seldom learned the restorative joy of fiction and fantasy

in school I learned to colour inside the prescribed lines
but I seldom learned about wild places beyond, elsewhere

in school I learned the denotative definitions of words
but I seldom learned the magic of capacious connotation

in school I learned to be good, an anaesthetic obedience
but I seldom learned to ask with aesthetic wonder, what is good

in school I learned to be neat tidy clean even pristine
but I seldom learned to enjoy the body's erotic energies

in school I learned to grow my brain-mind-head like a cabbage
but I seldom heard my heart beat or the hearts of anyone else

in school I learned to fear the arts like wild lions, lacking logic,
but I still caught glimpses of dandelions in the cracks of sidewalks

and so I dance with lines, straight and slant, curvaceous and cursive
and I dance with dandy lions, too, no longer fearing their ferociousness

Some writing teachers have the notion that they are guardians of the grammar garden. Some teachers see themselves as angels with flaming swords outside the garden, policing and securing traditions of correctness. They have grown up in a system where they are constantly grading students with letters and numbers and are constantly assessing

---

* "Spelling" by Carl Leggo. Copyright © 2012 Carl Leggo.

students according to prescribed standards. They understand grammar as the science of language, or a set of rules, or a system of standards or general principles, or a compendium of preferred and prescribed forms. They understand grammar in the ways they learned grammar in school.

I always felt like grammar involved more than strict rules for the use of the semicolon. So, I was happily surprised when I learned that the word "grammar" is derived from the word *gramarye* (which is now called an archaic word), related to the Old French *gramaire* or "learning." *Gramarye* means magic, occult knowledge, alchemy, necromancy, and enchantment. So, grammar is really about spells and spelling. Understanding grammar in this more accurate and creative way, I promote a poetic return to language that acknowledges purposeful play and playful purpose. Instead of simply being a system of rules and correctness, grammar can acknowledge the wild creativity that is the heart of language. Many years ago, as a grade 7 teacher, my students often called me "Mr. Grammar" because I emphasized the mystery of punctuation, syntax, and parts of speech. Today, I continue to celebrate the wonder of grammar. I am always urging writers to attend to grammar as magical, as full of wonder, as a significant part of the dynamic energy of language. I thoroughly enjoy reading grammar handbooks because I am always attracted to the playfulness of language and the ways that language changes and evolves. I am glad when young people write in any medium or in any language, including slang and text-messaging. I always trust that, if students write, they will grow as writers. In turn, through the active experience of writing and growing as writers, I believe that students will want to learn all they can in order to make their writing as effective as it can be. That includes paying attention to standard language use in those kinds of texts and situations where formal language is expected and needed.

We become readers and writers by engaging with the spells and mystery of language. I think we ought to emphasize the mystery rather than the mastery of language. None of us ever masters language. We can never rest assured there's nothing more to learn. If we embrace the mystery and the playfulness of language, then we remain humble. I embrace Ted Aoki's (2005) wise call for "the voice of play in the midst of things—a playful singing in the midst of life" (p. 282).

In order to grow in confidence about our writing, we need to *own* our writing. Good writers must take responsibility for their writing. Otherwise, they will always be seeking to please the dictates of others—teachers, editors, professional writers. Therefore, an approach to teaching writing where a teacher identifies the writers' errors and demands correction will be counterproductive because the writers will not learn to identify errors on their own. They will not learn to take responsibility for their writing. They will not learn to own their writing, or to care about their writing. This approach does not mean that there is no place for teachers in the writing process; in fact, teachers are essential to the writing process. This view, though, does suggest that there will be more than just one teacher. I like the notion of a group of writers as a group of students and teachers or, even more accurately, student-teachers: everybody is both a student and a teacher, helping and guiding and responding to her or his own writing and to the writing of one another. I object to the common assumption that one person in a group is the teacher with a mantle of authority and expertise that makes this person the writer, evaluator, or judge. All writers need to learn that each act of writing is a new challenge with unique questions, demands, and problems. Hence, writers need to enter each experience of writing with an interrogative spirit open to wonder and surprise; with a bold, even reckless spirit open to uncertainty and change; and with a confident spirit open to the pleasure and power of word-making. But so often, beginning writers or writers who lack confidence will throw up their hands in frustration or befuddlement because they do not know how to proceed and have seldom, if ever, known much success in their writing. Therefore, it is important to demystify the writing process at the same time that the mystery is acknowledged, even celebrated.

Seven Basic Stages of the Writing Process

The following questions can be asked at the beginning of a writing assignment as well as throughout the process of drafts, or even at the end of the assignment. I suspect that some students will need to be led through a more structured process than others. What I like about the following list is that students can use it according to their needs. Some will then use it more frequently than others. I also think that many of the stages are internalized as the writer writes and grows in confidence about writing.

1. Identifying the subject and purpose

   What do I want to write about? What topics, issues, ideas, people, places, experiences, questions concern me? What do I care about? What do I want to learn? What do I want others to learn? Why should I write about this subject? Is it worthwhile? Will anyone else be interested? What do I hope to accomplish by writing on this subject?

2. Considering the audience

   Who am I writing for? Who will be interested in my writing? What do I know about my audience? What does my audience already know? What does my audience want or need to know? What kind of audience response do I hope for? Do I care about my audience?

3. Determining the genre

   Should I write narration, description, exposition, poetry, drama, fiction, creative non-fiction? Do I want to tell a story or argue a point or explain a procedure or describe a place? Which genre is most appropriate for my subject, purpose, and audience? What would I accomplish by writing in a genre that is not typically considered appropriate? What are the conventions of different genres? What is the effect of contravening conventions?

4. Collecting data

   What do I know about the subject? Where can I find out more? What questions do I want to address? What citations, stories, illustrations, comparisons, facts, statistics, evidence, details, examples, or reasons will support the development of my subject?

5. Examining the organization

   What design, order, or shape best serves my purposes in this writing? Can I represent the organization in an outline or graphic organizer? Where do I want to go in the writing? Where do I begin? Where do I end? What are the main points of interest on the journey? What are the main questions to be asked or answered? Are my points relevant? What signposts are provided to guide the reader on the journey? Does the writing flow in a logical or convincing or entertaining way? What relationships exist among the different parts of the writing? Do I use effective transitions between paragraphs and between sentences? Do I incorporate supporting evidence into the text in a way that flows?

6. Observing the style

   What point of view do I use? What tone do I use? What voice do I use? Is my voice conversational and intimate, or formal and objective? What is the pace of the writing? Is information given to the reader too quickly or too slowly? Is the writing confusing or boring? Is each point sufficiently dealt with? Is there balance in the writing? Do main points receive sufficient development while minor points are treated appropriately? Is the writing superficial or dull? Is the writing full of clichés or stereotypes? Are words wasted? Are there places where words could be deleted? Does the writing indicate a desire for readers? Is it lively and energetic? Is it a pleasure to read? Do I use a variety of sentence types and lengths? Do I use adjectives and adverbs effectively?

7. Polishing to bring out the finish

   Have I accomplished my purposes in the writing? Have I adhered to standard rules of spelling and punctuation and grammar? If not, why not? Is the documentation accurate? Do I like the writing?

To focus only on writing for the purposes of composing a final product is to limit the experience of writing; but, to focus only on writing as a process is also constraining. What's needed is a balanced approach where teachers and students engage in worthwhile writing experiences that serve a wide range of purposes. These writing experiences should invite exploration and experimentation, as well as the development of useful strategies and skills for writing in diverse genres and for diverse audiences. Above all, the classroom needs to be a location where teachers and students know vibrant experiences with words and word-making. The classroom is an integral part of the larger world that both teachers and students live and grow in. Therefore, the classroom needs to promote engagement with language and literacy that intersects with and extends into the world outside the classroom.

All Writing Creates/All Writing Is Created

Each of the many kinds of text has its own conventions—its own set of expectations, constraints, and purposes. In order to learn how to write well in each of the different kinds of text, it is necessary to know the expectations, constraints, and purposes of different kinds of text. In other words, we need to know about the rhetoric of texts—their art and their science—encompassing how texts are designed, organized, and constructed. The kinds of text seem without end, and new kinds of texts like graphic novels and "movels" (novels based on movies) are being created all the time. Pragmatics is the study of the use of different kinds of texts. It asks questions like: Who is the audience? What are the purposes of this kind of text? What are the conventions that govern this kind of text? What are the qualities of this kind of text? Finding these answers, a writer can pragmatically investigate the rhetoric of any of the following kinds of written texts:

> abstracts, acknowledgments, acronyms, addresses, advertisements, advice columns, agendas, album covers, alphabets, Alphagetti, anagrams, announcements, aphorisms, applications, autobiographies, awards, ballads, balloons, bibliographies, billboards, bills, biographies, bird bands, books, Braille, briefs, brochures, bulletins, bumper stickers, buttons, calendars, captions, cards, cartoons, certificates, charts, checklists, chemical equations, cheques, clothing labels, codes,

collection notices, colloquialisms, columns, comics, commands, commentaries, commercials, computer programs, concordances, consent forms, constitutions, contracts, coupons, creative non-fiction, credit cards, credit vouchers, creeds, critiques, crosswords, data, debates, deeds, description, diaries, dictionaries, digital pagers, diplomas, directions, dirges, dissertations, documents, doodling, doormats, doublespeak, drama, edicts, editorials, electronic mail, embroidery, encyclopedias, engraving, epics, epitaphs, equations, erotica, essays, eulogies, euphemisms, eviction notices, examinations, exposition (interpretation, argument, analysis, persuasion), fables, fiction, financial statements, flyers, fonts, forms, formulae, fortunes, games, glossolalia, gossip, graffiti, grammars, graphics, graphs, greeting cards, guides, handbooks, headlines, hieroglyphics, history, horoscopes, hymns, identification, inscription, instructions, interviews, invitations, itineraries, jargon, jokes, journals, junk mail, keys, labels, lab reports, languages, laws, lecture notes, legends, letters (Dear Abby, business, application, friendly, thank-you, chain), licences, lifewriting, limericks, lists, literature, logos, logs, lyrics, magazines, magnets, manifestos, manuals, maps, marginalia, marquees, memos, menus, monologues, morse code, movels, music books, mysteries, myths, names, napkins, narratives, newsletters, newspapers, non-fiction, notes, notices, novels, obituaries, odes, orders of service, overheads, packages, pamphlets, parables, placards, poems, policies, pornography, posters, prayers, prescriptions, programs, promises, pronouncements, propaganda, proposals, proverbs, psalms, puns, queries, quizzes, quotations, rebus books, receipts, recipes, reports, research papers, resumes, reviews, riddles, romances, rules, sand-writing, scales, science fiction, screenplays, scripts, scriptures, semaphore, sermons, shorthand, sidewalk chalk messages, signet rings, sign language, signs, skywriting, slang, slogans, songs, speeches, spells, sports cards, stamps, subtitles, summons, symbols, tales, tapestries, tattoos, tests, textbooks, theorems, thesauruses, theses, tickets, titles, tracts, translations, T-shirts, ultimatums, utterances, valentines, vignettes, vows, wallpaper, warnings, wills, write-ups, writs, X-rays, xylographs, yarns, yearbooks, zeugmas, zincographs, zip codes.

Revelling and Revealing: Why Write?

I have developed a long list of reasons for writing, but I know that my reasons are born out of my own happy experiences as a writer. I know personally how writing is integrally connected with pleasure and possibility. When I ask my students about their experiences with writing, many of them articulate a long list of reasons for *not* writing. Some fear evaluation, judgment, errors, misunderstanding, and failure. Some prefer to avoid confronting and revealing personal memories and experiences because they fear exposure and vulnerability. Some lack confidence, will, energy, motivation, encouragement, skills, or time. Some prefer simply to speak, and some prefer to read and listen. Some have had unhappy experiences with writing in school where writing was perceived as work, and where creativity was stifled by rules. Some are concerned that writing leaves a permanent record that might lead to legal culpability. Some question whether or not writing is really all that important in the contemporary world of technological wonders. While acknowledging my students' reasons for not writing, I invite them to consider carefully the countless reasons for writing.

I write in order to

account, accuse, administrate, admonish, advertise, advocate, affirm, aggravate, agree, alleviate, analyze, argue, bind, beg, calculate, change, claim, clarify, classify, command, commend, communicate, compare, complain, compliment, compute, conceal, conclude, connect, constitute, construct, contrast, contradict, control, convince, create, criticize, decide, declare, dedicate, defend, define, denounce, deny, deconstruct, describe, direct, disseminate, earn, empower, encourage, endorse, enlighten, enrich, entertain, evaluate, evoke emotion, excite, expand, explain, explore, expose, express self, fabricate, fantasize, focus, gain fame, gauge, grade, grasp, guard, hail, heal, help, humour, hypothesize, imagine, immortalize, impress, influence, inform, inspire, instruct, interpret, join, joke, judge, justify, keep, know, label, launch, lead, learn, legalize, libel, lie, maintain, make money, manage, manifest, mean, minister, name, narrate, negotiate, observe, organize, pass time, persuade, placate, plan, play, please, preserve, project, propagandize, protect, protest, prove, purge, qualify, question, quicken, reason, recall, record, relieve, remember, remind, report, research, resolve, respond, reveal, review, seduce, select, sell, share, speculate, spur, store, subvert, summarize, support, symbolize, synthesize, teach, tease, tell, test, think, train, translate, understand, undo, utter, value, verify, vindicate, vouch, wail, waken, warn, wonder, X-ray, yammer, yarn, yield, yoke, zero, zigzag.

In order to simplify this expansive list of reasons for writing, I like to focus on five main reasons. I call the first reason **epistemic**, by which I mean that I write in order to know. I know my life as an episodic narrative, more extensive in scope and more intricate in interrelated details than Cervantes' *Don Quixote* (and probably with the same mixture of illusion and delusion). I know my life as an inexhaustible library of stories. In story after story I am protagonist and antagonist, narrator and listener, participant and spectator. In story after story I am the writer/reader collecting, connecting, projecting, constructing, deconstructing, reconstructing, drawing themes, seeking totality, making sense. In my story-making I seek to know.

My second reason for writing is **pedagogic**. I write in order to become. I am a subject in process. My stories do not describe events in the way they happened. They're not autobiographical with claims to empirical veracity. About my stories I am always asking, am I expressing myself or constituting myself or constructing a plurality of selves—sites from which to observe my world or, more cogently, sites where my world is disclosed. Perhaps my life is composed out of the scraps and traces that I seize, not unlike Newfoundland yard art, a menagerie of flotsam from the beach and the forest, gaily painted in the bright colours nobody else wanted at the general store.

My third reason for writing is **revelatory**. I write in order to be true. We need to be open, to take risks in our writing. I know that when I invite people to write about their lives, I invite the opening of Pandora's box. I know that when I invite people to write about their lives, I invite them to write about the death of loved ones, the loss of love, the brokenness of homes, the abuse and loneliness and despair that characterize many lives, young and old. I know that when I invite people to write about their lives, I invite hot tears and overwhelming hurt and unsettling questions, but I am convinced that whatever there is of hope and wisdom and goodness in our world is known as we write our lives truly. I tell my students that I am a writer trying to make sense out of chaos, and I invite them to join me in wording our worlds together.

My fourth reason for writing is **ludic**. I write in order to have fun. I love to play with words. I like to feel words rolling on my tongue. I like to write lists of words that rhyme. I like to read dictionaries. I like to sit in public places and write whatever comes into my head. I like eavesdropping. I like to write sentences that go on and on and on. I like to shape words on the page. I like using different kinds of pens. I like to make up words. I claim that writers are the happiest people in the world. When I was a kid I played with wooden blocks engraved with the 26 letters of the alphabet. I no longer have the blocks, but I'm still playing with the 26 letters of the alphabet. And, like a kid, I remain open to the wonder around me.

My fifth reason for writing is **utilitarian.** I write in order to get things done. This might seem like the most common kind of writing that people do—resumes, business letters, memos. While this reason for writing is significant, I do not think that it should be the main reason that people write. I am committed to nurturing writers filled with desire, writers who take risks in their meaning-making, writers who revel in the wonder of words, writers who know that they weave their worlds as they weave their words as words weave them in worlds spilling and spelling without end.

Leaning into Learning

I am critical of my school education, and I am especially critical about the ways that, as a writer, I was constrained and even wounded by the kinds of experiences that comprised my senior language classes. What I remember most vividly are the repetitive exercises and the focus on drills, discrete activities, and correctness. What I remember least are opportunities to write in innovative and creative ways, to take risks in writing, or to experiment with diverse discourses. David Bohm (2004) does not mince words in his judgment that "generally speaking, what we learn as children, from parents, teachers, friends, and society in general, is to have a conformist, imitative, mechanical state of mind that does not present the disturbing danger of 'upsetting the apple cart'" (p. 20).

As a poet and language educator, I invite and encourage writers to take risks in their writing; to engage innovatively with a wide range of genres; to push boundaries in order to explore creatively how language and discourse are never ossified but always organic, and how language use is integrally and inextricably connected to knowledge, identity, subjectivity, and being in the world. I invite writers, whether English is their first language or an additional language, to know themselves in poetry, to know themselves as poets. We live in a contemporary culture that mostly ignores poetry, at least traditional forms of written poetry. This is very unfortunate because poetry invites alternative ways of knowing and being and becoming. I encourage all educators and students of language and literacy to write poetry because poetry is a capacious genre that opens up endless possibilities for expression and communication.

All writers need to approach every writing project as an adventure with both challenges and joys. But, as I suggested earlier, beginning writers or writers who lack confidence will throw up their hands in frustration or befuddlement because they do not know how to proceed in their writing and they have seldom, if ever, known the wonderful mystery of writing.

So, my advice to young and older writers is simple:

1. Believe in your writing and yourself as a writer.
2. Commit yourself to writing every day.
3. Cultivate a keen sense of your voice.
4. Seek to know the world in writing.
5. Share your writing with others.
6. Always read lots of other writers.
7. Explore and experiment and take risks.
8. Engage innovatively with a wide range of genres.

In Part 4, focused on processes and products of learning, all the authors ask thoughtful and unsettling questions and recommend the kind of creative and engaging approaches to working with diverse texts and discourses that honour language learning as vibrant and vital. After reading the entries in this section, English language arts educators will be inspired and encouraged to lean into old and new adventures with the wild possibilities of language learning.

References

Aoki, T. (2005). *Curriculum in a new key: The collected works of Ted T. Aoki.* W. F. Pinar & R. L. Irwin (Eds.). Mahwah, NJ: Lawrence Erlbaum.

Bohm, D. (2004). *On creativity*. London, UK: Routledge.

Lane, P. (2004). *There is a season: A memoir*. Toronto, ON: McClelland & Stewart.

Miller, R. E. (2005). *Writing at the end of the world*. Pittsburgh, PA: University of Pittsburgh Press.

Stegner, W. (1988). *On the teaching of creative writing: Responses to a series of questions.* E. C. Lathem (Ed.). Hanover, NH: University Press of New England.

SECTION 1

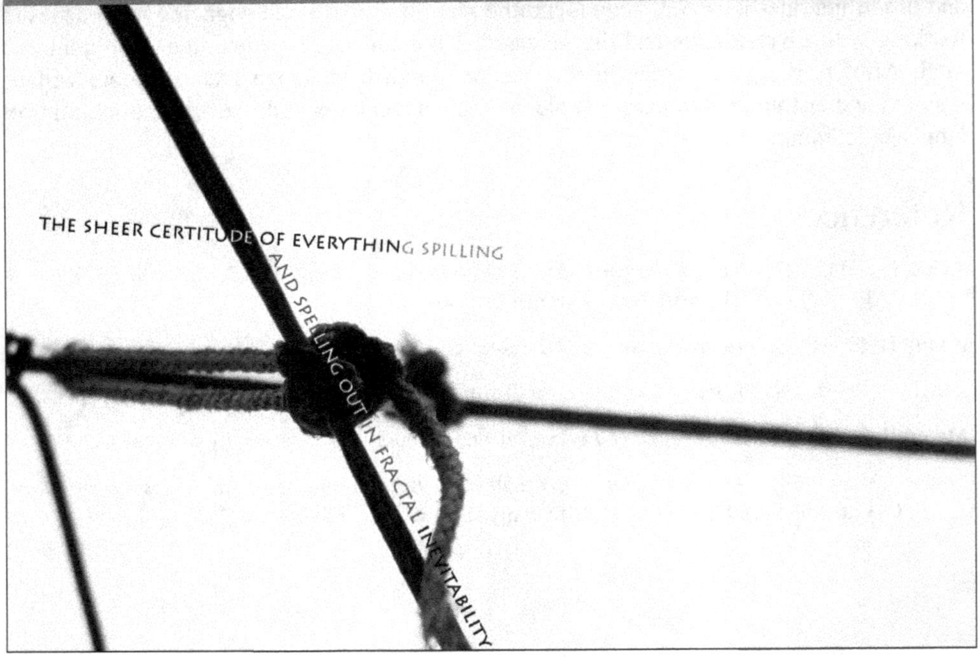

Roots of Learning

Why Is Poetry Still Relevant in School?

By Rebecca Luce-Kapler, Queen's University

> It is difficult to get the news from poems yet men die miserably every day for lack of what is found there.*
>
> —William Carlos Williams

This epigraph, recalling poetry's vital yet subtle contributions to humanity, seems as relevant today as it did when first written in the 1950s. Jane Hirshfield characterizes such a sensibility as "a fidelity to the ungraspable [that] lies at the very root of both biological existence and what we experience as beauty" (2008, p. 9). Poetry acknowledges the mystery of living—that unknowable presence with which we grapple—even as it encourages a more complex seeing of the shadow and the light.

As a poet, this argument for the importance of poems resonates with me, but as a teacher of poetry, I typically rely on more concrete reasoning. I want my students to see that poetry offers the opportunity to experience life from a different rhythm, that it encourages our most precise expressions of experience, and that it hones the imagination for more creative and critical thinking. I build my argument for poetry not through

---

* By William Carlos Williams, from *The Collected Poems: Volume II, 1939-1962*, copyright ©1994 by William Carlos Williams. Reprinted by permission of New Directions Publishing Corp.

presenting the world's "best" poems and asking students to discover the meter, the imagery, and the theme. Rather, I use poetry to teach the mindsets and skills of the craft, slowly building an educated appreciation that finds its way to reading and writing poetry.

Experiencing Life at a Different Rhythm

Thirty days hath September, April, June, and November.

—Traditional mnemonic rhyme

When we listen to and recite poetry, its sound comes into our bodies and its rhythms help us remember. The verbal forms have their genesis in oral story traditions that predate written language. Poems are "carried in our memory like a small stone in the pocket" (Steffler, 1995, p. 51), their heartbeats calling us to action and remembrance. Every poem offers a new way of breathing in the world and a different way of understanding experience as its rhythm becomes a "syntax for knowing" (Lee, 2002, p. 20). The oral celebration of poetic rhythm brings energy to a classroom where students' patience for stillness is often stretched.

Although poetry has seen some revitalization in popular culture, students too often see it as dead anthology entries followed by comprehension questions. As teachers, we have to set the poetic context for students so our classrooms can become a culture where oral language—especially poetry—flourishes. The key is to begin with low-risk activities such as pointing out the vibrant poetic forms accessible in current music popular with students. Not only does this poetry need to be acknowledged, it also needs to be heard and performed in class. From that starting point other poems can be read aloud, their rhythms and sounds played with and enjoyed. This process can be as simple as each student bringing their favourite word to a small group who creates a sound poem or rap using those words. Language ceases to be transparent as students develop an appreciation for its malleable, rhythmic beauty.

Expressing Experience

Sleep lingers all our lifetime about our eyes, as night hovers all day in the boughs of the fir tree.

—Ralph Waldo Emerson

Poetry teaches the workings of language and its power to bring witness to the emotional depth of experience. In no other genre is attention to language more critical. A comma and a dash vary by a breath and can change the impact, while a choice between someone "walking" or "striding" in a poem can alter the mood. Poetry is the womb of figurative language, especially metaphor. While poetic language demands the concrete, it also opens that image to the dimensions of imagination. Even though metaphor is often false at the literal level such as in these lines, "cold begins in the ears by breaking sticks,/its first fires carefully set" (Dickinson, 2006, lines 1–2), it indicates a greater truth in its accurate representation of frostbite (Lockett, 2010). In an age of tweets and texts, a greater facility in our students' use of short, pithy language would be a boon.

To attune students to the nuances of poetic language, I like to think of teaching poetry as engaging students in an apprenticeship. Why would we expect them to be able to read and write poetry without consideration of the decision making—the mindset of poetry—that is needed to create a poem? To teach line breaks, for example, I present a stanza of poetry written as prose. Students consult in groups to decide what punctuation to include and where the lines should be broken. When they have decided how that poem should appear, they post it for the class and read it aloud. I have never had two groups present a stanza in exactly the same way. What emerges is an exciting discussion about their thought processes: What happens when the line is broken in one place and not another? What happens to the meaning and the rhythm? What is the visual effect? Why might one use short lines or long ones? The beauty of this assignment is that the students begin to think like poets without having to write a poem. It also highlights the important and powerful connection between reading and writing. After discussing their choice of line breaks, we look at what the poet has chosen. By imagining first how the text may have looked and then seeing how the author chose to present it, the students begin to understand how literature can teach us to write and represent our own experience. There are a number of other poetic skills that I teach in similar ways to line breaks such as having students rewrite lines of a published poem using their own words. While they follow the set rhythm, they have to struggle with language choice, developing a deeper appreciation for a careful use of word and image so critical to poetic writing.

A much harder skill to teach is that of revising poems. This process requires all the skills students have learned, and it is where we begin, as a class, to talk about the art and the integrity of the poem where the writer moves beyond the "what really happened" to the cohesive experience of the poem. These are more sophisticated understandings that come later in the crafting, but if students have developed some appreciation of the skills they have learned, they are much better equipped to approach this process.

Honing the Imagination

Our seeing is a mirror or a sieve.*

—Zbigniew Herbert

Current studies in neuroscience have speculated on how humans develop empathy. An aspect of this research describes qualia—those rich sensory details that we experience but cannot fully share with other human beings through language. David Lodge (2002) has argued that the most powerful way to share qualia is through lyric poetry. While narrative is more concerned with ordering and taming experience, lyric affirms "memory as wilderness, as the raw music of experience" (Zwicky, 2006, p. 96). Poetry can open up experience to unexpected avenues as we try to represent what we have witnessed, and it invites imagining with others. The depth that young writers search for in their reliance on abstract terms such as love, hate, and angst can instead more deeply be felt through expressing the qualia of their own seeing.

If we engage students in the skills of poetry with an eye to using them for their own writing and to recognizing them in accomplished poets, it will not be a matter of the teacher asking questions hoping that students will notice details; rather, students can be turned loose with some well-developed skills to discover how poems invite them into rich moments of experience. Focusing on a very short piece of text can seem less intimidating to a student than reading or writing a story or essay. It can also teach the discipline of

---

* From *The Collected Poems 1956-1998* by Zbigniew Herbert. Translated & Edited by Alissa Valles. Copyright © 2007 by Alissa Valles. Introduction copyright © 2007 by Adam Zagajewski. Reprinted by permission of HarperCollins Publishers.

working with language through rewriting to more clearly evoke what one wants to portray. As students learn to think like poets, they will develop more creative and critical thinking skills that ignite their imagination and benefit them far beyond the enjoyment of a poem.

Poetry is a crucible that can forge an appreciation for the aesthetic, an ear for rhythm, a discipline of rewriting, an attention to the senses, an ethical witnessing of experience, and an understanding of many of the metaphors that have come to populate language. When teachers and students approach poetry first as a craft that can be taught and appreciated, students will begin to understand the meaning and beauty possible through poetry. While they may never become published poets themselves, this is not the goal of such teaching. Rather, when students experience the thought processes of poetic creation and imagine the mind of a poet, they understand language in a new way, they learn the craft of expression, and they make decisions about their writing to give words depth and power. Teaching poetry is not only relevant for students, it is empowering.

References

Dickinson, A. (2006). *Kingdom, phylum*. London, ON: Brick Books.

Emerson, R. W. (1983). Experience. In J. Porte (Ed.), *Emerson: Essays and lectures* (pp. 469–492). New York: Penguin Putnam.

Herbert, Z. (2007). *The collected poems: 1956–1998*. Edited and translated by Allisa Valles. New York: HarperCollins.

Hirshfield, J. (2008). *Hiddenness, uncertainty, surprise: Three generative energies of poetry*. Newcastle, GB: Bloodaxe Poetry Lectures.

Lee, D. (2002). Body music. In T. Lilburn (Ed.), *Thinking and singing: Poetry and the practice of philosophy* (pp. 19–58). Toronto: Cormorant Books.

Lockett, M. (2010). No narrow frith. An unpublished doctoral proposal. Kingston, ON: Queen's University.

Lodge, D. (2002). Consciousness and the novel. In D. Lodge (Ed.), *Consciousness and the novel* (pp. 1–91). New York: Penguin Books.

Luce-Kapler, R. (2009). Serendipity, poetry and inquiry. In M. Prendergast, C. Leggo, & P. Sameshima (Eds.), *Poetic inquiry: Vibrant voices in the Social Sciences* (pp. 75–78). Rotterdam: Sense Publishers.

Luce-Kapler, R. (Fall 2003). Orality and the poetics of curriculum. *Journal of Canadian Association of Curriculum Studies, 1*(2), 79–93.

Luce-Kapler, R. (1999). White chickens, wild swings, and winter nights. *Language Arts, 76*(4), 298–303.

Luce-Kapler, R. (2002). Dancing through light: Learning to read and write poetry. In M. Hunsberger & G. Labercane (Eds.), *Reader response theories and practices for the classroom* (pp. 55–67). Toronto: Allyn and Bacon.

Luce-Kapler, R. & Sumara, D. (2010) Taking shape: How reading (in)forms writing. In M. C. Courtland and T. Gambell (Eds.), *Literature, media & multiliteracies in adolescent language arts* (pp. 213–234). Vancouver, BC: Pacific Education Press.

Luce-Kapler, R. (2000). When reading meets writing: Understanding short stories and poetry. In M. C. Courtland & T. Gambell (Eds.), *Young adolescents meet literature: Intersections for learning* (pp. 178–200). Vancouver, BC: Pacific Educational Press.

Steffler, J. (1995). Language as matter. In T. Lilburn (Ed.), *Poetry and knowing: Speculative essays and interviews* (pp. 45–51). Kingston, ON: Quarry Press.

Williams, W. C. (1988). Asphodel, that greeny flower. In C. MacGowan (Ed.), *The collected poems of William Carlos Williams, Volume II, 1939–1962* (pp. 310–338). New York: New Directions.

Zwicky, J. (2006). Lyric, narrative, memory. In R. Finley, P. Friesen, A. Hunter, A. Simpson, & J. Zwicky (Eds.), *A ragged pen: Essays on poetry & memory* (pp. 87–108). Kentville, NS: Gaspereau Press.

What Are the Benefits for Teachers and Students of Reading Postcolonial Literature in Contemporary Secondary English Language Arts Classes?

By Ingrid Johnston, University of Alberta

From Multicultural to Postcolonial

Secondary school English language arts teachers are becoming increasingly familiar with a range of multicultural literature for their classrooms. Multicultural education has succeeded in focusing more attention on questions of culture by including texts from "non-mainstream" cultures as an add-on to the more familiar, canonical, well-loved texts. As Laurie Grobman (2007) has suggested:

> Since its emergence in literary studies in the 1970s, multiculturalism has transformed the teaching of literature and how we understand what it means to study literature. Curricula and syllabi have become more diverse and inclusive, and writers of color and their texts have received significant scholarly and popular attention. (p. xv)

This infusion of multicultural texts is represented, for example, in Alberta Education's recommended list of novels and non-fiction, which includes books like *Red Scarf Girl: A Memoir of the Cultural Revolution* (Jiang, 1998) for grade 9 students; *Road to Chlifa* (Marineau, 2003) for grade 10 students; *Tamarind Mem* (Badami, 2004) for grade 11 students; *The Joy Luck Club* (Tan, 2006), also for grade 11 students; and *The Hero's Walk* (Badami, 2001) for grade 12 students. In British Columbia, texts such as *Shabanu: Daughter of the Wind* (Staples, 2003) for grades 8 through 9; *Chanda's Secrets* (Stratton, 2004) for grades 9 through 10; *The Concubine's Children* (Chong, 2006) for grades 11 through 12; and *The Jade Peony* (Chow, 1995), also for grades 11 through 12, have been added to recommended lists over the past years. A number of these texts are being taught in Canadian junior and senior secondary school classrooms and are helping to promote diverse cultural perspectives among student readers.

All of these multicultural texts have the potential to offer adolescent readers valuable insights into ethnocultural experiences that may be different from their own. Readers can engage with characters whose backgrounds, belief systems, and cultural contexts open doorways into new worlds outside their own familiar and taken-for-granted contexts.

However, there may be the danger of teachers introducing such books as a form of "culture tour" for their students from European backgrounds, encouraging them to see how others live in the world, while maintaining a superior viewpoint that sees non-Western ways of life as inferior. Some multicultural books, often those written by Western writers who are outside the culture being described, may reinforce mainstream readers' views of themselves as being at the centre of the universe, as offering no challenge to their Eurocentric belief systems, thereby continuing to reinforce the marginalization felt by students from minority cultures. As Rabinowitz and Smith (1998) caution, "If multicultural literature is to challenge students' ethnocentricity, then [students] have to engage in looking at things, at least provisionally, through new perspectives" (p. 128).

I suggest that while the introduction of multicultural literature into secondary classrooms can be beneficial for student readers, English language arts teachers might also consider the value of introducing postcolonial literature and postcolonial reading practices into their classrooms. As Dimitriadis and McCarthy (2001) suggest, multicultural literary texts often resist the need to address complex issues of power relations as well as marginalized knowledges and practices in the classroom. In contrast, postcolonial literatures offer a more radical engagement with difference. Postcolonial texts invite teachers and students to consider the intersections of the aesthetic and the political in the study of literary texts. Reading "in-between" the aesthetic and the political might be a fruitful position from which to consider the fluid boundaries of culture, race, and subjugated knowledges. Dimitriadis and McCarthy (2001) explain further:

> Thinking in postcolonial terms about the topic of difference and multiplicity in education means thinking relationally and contextually. It means bringing back into educational discourses all those tensions and contradictions that we tend to suppress as we process experience and history into curricular knowledge. (p. 119)

Teachers' sensitivity to considerations of historical inequities and material contexts surrounding a text means that contemporary problems of political, social, and cultural domination enter the classroom alongside discussions of literary allusions, foreshadowing, metaphor, and metonymy. So, for example, we might consider the potential of teaching a novel such as *Bifocal* (Ellis & Walters, 2007) in a junior high classroom. This Canadian young adult novel is set in Toronto with the narrative told in the alternating voices of two secondary school students: Haroon, a serious, Muslim student of Persian descent; and Jay, a rising football star from a white European background. When the school is put on lockdown because of rumours of a planned terrorist attack, the police arrest a Muslim student on suspicion of terrorist affiliations. Along with the rest of the school, Haroon and Jay take sides about whether the boy is really guilty. The novel invites adolescent readers to consider how events such as 9/11 and the Toronto bomb plot of 2006 (on which the novel is based) have resulted in particular beliefs and assumptions being perpetuated about Muslims in Canada as potential terrorists.

Another junior high novel with potential to challenge Canadian students' complacency about the colonial past is the novel *47* by the African-American writer Walter Mosley. This evocative story of an escape from slavery combines magical realism and African-American myth with the reality of life on a slave plantation and the courage of resistance. The narrator claims to be telling a story of his youth, 170 years ago in 1832, when he was a 14-year-old slave named "47" in Georgia. He recalls being chained, branded, and whipped until the runaway Tall John, a supernatural being with the ability to fly between galaxies, inspires 47 to lead his people to freedom. The magical realism works effectively with Mosley's first-person narrative to bring the realities of slavery very close to the reader; the spiritual tall tale allows for flights of imagination that bring the characters hope of an escape from these shameful (but historically accurate) events.

Teachers in secondary school English language arts classes have the option of introducing selected adult postcolonial novels with characters that might resonate with adolescent readers. *The Kite Runner,* by the Afghani-American author Khaled Hosseini, is a postcolonial text that is already making appearances in many Canadian classrooms. Published in 2003, it was adapted into a film of the same name in 2007. *The Kite Runner* tells the story of Amir, a young Pushtin boy from Afghanistan who is tormented by guilt for abandoning and betraying his friend Hassan, the son of his father's Hazara servant. The novel evokes complex questions about the nature of guilt, atonement, and hybrid identities. Set against a backdrop of tumultuous historical events, the novel follows the main character's life from the fall of the monarchy in Afghanistan through the Russian invasion, the mass exodus of refugees to Pakistan and the United States, and the main character's return to Afghanistan during the rise of the Taliban regime. Issues of power relations, political domination, and racial and gender discrimination as well as questions of identity formation invite readers to question their own position in the world and their belief systems.

The Book Thief, by Australian writer Markus Zusak, is a darkly moving Holocaust novel that is both harrowing and lyrical in its depictions of life in Nazi Germany during World War II. Narrated by the character Death, the novel tells the story of Liesel, a young girl living near Munich in 1939. She arrives at her foster home having just stolen a book called *The Gravedigger's Handbook* from the cemetery where her young brother is buried. Her foster father reads it aloud to help her get to sleep whenever she is kept awake by nightmares. Once she develops a love of reading, Liesel begins to steal books from the mayor's wife and from Nazi book-burnings. When Liesel's foster parents hide a Jewish man in their basement, they use books and the power of storytelling to help keep them all alive. The novel is a compelling read for both adult and adolescent readers. From a pedagogical standpoint, it offers possibilities for teachers to consider how texts that bear witness to the horrors of the Holocaust may be considered alongside those that address issues of colonization more directly. Michael Rothberg (2010), speaking about his recent book *Decolonizing the Holocaust: Multidirectional Memory and the Legacies of Violence* (2009), argues that

> Like the literature of the Holocaust, the literature of the colonial and postcolonial conditions testifies to the underside of Western modernity. Both literatures bear witness to forms of extreme and everyday violence perpetrated in the name of racial ideologies and imperial political projects. Both literatures grapple necessarily with the burden of history, the destruction of cultures and communities, and the fracturing of time. (n. pag.)

Novels such as the ones I've mentioned encourage adolescent readers to understand in more meaningful ways the legacies of colonialism and historical marginalization, and to appreciate how issues of race, power, and class, together with questions of cultural difference, are valuable topics for classroom discussion alongside more aesthetic aspects of literary texts (Johnston, 2003). English language arts teachers who make spaces for introducing postcolonial literature as part of their curriculum create opportunities for re-reading existing canonical school texts through the aesthetic and political prism of newer, postcolonial literature in ways that can open up dialogue on the broader contemporary social issues raised by the texts.

References

Badami, A. R. (2004). *Tamarind mem.* Toronto: Vintage Canada.

———. (2001). *The hero's walk.* Toronto: Vintage Canada.

Chong, D. (2006). *The concubine's children.* Toronto: Penguin Canada.

Chow, W. (1995). *The jade peony.* Toronto: D&M Adult.

Dimitriadis, G. & C. McCarthy. (2001). *Reading & teaching the postcolonial: From Baldwin to Basquiat and beyond.* New York: Teachers' College Press.

Ellis, D. & E. Walters. (2007). *Bifocal.* Toronto: Fitzhenry and Whiteside.

Grobman, L. (2007). *Multicultural hybridity: Transforming American literary scholarship and pedagogy.* Urbana, IL: NCTE.

Hosseini, K. (2004). *The kite runner.* New York: Riverhead Trade.

Jiang, J. L. (1998). *Red scarf girl: A memoir of the cultural revolution.* New York: HarperCollins.

Johnston, I. (2003). *Re-mapping literary worlds: Postcolonial pedagogy in practice.* New York: Peter Lang.

Marineau, M. & S. Ouriou (Translator). (2003). *Road to Chlifa.* Red Deer: Red Deer Press.

Mosley, W. (2005). *47.* New York: Little, Brown.

Rabinowitz, P. & M. Smith. (1998). *Authorizing readers: Resistance and respect in the teaching of literature.* New York and London: Teachers College Press.

Rothberg, M. (2009) *Decolonizing the Holocaust: Multidirectional memory and the legacies of violence.* Stanford: Stanford University Press.

———. (n.d.) "Decolonizing the Holocaust: Multidirectional memory and the legacies of violence." http://www.dubnow.de/Michael-Rothberg.273.0.html (accessed December 30, 2010).

Staples, S. F. (2003). *Shabanu, daughter of the wind.* New York: Laurel Leaf.

Stratton, A. (2004). *Chanda's secrets.* Toronto: Annick Press.

Tan, A. (2006). *The joy luck club.* New York: Penguin.

Zusak, M. (2006). *The book thief.* New York: Knopf.

How Can Language Study Be Integrated into Writing and Content Instruction?

By Kedrick James, University of British Columbia

Mention the word "grammar" in front of a group of students and see how quickly their excitement deflates. Few schools today offer courses in grammar, but somehow the dread legacy of those English classes, of the taxonomic parsing through hacking written language to bits, remains in collective memory. Perhaps it is the prescriptive tendencies of the grammarian that have led to this widespread rejection of all things grammatical in adolescent education. And that's unfortunate. Language study should be fun, collaborative, and learned through use—it shouldn't be a rote memorization of rules that almost inevitably have exceptions. In an English class, it is useful to conceive of everyone as English language learners: the ESL students, the other students, and even the teacher.

Language study can be integrated seamlessly into all aspects of English language arts instruction as a generative tool for analysis and composition. When grammar becomes a descriptive tool rather than a prescriptive set of rules that must be memorized, language learning is enhanced through contextual and critical understanding, playful engagement, and strategic compositional practice (Ehrenworth & Vinton, 2005). Photocopying pages out of a language workbook in order to provide specific exercises to develop fluency among given parts of speech can be highly beneficial. As a routine for an entire class, though, it is less useful. Instead, such a "workbook approach" (Azar, 2009; Murphy, 2004) is most beneficial when individual needs have already been assessed and strategic language support can be handled quickly and efficiently. This way, a teacher won't have to make all students engage in a skill-drill that for many will not be challenging or particularly helpful.

In 2003, I conducted research in an adult language school to explore the efficacy of the grammar workbook approach in comparison to a context-enriched method that exclusively used various kinds of literature and creative writing exercises (James, 2003). The study involved experimental and control groups of students with equivalent entry levels of English fluency, tested over a three-month period to measure rates of language acquisition. There was no significant difference in the rates at which both groups learned language. However, students who learned using literature had increased verbal expression and had acquired culturally sophisticated phrasing. They not only learned typical rule-based patterns of words, but also acquired more idiomatic language like phrasal verbs, collocations, and colloquial expressions. This added confidence to their conversational and communicative practices in English. They accomplished language learning while engaging with works of literature—from science fiction to translating poetry from home languages.

I mention this to embolden English teachers to treat language study not as something *added* to a curriculum, but instead as a fundamental aspect of everything they do. Although in the present discussion it is not possible to explore the myriad ways to integrate language study into English language arts classroom activities, the following section provides a few approaches and activities that a teacher might use to engage students in learning about the English language without getting too caught up in teaching "grammar" per se.

Playing with Language Forms

We can put language study into four categories: texts, sentences, words, and sounds (Thornbury, 1999). Each category offers different kinds of language learning opportunities for teachers to integrate into their instruction. However, none of these levels are ever taught independently; all of them are engaged each time we make meaning linguistically. Ideally, in the process of discussing the larger discourses surrounding a given text (themes, genre, and style), the teacher focuses analysis on the patterns of language being used (syntax), the word choice (vocabulary), and even the sounds of the words put together (phonetics). Like a pendulum, the classroom focus should return to how these details affect readers' comprehension of the text, thereby situating the details within a larger context. As a generative practice, teachers can start with tonal sounds of words that suit the context of a composition, develop useful vocabulary, and discuss innovative ways to formulate sentences (topic sentences, transitions, complex sentences types). In this way, teachers can build up to the compositional process itself. Once finished with composing, revision begins and the pendulum swings back again, changing the classroom focus to sentence construction, word choice, and tone.

We often take the sounds (or phonemic aspects) of language for granted—until we are presented with an unusual dialect or heavily accented speech. Moreover, when students are presenting their work, speaking in public, rapping, or dramatizing a script, their lack of confidence, monotone delivery, mumbling, or other common problems with delivery can become hindrances to success (if they're being evaluated). Practising expression collectively as a class prevents individual students from feeling embarrassed. Further, voicing texts and physically engaging with language deepens the pleasure of reading. Having the whole class stand up, move around, warm up their vocal cords, and make sounds together is a great way to bond, get excited, and find joy in language. The following activities can help make this happen.

Sounding Language: A Suggested Activity

Draw a shape that looks like a simple sine wave. Use the sound "oh" or "ah" or "wow," and collectively, loudly, with exaggeration, follow the waveform as a notation of pitch. The result is meaningful—an emotive utterance that expresses realization and understanding. The greater the range of pitch used, the greater the epiphany. Then draw a vertical line bisecting the waveform at its apex, and vocalize the first part. This embeds a questioning intonation—it is expectant, anticipatory, and requests a response for more dialogue. Then, vocalize the second part. Hear the sound of resignation, of acceptance, closure to a thought. The utterance changes from interrogative to declarative. The following figure shows the visual component of this exercise:

FIGURE 1 Waveform Exercise

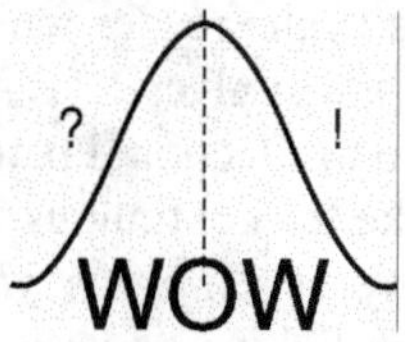

Source: Waveform exercise by Kedrick James. Copyright © 2012 Kedrick James.

Next, take a section of text being studied. Underline all the adverbs in the text. Have students take turns reading the text so that all the adverbs get the full, exaggerated glissando (the rise and fall of intonation). Note how much more emphatic the speaker sounds and how, if too many such uses occur in a sentence, the listener will likely become confused: What part of the sentence does the speaker want me to pay attention to? Such intonation places emphasis on the part of the sentence the speaker wants the listener to respond to. To connect this practice with the study of a text, have students select one word (or phrase) per sentence or line of text that they think carries the most important meaning. Read aloud several different choices, hear how this changes the meaning and discuss. This exercise engages students in close analysis of language and is excellent preparation for verbal delivery of the text. However, another, equally important focus in the English classroom lies in vocabulary.

Selecting Words to Teach

The eight parts of speech generally taught in schools are nouns, verbs, adjectives, adverbs, prepositions, pronouns, conjunctions, and interjections. One of the most important aspects of the language teacher's job is to help students develop their vocabulary in all parts of speech. English recently crossed the threshold of one million unique words, and it is doubtful whether anyone could or would want to actually use all those words. So what words should we teach? Vocabulary from the texts or contexts being studied and from the immediate environment should be the highest priority. Get students looking for "language curiosities," as Koch and Brazil (1978) call them, those strange words and expressions that catch our attention or have cachet and style. It is also important to get students using new words, recycling them in their own speech and writing. This is a key to retaining new vocabulary. One way to build on students' word stocks is to develop activities using morphology (or the study of how word roots change their form in different parts of speech) to add new uses to the words students have already acquired.

Morphology: A Suggested Activity

Begin by going through a text the class is studying and identifying all the nouns that can also be verbs (e.g., trigger, fold, set, transfer, party), some of which are also adjectives or adverbs (e.g., still, like, last, mine, single). As homework, assign students to list as many such words as they can. In the next lesson, ask them to organize their list into groups of three noun/verb words which together make particular sense to them. With three different words per line (*lie still trigger*), put three lines together into a stanza, and with three stanzas, or 27 words on nine lines, you have a *morpho-poem.* By adding an "s" (inflection) at the end of the words, many nouns become plural and many verbs are conjugated for third person. This process of deciding which words to add an "s" to is inventive because it changes the meaning—it suggests to the reader which words are nouns and which are verbs (even though they are all both), and gives ESL students a chance to practise identifying words that don't fit the common inflectional patterns. Add punctuation. Then introduce the "ing" endings that can make the continuous tense of a verb or the adjectival and gerundive (noun) forms of many verbs (*She is walking/with a walking stick/because walking is good*). Continue to morph the words until a sensible poem begins to emerge. Then reintroduce each different class of words, one at a time, until satisfied.

Instead of having to learn many unique words, a single word can be used to generate multiple vocabulary items. This also teaches students how to discover the meaning of unfamiliar words by breaking them down to an etymological root word, and builds comprehension tools for vocabulary across the curriculum. The main point, however, is to have students start exploring and experimenting, free of the worry that they are "not doing it right." Another way to alleviate this concern is to have them create poems using a collection of phrases from a random word generator and then compose by deleting words, or parts of words, that they don't want to use. A surprise awaits students when they read the results aloud and realize how many different meanings and texts can be derived from the same collection of words; each poem will have the student's particular twist and style, even though they didn't write it "in their own words." This method, called "cut-up," is much more fun than filling in the deleted words from prewritten paragraphs, and can be done with digital or physical texts (James, 2009). Creating poems out of the scrambled words from a page of text that the students will be studying later is an excellent way to augment personal engagement in language study and literary analysis.

The possibilities are limitless, and many of these activities can be accomplished with a very basic linguistic knowledge. Above all, don't tell students that they are going to be studying grammar. They are going to be playing with words: reading, writing, chanting, inventing new words, cutting things up, and seeing how far they can push language as they discover their voices within.

References

Azar, B. S. (2009). *Understanding and using English grammar (4th edition).* White Plains, NY: Pearson Education.

Ehrenworth, M. & Vinton, V. (2005). *The power of grammar: Unconventional approaches to the conventions of language.* Portsmouth, NH: Heinemann.

James, K. (2003). *The effect of literature-based instruction on ESL acquisition rates.* Unpublished master's thesis, University of British Columbia, Vancouver, British Columbia, Canada.

James, K. (2009). Cut-up consciousness: Poetic inquiry and the spambot's text. In M. Prendergast, C. Leggo & P. Sameshima (Eds.), *Poetic inquiry: Vibrant voices in the social sciences* (pp. 59–74). Rotterdam: Sense Publishers.

Koch, C. & Brazil, J. M. (1978). *Strategies for teaching the composition process.* Urbana, IL: National Council of Teachers of English.

Murphy, R. (2004). *English grammar in use with answers: A self-study reference and practice book for intermediate students of English (3rd edition).* Cambridge, UK: Cambridge University Press.

Thornbury, S. (1999). *How to teach grammar.* Essex, England: Pearson Education.

SECTION 2

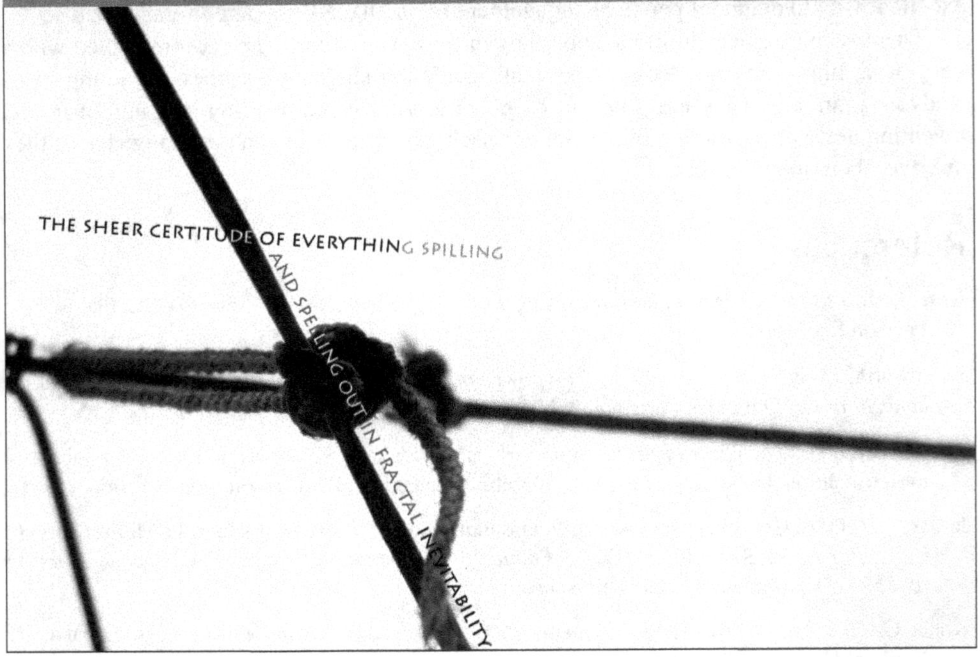

Expressing Understanding

What Do Hip-Hop, Spoken Word, and Slam Poetry Have in Common and How Might They Be Used in a Secondary School English Classroom?

By Bronwen E. Low, McGill University

I attended my first poetry slam in 1999. Thirty teen poets, representing schools and community centres across the New York City boroughs, competed in a war of words—a poetry "mock Olympics." It was New York's first youth slam, and the poets paraded on and off the stage, some dreadlocked and ponytailed, some braided and buzzed, some squeezed into stretch pants and baby T-shirts, while others, in the words of poet Patricia Smith, were "drooped in drapery." Iolet, head-wrapped and regal, told of police brutality. A boy from New Jersey dedicated his poem (about being "surrounded by a raging sea called heterosexuality") to "anyone who's ever felt left out of societies' categories, or been to a really boring sweet 16 party in Westchester county." There was a poem about Puerto Rican nationalism, an ode to a mother, another to a jailed brother, and many tales of sex and heartbreak. The crowd hollered its approval and disagreement with the judges' scoring. Asheena McNeil, who wrote her poetry on the 125th Street bus she took to and from school in Harlem, won the slam with a perfect score for her "125th Street Blues." She cited as inspiration Maya Angelou and her own grandmother who "lives poetry rather than writes it." And like most of the other student poets, she credited rap music and hip-hop culture in general as having made poetry "cool." This experience prompted my interest in slam, hip-hop, and education. I explored this interest in teaching practice with two co-researchers, a secondary school language arts teacher and a teaching artist. We developed and taught a course that drew upon hip-hop culture, spoken word, and slam poetry.

What is hip-hop? Although sometimes used interchangeably with "rap music," "hip-hop" refers to a global youth arts movement and culture with four basic elements: visual arts (graffiti), dance (breakdancing), rhythmic/musical collage (DJing), and poetry (rhyming, rhythmic, and chanted rap). "Rap music" brings together the beats and music of the DJ with rapped lyrics. Rapper and educator KRS-One (2001) has famously described hip-hop as "not just a music, [but] an attitude, . . . an awareness, . . . a way to view the world. So rap music is something we *do,* but hip hop is something we *live.*" Hip-hop is rooted in Afro-diasporic traditions. One popular version of its history begins with DJ Kool Herc, a Jamaican who brought the "toast and boast" tradition of roots reggae to the Bronx. The Jamaican "Yard DJ" would spin records on a sound system that included the recognizable hip-hop icons of turntables and speakers. He would talk or "rap" over the "ska," the reggae beats. In the spirit of hip-hop invention and "making do," Kool Herc and other early DJs would power these sound systems by tapping into any publicly accessible power source, like a street lamp, and entertain crowds at open-air block parties.

Rap music is also a subset of "spoken word culture," a category used to describe forms of poetry and performance in which an artist recites poetry, often to musical accompaniment ranging from a jazz ensemble to a bongo drummer. The 1960s-style coffeehouse is back with force and in a multitude of forms from "open mic" nights at cafés or bars in urban centres to HBO's weekly half hour of spoken word poetry (called *Def Poetry Jam,* it ran from 2002 to 2007). One of the most dynamic branches of spoken word is slam poetry. In a slam, poets perform original works before a live audience and are ranked from 1 to 10 by a panel of judges. In its original form, this panel is selected at random from the audience. Poets use neither props nor musical instruments in this war of words, relying instead on the expressiveness of their bodies and voices. No performance can exceed a three-and-a-half-minute time limit. Slam poetry emerged in the 1980s, first in Chicago and then in other major urban centres. Venues such as the Nuyorican Poets Café in New York City host regular slam poetry "open-mics." Slam poetry is populist, designed to win the hearts and minds of the audience: it tells stories that blend and move between the personal and the socio-political; it is often urgent, sometimes sexy, and regularly funny, and its language tends to be vernacular and reflect the multilingual contexts of its emergence (Low, 2006). The yearly Slam Poetry National competition, which is held in a different U.S. city each year, brings together approximately 80 teams representing different cities across North America. Individual poets can compete at the World Poetry Slam and the Women of the World Poem Slam. Central to the slam youth movement, and linking schools and community centres across cities in North America and elsewhere, is the Brave New Voices International Teen Poetry Slam Finals, held every summer in a different U.S. city. The festival attracts more than 500 poets from more than 50 cities, and the final rounds can be performed before audiences of thousands. A key appeal of slam poetry to youth is performance—a return to the oral traditions of the bard or "griot"—and competition, encouraging audience participation and investment in response to the judges' scores and offering an infrastructure of local, regional, and national events.

There has been an explosion of academic interest in the pedagogical possibilities of hip-hop, spoken word, and slam. Scholars focused on the uses of rap lyrics and English language arts include Morrell and Duncan-Andrade (2004), whose language arts unit works to support students' learning of canonical poems by matching them with raps on related themes. Another is Hill (2009), whose language arts course aims to teach students the elements of literary analysis through close examinations of rap lyrics as poetry. A key member of the popular hip-hop education movement is Marcella Runnel Hall (2007), co-author with Martha Diaz of *The Hip Hop Education Guidebook: Vol. 1* (2009), which brings together hip-hop-related lesson plans and state curriculum standards in the United States. Committed to popular poetics, Jocson (2005) documents the June Jordan Poetry for the People program and Fisher (2007) studies an after-school "Power Writers'" spoken word club; the club's teacher held a vision for literacy education as grounded in a respect for the experiences of students, multilingualism (including "Bronxonics," or the spoken dialectical features of a Bronx accent), poetic traditions, and the potential of youth to "aspire beyond 'ascribed lives'" (p. 19). A new and very valuable resource for teachers interested in slam poetry and spoken word is the curriculum guide created to accompany the documentary film *Louder Than a Bomb* (which explores the youth slam scene in Chicago).

To give you a sense of what a spoken word and hip-hop curriculum might look like, I will share with you some details of the course that I helped develop and teach. The teacher, teaching artist, and I designed a unit (once taught in six weeks, once over a whole term) for senior English students. The unit drew upon student interests in hop-hop but also extended the lessons to include spoken word and slam poetry. During the class we immersed students in spoken word forms through videos, CDs, visits by local poets, and a series of workshops in which students developed and rehearsed their own poems. We explored some of the history of Black poetics including spirituals, the blues, and poetry from the Black Arts Movement. This unit included having the students do choral performances of selected works (e.g., Nikki Giovanni's "Ego-Tripping"). We invited students to bring the rap music they cared about into class and examine the poetry of the lyrics. In one year of the course, we invited a local hip-hop radio DJ to give the students a history of hip-hop culture. We also examined various contexts in the history of poetics for thinking about rap's experimentation with word and sound including Dadaist sound poetry, Gertrude Stein's modernist decompositions of language, jazz poetry, and blues poetry.

However, the bulk of the course was dedicated to writing and performance workshops. Integral to the course were journals within which students free-wrote in response to various creative prompts, wrote drafts of poetry to be workshopped in class, and responded to textual, audio, and visual recordings of poetry as well as to their classmates' performances. Classes often began with a "writing practice" about which the teacher would say: "Don't edit yourselves. Be adventurous with your language. No talking." In their journals, the students sometimes wrote to specific prompts, such as William Carlos Williams' "Men die every day for what they miss in poetry," "Poetry heals the wounds inflicted by reason," or "Write down the words for a song or poem you wish you'd written. Then explain why." In order to help them respond to work we had read or listened to, the students were given sentence openers such as: "I don't understand," "I noticed," "I wonder," "I was reminded of," "I think," "I'm surprised that," "I'd like to know," "I realize," "If I were," "The central issue here is," "One consequence of _______ could be," "If _______ then _______," "I'm not sure," or "Although it seems." They were also encouraged to experiment with particular kinds or genres of poems such as a "persona" poem, spoken in the voice of another, or an epistolary "Dear America" poem. So that students were better able to respond constructively to each other's works in progress, they were given concrete strategies such as "pointing," where the students write down words and phrases that jump out at them from the poem. The language arts teacher also recommended that the students initially structure their responses around one or more of the following prompts:

> "I believe your poem because _______."
> "I doubt your poem because _______."
> "When I hear your poem, what goes through my head is _______."

These prompts ask the students to be specific in their feedback and help them avoid simplistic judgments about something being either good or bad. They also make clear the subjective nature of all responses.

The course culminated in a poetry slam at the end of the school year in an auditorium filled with all of the senior students, select classes of juniors, and some invited members of the community. Judges were picked based on a formula in which two or three were selected from inside the school (such as teachers, librarians or current students) and two or three from the larger community (including local artists and community arts members, parents, and school alumni). This formula strays from the original slam rules in which judges are picked randomly from the audience, a move designed to increase the probability of balanced and disinterested scoring. The slams I have witnessed usually have a hip-hop element or style to them; in one at the school, a student DJ played between performances, and a number of poems regularly referred to or discussed hip-hop.

An important consideration for teachers interested in drawing upon rap lyrics is their own familiarity and comfort with the material as well as their particular teaching context. Many teachers and administrators shy away from hip-hop culture in the classroom (despite its evident popularity among youth) due to some of its very harmful depictions of women, sexuality, and homosexuality, or its explicit language and its celebrations of violence and materialism. While these representations reflect widespread problems in culture more generally, they can be particularly explicit in rap music. Nevertheless, the recently published *Anthology of Rap* makes it clear that there is an abundance of "conscious" and positive rap easily found for use in a classroom (including the work of Lauryn Hill, Mos Def, and Common). We also found that critical discussions about some of these contentious elements of hip-hop, taking the form of critical media literacy, was a very important aspect of the course for both students and teachers (see Low, 2011, for an extended discussion of this). For teachers who do not feel they are able to learn enough about rap music or even spoken word poetry, a "teaching artist model" would be ideal: many cities and programs, working in partnership with teachers, will sponsor local poets to offer workshops in classrooms. As well, one of the most valuable aspects of exploring youth culture with students is that they usually know more about it than the teacher, providing excellent opportunities for the sharing of expertise and authority.

References

Fisher, Maisha. (2007). *Writing in rhythm: Spoken word poetry in urban classrooms.* New York: Teachers College Press.

Hall, Marcella Runell. (2009). Hip hop education resources. *Equity and Excellence in Education* 42(1), 86–94.

Hall, Marcella Runell, and Martha Diaz. (2007). *The hip hop education guidebook: Volume 1.* New York: Hip Hop Association.

Hill, Marc Lamont. (2009). *Beats, rhymes, and classroom life: Hip-hop pedagogy and the politics of identity.* New York: Teachers College Press.

Jocson, K. M. (2005). "Taking it to the mic": Pedagogy of June Jordan's Poetry for the People and partnership with an urban high school. *English Education*, 37(2), 44–60

KRS-One. (2001). Hip hop knowledge. On *Sneak attack.* Prod. Kenny Parker.

Low, Bronwen. (2006). Poetry on MTV? Slam and poetics of the popular. *Journal of Curriculum Theorizing* 22(4), 97–111.

Low, Bronwen. (2011). *Slam school: Learning through conflict in the hip-hop and spoken word classroom.* Palo Alto: Stanford University Press.

Morrell, Ernest, and Jeff Duncan-Andrade. (2004). What they do learn in school: Hip-hop as a bridge to canonical poetry. In *What they don't learn in school: Literacy in the lives of urban youth*, ed. Jabari Mahiri (pp. 247–268). New York: Peter Lang.

Poetry slam: The competitive art of performance poetry. (2000). Ed. Gary Glazner. Manic D Press.

Additional Resources

ALOUD: Voices from the Nuyorican Poets Café. (1994). Eds. Miguel Algarín and Bob Holman. New York: Henry Holt.

Coval, Kevin, Anna Festa, and Greg Jacobs. (2012). *Louder than a bomb study guide.* Sausalito: Ro*Co International.

Poetic license. (2001). Directed by David Yanofsky. San Francisco: Independent Television Service.

Rose, Tricia. (1994). *Black noise: Rap music and Black culture in contemporary America.* Middletown, CT: Wesleyan University Press.

Russell Simmons presents brave new voices. (2009). Directed by Stan Lathan. Los Angeles: Simmons Lathan Media Group.

Slam. (1998). Directed by Marc Levin. New York: Offline Entertainment.

SlamNation: The sport of spoken word. (1998). Directed and produced by Paul Devlin.

The anthology of rap. (2010). Eds. Adam Bradley and Andrew Dubois. New Haven: Yale University Press.

Why Teach Writing?

By Robin Bright, University of Lethbridge

The ability to write in and out of school is as important as ever (Ippolito, Steele, & Samson, 2008). While traditional writing in the form of essays, letters, memos, poetry, short stories, and book or film reviews tends to fall under the schools' mandate to teach, new forms of writing have emerged in electronic environments that include texting, blogging, instant messaging, tweeting, and countless other evolving texts and modalities. Given the pervasiveness of these kinds of text both in school and outside school, it is crucial to examine and reconfigure both what it means "to master the complex set of skills and knowledge called writing" (National Writing Project & Nagin, 2003, p. 1), as well as the teaching practices that might be employed in working with such diverse written forms.

There is widespread awareness that communication skills are crucial in the workforce. Also important is the belief among educators and writing theorists such as Peter Elbow (2000) that all children *can* learn to write. Elbow's thesis is that it is important to have students learn to both comply with and resist the kinds of instruction they receive in classrooms. According to Elbow, too much compliance means that the writer has not found his or her voice and is overly intent on writing for the teacher, but too much resistance could mean that the writer produces little writing or nothing at all or, worse, does not care about the writing. The aim for teachers of writing is to balance these two forces so that students find their writing voices and learn to write using a variety of forms and for various audiences and purposes. Simply put, writing is central to the success of future generations as a means of inquiry and expression.

How Should We Teach Writing?

The teaching of writing is informed by more than three decades of research beginning with works such as Janet Emig's (1971) study of grade 12 students engaged in a writing task over time. For the first time in the history of writing pedagogy, Emig—and, later, Donald Graves (1983)—showed an interest in not only looking at the products of writing but also the process in which writers engage. Their early work demonstrates that writing pedagogy was and is influenced by cognitive (Flower & Hayes, 1980) and social (Vygotsky, 1978) perspectives. These theories focus on how students think while writing and the importance of writing as a social act, a way of interacting with others in the various social contexts in which adolescents write.

This research led to the development of "the writing process," a series of stages that guide writing and continue to inform teachers of writing today (e.g., see Bright, 2007). These stages include prewriting, drafting, revising, editing, and publishing. Prewriting is the time a writer spends on developing his or her ideas about topics for writing, the purpose of writing, the audience for whom writing is intended, and the form of writing. Teachers use specific strategies in each stage of the writing process to support writers. For instance, in the prewriting stage, students learn to brainstorm ideas for writing, create webs to link those ideas, and draw pictures or locate images or music to help them think about ideas.

In the drafting stage, writers are encouraged to get their ideas down on paper or screen without much concern for the mechanics of language (spelling, grammar, punctuation), which can come later. Next, student writers are encouraged to revise by examining their own drafts or by working with peers on their writing in order to make decisions about the overall meaning and organization of their writing. Usually, in this stage writers will make significant changes to their writing that help to communicate the meaning they intend. In the editing stage, writers, alone or with peers, work to identify and correct the mechanics of the writing. This is where they attend to spelling, grammar, punctuation, paragraphing and other aspects of language correctness. The publishing stage involves students sharing their writing with others. Teachers can use the stages of the writing process to flexibly show students how these stages might improve their writing. However, there are some mistaken assumptions associated with this process. For example, the writing process could be viewed as a formula for producing writing. Believing in the simplistic nature of a defined process does not address the complexities of learning to write. The intent is not to reify the writing process as a formulaic method but to show students how the stages can be utilized in a recursive manner to help them write with power, purpose, and pleasure.

Teachers' knowledge of the writing process is supported and enhanced by a worthwhile approach to writing instruction called the writers' workshop. Teacher and researcher Nancie Atwell (1998) helped to change the way in which writing is taught in middle and secondary school classrooms through her book *In the Middle: New Understandings about Writing, Reading, and Learning,* which was first published in 1987. Of importance in this approach are routines and procedures such as mini-lessons, strategy instruction, collaboration, and conferencing in writing.

Since Atwell's work first emerged, technologies for writing have changed and it is important that students learn how to write in different modalities. This has led to instruction that helps link written communication with visual and aural communication. Writing in new modalities may include digital storytelling, video conferencing, blogging, and writing fan fiction (Barone & Wright, 2007; Coiro, Knobel, Lankshear, & Leu, 2008; Knobel & Wilber, 2009). Yancey (2005) suggests that these developments in writing have contributed to a "textured literacy" and that when these are attached to curriculum outcomes they can have positive effects on writing.

Another perspective on writing is the importance of "writing across the curriculum" (WAC), an idea that first developed in the 1980s and continues to gain momentum in writing pedagogy (Tierney, 1981). WAC highlights the observation that all teachers are teachers of writing and that writing is fundamental to all learning. This means that writing is no longer thought of as a separate subject to be taught solely in English language arts classrooms but is the work of all teachers. Teachers approach writing across the curriculum in a number of ways in order to show its importance in communicating and constructing meaning. A great deal of research supports the value of teaching the various forms of conveying written information across subject areas—the writing of lab reports, explanations of solutions to problems, scientific articles, learning logs, summaries, business plans, and biographies—to promote thinking and learning (Vacca & Vacca, 2000).

In terms of assessment and evaluation, writing improvement depends on instruction that shows progress over time and allows for thoughtful and timely feedback. To that end, portfolios are extremely useful ways for students to maintain their writing. Students place their writing in the portfolio, selecting pieces that they would like to work on and have the teacher evaluate. They are given the opportunity to reflect on their work and their processes individually or with peers. Using this approach, teachers do not evaluate everything that the student writes; instead, they ask students to select, for instance, two pieces each month to be assessed and later evaluated. Teachers (and peers) provide comments on writing through conferences and students revise their writing based on the feedback they have received. This type of feedback is essential before the teacher assigns a grade. According to Calfee (2000), exemplary practice with portfolios means teachers do not only evaluate final products but also record the "progress from the students' starting point through drafts and revisions, through to the final version" (p. 285).

Finally, writing instruction must continue to evolve. Solomon (2009) suggests that traditional writing workshops will extend to online writing workshops, in which students use new literacies together with components related to the three Cs of online writing: *composing, computers,* and *commotion.* Writing will continue to mean composing, but perhaps not the linear composition associated with print owing to the introduction of writing technologies that allow for alternate presentation of text. Finally, writing and its instruction must extend to take account of the notion of writing as an active social process engaged in by groups of writers in, for example, online settings, rather than a quiet independent enterprise undertaken by individuals in isolation from one another.

References

Atwell, N. (1998). *In the middle: New understandings about writing, reading and learning* (2nd ed.). Portsmouth, NH: Boynton/Cook Publishers.

Barone, D. and Wright, T. (2008). Literacy instruction with digital and media technologies. *The Reading Teacher 62*(4), 292–302.

Bright, R. (2007). *Write through the grades: Teaching writing in secondary schools.* Winnipeg, MB: Portage & Main Press.

Calfee, R. (2000). Writing portfolios: Activity, assessment, authenticity. In R. Indrisano and J. Squire (Eds.), *Perspectives of writing: Research, theory and practice* (pp. 278–304). Newark, DE: International Reading Association.

Coiro, J., Knobel, M., Lankshear, C., and Leu, D. (Eds.), (2008). *The handbook of research in new literacies.* New York: Routledge.

Elbow, P. (2000). *Everyone can write: Essays toward a hopeful theory of writing and teaching writing.* New York: Oxford University Press.

Emig, J. (1971). *The composing processes of twelfth graders* (Research monograph no. 13). Urbana, IL: National Council of Teachers of English.

Flower, L. and Hayes, J. (1980). The cognition of discovery: Defining a rhetorical problem. *College Composition and Communication 31,* 21–32.

Graves, D. (1983). *Writing: Teachers and children at work.* Portsmouth, NH: Heinemann.

Ippolito, J., Steele, J., and Samson, J. (2008). Why adolescent literacy matters now. *Harvard Educational Review*, Spring. http://www.hepg.org/her/abstract/638 (accessed December 30, 2011).

Knobel, M. and Wilber, D. (2009). Let's talk 2.0. *Educational Leadership,* March, 20–24.

National Writing Project and Nagin, C. (2003). *Because writing matters: Improving student writing in our schools.* San Francisco, CA: Jossey-Bass.

Solomon, M. (2009). True adventures in students' writing online: Mummies, vampires, and schnauzers, oh my! In A. Herrington, K. Hodgson, and C. Moran (Eds.), *Teaching the new writing: Technology, change and assessment in the 21st-century classroom* (pp. 21–38). New York: Teachers College Press.

Tierney, R. (1981). Using expressive writing to teach biology. In A. Wotring and R. Tierney (Eds.), *Two studies of writing in high school science* (pp. 47–73). Berkeley: Bay Area Writing Project, University of California.

Vacca, R. and Vacca, J. (2000). Writing across the curriculum. In R. Indrisano and J. Squire (Eds.), *Perspectives of writing: Research, theory and practice* (pp. 214–232). Newark, DE: International Reading Association.

Vygotsky, L. (1978). *Mind in society: The development of higher psychological processes.* Cambridge, MA: Harvard University Press.

Yancey, K. (2005). Using multiple technologies to teach writing. *Educational Leadership 62,* 38–40.

How Can English Language Arts Teachers Get Students to "Buy Into" the Value of Engaging in a Process-Based Approach to Writing?

By Jeff Park, University of Saskatchewan

The theory of writing as a process has been widely accepted in English language arts pedagogy and curriculum design. Yet, despite this acceptance, there has been an incomplete implementation of the theory in the classroom setting. There are two practical issues that often stall both students and teachers who are trying to fully engage with writing as a process-based act. The first is the question of how to motivate students to actually engage with and get involved in the act of writing. The second is how educators themselves can successfully teach students to see writing as an ongoing process, a process that is valuable in itself as a means of communication and expression rather than merely as an assignment to be completed.

What Is the Background to Writing Process Theory?

In 1982, Maxine Hairston declared that a paradigm shift had occurred in the teaching of writing as educators began to perceive writing as a process rather than simply the production of a product. This "writing process movement" shifted the pedagogical focus from an emphasis on essay structures, text, grammar, and themes to the interests of the individual writer and how he or she creates, values, and conceptualizes writing. Working to understand the needs of individual writers is central to this shift in pedagogical thinking. Educators began looking at how individual writers "processed" ideas into the final products. Britton (1972) envisioned the writing process as a three-step model: conception, incubation, and production. This structural model corresponds to Rohman's (1965) three-stage writing model: prewrite, write, and rewrite. Moreover, the theoretical shift to writing-as-process has led to changes in pedagogical practice. For example, if writing is understood to occur in stages, then teaching the stages of such writing in the classroom has a distinct advantage over a product-oriented approach.

Indeed, a number of other researchers began to conceptualize how the writing process works in the practice of teaching. Donald Graves (1973, 1975), Nancie Atwell (1987), and Lucy Calkins (1983, 1986) were among the first to bring the movement to elementary and middle schools. Janet Emig (1971) explored the composing processes of grade 12 students and also examined writing as a mode of learning (1977). At the university level, Donald Murray (1968, 1984), James Moffett (1968, 1973), Peter Elbow (1973/1998, 1981, 1986), and Ken Macrorie (1970, 1974) began using process theory in their teaching. Murray (1968, 1982, 1984, 1985) developed one-to-one conferencing and the notion of writing to learn. He even publicly adopted the slogan, "Teach writing as a process, not a product."

Many of the latest North American curriculum guides incorporate writing-as-process theory and writing workshops as basic assumptions or underlying frameworks. Writing-as-process theory is extremely valuable in terms of teacher planning and organizing by framing writing as a means of discovery; however, the application of the theory remains in need of further examination. As well, the writing process as taught by many writing teachers is still focused on revising a final or future product, rather than developing an individual writing process for each individual student writer. A five-step model of the writing process (prewriting, drafting, revising, editing, and publishing) has been almost standardized in many cases, both by textbook writers and teachers. A typical example of this can be found in Tompkins' (2000) widely used university textbook for teachers of writing, *Teaching Writing: Balancing Process and Product*. Though the book attempts to balance process against product, Tompkins' assumption is that writing can be taught simply as a process based on a limited number of steps. Teachers usually interpret these steps to be sequential and, in extreme cases, may even use the five steps of the writing process to correspond to the five days of the school week. What such teachers need to understand is that there is no single writing process that applies to every individual in every classroom. To address this diversity, educators will require a variety of resources that can facilitate meaningful writing in the classroom.

How Can Educators Get Students Writing in Meaningful Ways?

Thus, despite the acceptance among educators of writing process theory, there are still a number of pragmatic issues regarding the implementation of the writing process in the classroom. Students often see writing-as-process activities (such as prewriting or revising) as meaningless and time-consuming; teachers themselves often do not fully understand the value of having students engage in prewriting activities, especially when class time is already so constrained simply trying to cover the curriculum. Perhaps the first point that needs to be addressed is allowing students a choice in their writing topics and finding other such ways to make their writing more meaningful. Writing needs to become a meaningful and, yes, even an exciting part of the day-to-day activities in the classroom.

Prewriting activities can take some of the pressure off students since the techniques aren't expected to yield a finished product immediately. Murray (1997) maintained, "Prewriting is everything that takes place before the first draft. Prewriting usually takes about 85% of the writer's time. . . . [it] may include research and daydreaming, note-making and outlining, title-writing and lead-writing" (p. 4). While the percentage he provides might be a little exaggerated, Murray does invite educators to look at the importance of prewriting as a valid use of time. One technique that is very effective in getting students involved in the immediacy of the act of writing is *freewriting*.

Ken Macrorie (1974) and Peter Elbow (1973/1998) developed the use of freewriting as a means of opening up student writing to the writer within. Students need to feel that writing is an effective means of communicating ideas and expressing their thoughts and feelings. Freewriting allows students to "get their ideas out there" and start exploring them. Freewriting is highly effective because it is a rapid way for students to develop a starting point for a writing project. Usually 10 or 15 minutes will suffice for most students to begin articulating their ideas. Elbow (1998) comments that "freewriting improves your writing. It doesn't always produce powerful writing, but it *leads* to powerful writing" (p. 15, my emphasis).

There are other valuable prewriting activities that can engage students immediately. Brainstorming, or simply creating a list of ideas, is also an effective way for getting writing to ferment. The significance for students is that they are able to gather their ideas in a non-threatening manner. Teachers can give the class a few minutes to collect their ideas on paper. Sometimes the simple fact that students are able to refer to a list of ideas generated beforehand can provide momentum to their initial draft. After students have finished collecting ideas, they can then be shown how to organize the ideas into sections. Clustering is another simple activity where students collect ideas. Clustering indicates the connections among the central and subordinate ideas in a writing project. This can be done by cutting and pasting on a word processor or simply drawing arrows by hand (yielding an outward-radiating, web-like pattern) to designate connections among ideas. Students can also use numbers or letters to label similar ideas and thereby begin to organize ideas into concepts that could later be expanded into paragraphs. In a similar manner, students could colour-code ideas or circle similar concepts as an organizing process, an activity which could then lead to the creation of a more formal outline.

Students need to be exposed to a number of prewriting activities to get them started generating text on paper. Each individual student might have a slightly different approach to a piece of writing, and teachers should be aware that what works for one student might not work for another. The important thing to remember is to focus your students on the writing process.

How Can Educators Get Students to "Buy Into" the Need for Revision and the Need to See the Initial Draft as a Work-in-Process?

Once students have completed a number of prewriting activities, they are ready to write the first draft. In traditional writing classes, the writing of the draft (in order to create a final product) was the central focus, and often the only step in writing. Yet, to Murray (1997) this step should account for only 15 percent of the total writing time. English language arts teachers need to allow students first to engage *creatively* with writing in the prewriting activities, and only later encourage them to engage *critically* with their work during the postwriting and revision stages. Elbow (1998) suggests that "it helps to separate the creating and criticizing processes so they don't interfere with each other" (p. 7). Educators and students often conflate the two very different processes, resulting in much confusion. It is much better to have students focus first on writing, and only later on rewriting.

Revision is in many ways the heart of good writing. Zinsser (2006), in *On Writing Well,* states: "Revision is the essence of writing well; it is where the game is won or lost" (p. 83). Revision is more than editing and proofreading for correct spelling and sentence structure. "Writing *is* revising," writes Murray, "and the writer's craft is largely a matter of knowing how to discover what you have to say, develop, and clarify it, each requiring the craft of revision" (Murray, 2003, p. 2). Students need to be informed of the value of revision: the re-seeing and re-conceptualization of their original draft. Most students honestly believe they have completed the required work by writing the draft, and this perspective is at least partially caused by our current educational system's focus on the evaluation of the final product. Students often ask two questions about an assigned piece of writing: one, "How long does this have to be?"; and two, "What is it worth?" Educators need to refocus on the intrinsic value of the act of writing itself, rather than on the extrinsic evaluation. At the very least, educators can shift the evaluation process to include more emphasis on the prewriting and revision stages of the writing process.

Students are often hesitant to revise their work, sometimes for reasons other than marks or evaluation. Fear is one factor that educators need to consider. Writing can be revealing of the writer's innermost thoughts, and sometimes students believe that any criticism of their writing is a criticism of themselves. Educators need to reassure students that any suggestions for improvement are for the purposes of clarifying the student's ideas, and are always meant to value the writing. Murray (2003) says that many writers "fear rewriting because of inexperience. We have not been taught how to rewrite" (p. 2). Guiding students through revision processes as a group is often helpful, especially when teachers can show how they revise their own work. Showing examples of how famous authors have revised their writing is also very helpful. One-on-one teacher-student conferences are invaluable as a means to build rapport and trust. In the beginning, the conferences may appear to be time-consuming, but as the rapport builds, time is actually saved. Student-teacher conferences can lead to writers' workshops and peer evaluation where students read over and comment on each other's writing in order to make improvements and fully develop their work. Conferencing and writers' workshops make for meaningful writing because "[r]evising with feedback is the most powerful way to revise, and happily enough it is also the most interesting and enjoyable technique" (Elbow, 1981). Showing students that writing and rewriting is enjoyable and valuable is probably one of the greatest challenges educators face today and yet it can be one of the most rewarding.

In my book *Writing at the Edge,* I suggest educators "position writing as an active, meaningful practice that involves engagement with learning, rather than a passive response to something that is happening 'outside' the individual student" (Park, 2005, p. 160). If educators make writing meaningful, students will "buy into" prewriting and revision activities and finally begin to see themselves as authentic writers whose voices will be heard.

References

Atwell, N. (1987). *In the middle: Writing, reading and learning with adolescents.* Portsmouth, NH: Boyton/Cook Publishers.

Britton, J. (1972). Writing to learn and learning to write. In G. M. Pradl (Ed.), *Prospect and retrospect: Selected essays of James Britton* (pp. 94–111). Upper Montclair, NJ: Boynton/Cook.

Calkins, L. (1983). *Lessons from a child: On the teaching and learning of writing.* Exeter, NH: Heinemann Educational Books.

Calkins, L. M. (1986). *The art of teaching writing.* Portsmouth, NH: Heinemann.

Elbow, P. (1973/1998). *Writing without teachers* (2nd ed.). New York: Oxford University Press.

Elbow, P. (1981). *Writing with power: Techniques for mastering the writing process.* New York: Oxford University Press.

Elbow, P. (1986). *Embracing contraries: Explorations in learning and teaching.* New York: Oxford University Press.

Elbow, P. (1998). *Writing with power: Techniques for master the writing process.* New York: Oxford University Press.

Emig, J. (1971). *The composing processes of twelfth graders. Research Report no. 13.* Urbana, IL: National Council of Teachers of English.

Emig, J. (1977). Writing as a mode of learning. *College Composition and Communication* 28(2), 122–128.

Graves, D. (1973). *Children's writing: Research directions and hypotheses based upon an examination of the writing processes of seven year old children.* (Ed.D dissertation from State University of New York at Buffalo.) Retrieved from ERIC database (ED095586).

Graves, D. (1975). An examination of the writing processes of seven year old children. *Research in the Teaching of English* 9, 227–241.

Hairston, M. (1982). The winds of change: Thomas Kuhn and the revolution in the teaching of writing. *College Composition and Communication* 33(1), 76–88.

Macrorie, K. (1970). *Telling writing.* New York: Hayden Book Co.

Macrorie, K. (1974). *A vulnerable teacher.* Rochelle Park, NJ: Hayden Book Company.

Moffett, J. (1968). *Teaching the universe of discourse.* Boston: Houghton Mifflin.

Moffett, J. (1973). *A student-centered language arts curriculum, grades K-13: A handbook for teachers.* Boston: Houghton Mifflin.

Murray, D. (1968). *A writer teaches writing: a practical method of teaching composition by Donald M. Murray.* Boston, Houghton Mifflin.

Murray, D. (1982). *Learning by teaching: Selected articles on writing and teaching.* Montclair, NJ: Boynton/Cook.

Murray, D. (1984). *Write to learn.* New York: Holt Rinehart and Winston.

Murray, D. (1985). *A Writer teaches writing* (2nd ed.). Boston: Houghton Mifflin Co.

Murray, D. (1997). Teach writing as a process not product. In V. Villanueva (Ed.), *Cross-talk in comp theory: A reader* (pp. 3–6). Urbana, IL: National Council of Teachers of English.

Murray, D. (2003). *The craft of revision* (5th ed.) Belmont, CA: Wadsworth Publishing

Park, J. (2005). *Writing at the edge: Narrative and writing process theory.* New York: Peter Lang.

Rohman, D.G. (1965). *Pre-writing: The stage of discovery in the writing process.* College Composition and Communication, 16(2), 106-122.

Tompkins, G. E. *Teaching writing: Balancing process and product* (3rd ed.). Columbus, OH: Prentice-Hall, 2000.

Zinsser, W. (2006). *On writing well.* New York: HarperCollins.

SECTION 3

Changing Modes of Expression

What Do Multimodal Textual Practices Tell Us about the Family Understandings, Beliefs, and Practices That Inform Our Students' Experiences of Literacy?

By Anne Burke, Memorial University of Newfoundland

The following entry will look at two adolescents' multimodal school literacy practices, illustrating how their choices of reading material and their authoring of multimodal texts may be traced to the primary discourses of the home. By discussing and examining the students' situated literacy practices, we can see how teachers may engage students in textual representations that are more in tune with students' lifeworlds. To frame this exploration, I ask the critical question, "What do multimodal textual practices tell us about family understandings, beliefs, and practices that inform our students' experiences of literacy?"

Changing Texts and Changing Space

> I try to incorporate a lot because I recognize that literacy involves many things . . . through the use of computers—[but] obviously we have to stick with your typical textbooks . . . that's what is expected.
>
> —Chantelle, classroom teacher

Modern language arts teaching is no longer confined to the reading and writing found in anthologies of short stories or Shakespeare's plays, or to analyzing argumentative essays. More importantly, neither are the literacy experiences of contemporary students likely to be confined to the printed page. Many teachers and classrooms embrace textual practices that engage new forms of student response. These might include digital media such as photo-stories and PowerPoint presentations, or artifacts such as graphic novels and homemade videos. Current research with adolescents (Alvermann, 2008, Burke & Hammett, 2009; Carrington & Robinson, 2009; Hagood, 2009; McGinnis, 2007; Sarroub, Pernicek, & Sweeney, 2007) has illustrated that students can become motivated to take hold of their own literacy when educators harness the skills that students have developed at home and out of school. To show how students engage in literacy practices that are not necessarily welcomed in language arts classes, this essay will situate these engagements in the conceptual framework of multimodality—keeping in mind that literacy is a social practice that engages learning, life experiences, and global relationships.

As pre-service teachers, it is likely that technology is strongly connected to your literate lives. You are part of the textual renaissance that is occurring as a result of technology and globalization. However, your classroom's texts (as the preceding quote from Chantelle brings to the fore) may not take account of the social and political struggles inherent in literacy practices generally and in the individual lives of the adolescents we teach. We need to think of literacy in terms of what is *done* with the skills, and not just as a set of skills and techniques that must be practised and memorized. Changing forms of text embedded within life practices are better understood when considered as "multimodal" forms—a category that Bearne (2009) defines as the "combination of image, sound gesture, movement and writing or print [whether] communicated through paper, the screen, face to face meetings, or performative spaces" (p. 157). Many studies in the last decade (Hull & Shultz, 2002; Jewitt, 2008; Knobel, 1999; Mills, 2010; Pahl, 2003; Thompson, 2008; Vincent 2006) have shown that reaching beyond traditional literacy practices by using multimodal pedagogies in the classroom can make the boundary between home and school language practices much more permeable. Framing literacy in these terms requires us to look closely at the home and family experiences that adolescents bring to their literacy engagements.

Literacy is connected to the social and cultural spaces of people's lives; it is more than a set of decontextualized skills. An examination of the lived engagements with literacy that substantially frame young people's lives reveals engagement with multiple forms. A student may be reading a novel, commenting on it through Facebook, or tweeting her or his passing thoughts. Multimodal textual engagements like these have become possible through new technologies that enable students to engage with new and sophisticated skills—skills that, unfortunately, are not always accepted or invited into our classrooms. These everyday literacies often define the social fabric for the children we teach. It is the world in which they live and learn.

Theoretical Constructs

These ideas stem in part from the work of scholars in New Literacy Studies (Street, 1984; Gee, 1996; Barton & Hamilton, 2000) who established that literacy is situated within the social, political, and cultural spaces in which it is practised. In other words, "literacy" is the events and practices in which people engage in their everyday lives to make meaning

(Barton & Hamilton, 2000). Street's research shows how literacy is a socially situated practice (Street, 1984). Working as a social anthropologist led Street to the realization that literacy was viewed by policy-makers as either autonomous (applied across all contexts) or ideological (grounded in social, historical, cultural, and political contexts). In an ideological model, literacy is a set of social practices that are shared within a particular cultural group and linked to power structures within society (Street, 1993). As it stands, the autonomous model of literacy dominates Western perspectives on schooling and determines the standard, governmental literacy definitions and goals. Street's work challenges us to see how reading and writing are both linguistic and social practices.

The writings of Gee (1996) illustrate that in order to be literate in society, one must understand the "discourses" that a particular language carries in its community. For Gee, "Discourses are ways of being 'people like us'. They are 'ways of being in the world'; they are 'forms of life'. They are . . . always and everywhere social and products of social histories" (1996, p. 8). Discourses are made up of social languages that can range in form from the way we use words to gestures and acts, and even to the clothes that we wear. Once understood, they allow us access to group values, purposes of being, and ways of acting. Most importantly, Gee (1996) claims that being literate is not just a mastery of the language within a community, but also being able to use the "right language in the right ways" within a particular context.

Multimodality

When students actively engage modes of language that connect with their own social realities—perhaps through their busy online interactions—then the written word transforms the world *told* into the world *shown* (Kress, 2003). This is the basis for discussions about multimodality. Discourse, defined earlier as the social use of language, carries messages represented by the texts that one reads and writes as well as the spaces, contexts, and relationships that one encounters. The prevalence of online literacy practices means that the nature of these discourses is changing. As we've seen, definitions of literacy have expanded to include many literacy practices that students use in their contemporary lifeworlds beyond traditional notions of reading and writing. Teachers who wish to embrace these new literacies need to make a conscious connection between students' out-of-school literacy practices (many of which are multimodal in nature) and their in-school literacy practices.

Literacy as Events in Two Adolescent Lives

George and Sienna were in Chantelle's junior-high language arts class at the time of the study; both were from middle-class homes and both usually had good grades. Typical for their age group, they both enjoyed access to computers and were avid consumers of TV, music, and other digital media. Their literacies were profiled through a series of questions. Their answers to these questions illustrated the multimodal literacy practices of their lives. During the study, they were asked to respond to questions such as: (A) Do you write or draw in your spare time?; (B) Do you work with images or music?; (C) Do you share what you read at home (webpages, books, newspapers, email, etc.); and (D) What do you like to do after school with friends and family? Their responses illustrated the rich tapestry of their cultural and home literacy practices and provided some key insights into the varied practices of home literacy. Their literacy practices outside the classroom included reading and communication using a variety of print and online resources, video gaming online, downloading music, and creating multimodal artifacts using software like PowerPoint and PhotoShop. Some of their home literacy practices connected to their school literacy practices, but others did not.

TV as Literate Practice

George was an avid TV viewer. He demonstrated a strong critical awareness of the construction of media, such as the satirical cartoon *The Simpsons*. He shared that his entire family loved this show and enjoyed deconstructing its plots and jokes (with the exception of his mother, who "doesn't get it"). George used the Internet to find designs to create his own visual representations of the show's characters and to develop a trivia quiz for his family. This was later turned into a PowerPoint presentation for a class project. In finding such powerful "secondary discourses" to the primary discourse of *The Simpsons,* he engaged in redesign or a transformation of the materiality of the show (Cope & Kalantzis, 2000; Kress, 2003), thus appealing to his family's interests. As a "code breaker" (Luke & Freebody, 1999), he came to understand satire and how the show's writers designed the satire of *The Simpsons*. In creating his quiz, George showed his awareness that texts are not neutral and do not represent certain viewpoints and discourses. As a text-maker, he renegotiated the cultural forms of the texts and critically analyzed and transformed the text through the use of PowerPoint (Cope & Kalantzis, 2000). The pop quiz he created would appeal primarily to the family's literacy practice of trivia game playing. However, his redesign of the television show also showed how he transformed himself, constructing a new identity as quizmaster and TV critic through his PowerPoint presentation. In fact, his home literacy practice of watching television may have even been redesigned to show his mother the value of the cartoon genre. This activity supports the Barton and Hamilton (1998) claim that "Literacy practices are purposeful and embedded in broader social goals and cultural practices" (p. 7). Despite its mundane origin, George's out-of-school literacy was critically engaged using multimodal forms and allowed him to find classroom value in a home practice.

Teen Idols and Cultural Practices

As a class assignment, Chantelle asked her students to research a personal hero. Sienna, who had recently emigrated from Latin America, used research and multimodal artifacts she found on the Internet to create a presentation about her love of Spanish music and to describe the life of the late musician Selena. Sienna explained that she wanted to do research on someone who was of her own culture and who spoke Spanish, and that the recordings of this singer in particular were often played at community gatherings and celebrations. This local literacy practice (playing Spanish music at parties) was of great importance to Sienna. She also explained that the singer Selena had been very poor and deserved the success she had attained. Sienna identified with the singer's work ethic as it reflected her own belief that hard work would translate into personal success. Sienna's confidence in the assignment showed the personal value of literacy learning when it draws on home and local literacies, such as her own Latin American cultural reference points (Barton & Hamilton, 1998; Gee, 2003; Street, 1993). Sienna connected with the struggles of this singer, associating Selena's confidence and bravery with her own everyday struggles. Sienna said at one point, "by the time Selena was six, she was already singing like a professional in English and Spanish. Even though she did not speak English, she still (sang) in both languages." For Sienna, public speaking in English and being able to adequately express her ideas were challenges she was struggling to overcome in her own life. The singer Selena's personal challenges aligned with many of Sienna's social challenges (Holland, Lachiotte, Skinner, & Cain, 2001). Like George, she was able to use the designs available on the Internet to empower herself *within* the classroom using a home literacy to bring her own family experience to school and in so doing becoming a proud advocate for her own culture.

Conclusion

Through an examination of their literate engagements, we can see how Sienna and George used non-traditional texts to bring their home understandings to school and how the multimodal texts they used and produced were shaped within spaces where their meanings had personal value. It is very important to note how they engaged in the design and redesign of their literate engagements in order to bring deeper meaning to their own lives and display it to others. In both cases the act of design, redesign, and transformation of their social futures was evident in how they harnessed their literacy to engage the multiple discourses they mobilized within their lives. By embracing this multimodal approach to classroom assignments, and by encouraging her students to bring their home literacies into the school, our teacher Chantelle, the classroom teacher, was able to tap into a powerful reserve of creative energy. While the theory behind this method may be complex, for teachers the action is relatively straightforward: keep an open mind to technology and multimodal approaches combined with a ready willingness to bring both home and other out-of-school literacies into the classroom. Ultimately, this offers students a chance to empower themselves and expand their skills to embrace new levels of literacy.

References

Alvermann, D. E. (2008). Why bother theorizing adolescents online literacies for classroom practice and research? *Journal of Adult and Adolescent Literacy 52*(1), 8–19.

Barton, D. & Hamilton, M. (1998). *Local literacies: Reading and writing in one community.* London: Routledge.

Barton, D. & Hamilton, M. (2000). Literacy practices. In D. Barton, M. Hamilton, & R. Ivanic (Eds.), *Situated literacies: Reading and writing in context* (pp. 7–15). New York: Routledge.

Bearne, E. (2009). Multimodality, literacy and texts: Developing a Discourse. *Journal of Early Childhood Literacy* 9(2), 156–187.

Burke, A. & Hammett, R. (2009). *Assessing new literacies: Perspectives from the classroom.* New York: Peter Lang.

Carrington, V. & Robinson, M. (2009). (Eds). *Digital literacies: Social learning and classroom practice.* London: Sage

Cope, B. & Kalantzis, M. (2000). (Eds). *Multiliteracies: Literacy learning and the design of social futures.* London: Routledge.

Cope, B. & Kalantzis, M. (2000). Introduction: Multiliteracies: The beginnings of an idea. In B. Cope, & M. Kalantzis (Eds.), *Multiliteracies: Literacy learning and the design of social futures* (pp. 3–8). London: Routledge.

Gee, J.P. (1996). *Social linguistics and literacies: Ideology in discourses* (2nd ed.). London: Taylor & Francis.

Gee, J. P. (2003). *What video games have to teach us about learning and literacy*? New York: Palgrave.

Hagood, M. (2009). (Ed). *New literacies practices: Designing literacy learning*. New York: Peter Lang.

Holland, D., Lachicotte, W., Skinner, D., & Cain, C. (2001). *Identity and agency in cultural worlds.* Cambridge, MA: Harvard University Press.

Hull, G. & Shultz, K. (2002). *School's out! Bridging out of school literacies with curriculum practices.* New York: Teacher's College Press.

Jewitt, C. (2008). Multimodality and literacy in school classrooms. *Review of research in education* 32(1), 241–267.

Jewitt, C. & Kress, G. (2003). *Multimodal literacy*. New York: Peter Lang.

Knobel, M. (1999). *Everyday literacies: Students, discourses, and social practices.* New York. Peter Lang.

Kress, G. (2003). *Literacy in the new media age*. London: Routledge.

Luke, A. & Freebody, P. (1999). A map of possible practices: Further notes on the four resources model. http://www.readingonline.org/research/lukefreebody.html (accessed December 29, 2011).

McGinnis, T. (2007). Khumer rap boys, X men, Asia's fruits, and Dragon ball Z: Creating multilingual and multimodal classroom contexts. *Journal of Adolescent and Adult Literacy* 5(7), 570–579.

Mills, K. A. (2010). Filming in progress: New spaces for multimodal designing. *Linguistics and Education: An International Research Journal* 21(1), 14–28.

Pahl, K. (2003). Children's text making at home: Transforming meaning across modes. In C. Jewitt & G. Kress (Eds.), *Multimodal literacy* (pp. 139–154). New York: Peter Lang.

Sarroub, L., Pernicek, T., & Sweeney, T. (2007). I was bitten by a scorpion: Reading in and out of school in a refugee's life. *Journal of Adolescent and Adult Literacy* 50(8), 668–679.

Street, B. V. (1984). *Literacy in theory and practice.* Cambridge, England: Cambridge University Press.

Street, B. V. (1993). The new literacy studies: Guest editorial. *Journal of Research in Reading* 16(2), 81–97.

Thompson, M. (2008). Multimodal Teaching and Learning: Creating Spaces for Content Teachers. *Journal of Adolescent and Adult Literacy* 52(2), 144–153.

Vincent, J. (2006). Children writing: Multimodality and assessment in the writing classroom. *Literacy* 40(1), 51–57.

How Do I Teach Writing in a Digital and Global World?

By Sean Wiebe, University of Prince Edward Island

We Cannot Ignore How the Online World Is Changing What It Means to Write

The digital turn has so profoundly increased the possibilities for teaching writing that traditional writing assignments, on their own, often feel too static, too structured, and too limited. In an age of connectivity, young people are clearly accessing information outside of school and comfortably use a variety of tools associated with new technologies to transform, create, and distribute knowledge (Knobel & Lankshear, 2007). But inside the classroom, very little has changed with respect to writing pedagogy (Wiebe & McAuley, 2010). Many English teachers, content to deploy traditional paradigms, have yet to imagine how writing functions differently for today's youth who are digitally connected to a vast public. Hayles's (2005) comment, "I think therefore I connect with all the other cognizers in my environment" (p. 213), illustrates how being connected offers an entirely different form of expression. How can English teachers utilize the online world in the classroom without sacrificing traditional writing expectations?

Old Concerns, New Concerns, and How the English Teacher Can Help

Ten to 15 years ago, the increasing prominence of technology in education may have created the impression that English teachers had to fight against the Internet in order to preserve formal writing conventions. Abbreviations, emoticons, and online code words were said to be too often appearing in formal assignments. Teachers worried that plagiarism might be on the rise: cut, paste, and submit. Today's online world includes Kindle and YouTube, novelists who "tweet" and "facebook": such new verbs are recorded in dictionaries, reflecting the scope of the change; even newspapers now blend content between blog and print. Quality fiction and non-fiction are easily accessed online. The new online world calls for new concerns and new approaches.

One primary concern is that while research on the social dynamics of Web 2.0 confirms that students are *consuming* more information, their participation in content *creation* lags behind (Gabriel, Wiebe, & MacDonald, 2009; Kumar, 2010). A second, related concern is that the quality of online content, such as tweets, text messages, blog comments, and Facebook posts, reflects a trend of instant publication (Klages & Clark, 2009) that is devoid of deeper thought (Wiebe, in press; Hegarty, 2004). Fortunately, it is possible for English teachers to counteract these two disturbing trends by (1) creating opportunities for collaborative content creation, and (2) embedding specific writing tasks within content creation.

Creating Opportunities for Collaborative Content Creation

The Internet is not only for finding information, but for sharing information as well. Universities, private corporations, and savvy, tech-minded individuals are leveraging online spaces in ways that are creating social and economic value (Tapscott and Williams, 2010). Willinsky (2009) reminds us that students are entitled to opportunities that advance their interests and rights to expression. This means "the 'ethos' and 'technical' affordances of Web 2.0 have the potential to catalyze the aesthetic creativity of youth" (Vasudevan, 2010, p. 44).

If I were teaching at the local secondary school tomorrow, my students would be online during class, and my hope would be that our classwork would be a genuine, real-world contribution to knowledge. Current research tells us that the online experience should be collaborative, inviting, and accessible (Gagne & Fels, 2007), that it should provide opportunity for personal expression (Rutherford & Figg, 2008), that it should include the teacher's involvement as a class or group member (Senior, 2010), and that pedagogy involving online experience should focus on learning the course objectives rather than learning "online learning" (Gustafson, 2004). Therefore, I would begin a new writing assignment by directing students to collect data. They could scour YouTube, Twitter, Facebook, blog sites, online newspapers, and so on. What I would make clear is that they are conducting research, and I would briefly teach them some criteria for collecting quality data that is compelling, influential, and relevant. Students would need a research question related to our unit of study, and for the purposes of this present example the question would be, "What skills do today's youth need in order to prosper in the twenty-first century?"

For an entire class period, the students would upload data to a collaborative online space (such as Google docs, Moodle, or Knowledge Forum), and for homework I would assign the task of analyzing the data, which would involve commenting on the content they uploaded during class. I would be active in the online space, available for questions via chat, and also commenting on the data. What I would seek to foster in this collaborative online space is a process of conversation where students are analyzing, comparing, extending, and evaluating. Through such a collaboration, Siemens (2005) theorizes that new competencies would arise; Goodwin-Jones (2008) suggests that students would take more responsibility for their learning; and Sheetz and Curcher (2008) have shown how online conversations can carry over and improve face-to-face conversations. During class the next day we would discuss what we have discovered so far, and, with a view to students being active, literate, and worldly citizens, we would then zero in on the data, which could then serve as a springboard for our own contributions to the vast public of the Web 2.0 world.

Supposing that the class picked a popular YouTube video as being the most compelling, influential, and relevant piece of data, the online space for content creation would then be the comment section below the YouTube video and the space for posting a video reply. It would be a mistake to now set the students loose to upload content. Research clearly states that students need scaffolded writing instruction matched to their ability level in order to support the online creation process (Sheetz & Curcher, 2008). The design and composition processes should involve writing instruction and writing practice.

Embedding Specific Writing Tasks within Content Creation

Multimedia tools make it possible to communicate a highly sophisticated message with minimal technical learning, thereby making the production process more accessible.

Vasudevan (2010) has found that multimodal project work matters outside the classroom. For students it is interesting and enjoyable, and it fits within the social sphere of their own lives in ways that traditional text-only assignments may not.

To maintain a focus on writing, I would embed specific writing tasks within online content production. Continuing with the example above, I might have students write five thesis statements based on their analysis of the collected data. With partners, they would then compare, evaluate, and choose a thesis statement. I would offer feedback on ways of narrowing the topic and avoiding stating the obvious. Important is how participation in the online space might reveal to teachers new pedagogies for working with students in face-to-face settings. First-order critical thinking work of composing and evaluating claims would take one class period, and for homework students would upload a textual or video comment to the YouTube space. Acting individually and collectively, the students would be contributing their message to a public space. Young (2009) confirms that mini-messages can explore, clarify, and refute societal norms. As teachers and students engage together with these messages and conversations about the data, there are endless possibilities for more writing and communicating.

Concluding Thoughts

As I see it, the above example has some key elements that both critique the online space and utilize it in the classroom:

1. Students are required to critically evaluate the content they encounter.
2. The students' online world matters as they can research data that connects with them and their world.
3. Students work collaboratively in the gathering, analyzing, and producing of content.
4. Both traditional texts and multimodal texts are valued.
5. Students still learn how to write well and how to support their claims. As well, they write for an authentic audience.
6. Students learn skills that prepare them for the changing cultural conventions of communication.
7. Students' work is out there in the real world, being critiqued by real people on issues that matter beyond the typically closed classroom space.
8. Students are no longer just knowledge consumers but are participating in knowledge production, and, while doing so, are hopefully being prompted to deeper thought in their personal online lives as well.

References

Gabriel, M., Wiebe, S., & MacDonald, R. (2009). Net generation expectations for technology—mediated learning at the university level. *Research, Reflections and Innovations in Integrating ICT in Education* 1, 996–1000.

Gagne, C. & Fels, D. (2007). Learning through weblogs. In T. Bastiaens & S. Carliner (Eds.), *Proceedings of World Conference on E-Learning in Corporate, Government, Healthcare, and Higher Education* (pp. 2518–2526). Chesapeake, VA: AACE.

Gustafson, K. (2004). The impact of technologies on learning. *Planning for Higher Education* 32(2), 37–43.

Godwin-Jones, R. (2008). Web-writing 2.0: Enabling, documenting, and assessing writing online. *Language Learning & Technology* 12(2), 7–12. Retrieved March 23, 2009 from ERIC database.

Hayles, K. (2005). *My mother was a computer: Digital subjects and literacy texts.* Chicago: University of Chicago Press.

Hegarty, M. (2004). Dynamic visualizations and learning: Getting to difficult questions. *Learning and Instruction* 14, 343–351.

Klages, M. & Clark, J. (2009). New worlds of errors and expectations: Basic writers and digital assumptions. *Journal of Basic Writing (CUNY)* 28(1), 32–49.

Knobel, M. & Lankshear, C. (2007). *A new literacies sampler.* New York: Peter Lang.

Kumar, S. (2010). The net generation's informal and educational use of new technologies. *In Education: Technology & Social Media (Special Issue, Part 2).* 16(1). Retrieved from http://ineducation.ca/issue-2.

Rutherford, C. & Figg, C. (2008). Tech use and teacher candidates: The impact of new online tools on attitudes. In K. McFerrin et al. (Eds.), *Proceedings of Society for Information Technology and Teacher Education International Conference* (pp. 679–683). Chesapeake, VA: AACE.

Senior, R. (2010). Connectivity: A framework for understanding effective language teaching in face-to-face and online learning communities. *RELC Journal* 41(2), pp. 137–147.

Sheetz, D. & Curcher, M. (2008). Using blogs to enhance content learning for students who are learning in a second language. In G. Richards (Ed.), *Proceedings of World Conference on E-Learning in Corporate, Government, Healthcare, and Higher Education* (pp. 1254–1259). Chesapeake, VA: AACE.

Siemens, G. (2005). Connectivism: A learning theory for the digital age. *International Journal of Instructional Technology and Distance Learning* 2(1). http://www.itdl.org/Journal/Jan_05/article01.htm (accessed January 2, 2012).

Tapscott, D. & Williams, A. D. (2010). Innovating the 21st-century university: It's time! *EDUCAUSE Review* 45(1), 16–29.

Vasudevan, L. (2010). Literacies in a participatory, multimodal world: The arts and aesthetics of Web 2.0. *Language Arts* 88(1), 43–50.

Wiebe, S. (under review). A limit case narrative on post digital student inquiry in elementary education. *Journal of Curriculum and Pedagogy.*

Wiebe, S. & McCauley, S. (2010). Harnessing new technologies to teach academic writing to the net generation. *In Education* 16(1), n. pag. http://ineducation.ca/article/harnessing-new-technologies-teach-academic-writing-net-generation (accessed December 30, 2011).

Willinsky, J. (2009). The intellectual properties of literacy. *LEARNing Landscapes* 3(1), 17–27.

Young, K. (2009). I have a student who...: An exploration of societal norms embedded in co-constructed narratives. *Narrative Inquiry* 19(2), 356–371.

How Can I Keep Up with the Changes in the Literacy World? How Can I Know What to Do Regarding New Forms of Composition?

By Jill Kedersha McClay, University of Alberta

Professional Development and New Literacies

Now is an exciting time to be a literacy teacher. The contemporary literacy world offers adults and adolescents a dizzying array of new forms of composition and expression. We barely become aware of one new form—Twitter or webinars, for example—when another new form ("vooks," anyone?) comes into view. However, for beginning and experienced teachers alike, this exciting time is also fraught with anxiety. Teachers face competing pressures from educational mandates and public opinion: we are expected to maintain traditional practices of literacy, to be up-to-the-minute and engage students with twenty-first century literacies, to prepare students for digital work environments, to firewall objectionable online practices from our classrooms, and so on. Scholars argue about exactly what it now means to be a "literate" person while agreeing with Frank Zingrone (2001) that "the one-medium user is the new illiterate" (p. 237). Multimodal composition is the norm and literacy researchers are now focused on the ways in which literate people engage in social communities online. The provincial standardized assessments that govern teachers' classroom practices, however, remain stubbornly print-based; they do not require or allow for multimodal composition.

Conscientious teachers grapple with many questions regarding contemporary literacy education: Which new literacy practices ought to be included in the English language arts curriculum? Is tweeting, for example, a silly fad or is it here to stay? How can we teach students to be responsible online citizens when the social practices of literacy change so rapidly? How can we fit anything else into the already overcrowded list of expectations for teachers? What can we give up if we want to add something new to our programs? No educator, administrator, theorist, or researcher knows the answers to these questions, just as no one knows which literacy practices will prove to be enduring and valuable for students in their future lives.

Teachers do not have the luxury of waiting five or ten years to see which of these new forms of expression will "stick" and which will disappear with the next fad. We have to make decisions each day about what to include in and exclude from classroom life. Most teachers must make these decisions without much expertise in a given new form of expression. As forms and social practices of literacy evolve rapidly, we are unable to keep abreast of each new form, much less evaluate its usefulness presently or for the future.

The dilemma thus facing literacy teachers is enormous: How can I keep up with the changes in the literacy world? How can I know what to do regarding new forms of composition? The dilemma rests upon a central paradox of contemporary literacy education: How can we teach and assess that which we do not truly understand? Teachers must teach and assess students' work in new multimodal forms and social practices of composition when we do not have much (or sometimes any) experience in creating these forms or engaging in these practices ourselves. I want to suggest a starting point to help new and experienced teachers develop strong practices to solve this paradox.

Arthur Applebee (1996) writes of this dilemma when he discusses the need for teachers to develop "knowledge-in-action": "The paradox of knowledge-in-action is that in order to learn something new, one must do what one doesn't yet know how to do. The way out of this paradox is to realize that learning is a social process: we can learn to do new things by doing them with others" (Applebee, 1996, p. 108). The starting point that I propose for new and experienced teachers alike is to develop "knowledge-in-action" in social groups through collaborative teacher inquiry.

Collaborative inquiry groups can be developed sensibly and richly by teachers working together to consider teaching and literacy practices systematically and critically. Learning together, exploring questions and issues of common interest to the group, teachers can attend carefully to students' abilities and needs; they can focus on questions of great relevance to students' literacy rather than on excessive and narrow preparation for outmoded standardized examinations.

Additionally, collaborative learning approaches that involve teachers and researchers working together are often highly productive (Cochrane-Smith & Lytle, 2009; Wells, 2009). Collaborative inquiry allows teachers and researchers to bridge a gap between theoretical understanding and classroom practice as it allows teachers and researchers to explore complex issues together, achieving a "bifocal vision" (Bateson, 1994) in a relationship of "collaborative resonance" (Cochran-Smith, 1991). Together, they can achieve a broader and deeper perspective than either group could accomplish alone (McClay, 2006). There is a strong dialectic between practice and theory in the actual conduct of collaborative inquiry among teachers and researchers as theory provides a framework for teachers' decision making and for their systematic collection of data. Collaborative inquiry provides opportunities for teachers to reflect on their practice in a social group and to benefit from each other's experience and perspectives.

Teacher inquiry groups that include a researcher can manage a productive and systematic means of collecting information. While the teachers are responsible for teaching and assessing their students, a researcher can be responsible for the organized collection of data during a project. Participants in experienced teacher inquiry groups have learned that it is essential to take student work into account when exploring their teaching practices; student work is the evidence that draws teachers into genuine discussion and opens new avenues of thought (Bearne, Graham, & Marsh, 2007). With a researcher among the members, collaborative inquiry groups have the ability to collect evidence systematically and to include student perspectives through interviews and observations.

In creating a safe space for exploration of new forms and practices in literacy, teachers can approach their learning both as individual literate beings and as teachers responsible for the education of students. We learn through purposeful, exploratory talk and consideration of the data at hand: student work, student perspectives, teacher reflections, classroom observations, and professional reading. Because we genuinely do not know the answers to the difficult questions posed above, the focused, professional talk of teacher inquiry groups is vitally important. These are opportunities for pragmatic discussion of multimodal composition, of what we intend and what we create in our compositions, of how audiences respond to our creations.

Questions of assessment arise naturally and inevitably in these discussions—how do we appraise the quality of our own compositions and those of our students? What standards are appropriate for the work my students create? When teachers evaluate according to standards that students either do not know or do not understand, there is very little teaching that comes with assessment; however, when teachers genuinely participate in a discussion about quality and what is "good" in a given form of composition, assessment can be an authentic aspect of teaching and learning.

Vygotsky's "zone of proximal development" (ZPD) is a much-cherished concept among educators. Vygotsky defined the ZPD as "the distance between the actual developmental level as determined by independent problem solving and the level of potential development as determined through problem solving under adult guidance or in collaboration with more capable peers" (1978, p. 86). Too often, however, we forget that with respect to new literacy forms and practices, teachers and researchers also live in a perpetual zone of proximal development, and the zone is multidirectional (McClay & Mackey, 2009). In a lively and supportive teacher inquiry group, teachers and researchers can learn together in a shared zone of proximal development where everyone performs at a higher level than he or she could manage unassisted. Vygotsky also taught teachers the importance of talk and play; for us to make good pedagogical sense of new literacy practices, talk and play are vitally important—both with colleagues and in our classrooms. We need to allow ourselves the freedom to acknowledge our lack of answers. Nobody is an expert in a literacy form that is brand new!

We cannot begin to develop realistic and appropriate assessment practices unless we take development into account. Therefore, we need to ask, "What do multimodal composers *do*?" Eve Bearne and Helen Wolstencroft (2007) have developed a very useful categorization to explain what producers of multimodal texts must be able to do. They must be able to:

- Make decisions about mode and content for specific purposes and audiences
- Structure texts
- Use technical features for effect
- Reflect

(adapted from Bearne and Wolstencroft, 2007, pp. 168–172)

When we engage in these practices ourselves, we can begin to create appropriate assessment practices for multimodal work and work in contemporary literacy env ironments with and for our students. Jenkins et al. (2006) also categorize some of the new skills that literate people need in contemporary literacy environments. Their list includes:

- Play
- Performance
- Simulation
- Appropriation
- Multi-tasking
- Distributed cognition
- Collective intelligence
- Judgment

- Transmedia navigation
- Networking
- Negotiation

(adapted from Jenkins et al., 2006, p. 4)

It is a daunting list, to be sure, and it is unlikely that any teacher or researcher feels truly competent with all these skills. We need opportunities to play with a form or medium before we can assess creations in it. We must have opportunities to learn the affordances of the medium and what the form lends itself to. Teachers need this time of exploration as much as students do, possibly more. Our collaborative inquiry groups, like our classrooms, can become places of literate play that will be the precursor to literate engagement in new literacies pedagogy.

Collaborative teacher inquiry offers teachers a lively and essential way to develop what Kevin Leander (2009) terms "parallel pedagogy," the concurrent reliance on traditional approaches and newer Web 2.0 sensibilities in classroom practices. When such professional and supportive inquiry groups include teachers and researchers working together to develop both theory and classroom pedagogy with regard to new literacies and multimodal composition, there are rich opportunities for students to learn well in our classrooms.

References

Applebee, A. N. (1996). *Curriculum as conversation, transforming traditions of teaching and learning*. Chicago: University of Chicago Press.

Bateson, M. C. (1994). *Peripheral visions: Learning along the way*. New York: HarperCollins Publishers.

Bearne, E., Graham, L., & Marsh, J. (2007). *Classroom action research in literacy: A guide to practice*. Leicester, England: United Kingdom Literacy Association.

Bearne, E. & Wolstencroft, H. (2007). *Visual approaches to teaching writing: Multimodal literacy 5–11*. London: Paul Chapman Publishing.

Cochran-Smith, M. (1991). *Learning to teach against the grain*. Harvard Educational Review, 51(3), 279-310.

Cochran-Smith, M. & Lytle, S. (2009). *Inquiry as stance: Practitioner research for the next generation*. New York: Teachers College Press.

Jenkins, H., Purushotma, R., Clinton, K., Weigel, M., & Robinson, A. J. (2006). *Confronting the challenges of participatory culture: Media education for the 21st century*. Retrieved on April 2, 2007 from http://digitallearning.macfound.org/.

Leander, K. (2009). Composing with old and new media: Toward a parallel pedagogy. In V. Carrington & M. Robinson (Eds.), *Digital literacies: Social learning and classroom practices* (pp. 147–163). Los Angeles/London: United Kingdom Literacy Association/SAGE Publications Ltd.

McClay, J. K. (2006). Collaborating with teachers and students in multiliteracies research: "Se hace camino al andar." *Alberta Journal of Educational Research,* 52(3), 182–195.

McClay, J. K., & Mackey, M. (2009). Distributed assessment in OurSpace: This is not a rubric. In A. Burke & R. Hammett (Eds.), *Assessing new literacies: Perspectives from the classroom* (pp. 113–132). New York: Peter Lang.

Vygotsky, L. S. (1978). *Mind in society: The development of higher psychological processes.* Cambridge, MA: Harvard University Press.

Wells, G. (2009). Dialogic inquiry as collaborative action research. In S. Noffke & B. Somekh (Eds.), *The Sage handbook of educational action research* (pp. 50–62). Thousand Oaks, CA: Sage Publications.

Zingrone, F. (2001). *Media symplex: At the edge of meaning in the age of chaos.* Toronto: Stoddart.

SECTION 4

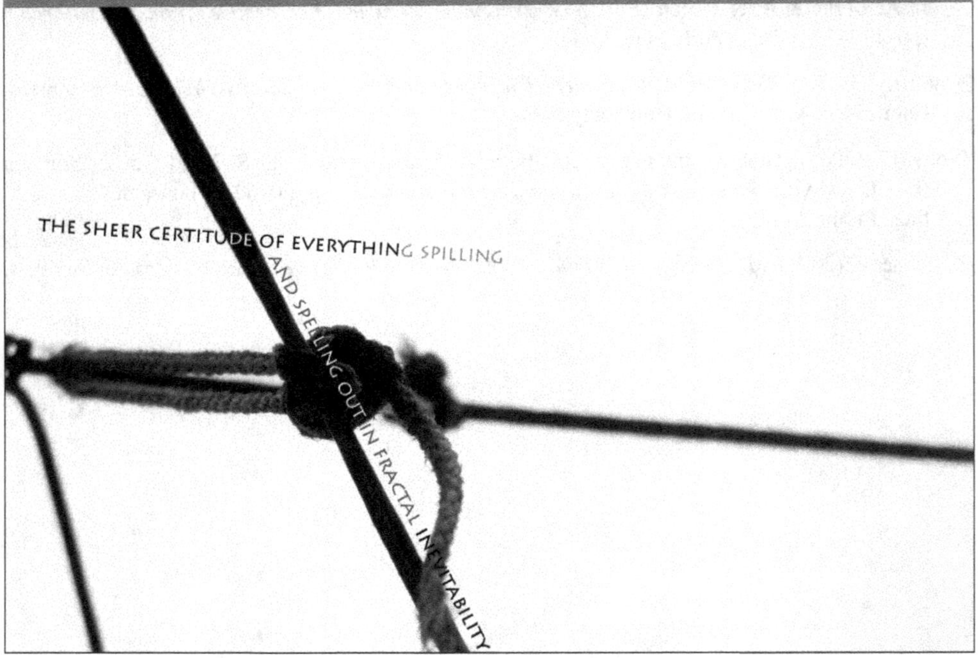

Assessing and Shaping Progress

How Can Feedback to Students on Their Writing Function as a Pedagogical Practice?

By Shelley Stagg Peterson, Ontario Institute for Studies in Education

Providing feedback on written assignments is an assumed part of middle and secondary school English teachers' workload. Teachers are expected to assign grades and write comments on assignments (Smith, 1997). As such, feedback is often seen as an assessment tool to justify the assigned grade. Yet, it can also be a powerful teaching tool if the feedback is provided while students are in the process of writing drafts.

Indeed, feedback on writing can be viewed as individualized writing instruction. Working within students' "zones of proximal development" (Vygotsky, 1986), teachers use the students' own writing as instructional material to teach elements of style, organizational and formatting approaches, voice, writing conventions, and other aspects of composing. Feedback has the greatest impact on students' growth as writers when it is provided while students are drafting and revising their writing, rather than after they have handed in a completed composition for a grade (Ferris, 1997). The feedback gives students a sense of the possibilities for revising the writing in the moment. More importantly, the feedback supports students' learning at a time when it is most helpful to their development as writers. They have an immediate opportunity to apply what they learn from the feedback as they continue to draft and revise their written compositions. In this way, the feedback supports students' overall writing development.

Teacher feedback should accomplish two aims (Elbow, 1998): providing students with an indication of how well the writing meets the grading expectations (criterion-based feedback) and giving students a sense of the effect of the writing on the reader (reader-based feedback). When providing reader-based feedback, teachers might describe for students the visual images or the emotions that the writing evokes. Teachers may summarize what they feel the student is saying or trying to achieve, or they may talk about a personal remembrance that a student's narrative has jogged. Reader-based feedback helps students to get a sense of how well their writing entertains, informs, persuades, or achieves other communicative purposes (Elbow, 1998). Knowing that they will be evaluating the writing at a later date, teachers often feel that students would be better served if their teachers talk about students' writing in terms of the evaluation criteria. However, reader-based feedback should not be disregarded, as criterion-based feedback on its own cannot provide a complete sense of how well the writing achieves the writer's purpose.

When determining the purpose and content of their feedback, teachers should identify the elements of the writing that clearly communicate the intended ideas, information, and perspectives as well as areas where students could potentially revise their writing to clarify meaning and engage readers in intended ways (Haswell, 2006). Because the goal of the feedback is to enhance students' growth as writers, teachers should build on what students demonstrate that they do well and determine what they need to learn, extending students' knowledge and skills in new directions. For example, teachers may praise a student for including relevant details or choosing a provocative point of view, and then indicate where the organization of an argument was confusing or where the choice of vague words weakened the argument.

Although students commonly report that positive comments do not help them to improve their writing, they appreciate receiving praise to nurture their confidence as writers and their motivation to write. Unambiguous, elaborated, specific feedback is most helpful in guiding students' revisions (Beedles & Samuels, 2002; Straub, 1997) and has been shown to lead to more substantive revisions (Ferris, 1997). It is preferable to give feedback on the content, organization, and style features of the writing in early drafts and wait to give feedback on the writing conventions until the writing is almost complete. If students focus on writing conventions early on in their writing processes, their flow of ideas may be curtailed. In addition, students may be editing sentences that will later be cut as they revise.

Spelling, punctuation, and grammar may be the focus of criterion-based feedback, but they should not be the sole focus. When providing feedback on writing conventions, teachers should identify patterns of errors, rather than point out every error on the page (Haswell, 2006). Students can then attend to and learn one or two types of spelling, punctuation, or grammar patterns as they edit and continue with their writing. It is also important to identify patterns that students have recently mastered so that students get a sense of how much they already know, as well as what they have yet to learn. For instance, teachers may highlight students' correct use of apostrophes in contractions while identifying patterns in sentence fragments created when starting sentences with subordinating conjunctions.

Students' sense of ownership of their writing needs to be considered when providing feedback (Graves, 1994; 2004). Revising and editing are difficult, time-consuming processes for many students. When students have the autonomy to decide how they will use their teachers' suggestions and observations, they are more likely to feel a sense of commitment to improving the writing and to becoming better writers (Bright, 2007).

Feedback is most useful when teachers discuss the assessment criteria with students to ensure that students have a clear understanding of the expectations. This might take the form of examining a sample of writing together with students to identify how specific features of the writing would be assessed using the criteria. Ideally, students should have an opportunity to participate in determining the assessment criteria (Black, Harrison, Lee, Marshall, & Wiliam, 2003). For example, students and their teachers might co-create scoring guides by modifying existing criteria (e.g., Spandel's [2005] "6 Traits") to fit with the purpose and context of particular writing assignments.

Creating Opportunities to Provide Ongoing Feedback to Students on their Writing

When establishing routines for providing feedback to middle and secondary school students on their writing, English teachers should consider the volume of writing that students will be producing and the number of students they are teaching. It may be possible to provide all students with verbal feedback in student-teacher conferences, with informal feedback given "on-the-spot" while students are writing. However, it may be more realistic to provide one type of feedback for some assignments and another type of feedback for other assignments. For instance, focus on organization for one assignment and matters of style or matters of convention for another.

Ideally, teachers should provide verbal feedback to each student in 5-to-10-minute student-teacher conferences at least once for each major writing assignment (Graves, 2004; Murray, 1979). Students either sign up to meet with their teacher when they feel ready for feedback or meet at a scheduled time. Four or five student-teacher conferences could be scheduled in any one English class, replacing a portion of the whole-class instruction time. The conferences take place while the rest of the class works on assignments independently or in small groups. The teacher asks students to hand in their drafts prior to the student-teacher conferences so that they don't take up conference time reading the draft. The conference is meant to be interactive so teachers can not only provide feedback but also encourage students to ask for help, to request feedback on particular aspects of the writing, or to talk about their intended purposes, and so forth (Anderson, 2005).

Routines for providing written feedback can also be incorporated into the rhythms of middle and secondary school English classes. To encourage revisions that draw on teacher feedback and to ensure that all students are benefiting from receiving feedback, teachers may choose to allot a small percentage of the final grade to handing in a draft by a certain date. This provides a formal opportunity for the teacher to write comments on the drafts and encourage students to revise the drafts before handing in the final compositions for grading. Students could submit a "revise-and-resubmit" letter explaining how the feedback influenced their revisions, providing teachers with insight into their thinking and enhancing students' metacognitive awareness of their writing processes and intentions (Ferris, 1997).

Teachers are not the only potential feedback providers in English classes (Peterson & McClay, 2010). Not responsible for formally assessing the writing, peers are well positioned to provide reader-based feedback. Students might ask peers for feedback spontaneously as they feel it is needed, or teachers might set up formal routines where students exchange their writing with each other to elicit peer feedback.

Capitalizing on the teaching potential of feedback on student writing requires changes in English classrooms. Student-teacher conferences become part of everyday instruction, and written feedback is provided *while* students are working on drafts rather than after they hand in completed writing. Teachers *and* peers can provide criterion-based and reader-based feedback. Feedback then becomes a pedagogical practice that is responsive to students' immediate needs and enhances their writing development.

References

Anderson, C. (2005). *Assessing writers.* Portsmouth, NH: Heinemann.

Beedles, B. & Samuels, R. (2002). Comments in context: How students use and abuse instructor comments. In O. Ogede (Ed.), *Teacher commentary on student papers* (pp. 11–20). Westport, CT: Bergin & Garvey.

Black, P., Harrison, C., Lee, C., Marshall, B., & Wiliam, D. (2003). *Assessment for learning: Putting it into practice.* Berkshire, England: Open University Press.

Bright, R. (2007). *Write through the grades: Teaching writing in secondary schools.* Winnipeg, MB: Portage & Main Press.

Elbow, P. (1998). *Writing with power: Techniques for mastering the writing process.* New York: Oxford University Press.

Ferris, D. R. (1997). The influence of teacher commentary on student revision. *TESOL Quarterly* 31(2), 315–339.

Graves, D. (1994). *A fresh look at writing.* Portsmouth, NH: Heinemann.

Graves, D. (2004). What I've learned from teachers of writing. *Language Arts* 82(20), 88–94.

Haswell, R. (2006). The complexities of responding to student writing; or, looking for shortcuts via the road of excess. *Across the disciplines, 3.* http://wac.colostate.edu/atd/articles/haswell2006.cfm (accessed March 25, 2010).

Murray, D. (1979). The listening eye: Reflections on the writing conference. *College English* 41(1), 13–18.

Peterson, S. S. & McClay, J. (2010). Assessing and providing feedback for student writing in Canadian classrooms. *Assessing Writing* 15(2), 86–99.

Smith, S. (1997). The genre of the end comment: Conventions in teacher responses to student writing. *College Composition and Communication* 48(2), 249–268.

Spandel, V. (2005). *Creating writers through 6-trait writing assessment and instruction* (2nd ed.). Boston, MA: Pearson/Allyn & Bacon.

Straub, R. (1997). Students' reactions to teacher comments: An exploratory study. *Research in the Teaching of English* 31(1), 91–119.

Vygotsky, L. (1986). *Thought and language.* Cambridge, MA: MIT Press.

What Approaches Might Be Taken to Assessing Multimodal Assignments?

By Roberta F. Hammett, Memorial University of Newfoundland

Teachers are involved with a variety of assessment practices both within and beyond their control. Increasingly high-stakes, standardized testing (for example, PISA, the international assessment of the reading, science and mathematics achievement of 15-year-old students) is influencing classroom instruction as teachers begin to realize that their futures may be on the line in accountability practices that tie students' test scores to merit pay and tenure, as recently suggested by the Fraser Institute (a conservative think tank that largely represents free enterprise, including the privatization of schools; see, for example, Cowley and Veldhuis, 2011). PISA (Programme for International Student Assessment) ranks schools yearly based on standardized test scores. Understandably, teachers may decide that teaching to those external tests is their highest priority; what is tested, they will assume, is what must be taught. Unfortunately, this may mean learning activities that might be more interesting and engaging for students are given even less time in classrooms. The same may be true of activities that connect with students' creativity, like multimodal assignments; after all, there's often little opportunity for creativity in standardized tests, even those that require written responses (see http://pisa-sq.acer.edu.au/ for a sample reading test). As teachers of literacy, we must negotiate this contradiction and hopefully find a way to prepare students for tests while still engaging them in creative, multimodal literacy practices.

Another challenge faced by teachers is negotiating formative and summative assessments within their classrooms. Teachers are encouraged to utilize assessment *for* learning and *as a path to* learning (formative), as opposed to exclusively *of* learning that has already occurred (summative). Multimodal assignments, engaging with new literacies which are often collaborative, social, participatory, challenging, reflective, and creative, are well suited to formative assessment for the purpose of learning, but may also have to be assigned a final, summative grade. Before discussing some specifics of the assessment of multimodal assignments, let me review some of the characteristics of (new) literacies. As described by Lankshear and Knobel (2006), new literacies are "socially recognized ways of generating, communicating and negotiating meaningful content through the medium of encoded texts within contexts of participation in Discourses" (p. 108). That they are "socially recognized ways" suggests that they are engaged within everyday social activities; goals and patterns of communication are thus "built in" to the literacy practices. Often the practices are constituted within particular "discourses," or ways of doing and being in the world. That is, belonging to a discourse means that we can take up an identity within an "insider" group, with its conventions and culture—including "ways of thinking, acting, feeling, moving, dressing, speaking, gesturing, believing, valuing . . . [as well as its associated] tools, objects, institutions, networks, places, vehicles, machines, physical spaces [and] buildings" (Lankshear & Knobel, 2006, p. 70). The term "encoded texts" broadens our sense of texts beyond written (linguistic) works to multimodal texts that can combine linguistic, visual, aural, and gestural elements through digital technologies. Lankshear and Knobel's description of new literacies also includes what they call *new technical stuff,* the knowledge and use of various digital tools and resources; and *new ethos stuff,* a different mindset that entails a concept of compositions and activities as inherently participatory, collaborative, distributed, evolving, and inclusive (2006, pp. 73–103). Often, such activities are a digital remix of images, sound, and video that even challenge conventional notions of ownership and copyright (Lankshear & Knobel, 2006, p. 108).

Now to assessment: if, as I believe, multimodal assignments enact many of the characteristics of new literacies, their assessment in the classroom must go beyond a summative numerical or letter grade assigned as if to a completed product. Rather, the grade should to take into account the composition process, its context, and the new literacies it incorporates. Such complex considerations have made rubrics popular, for rubrics afford consideration of multiple aspects and elements of the composing process and composition. Considering the above discussion of new literacies, the rubric categories might include goals and conventions of the related discourses and social contexts, the meaningfulness of the content, the *technical stuff* (use of digital technologies and evidenced knowledge of their features and affordances) and the *ethos stuff* (for example, being collaborative both in the sense of collaborating with fellow students and with other composers who have posted texts online that are downloaded and incorporated in this "new" composition).

As is the nature of a rubric, these categories require a description and gradation of what might be expected in the particular genre of the text (perhaps including what components were emphasized in the assignment), what content is necessary, what levels of understanding are exhibited, what aspects of discourse might be built in, and what technical features are used to what effect (i.e., elements of design). Therein lies the rub. When it comes to new literacies, particularly with regard to the "technical stuff," students often know more than teachers; thus teachers may rely upon students to teach one another—and sometimes the teachers themselves—how to do technical things. As Kimber and Wyatt-Smith remind us, "young people have developed skills, capabilities and technology-mediated social practices that have often been extended by their peers, not the classroom teacher" (2009, p. 134). Within a collaborative classroom environment where students construct knowledge in social ways, it seems appropriate for students to collaborate with teachers to learn and assess—to co-construct, that is, knowledge of the features of new literacies' processes and products. When students and teacher develop rubrics together and use them for self and peer assessment during the composition of multimodal texts, they are likely "to develop metacognitive and critical awareness of the work under consideration" (McClay and Mackey, 2009, p. 118).

Kimber and Wyatt-Smith (2009) lay out what they call "Essential Digital Learnings" that may assist students "to becom[e] more digitally proficient, critical evaluators, creative producers and ethical users of new technologies." They advocate a shift in focus "to develop the learner's cognitive, metacognitive, performative and transformative capabilities" (p. 142). Their "Essential Digital Learnings (EDLs) . . . include *e-proficiency, e-credibility* and *e-designing,* extending to *metalearning*" (p. 142, emphasis in original). They frame these EDLs within the context of knowledges that include curricular knowledges, curriculum literacies, community knowledges, and criterial knowledges with the latter identified in a "collaborative, negotiated process where expertise is shared between teachers and students" (p. 140). I suggest these EDLs and knowledges could inform composition and assessment of multimodal assignments, including rubrics.

Thinking beyond rubrics, however, McClay and Mackey (2009) offer peer-to-peer learning networks and sideshadowing as approaches to "distributed assessment" (p. 119). Following the practices of peer-to-peer learning networks, students would seek instruction as needed, specialize in niche skills and knowledge, and receive feedback, review, critique, and encouragement throughout the process (p. 119). Sideshadowing is a reflective process "for uncovering a person's appraisals and intentions in his/her own literate work" whether in progress or completed (p. 120).

During our collaborative research, a grade 9 teacher and I used the features of a social networking site (www.ning.com) for students to plan, compose, display, and reflect upon digital responses to *Romeo and Juliet.* The students used the group discussion feature of the Ning site to plan their collaborative (group) composition and the blog feature to reflect on their finished product, which they had either uploaded or linked to the Ning (giving insight into their "appraisals and intentions"). Their compositions included an e-zine, several digital movies created from images and songs with Photostory3, a digital video recording of a modernized version of the play, a digital "flip book" of photos of events from Juliet's perspective, and a sound-enhanced PowerPoint slide show. With their teacher, the students developed a rubric for use in assessing their digital compositions (developing and exhibiting "criterial knowledge"). Although not evaluated for a grade, their blog reflections on the assignment and working process, as well as their "wall" comments to one another, provided us (teacher and researcher) great insight into their depth of learning, their self and peer assessment, their insights into the play, their knowledge of the play, their composing processes, and their perceptiveness about group work, digital tools and resources, creativity, and engagement. Curriculum guides and outcomes, student interest, expanding new literacies, and proliferating digital technologies and resources all enable teachers to integrate multimodal assignments in their pedagogical practices. Assessment should not dissuade teachers from engaging in collaborative digital composing and providing a wide variety of rich literacy practices; external standardized tests should not narrow learning possibilities and enjoyment. Rather, teachers can continue to find spaces for new literacies and multimodal assignments within whatever accountability systems are in place at their institutional settings.

References

Cowley, P. & Veldhuis, N. (2011). Properly designed, merit pay for teachers will pay off for students. *Fraser forum.* Retrieved from: http://www.fraserinstitute.org/uploadedFiles/fraser-ca/Content/research-news/research/articles/properly-designed-merit-pay-for-teachers.pdf

Kimber, K. & Wyatt-Smith, C. (2009). Valued knowledges and core capacities for digital learners. In A. Burke & R. Hammett (Eds.), *Assessing new literacies: Perspectives from the classroom* (pp. 133–155). New York: Peter Lang.

Lankshear, C. and Knobel, M. (2006). *New literacies: Everyday practices and classroom learning* (2nd ed.). Maidenhead & New York: Open University Press.

McClay, J. K. & Mackey, M. (2009). Distributed Assessment in OurSpace: This Is Not a Rubric. In A. Burke & R. Hammett (Eds.), *Assessing New Literacies: Perspectives from the Classroom* (pp. 113–132). New York: Peter Lang.

Index